W0050211

PENGUIN MODERN CLASSICS
Letters from a Young Poet

RABINDRANATH TAGORE (1861–1941) was a key figure of the Bengal Renaissance. He started writing at an early age and by the turn of the century had become a household name in Bengal as a poet, a songwriter, a playwright, an essayist, a short-story writer and a novelist. In 1913 he was awarded the Nobel Prize for Literature and his verse collection *Gitanjali* came to be known internationally. At about the same time he founded Visva-Bharati, a university located in Santiniketan, near Kolkata. Called the 'Great Sentinel' of modern India by Mahatma Gandhi, Tagore steered clear of active politics but is famous for returning his knighthood as a gesture of protest against the Jallianwala Bagh massacre in 1919.

Tagore was a pioneering literary figure, renowned for his ceaseless innovations in poetry, prose, drama, music and painting—which he took up late in life. His works include some sixty collections of verse, nearly a hundred short stories, several novels, plays, dance dramas, essays on religious, social and literary topics, and over 2500 songs, including the national anthems of India and Bangladesh.

ROSINKA CHAUDHURI is Professor in Cultural Studies at the Centre for Studies in Social Sciences, Calcutta. She has been Visiting Fellow at the Southern Asian Institute, Columbia University, and Charles Wallace Fellow at Cambridge University. She is the author of *Gentlemen Poets in Colonial Bengal*, *Freedom and Beef-Steaks* and *The Literary Thing*. She has edited *Derozio, Poet of India* and co-edited *The Indian Postcolonial*. Her articles have appeared in various reputed journals including *Journal of Asian Studies*, *Social Text*, *Modern Asian Studies* and *Economic and Political Weekly*; she reviews for the *Book Review* and the *Times Literary Supplement*.

RABINDRANATH TAGORE

Letters from a Young Poet
1887–1895

Translated from the Bengali
by Rosinka Chaudhuri

PENGUIN BOOKS

An imprint of Penguin Random House

PENGUIN BOOKS

USA | Canada | UK | Ireland | Australia
New Zealand | India | South Africa | China | Singapore

Penguin Books is part of the Penguin Random House group of companies
whose addresses can be found at global.penguinrandomhouse.com

Published by Penguin Random House India Pvt. Ltd
4th Floor, Capital Tower 1, MG Road,
Gurugram 122 002, Haryana, India

First published in Bengali as *Chinnapatrabali* by Visva-Bharati Press,
Kolkata 1960
First published in English by Penguin Books India 2014

Translation and introduction copyright © Rosinka Chaudhuri 2014

10 9 8 7 6 5 4 3 2

ISBN 9780143415763

Typeset in Bembo by Eleven Arts, Delhi

Printed at Manipal Technologies Limited, India

To the memory of my grandfather,
Satis Ranjan Khastgir (1898–1973),
who went to live in Santiniketan because
he loved Rabindranath.

I celebrate myself, and sing myself,
And what I assume you shall assume,
For every atom belonging to me as good belongs to you.

I loafe and invite my soul,
I lean and loafe at my ease observing a spear of summer grass.

Walt Whitman, 'Song of Myself', *Leaves of Grass*, 1855

Contents

Acknowledgements

While translation is always generally acknowledged as a difficult task in itself, translating from Tagore, it has been readily conceded, is an endeavour most peculiarly susceptible to failure. My work here has been made easier by the patience and cooperation of colleagues and friends who have answered queries, listened to passages, and provided references, chiefly Sibaji Bandyopadhyay, Partha Chatterjee, Manabi Majumdar and Dwaipayan Bhattacharya. I presented a portion of the introduction at a seminar at the Centre for Studies in Social Sciences, Calcutta, in September 2013, and I am grateful for the keen response of faculty and students there. Dipesh Chakrabarty had read the first draft of some of these letters, and to him I owe the illuminating thought that these wonderful letters actually allow you to be, for a moment, as if 'in the company of the man'. Amit Chaudhuri—'*il miglior fabbro*'—was available on demand to test the sound of the sentence on the page; for that I am, as always, grateful.

Two of these letters have been previously published in the *Telegraph* under the title 'Letters from Another Autumn', on 4 October 2011; they have been further revised since. Radha Chakravarty and Fakrul Alam are to be thanked for the freedom they allowed me in choosing what I wanted to translate for *The Essential Tagore* (Harvard University Press and Visva-Bharati, 2011). The original selection I made for them was the seedbed for this entire project, setting in motion the process that would ultimately result in this book. I must also thank Supriyo Tagore and Supurna Devi (via Srimanti) for responding to my queries, as also my uncle, Kamal Ghosh, for his help. Most of all, my gratitude to Diya Kar Hazra at Penguin for having the foresight and generosity of a great commissioning editor, and having so readily agreed to my suggestion of publishing these letters in translation; to Sivapriya and Ambar Chatterjee for having attended to innumerable workable and unworkable suggestions with patience and courtesy; and to Richa Burman for an admirable job at the proofs stages.

Note on Transliteration

In transliterating Bengali words the Bengali Romanization table from the Library of Congress (http://www.loc.gov/catdir/cpso/romanization/bengali.pdf) has been used, with the exception of content within quotation marks, where the original spellings within the quote have been retained, and, of course, most proper nouns. The only departure has been that the implicit vowel *a* that is mandatory after all consonants and consonant clusters in transliteration has generally not been used at the end of a word unless pronounced. Titles of Sanskrit works have been represented in their Bengali pronunciation. Bracketed Bengali words have also been inserted on occasion to both clarify particular terms difficult to translate and sometimes to instantly remind the reader of well-known lines from Tagore.

Key to Transliteration and Pronunciation

In preparing the pronunciation guide, examples have been provided where possible: these are arbitrary and merely indicative. The words provided as examples are sometimes taken from proper nouns that make it comprehensible to the South Asian reader. Similarly, the examples given for aspirated sounds that are routinely not

aspirated in this region (such as the 't' in *table*) make it a guide
only for those familiar with English pronunciation here—which
the Western reader will have to have a knowledge of in order to
comprehend the key.

Vowels and Dipthongs

(With the exception of two vowels, pronounced *rhi* and *li*, which
have not been used here)

a	pronounced like *aw* in *awful*
ā	pronounced like the *a* in *far*
i	pronounced like the *i* in *it*
ī	pronounced like *ee* in *steel*
u	pronounced like the *u* in *put*
ū	pronounced like the *oo* in *scoot*
r̥	pronounced like the *ri* in *Hrithik*
e	pronounced like the *a* in *day*
ai	pronounced approximately like *oi* in *hoi-polloi*
o	pronounced like the *o* in *onerous*
au	pronounced approximately like the *au* in *Kaurava*, but with an 'o' sound as above

Consonants

Gutturals

ka	pronounced like the *k* in *kite*
kha	pronounced like the *kh* in *khaki*
ga	pronounced like the *g* in *goose*
gha	pronounced like an aspirated 'ga' sound, as in *Ghana*
ñ	used in conjunction with a consonant like 'ga', pronounced like the *ng* in *thing*

Palatals

ca	pronounced like the *ch* in *change*

cha	pronounced like an aspirated 'ca' sound, as in *Chhattisgarh*
ja	pronounced like the *j* in *jam*
jha	pronounced like an aspirated 'ja' sound, as in *Jharkhand*
ña	used in conjunction with a consonant like 'ca', pronounced like the *n* in *trenchant*

Cerebrals

ta [ṭ]	pronounced as in *table*
tha [ṭh]	pronounced like an aspirated 'ta' sound
da [ḍ]	pronounced as in *dog*
ra [ṛ]	pronounced like an aspirated 'ra' sound
dha [ḍh]	pronounced like an aspirated 'dha' sound, as in *Dhaka*
rha [ṛh]	pronounced like an emphatic aspirated 'ra' sound
na [ṇ]	pronounced like a cerebral 'na' sound

Dentals

ta	pronounced as in *entente*
t [ṱ]	pronounced like an aspirated 'ta' sound
tha	pronounced like an aspirated 'ta' sound, similar to above, as in *thing*
da	pronounced like a soft *d* as in *rendezvous*
dha	pronounced as in *dharma*
na	pronounced as in *not*

Labials

pa	pronounced like the *p* in *rapt*
pha	pronounced like an aspirated 'pa' sound
ba	pronounced like the *b* in *Bombay*
bha	pronounced like an aspirated 'ba' sound, as in *Bharat*
ma	pronounced like the *m* in *mother*

Semivowels

ya	pronounced like the 'ja' sound

ẏ	pronounced like the *y* sound in *yacht*
ra	pronounced like the *r* sound in *river*
la	pronounced like the *l* sound in *love*
ba	pronounced like the *b* in *boat*

Sibilants

śa	pronounced like the *sh* sound in *shame*
sha	same as above
sa	same as above

Aspirate

ha	pronounced like the *h* in *happy*

Anusvār: ṃ	pronounced like *ng* in *thing*
Bisarga: ḥ	pronounced like *h* in Utah
Chandra-bindu:	the half-moon sign with a dot over it above the concerned letter being unavailable, the symbol ñ has been used to indicate the use of the *chandrabindu* or *anunāsika*.

Bengali Months and Seasons

The Bengali year begins on the first of Baiśākh or Paẏlā Baiśākh, which corresponds to 15 April. The months that follow are:

Baiśākh	mid–April to mid–May
Jaiẏshṭha	mid–May to mid–June
Āshāṛh	mid–June to mid–July
Śrāban	mid–July to mid–August
Bhādra	mid–August to mid–September
Āśvin	mid–September to mid–October
Kārtik	mid–October to mid–November
Agrahāẏan	mid–November to mid–December
Paush	mid–December to mid–January
Māgh	mid–January to mid–February
Phālgun	mid–February to mid–March
Caitra	mid–March to mid–April

There are six seasons in the Bengali calendar:

grīshma	summer
barsha	rainy season
śaraṯ	end of rains, roughly autumn
hemanta	autumn leading to winter
śīt	winter
basanta	spring

Introduction

> Of all of Rabindranath's prose, I have read *Chinnapatra* the most
> frequently throughout my life. When I first went abroad, I was
> very careful to keep it with me always—so that, from a distance
> of twelve thousand miles, I could sometimes touch the heart of
> Bengal—Buddhadeva Bose[1]

The letters collected in *Chinnapatrābalī* were written by
Rabindranath Tagore to his niece, his brother's daughter Indira,
between September 1887 and December 1895, from when he was
twenty-six to the age of thirty-four, a period he later described as
being 'the most productive period of my literary life'.[2] At first they
were put together in Indira's own hardbound exercise books (there
were two), into which she copied out all the letters written to her
by him in this period. These were a present from her to the uncle
who was, by then, a well-known literary figure, soon to be Nobel
laureate and knight of the realm. The idea of copying the letters
into exercise books is one he expressed himself in these letters:

> Give me your letters once, Bob, and I'll copy out just the
> experiences of beauty from them into an exercise book. Because

if I live for a long time then I'm sure to grow old; then all these days will become things of remembrance and consolation. . . . Then this Padma's sandbank of today and the soft, peaceful, spring moonlight will return to me afresh in exactly the same way. My days and nights of joy and sorrow are not woven together like this anywhere else in my poetry or prose.*

When a selection of these letters was first published in 1912 as *Chinnapatra*, they had been revised and edited by Rabindranath himself from the version that existed in the exercise books at the time, giving them a 'literary' shape, and arguably turning them into a distinct fictional narrative of his own.[3] In that collection, the first eight letters were written to his friend Srishchandra Majumdar, and the rest to Indira Debi. The volume could almost be thought of as a prose companion to the English *Gitanjali* that had been published exactly in the same year, 1912. In it, every element of the personal, the angular, the obstreperous and the banal was carefully pruned from the letters so as to present a public face to the curious reader; all that remained in them—'just the experiences of beauty'—seemed to belong largely to the domain of the scenic and the spiritual. Even so, because the letters were so irrevocably grounded in the local, the particular and the everyday, some element of the original impulse filtered through in the letters that spoke specifically of the countryside, the river landscapes and the people in it. An English translation of *Chinnapatra* appeared under the title *Glimpses of Bengal* in 1921 and, in the short introduction to it, Rabindranath spoke of his own reasons for putting these letters before the public: 'Since these letters synchronise with a large part of my published writings, I thought their parallel course would broaden my readers' understanding of my poems as a track is widened by retreading the same ground.'[4]

* For an explanation regarding the name he uses for her—'Bob'—see the following section, 'The Young Woman'.

The *Chinnapatrābalī* is a different edition from the *Chinnapatra* and its English translation, *Glimpses of Bengal*, and was first compiled and published in October 1960, almost twenty years after Rabindranath's death, as part of the centenary-year publications; its editor was Kanai Samanta, and he was helped in this work by Subimal Lahiri. Here we have only the letters to Indira Debi in their fullest form, with an additional 107 letters to her that were left out of the earlier edition—thus, this publication was faithful to the original exercise books to the maximum extent possible. As the editor said at the time: 'In the present day, there can be no conceivable reason for us to discard any part of Rabindranath's own writings at all.'[5]

The English title, *Glimpses of Bengal*, was an apt one for *Chinnapatra*: the subject matter of these edited letters was Bengal—riverine, beautiful, green and vast—and the trope of seeing, or 'glimpsing', some of the wonder that was Rabindranath's Bengal came through exactly in that choice of title. It had, as it happens, no relation at all to the Bengali title, *Chinnapatra*, which is a compound word, a neologism made up of two words—*chinna*, or torn, and *patra*, or leaves. Characteristically, the words could also legitimately denote 'scattered' or 'fragmented' for the first word and 'letters', denoting correspondence, for the second. Torn leaves, scattered letters, pieces of a whole, falling leaves—a plethora of images jostle the imagination in the context of the volume of letters published under this Bengali title. The inconsistent and the fragmentary are the predominant metaphors here, and the word itself is a non-word, impossible to translate or to replicate in another language. To this compound word, the editor of the 1960 edition added a suffix, so that the last part of the word became *patrābalī* from the original *patra*. Now '*ābalī*' is a suffix that denotes collectivity—so *patrābalī* would mean collected letters, *padābalī* collected verse, *granthābalī* collected works, etc. So this title, *Chinnapatrābalī*, may be translated as 'collected fragments of letters', once again a neologistic compound word, adding, with that suffix, a notion of narrativity and flow, a sense of substance and collection, except that the word does not exist in the Bengali language. This was not exceptional as far as Rabindranath was concerned; the Bengali title he gave his *Selected Poems*, *Sañcayitā*, or his collected songs, *Gītabitān*, were grammatically legitimate but simply not extant words in the language. So, a narrative told in fragments of letters or a collection of torn letters or, again, stories in a collection of scattered letters—the title *Chinnapatrābalī* would signify all of these things unconsciously to the lay Bengali reader, well versed, by 1960, in the indeterminacy of the Tagorean trope.

*

The two exercise books, of which the contents of the *Chinnapatrābalī* are an exact replica, are currently in the Rabindra-Bhavana library in Santiniketan. They are hardbound copies with ochre and red covers of about A4-size length, ruled, with Indira Debi's neat, somewhat schoolgirlish handwriting running inexhaustibly across the pages. The letters copied out in the exercise books are by no means complete in themselves, with the beginning and end lopped off, and the remaining matter edited according to the recipient's (and later perhaps her uncle's) discretion. Sometimes, intriguingly, a blue or red pencil has deleted or bracketed off portions of the text, marking subtle changes made perhaps by Rabindranath when he was revising them for publication. Comparing the notebooks to the two editions, we see that the portions cordoned off within square brackets had been edited out of the *Chinnapatra* completely; these have been restored in the text of *Chinnapatrābalī*, while the dates and places the letters were sent from and received at have been inserted at the top and bottom of the individual letters.* Looking at the first letter alone, we observe an understandable impulse to screen

* The dates at the bottom of the letters indicating when and where they were received have not been included here. There was a great deal of confusion about dates and days, as Rabindranath himself was wrong in many instances, so the dates deemed to be correct by the editor of *Chinnapatrābalī* have been maintained.

anything that might be hurtful to any constituency, whether public or private—so, from 'and Sarala is unhappy that Rabi-mama didn't get to see it, although Rabi-mama is quite unrepentant', the last bit ('although Rabi-mama is quite unrepentant') has been edited out, while, following this, an entire sentence disappears from this letter written in Darjeeling: 'Forests, hilltops, mountains, streams, clouds, and a vast number of flat noses and slant eyes began to be seen.' This emaciates the text, taking out the angularities, the opinions or prejudices, the exasperation and, above all, the humour of the original. Once we have seen all of it, it is impossible to be satisfied with the anodyne quality of what was deemed fit for consumption and therefore left on the page in *Chinnapatra*.

What happened to the original letters themselves? Were they written on long sheets or short ones, ruled sheets or plain ones, white or blue? What colour ink was used, what did they physically look like, what sort of envelopes enclosed them? To these questions I could find no answer, as I put them repeatedly to the descendants of the family as well as to researchers, teachers and historians. The exercise books are heavily edited, sometimes with a pencil or ink-black line running through the lines, mostly with each word individually covered over with squiggles of black ink, and, sometimes, running across an entire page or two, a thin sheet of fine white muslin fabric has been pasted over the cut-out lines to further obscure their original content. It was suggested that technology could now be used to see through all these layers—somehow that invasiveness seemed undesirable for the purposes of this translation, and will have to remain for future generations to do if they so desire.

The Young Man

The first thing that strikes you about these letters is the youth of the person writing them; as Rabindranath put it himself, the period when these letters were written was one 'when, owing to great good fortune, I was young and less known'.[6] 'A Portrait of the Artist as a Young Man' would have been a good title for the volume, indicative of the shift in focus from the motifs of seeing or glimpsing, or of fragmentation and narrativity, to the man himself, and, even more particularly, to a young man at a formative age, in mature adulthood as a man and a writer, a poet in full possession of his voice.

Rabindranath was twenty-six years old at the time of writing the first letter of the *Chinnapatrābalī* dated September 1887 to Indira from Darjeeling. Almost exactly a year before, his first child, daughter Madhurilata (Bela or Beli), was born, on 25 October 1886. In that year of her birth he had published a collection of poems, *Kaṛi o komal* (Sharps and Flats), which, he later said in his memoir *Jibansmṛti*, marked that point in his life from when 'the harvest grain had begun to be reaped', when he had left the mist-laden vicissitudes of adolescence behind and begun to do business with the 'real world'. He had also published a novel (his third), *Rājarshī*, apart from editing a selection of medieval Vaishnava poetry, *Bidyāpatir padābalī*, composing innumerable songs of astonishing accomplishment, as well as writing reviews, articles, dramatizations and prose pieces in the family-run journals.

At twenty-six, when we first encounter him in these letters, he is little more than a youth, even if we take into account the fact that in the nineteenth century you were older at that age than you are now. Nevertheless, the letter writer here is a young man, a youthful husband, younger brother, father of infant children, maturing poet and growing literary sensation. The tone in the early letters is somewhat hesitant, slightly diffident, often embarrassed, and, equally, hugely amused and often quite wicked. This is the young man he was before he won the biggest literary prize in the world, before he was knighted, before he had established himself in the social and literary world; in short, this was, figuratively speaking, Rabindranath before he became 'Tagore'.

He was a good-looking man all his life, but at this age, his striking handsomeness awed friends and family alike. Pramatha

Chaudhuri, later to be Indira's husband, has left a record of the first time he met him in 1886, saying, 'I had never seen a man as good-looking as Rabindranath before. He was fair and tall, with black shoulder-length hair, a muscular body, a smooth, glowing complexion, and very beautiful eyes and nose . . . In those days Rabindranath went about bare-bodied. He used to wear a *dhuti* and *chādar* . . . He was full of life; his body and his face would brim with life. He was like a living picture. If beauty can be incarnate, his body was living proof that it was.' Another description by contemporary poet Dineshcharan Basu corroborates this evidence. Going to see Rabindranath at Jorasanko on 27 April 1886, he 'met him at the foot of the first-floor stairs. . . . Tall and graceful, very fair, with a lean face and beautiful nose, eyes and eyebrows, as if painted with a brush. Bunches of curls flowed upon his shoulders. Attire: dhuti.'[7]

Attire, however, was not always the dhoti alone, of course. Written from the boat at Baliya in 1893, we have a wonderful description of a dishevelled and sleepy young man in a state of absolute and relaxed lassitude:

Today neither the winter nor civilization has any purchase with me—the cāpkān and *cogā* [outer garment] hang from the hook in an extreme embrace—I'm blithely spending the morning in a blue-and-red striped *jin* night suit, the bell isn't ringing, the uniformed khansama isn't coming in to salaam—I'm enjoying the untidy, relaxed state of the half-civilized. The birds are calling, and on the shore the two big banyan trees' leaves make a shivering sound in the breeze, the sun on the surface of the trembling water flashes and shines when it comes inside our *boat*, and the morning proceeds in this loose sort of way.★

★ All the English words in italics in the text of the translations in this book indicate that the English word was originally used in the letters, either in Bengali script or spelt in English.

Rabindranath in denim! Almost but not exactly: the material available in colonial Calcutta, which is being referred to, is described in Subal Mitra's *Saral bāṅgālā abhidhān* (Easy Bengali Dictionary, 1906), as a 'thick material of closely woven thread'. Strikingly, this description also takes us to the physical sensuality of the youth writing these letters. Although he never actually speaks of physical contact with another, nor dwells upon any intimacy with a loved one, there are moments in the letters that make you wonder. In a letter from Shahjadpur written on a night flooded with moonlight, he writes:

> I rest my head upon the window—like the affectionate hand of nature, the breeze slowly runs its fingers through my hair, the water flows past with a rippling sound, the moonlight shimmers, and sometimes 'the eyes spontaneously overflow with tears'. Often when you're deeply hurt inside, tears well up as soon as you hear the sound of an affectionate voice. The lifelong hurt that we feel against nature for this unfulfilled life turns into tears and flows silently the moment nature turns sweetly affectionate. Then nature caresses you all the more and you hide your face in her breast with even more fervour, and you attain a sort of melancholic peace that comes from 'disinterested wisdom'. Such are my evenings.

The sentence preceding this declares: 'There is one lot that becomes restless thinking, "Why can't I know everything about the world?" and there is another lot that is frustrated wondering, "Why can't we say everything that's on our minds?"—in between, what the world has to say stays within the world and the inner thought stays within . . .' The ellipsis that marks the elision in the text at this point are portions in Indira's notebooks that she did not copy down, marking the break with three asterisks instead. The deeply personal nature of the words that are left on the page here make it obvious why whatever was expressed in the missing section would have been censored. What is important about what remains is not the obvious shallow speculation on the cause or object of intimacy and pain but, rather, the startling sensuality expressed by the feeling, suffering correspondent, and the utter physicality of the sensory experience in the body.

The body is also felt as encumbrance and pain—the second letter describes a bad back, a condition that leads him to rue: 'Never again shall I think of the back as merely a place to tuck in the ends of one's *dhuti*—man's humanity is sheltered in his back'—but it is also, entertainingly, the primary locus in relation to his children. In the latter instance, the tactility of the infant body—its softness and chubbiness, its sharpness in infant scratches or bites, its funniness of movement and gesture—is recorded with incredible warmth of humour and affection. At the end of a long train journey, he delights in his six-month-old son at home, who appears to him 'an absolute simpleton [*nitānta hāṅdā*]', 'quite dark', with 'chubby cheeks', 'plump hands curled into fat fists' and a 'constantly wavering look on his face and eyes . . . of complete brainlessness' which are the '*general characteristics*' common to the young of humankind. Three years later, we have a vignette of the three children—elder daughter Bela, elder son Khoka, and second daughter Renu—in Bolpur:

The other evening, Bela and Khoka got into an argument on a subject that's worth citing. Khoka said, 'Bela, I'm feeling hungry for water' [*Jal kshide peẏeche*]. Bela said, 'Nonsense, gap-tooth [*dhūr, phoklā*]! You don't say hungry for water! Thirsty for water.' Khoka, very firmly—'No, hungry for water.' Bela—'*Āyei*, Khoka, I'm three years older than you, you are two years younger than me, do you know that? I know so much more than you!' Khoka, suspiciously, 'You're that old?' Bela—'Okay, why don't you ask Baba?' Khoka, suddenly excited, 'And what about the fact that I drink milk and you don't?' Bela, scornfully, 'So what? Ma doesn't drink milk—does that mean she isn't bigger than you?'

Khoka, completely silent, with head on pillow, thinking. Then
Bela began to say, 'O father, I have a tremendous, tremendous
friendship with somebody! She's mad, she's so sweet! Oh I can eat
her up!' Saying this, she runs to Renu and hugs and kisses her
till she starts to cry.

The italicized portions, spoken originally in English by the child,
show how fundamentally bilingual the family was at this time even
in—perhaps especially in—moments of intimacy. Seeing his third
daughter, Meera, his 'youngest hatchling' in July 1894, he finds
that 'the thing is almost exactly as it was before', and attempts to
start up an acquaintance, an attempt that proceeds uproariously
rapidly as, 'in no time at all, she began to lay her soft fat hands
with their sharp nails upon my nose, face, eyes, hair, moustache
and beard . . . and not only that, she then began to roar and try to
put my nose and eyes into her mouth to eat it all up'. And again
in another letter: 'Her fat little hands feel so sweet on my body!'
The utter joy in children that Rabindranath was known for in his
lifetime is manifest here in the fun and physicality of play and in
the mocking, loving tone so typical even today in Indian attitudes
to little children.

Physicality is not only present in the domain of the romantically
sensuous in relation to the landscape or the rumbustiously comical
in relation to children—with his own body he is constantly
uncomfortable and dissatisfied. In relation to women, he is awkward
and shy, even at the age of thirty-two:

I don't think I'd be able to conduct a conversation with the
weaker sex with such absolute ease and sweetness and confidence
even now that I'm almost thirty-two years old. I stumble when
I walk, stutter when I must speak, can't decide where to keep
my hands, feel it's my duty to arrange my long legs somehow,
but always fail to do anything about them—by the time I've
decided whether to keep them tucked away under me, or in

front, or behind, I'm unable to match the correct answers to the appropriate questions. In the presence of three gas lamps and a roomful of people, to establish one's self solidly by the side of some young woman in an instant, without hesitation, like a piece of iron attracted to a magnet, is impossible for timid, anxious creatures such as myself.

The 'three gas lamps and a roomful of people' in presumably a drawing room also serve to remind us of the colonial appurtenances that were inevitably a part of his life at this time. This is a tennis-playing young man; as a journalist visiting Shilaidaha and Shahjadpur in 2010 said when he found the tennis racquet used by Rabindranath kept carefully in the Shahjadpur bungalow in Bangladesh: 'In this one department, he would have effortlessly beaten every one of his successors, from Jibanananda to Shakti Chattopadhyay to Joy Goswami. The only tennis-player poet in Bengali literature!'[8] Tennis was not the only colonial accomplishment in his life—listening to the piano being played, often by Indira, was also a large part of his life at the time. Writing from Shahjadpur in June 1891, he says to her:

> Nowadays the nights here are full of such marvellous moonlight, what can I say! Of course, I don't mean to say that you too don't have moonlit nights at your place—it has to be admitted that at your place the moonlight slowly spreads its silent authority over the meadow you have, that church spire, the silent trees and bushes. But you have many other things besides the moonlight— you have your *harmony* and *discord*, your *tennis*, your *marble tables*, the song and music sessions in the *drawing room*—but I have nothing except this silent night.

This feeling of distance from the colonial presence and the public was one that he expressed in a letter from Shilaidaha as well, when he wrote: 'I was walking as if I was the one and only last-remaining pulse of a dying world. And all of you were on another shore, on the banks of life—where there's the *British government* and the nineteenth century and tea and *cheroots*.' The words in the original English here gesture at the English presence in India and, inevitably, at his life in these years as a member of the elite, almost aristocratic, class—a conjunction from which he self-consciously drew away in his later years.

If a partly English way of life was inevitable for someone of his class, the harshness with which the colonial presence in his native countryside grated on his nerves must also have been felt by his compatriots, but few others have expressed themselves so urgently or vividly or humorously on the subject as he has in these letters. A classic in the genre is the letter in which he is forced to first interact with, and then give shelter to, the young English district magistrate in Shahjadpur in 1890:

> Exchanged a vast amount of felicitations with the saheb; said to him, 'Come and have dinner with me tomorrow evening.' He said, 'I'm leaving for somewhere else today itself to arrange for *pig-sticking*' (I was secretly pleased). Said I'm very sorry to hear that. The saheb said, 'I return on Monday' (which made me very gloomy). I said, 'Then make it on Monday.' He was instantly agreeable. Anyway, I sighed and reminded myself that Monday was still some distance away, and reached home.

A hilarious sequence follows: the description of an imminent storm, an invitation to the saheb to shelter on dry land, that is, at his home, the discovery that the guest room in the house is fit for a slum, of its eventual temporary renovation and, in conclusion, his fervent hope that cockroaches wouldn't tickle the soles of his guest's feet at night.

The brown man's burden—how to be hospitable to the white man in India—animates more than one letter. In one such (Letter 37), he laments:

Just a short while ago, the engineer from Pabna turned up with his mem and kids. You know, Bob, I don't find it easy to be a host—my head gets completely muddled—besides which, I never knew he was going to bring a couple of kids along. This time I was supposed to be living on my own, so I haven't even brought too many provisions. Anyway, I'm trying to shut my eyes and ears and get through this somehow. Additionally, the mem drinks tea, and I don't have any tea; the mem can't stand dal right from her childhood, and due to the absence of other food, I have ordered for dal to be made; the mem doesn't touch fish from *year's end to year's end*, and I have quite happily ordered catfish curry to be cooked.

He concludes: 'If I can bid goodbye to them tomorrow morning then I might just survive; if they say they're going to stay one more day then I'm going to die, Bob.'

Not all the portrayals of the English in India are humorous—most, in fact, sting with a bitter sharpness, describing a deliberate insult or unfair affront, as when an Englishwoman at a railway station tries to occupy the compartment he is trying to board, sniggering at him spitefully, or when in Puri the English magistrate's wife, Mrs Walsh, refuses his calling card because he is an unknown 'native'. His complaint is heartfelt:

In the first place, you know I can't stand the sight of these Englishmen in India. They habitually look down on us, they don't have an iota of *sympathy* for us, and, on top of that, to have to *exhibit* one's self to them is truly painful for me. So much so that I don't have the slightest inclination to enter even their theatres or shops (except for Thacker's). Even a great big cow born in an English home feels he's superior to every person in our country—that always hits me hard.

Very rarely does politics enter any of these letters, but in Letter 79, he comes up against an abrasive Englishman, 'the *Principal* of the *college* here' in Cuttack, whose opinions on the prospect of Indians being a part of the jury system in India render him speechless. This man's views leave him sleepless that night, and his head and heart hurt so much that he is helpless as he describes how, unable to make a fitting reply, when he had gone and sat down in a corner of that drawing room, it had all appeared like a shadow in front of his eyes:

> Yet in front of me were memsahebs in *evening dress* and the murmur of English conversation and laughter was in my ear—all together such discordance! How true our eternal Bhāratbarsha was to me, and this *dinner table*, with its sugary English smiles and polite English conversation, how empty, how false, how deeply untrue! When the mems were talking in their low, sweet, cultivated voices, I was thinking of you all, oh wealth of my country. After all, you are of this Bhāratbarsha.

A day later, he is still smarting from the experience.

> But, Bob, I've still not forgotten the audacity of that Englishman yesterday. He blithely said that we have no idea about the *sacredness of life*! These are the people who exterminated the *Red Indians* of *America*, who had no qualms in shooting down even helpless, weak *Australian* women like hunted animals for no reason and no fault of their own, who cannot be tried by one of our countrymen if they murder one of us; they come to the timid, pitiful Hindu and *preach sacredness of life* and *high standard of morals*?

This is an early and eloquent expression of an outrage familiar, of course, to many colonized peoples the world over as they've confronted the yawning gap between liberal preaching and violent practice in colonial and neo-colonial situations.

Yet, if anything is even more contemptible than the racist English men and women in India, it is Indians without self-respect. Against this class of men he is unforgivingly harsh—men in dinner jackets who flaunt their proximity to the English, speak in English and always fawn on the ruling class. He summarizes the politics of the period with acuity: 'All those *patriots* who make good speeches in English, how they look down on Bengali language and literature! And the temporary benefit from that one good English speech is so slight in comparison with all that is lost because of that scorn!' Rabindranath had pressed for putting a stop to the practice of making political speeches in English, as is well known, and his fierce fight for the heart and soul of his country—which he likens to the Pandavas in exile, preparing for war—is in evidence in some of these letters, which startlingly display a hot-headed youth (who addresses the English presence in India and says, 'Your affection is to me what the pig is to the Muslim. It makes me lose caste— really lose it'), not unlike his own future protagonist, Gora, in the eponymous novel written a decade later.

Unlike the character he went on to create in that novel, however, the persona in these letters is always vigilant against excess. Self-aware and sharp, his wry consciousness never allows him to ride the tidal waves of feeling in him to absurd or extreme levels. Following the section from the second letter quoted above, he observes:

Someone who has dressed up as an Englishman and been allowed to sit briefly at one side of an English table doesn't care an iota about winning the hearts of his countrymen any more! This is entirely natural. But we need to be extra careful exactly because it's natural. I know that if the Governor saheb spends two days on the second floor of our house reclining upon that easy chair of mine and calls me 'my dear' while puffing on his cheroot, then this Rabi that I am, who has assumed an aspect like a ball of fire in the mid-afternoon sun, I too may be swallowed up whole in a single ring of smoke expelled from those outcaste lips of Lansdowne. What a satisfied smile would spread over my entire face then, and what sticky sweetness drip from my speech! That's the chief worry! That's why the second-floor terrace needs to be locked (just in case our Governor saheb comes by to smoke a cheroot with his dearest friend *Tagore* under that tin roof!)!

The dangers of proximity to power assume a humorous aspect, and he laughs at the thought of himself curling up to bask in the glow of English approbation. This laughter—following upon the high seriousness with which he speaks of serving his country, to work among the people in secret and without acknowledgement, without 'the luxury of fame and honour' and without constantly thinking 'how do I get the English to read my book, how to get a slap on the back from the English'—is made piquant by the reader's knowledge of the great 'fame and honour' that was to come to him from them in the following years, and explains why it was so easy for him to repudiate those honours on behalf of his countrymen in situations such as those that followed the horrific events of 1919 at Jallianwala Bagh.

An undercutting of his own flights of fancy or imaginative and emotional excess is to be found again and again in these letters. Bathos inevitably follows pathos when he finds himself in the grip of sentiment or intense feeling; so much so that it would seem to be an intrinsic aspect of his character. As a poet he was both known and criticized for his aestheticization of feeling and of beauty, but as a man he is vehemently against the poeticism, the leaping sentiment, the flight of fancy. Immersed in his own thoughts in these riverine locations of eastern Bengal, he is often ardent, passionate about his thoughts and feelings. In a letter from Shilaidaha in 1892 he speaks of how beauty, for him, 'is a real drug! It really and truly drives me mad', describing the addiction of moonlit nights and the essential wildness of unbound nature, which makes him wonder why he wastes his life in polite conversation with neatly dressed gentlemen, for he is 'truly uncivilized, impolite', searching for 'beautiful anarchy' and for 'a festival of joy with a handful of madmen'. This is immediately followed, however, with: 'But what's all this poeticism I'm engaging in—this is the sort of thing that heroes of poems say—pronouncing their opinions on *conventionality* over the course of three or four pages, thinking they are bigger than the rest of human society. Really, it's quite embarrassing to say such things.' A year later, again from Shilaidaha, he describes the exquisite joy of composing songs by himself in that sun-drenched landscape and the list of groceries brought in the same breath:

> Here, I sing alone, with an entranced and liberated heart, my eyes half shut, and the world and this life appear to me touched by the sun's bright hands, swathed in the finest layer of tears, coloured like a seven-layered rainbow—one can translate everyday truths into eternal beauty, and sorrow and suffering too become radiant. In no time at all, the khājāñci appears with the accounts for two eggs, one sliver of butter, a quarter litre of ghī and six paisa's worth mustard oil. My history here is like this.

The history of the life in these letters, thus, is never far from the quotidian, the banal and the everyday. If the Multān *rāginī* is expressive of the afternoon with its tender high notes that evoke 'neither happiness nor unhappiness, only the melancholy of inertia and its inner secret sorrow' in the 'shining afternoon light' upon the river, then the thought is interrupted by 'another big problem—lots of mosquitoes'. 'It's impossible to preserve the sweetness of a feeling or the depth of a thought if you're constantly slapping your hands and legs and body', he sagely continues, going on to make an observation of even greater import: 'These sorts of small irritations—the mosquito's bite,

the helpful literary review, sand in the *mohanbhog*—do not teach
men to be brave in any way'. That he is an entirely secular man
who demands perfection in his food as much as in his art is clear
in the next sentence: 'I can say it especially because there was
sand in my mohanbhog today—and I can clearly recall how I felt
then—such feelings were unworthy of a Christian or a Brahmo
. . . or of a good Muslim too.'

Sometimes in the letters he speaks of himself in the third
person. This was an enduring habit, a technique he deployed even
in one of the last essays of his life, *Sāhitye aitihāsikatā* (Historicality
in Literature), and in his usage it has none of the pretension that
attaches to such use more generally. Rather, the distancing effect
created is often humorous, as we know from the famous instance
of his wedding invitation to a close friend, Priyanath Sen: 'Priya-
babu—/At an auspicious time and day on Sunday next, on the
24th of Agrahāyaṇ, my close relative Srimān Rabindranath Thakur
will be married. My relatives and I will be obliged if you could be
present on that occasion in the evening that day at Debendranath
Tagore's house at No. 6 Jorasanko to observe the wedding & c.
Yours/Gratefully/Sri Rabindranath Thakur.' In another letter
(4 August 1894), he describes how 'in a boat by an open window,
at the head of a *camp-table* upon a cane chair is the chief protagonist,
Sri Rabindranath'. If here he is a character in a story, elsewhere
he speaks almost of the existence of a double, as in Henry James's
famous story, 'The Private Life': 'It's very surprising, but nowadays
when I hear my poems being praised, I don't feel as happy as
I should. Actually, that's because I don't entirely grasp that the
person who is being praised by people is the same person who
writes the poems.'

Occasionally, the letters afford a fascinating glimpse of his own
notion of his character. Repeatedly, here, he describes a side of
himself as 'wild', 'uncivilized', even 'crazy', someone who writes
poetry when 'restless with joy, heedless and thirsty like an inebriated,
plaintive and self-forgetful madman'. He wishes to be as nomadic

as an Arab 'Bedouin' rather than a fussy Bengali. ('But I'm not a Bedouin, I'm a Bengali. I will sit in a corner and nitpick, I will judge, argue, turn my mind over once this way and then the other way—in the way one fries fish—you let one side splutter and sizzle in the boiling oil, and then you turn it over to let the other side sputter.') Over and over again, he rails against 'civilized society', polite company and the compunction of manners. On one occasion, he writes to Indira about this desire for freedom: 'Remember Satya had said to me, "There's a real air of luxury about you, like the Muslim nabābs"? That's not entirely true; in the sense that my nabābi is a mental nabābi—there, in my own kingdom, I don't want any restrictions on me, I want an unchecked right in my domain.' This luxury of mind, therefore, is premised on the exact opposite of material luxury, a mentality that took as a mantra Goethe's injunction to 'do without'; a temperament that spontaneously exclaims on a February afternoon in Shilaidaha: 'There's such a particular feeling of renunciation in the Indian sunlight that nobody has the power to evade it.' He continues again a few months later: 'You know how I cite the breezes of India as an excuse for rebellion against undertaking my duties? There's a deeper significance to that, Bob.' Doing nothing is serious business; it is what facilitates poetry; it is the foundation upon which poetry can be about 'the unnecessary'.

The Young Woman

The woman who receives these letters, affectionately called 'Bob' in some of them, is a silent but considerable presence in this book, an equal as an interlocutor, and not one to be written out of the narrative of its history. This is corroborated by Rabindranath himself repeatedly. As he said to Indira on 7 October 1894, he feels his letters achieve completion because they are addressed to her, and are expressive not only of his own inner essence but also of hers—just as Byron's letters to Thomas Moore express not just Byron's personality but Moore's as well:

Both the person who listens and the person who speaks are
together responsible for the composition—

> '*taṭer buke lāge jaler dheu,*
> *tabe se kalatān uṭhe.*
> *bātāse banasabhā śihari kaṁpe,*
> *tabe se marmar phuṭe.*'

> (The waves beat upon the shore's breast,
>   Only then does its murmur rise.
> The assembled woods tremble in the wind,
>   Only then does that rustle materialize.)

The letter had begun with a passage that was subsequently used as
a preface for the *Chinnapatrābalī*:

> I too know, Bob, that the letters I've written to you express the
> many-hued feelings of my heart in a way that hasn't been possible
> in any of my other writings. . . . When I write to you it never
> crosses my mind that you might not understand something I
> may say, or may misunderstand it, or disbelieve it, or think of
> those things which are the deepest truths to me as merely well-
> composed poeticisms. That's why I can say exactly what I'm
> thinking quite easily to you. . . . It's not just because you've known
> me for a very long time that I'm able to express my feelings to
> you; you have such a genuine nature, such a simple love for the
> truth, that the truth expresses itself spontaneously to you. That's
> by your particular talent. If the best writings of any writer are to
> be found in his letters alone then we must surmise that the person
> to whom they are written also has a letter-writing ability. I have
> written letters to so many others, but nobody else has attracted
> my entire self to themselves in writing.

Her 'genuine nature' and simple honesty have been attested to by
others apart from her favourite uncle, coming up unselfconsciously

in the letters exchanged between her and her fiancé before their marriage. 'You are such a very good girl, Bee—I wish I were like you,' she reports her friend 'Lil' (Lilian Palit, daughter of Loken Palit, family friend of the Tagores) saying to her in English one evening during an intense conversation around the news of her engagement. The person she's engaged to has no doubts in this regard, ruminating more than once on what a really good person she is—'*Tumi satyi bhāri lakshmi meẏe*' (You really are such a very good girl).[9]

As Chitra Deb has commented, 'Nobody else could attract the poet's entire self to themselves in writing. But Indira's identity does not end with this; rather, this is where it begins.'[10] Rabindranath's young, talented and beautiful niece was also an accomplished woman in her own right, only the thirteenth Bengali woman graduate, and the first Tagore from the male lineage (her cousin Sarala, daughter of Rabindranath's eldest sister, preceded her in this) to graduate. She read French and English honours, obtaining a BA degree in 1892, and was ranked first in her year and awarded the Padmavati gold medal. Both she and her husband were French scholars, and she called him '*Mon ami*' in her letters for lack of an appropriate Bengali equivalent (although, in the first instance, she did address him as '*suhṛdbar*' (friend/well-wisher), and then said defensively, '*Sambodhan dekhe hāṅscho?*' (Are you smiling at the form of address?). Her Bengali is alive and clear, sparkling and strong; her uncle described her language as 'lustrous'. Her tangible contribution to the culture of her time lay not only in the elusive arena of her influence and presence but also substantially in the fields of music (she notated a great many of Rabindranath's songs) and music theory, autobiography and memoir and, notably, in the domain of the essay form, at which she excelled, and in translations from English and French into Bengali.

Born in 1873, Indira Debi was twelve years younger than her uncle, the youngest brother of her father, the distinguished Satyendranath Tagore, the first Indian to enter the Indian Civil

Service. Satyendranath's family—his wife, Jnanadanandini Debi (an influential, educated and independent woman, a pioneering symbol of women's emancipation and creator of the modern Indian sari), son, Surendranath, and daughter, Indira—were very close to Rabindranath who often stayed with them in their home throughout his life. In his teenage years, preceding his voyage out to England, Rabindranath stayed with his brother in Ahmedabad, acquiring English customs and the English language. Subsequently, he spent time with them during Satyendranath's postings at Satara and Bombay, and even in the city of Calcutta, where he would escape the family home at Jorasanko to their quiet nuclear home in Park Street for long periods. His friendship with the children— Indira (five) and Suren (six)—began in England, when he went for the first time in 1878 to their home in Brighton as a seventeen-year-old.

Rabindranath had a lifelong attachment to children—he loved them and they loved him to a fault—and here he had the first opportunity in his life to give his heart to two children who would remain among the closest relations he would have amid so many in his family. In Brighton, they were amused by the strange Bengali accent in which he spoke English, but they got along famously. Indira wrote later that one of his tricks then with children was to sing songs in funny ways; so 'he would start singing the song *āju moraṇ ban bole* in a medium tempo and then go faster and faster, until towards the end, when his lips would seem to keep trembling and shaking, we would be in splits, simply helpless with laughter'.

At the time that these letters are being written to her, Indira is between the ages of fourteen and twenty-two, an eminently marriageable age, and it would be a dozen years after 1887 (when the first letter here is received) that she married the distinguished writer, editor and literary critic Pramatha Chaudhuri in 1899, unusually late for a woman of her times. In 1886, Rabindranath had dedicated three 'Letter-Poems' to her in *Kaṛi o komal*; all three were titled '*Patra*' (Letter), and all of them were dedicated to '*Srimati*

Indirā, Prāṇādhikāsu. Nāsik' or 'Miss Indira, Dearer than Life. Nasik'. In a letter-poem Rabindranath wrote to Suren, in Nasik at this time, published in *Bhāratī*, we have a riotous depiction of their relationship, written in a mix of Hindi and Bengali, where, addressing Suren, he says of Indira:

Merā upar julum kartā terā bahin bāi,
kī kareṅgā kothāẏ yāṅgā bhebe nāhi pāi!
bahuṭ jorse gāl ṭiptā dono āṅgli deke,
bilātī ek paini bājnā bājātā theke theke,
kabhī kabhī nikaṭ āke ṭhoṅṭme cimṭi kāṭṭā,
kāṅci le kar koṅkṛā koṅkṛā culgulo sab chaṅṭta, . . .

This woman, your sister, is torturing me so,
I can't think of what to do or where to go!
She pinches my cheek hard between her two fingers,
And keeps playing now and then upon some English piano thing;
Sometimes she comes up very close and pinches me on my lips,
Takes a scissor and begins to trim all my curly hair . . .[11]

Uncle and niece and nephew had many names for each other; among these, the most consistent nickname for her at home was Bibi, and he was their 'Robika' (a diminutive of Rabi-*kaka*; '*kaka*' being one's father's younger brother). Here, in these letters, however, he frequently addresses her as 'Bob'. The strange Englishness of the endearing nickname paradoxically seems typical of him, the committed Bengali man of letters. It could be speculated that this was an affectionate reference to the anglicized lifestyle of his brother's household. Indira's cousin Sarala has left an account of these children upon their return to Calcutta, already well travelled abroad, attending Loreto and St Xavier's schools respectively, going out in smart English clothes every evening in a carriage with a dog to take the air while the other children of the house gaped. Indira herself has remarked ruefully that she learnt to call her older brother

by his name in England as a child, a habit she retained, never using
the Bengali '*dada*' for him as custom demanded. 'Bob' might have
been a mocking variation on Bibi on account of all of this. It was
also private—in the notebooks, the name was scratched out in
blue pencil—as in 'It's quite a lovely day today, ~~Bob~~'—so that the
first edition, the *Chinnapatra*, or its translation, *Glimpses of Bengal*,
had no trace of it in them. Yet the use of it is so affectionate, so
engaging and particular in tone that its presence in the letters adds
an incalculable element that exactly captures the relation between
these two as nothing else could have done.

The Artist

Only two of the letters collected here in this book were written
in 1887, after which we skip a year and find a couple more from
1889, to be followed by four more from 1890. The flow of letters
picks up a more consistent speed from 1891 onward up to 1895.
Those were also the years when Rabindranath wrote some of the
best short stories in the Bengali language, published later in the
collection called *Galpaguccha* (Cluster of Stories), penned in close
contiguity to the Bengal countryside that gave them sustenance.
The landscape, in fact, demands a certain sort of art—'writing that
is quite simple, beautiful, sweet and generous'—not like the '*sickly*'
'convoluted' plots of Western novels such as *Anna Karenina* (an
opinion he excised from the *Chinnapatra*). In 'the calm current of
this small summer-worn river, the flow of the indifferent breeze, the
undivided expanse of the sky, the continuous peace of both shores
and the silence all around', the only reading that is appropriate are
'the shorter verses of the Vaishnava poets'; and the only writing that
is meaningful needs to be 'quite easy, beautiful, free or generous,
brightly tender, and rounded like a teardrop'.

The letters of the *Chinnapatrābalī* also contain vignettes of
many of the most memorable characters of his short stories. The
postmaster on whom the story '*Postmāstār*' was modelled makes

an appearance more than once—his wry character and sense of
the absurd are portrayed in satirical descriptions of the man and
his relationship with the village people—we also find out that he
was abashed and pleased at the same time about the story featuring
him as the protagonist. The young village tomboy who features in
another famous story, 'Samāpti' (The Ending), is also to be found
here in the original as the poet looks on as she is forcibly parted
from her natal family by the riverside and sent off to her distant
in-laws by boat. (Both stories were eventually filmed by Satyajit
Ray.) The process of a story being created around a character is
described in another letter:

> One of the pleasures of writing stories is that those I write about
> completely occupy my entire free time; they are the companions
> of my solitary mind—during the rains they drive away the sorrow
> of separation in my closed room, and when it is sunny, they roam
> around in front of my eyes like the bright scene on the shores of
> the Padma. That is why I have managed to make a small, proud,
> wheat-complexioned girl called Giribala descend into the world
> of my imagination this morning.[12]

If the characters in the stories are here, then so are their critics;
more than once we find Rabindranath exasperated with opinions
expressed by witless reviewers on the quality of his work. His
comments on the culture of reviewing in India, unfortunately, have
an even greater resonance today than they did then:

> The manner in which literary analysis is engaged with in our
> country is completely uneducated. There's no point in hearing:
> 'I liked it' or 'I didn't like it'. That only gives you a particular
> person's opinion; it doesn't give you the truth of that opinion. If
> that opinion comes from somebody who is sufficiently capable
> of appreciation or experienced in literary affairs then even that
> might make you think a little. But just any person's opinion has

no value at all. Our country lacks good reviewing skills—and the primary reason is that the people of our country do not have an intimate acquaintance with literature.

If reviewers are the bane of one's life, then being forced to write reviews unwillingly is a situation that invites the greatest sympathy, and the plight of a young man in the 'lonely leisure' of a 'tranquil Phālgun afternoon' in 1895, sitting on his private boat 'upon the still waters of the Padma, with the golden sunlight, blue skies and ashen sandbanks' in front of him, having to 'embark upon a review of *Dewan gobindarām* published by Sri Yogendranath Sadhu' is even more pitiable. The perfect day will 'be wasted' for a book as well as a review that nobody will ever read. A wonderful digression on 'a big, glossy, blue-coloured bee in a yellow cummerbund' follows, along with a meditation on the role of the bee in Indian literature, and the letter concludes: 'Just this moment another boat passed by mine. One of its Muslim oarsmen was lying flat on his back with a book on his chest and loudly and tunefully reciting from a poem. That man too has an appreciation for life—I'm sure you wouldn't be able to sit him down to review *Dewan gobindarām* even if you beat him up.'

The metaphoric beating he was taking at this time was in his bondage to the family-run journal *Sādhanā*; if the number of times he complains about editing, proofreading or writing for it in these letters is counted, it would come to no mean amount. The forced labour squeezed out of him in relation to the publication of this journal is time taken away not only from simply soaking in the beauty of the landscape—and Rabindranath has much to say about the virtue, even the indispensability, of leisure ('the complete rasa of idleness') here—but also from his most favoured vocation, that is, from writing his poems and songs, his *real* work.

Delightfully, we have a picture here of the posture and manner in which he composed his poetry, and even a description of the advantages of composing a tune in the bathroom for the song

Baṛa bedanār mata—quite a good song, he admits, and a favourite of his: 'Firstly, the seclusion; secondly, no other duty may claim you—if you pour a *tin* of water over your head and spend the next five minutes humming, your sense of duty doesn't suffer too much—and the greatest advantage is that since there's no possibility of an audience one can freely contort one's face as much as one wants.'* Contorting the face is common among Hindustani classical musicians, especially vocalists, and is indicative of the utter surrender to expression; fascinatingly, Rabindranath describes a similar abandon in the moment of composing poetry as well. Writing to Indira from Bolpur towards the end of May 1892, he says:

> This morning, getting out of bed a little late, I sat in the downstairs room leaning against a cushion with a slate on my chest and with my feet up, one on top of the other, and began to try and write a poem in the midst of the morning breeze and the call of the birds.

'It was all just beginning to gel—pleased expression, eyes slightly closed, head swaying frequently, and a rhythmic humming recitation growing progressively clearer—when suddenly', he is interrupted, but a brief period later, 'with a renewed nodding of the head and an indistinct humming', he resumes his 'poetic occupation'.

For Rabindranath here, there is 'more joy to be obtained from the completion of a single poem than in the writing of a thousand pages of prose'. Prose is 'an absolute specimen of a burden', while in poetry, 'one's thoughts attain a completion, almost as if one can pick it up with one's hands'. There's even a time for poetry and a time for prose—his 'short poems keep coming up spontaneously'

---

* *Baṛa bedanār mata bejecha tumi he āmār prāṇe,/mana ye keman kare mane mane tāhā manai jāne* . . . (Oh, you have played upon my heart like the deepest hurt/ Only the heart knows how dejected the heart feels, all on its own . . .)

in the heat of summer, and he is helpless before their demand. It will be winter, possibly, before he can deal with certain ideas for plays in his head, and this leads him to the realization that 'With the exception of *Citrāṅgadā*, all my other plays are written in the winter. That is the time when the passion of lyric poetry cools down a bit, and one can sit down calmly and quietly to write plays.' An entire letter on 20 November 1894 is devoted to the difference between prose and verse, of how prose belongs clearly to work and poetry to an immense ease or leisure, which is why poetry, indispensably, encapsulates the unnecessary.

Seeing (*dekhā*) is a trope that informs and illuminates the lines of these letters repeatedly, inexhaustibly and urgently. The mode in which his mind captures the images that fill these letters is one of stillness, of rest, of immobility and of meditation—'*Ei ye eklāṭi cup kare base ceẏe thākā*'—'this sitting quietly on one's own and looking' while the boat floats on in its journey to Goalundo. The rains, his favourite season always, transport him to another world. On the first day of the monsoon in Shilaidaha in 1892, thinking on the fact that a time will come when 'there will not be a single day remaining in my life of this day of Kalidasa, this day of *Meghdūt*, this first day of the rains in India for all of time past', all he wants to do is to look 'once again at this world very carefully'. Looking is also something that is inextricably tied to the landscape he traverses on his favourite houseboat. 'I am not yet satiated with what I have drunk of this sky,' he says, which is so expansive precisely because 'Bengal is on level ground', giving one a vast 'vista of its fields, [and] its riverbanks'. In short, 'there's no other place like this to keep looking and looking, and to fill up one's heart by looking'.

The seeing eye, however, is never far here from the inner eye of reflection and introspection, and the other theme of these letters is reminiscent of Rilke in more than one of his works. Although the more obvious correspondence may seem to be with *Letters to a Young Poet*, it differs from it in the immediacy and the affirmation of its own everydayness (the former, in comparison, more uniformly distant, lofty and advisory in tone). It is, rather, *The Book of Hours'* revelations of a lowly god, where god is but the embodiment of the artist's development and inspiration—'God, the rhyme'—and the astonishing, trembling life of the moment in *Notebooks of Malte Laurids Brigge* that come simultaneously to mind in the context of *Chinnapatrābalī*. Like Rilke, Rabindranath was an exceptionally prolific letter writer, and again, like him, all his letters 'are about himself, intimately, even when they are also about someone [or something] else', as Robert Vilain observed in his introduction to Rilke's *Selected Poems*. More than anything else, these letters of the *Chinnapatrābalī* are about the poet's own inner life, his struggle towards comprehension and, above all, of his perils *as a poet* or as an artist. Repeatedly, in these letters, we come across a determination to elucidate his own apotheosis of art, to clarify to himself the artist's role in society, to advocate that art and work are not dissociable, and to reiterate his belief in poetry's superiority. These themes play themselves out in letters crucial to our understanding of Rabindranath's writing.

The language of these letters is direct and unencumbered; compared with some of the poetry of the early period, the prose is straight and lean, conversational and contemplative. As we immerse ourselves in this luminous Bengali prose, the particular intimacy of the epistolary form allows us, for a moment, to be alone in the man's company. At the same time, it is worth remembering that the publication, in some part, of letters in conversational Bengali (*calti* or *calit bhāshā*) was first accomplished in Bengali literature in Rabindranath's *Europe prabāsīr patra* (Letters of Exile from Europe, 1879–80; 1881) at least a decade before these were written, and that eventual publication might well have been lodged in the interstices of his mind even as he was writing some of these letters to Indira. Another innovation with regard to the letters here was the use of Bengali dates in the original (sometimes alongside the English, sometimes not)—a practice the Tagore family helped popularize among English-educated Bengalis.

As we read, what is also worth remembering is that this is an unrevised manuscript published in full, with the exception of the censored sections. For someone who was famous for his endless and tireless revisions of his own writing—revisions whose shapes on the page acquired life to become artworks in time—the knowledge that the words here flow in an unselfconscious and unrestrained stream of thought (reminiscent of the term *nityaprabāhita cetanār mājhe* that he used in the context of children's rhymes in an essay written in this period at Shahjadpur)[13] is important, because the book does not merit a place in the world as a volume of Collected Letters, but rather as a literary work in its own right.

Often the sentences in these letters are very long, unbroken except for the successive commas or dashes,* continuing in their meandering way as they follow the thread of a thought:

> The ferries cross the river, travellers with umbrellas in hand walk
> by the road next to the canal, women immerse their wicker
> baskets and wash rice, the farmers come to market with bundles
> of tied jute on their heads—two men have flung a tree trunk
> on the ground and are splitting its wood with an axe, making a
> *thak-thak* sound, a carpenter works upon an upturned fisherman's
> boat under an *aśvattha* tree, repairing it with a chisel in hand, the
> village dog roams around aimlessly by the canal, a few cows lie
> lazily on the ground in the sun, swishing away flies with a languid
> movement of their ears and tails before they feed upon excessive
> amounts of fresh grass, and when the crows sitting on their backs
> irritate them beyond endurance, they shake their heads at them
> and express their annoyance.

* These long sentences, sometimes up to a page in length, have been kept intact along with their original punctuation of successive dashes or commas, wherever possible in these translations.

The cinematic image has a predecessor in such a paragraph, and the correspondences with the slow-panning camera movement in Satyajit Ray's visualization of village life in the *Apu Trilogy* cannot be coincidental. Along with the beauty of the camera's movement across this scene is the accompanying soundtrack that records, exactly and mesmerizingly, the incandescent nature of background sounds in the Bengal countryside; again something that Ray did path-breaking work on in his films. In a letter from Shahjadpur in 1893 Rabindranath records:

> The few monotonous *thak-thak thuk-thāk* sounds of this place, the cries of the naked children playing, the high-pitched tender songs of the cowherds, the *jhup-jhāp* noise of the oars, the sharp, sad sound of the oil mill hitting the *nikhād* note, all of these sounds work together and are in a sort of proportion to the bird call and the sound of the leaves—all of it seems to be some part of a long dreamlike *sonata* full of peace and enveloped in pity, somewhat in the mould of Chopin, but composed and bound to a very vast, spread-out, yet restrained metre.

The sensory is a source of delight, always. Again and again, he gives his thanks for being able to absorb with his senses the marvel of just being in the world; as he put it in a song many years later: *kān petechi, cokh melechi, dharār buke prāṇ ḍhelechi /jānār mājhe ajānāre karechi sandhān, /bismaẏe tāi jāge āmār gān.* (I hear, I see, I pour out my heart upon the breast of this earth/I have searched for the unknown in the midst of the known, /That is why my song awakens to wonder).

Repeatedly, he mentions the rustle of nature: 'This light and this air, this half-melancholy, half-happy feeling, this continuous trembling in the leaves of trees and fields of grain—', the 'shivering sound' of coconut fronds, or of the leaves of the *śiśu* trees in the south garden. On a Bolpur October day, when 'the endless cooing of the pigeons from within the dense mango orchards turns the entire field and sky and wind and dreamlike long hours of the dappled afternoon into a song of separation's sorrow', he feels that 'even the sound of the clock on my table seems to have merged with the tender melancholy of the afternoon's rustle of sound'. That feeling comes to him with special intensity in the afternoons ('These afternoons have made me fervent with feeling from my very childhood'), like a drone that resembles the buzzing of bees, bearing memories of his life, which have travelled to him 'borne upon a curious mixed rustle of sound' from very far away. The ancient Greek described by Hegel with which Barthes ends his brief essay 'The Rustle of Language' might well be a description of the poet Rabindranth: 'He interrogated, Hegel says, passionately, uninterruptedly, the rustle of branches, of springs, of winds, in short, the shudder of Nature, in order to perceive in it the design of an intelligence.'[14]

The responsiveness of this man to the sensory does not need the idylls of the countryside to find expression. In a letter from Calcutta in March 1895, he speaks of a morning spent in utter idleness, and of how, yet, he feels 'no regret at all for this laziness'—for 'this basanta morning breeze really wastes me'. He continues:

> Just letting this generous warm wind caress the whole body seems like a duty worth doing—it seems as though the flow of this sweet breeze is a conversation that nature holds with me. That I was born in this world, that the spring breeze came and touched me, that the smell of the kanakcāṁpā flower filled my head, that occasionally a morning such as this came to me in obeisance like a message from the gods—in the brief life of a man, how can this be insignificant!

Ruminating on the fact that 'all these forgotten unconscious moments too are an important part of a successful life', he has no regrets about the idle enjoyment of the morning, and also thinks, 'If this time had been spent in listening to a good song one would not have regretted that either.'

Songs are woven into this tapestry of letters like a recurrent motif; we see him write, compose, sing and reflect upon music repeatedly. Music and painting are two fields analogous to Rabindranath's poetic vocation that benefit from Theodor Adorno's remarks on the expressionism of Paul Klee, Franz Marc and Wassily Kandinsky and the music of Arnold Schoenberg, Alban Berg and Anton Webern in 'On the Relationship between Painting and Music Today'. 'A rebellion against reification' was how Adorno described the impulse of refusing any 'compartmentalization of the objective spirit's zones' in these artists, and while Rabindranath's creative accomplishments in these fields still await such inspired theorization, the fact that he forged an idiom in his painted work which, likewise, considered 'the material, indeed the sphere of aesthetic objectification itself, insignificant alongside the pure self-articulation of the subject' is evident to any viewer of his artwork. But that was much later. Now, in the years these letters are being written, he had not yet launched his career as an artist, although he reveals that, secretly, he wants to be a painter too, even though he is 'well known' as a 'colour-blind person':

> And then again, if one swallows one's pride and tells the absolute truth, then I have to admit that that thing called painting—I'm always looking towards it with the lustful glances of unrequited love—but there's no hope of winning it, the age for wooing it is past me now. Unlike the other knowledges, one cannot hope to acquire it easily—to attain it is like breaking the mythical bow; you cannot win its favour until you exhaust yourself with repeated strokes of the paintbrush.

The 'repeated strokes of the paintbrush' he mentions are with regard to the sort of painting being done at the time by Ravi Verma, whose paintings are mentioned in these letters, or, indeed, by his nephew Abanindranath Tagore. His subsequent discovery of the work of the Bauhaus painters—Klee and Kandinsky among them—that he was then instrumental in bringing to Calcutta in an exhibition in 1922 perhaps set him free from his own conventional notions, allowing him to refashion 'similarity to the object' in visual art.

The Land

Written from a variety of locations, as he travelled on work or on holiday, with family or on his own, the letters contained in this book are intensely visual, recording a landscape and countryside that contain, for the young man who writes of them, a narrative of discovery and belonging; and if he had been like Nehru in temperament, he too might well have called this very different book *The Discovery of India*. Even though a few of these letters were posted from London or Calcutta, the vast majority of them were from the towns and villages and even rivers of Bengal, and the litany of place names mentioned at the head of the letters may be said to constitute a poem in itself—from his boat on the Ichamoti or from Shahjadpur or Shilaidaha, from Boalia, Bolpur or Baliya to Cuttack, Dighapatia, Patishar or Natore.

The road or path so beloved of him, used so often as a metaphor in his poems and songs, here becomes incarnate; thus we have letters written 'On the way to Kushtia', 'On the road to Goalundo' or 'On the waterway to Dighapatia'. These place names now belong to Bangladesh, and that country has found new ways to reinvent the poetry of this text. In a play created from Rabindranath's letters in the *Chinnapatrābalī* titled *Bāṅglār māṭi bāṅglār jal* (Bengal's Land, Bengal's Water), itself a phrase from one of Rabindranath's best-known patriotic songs, Sayyed Shamsul Haq has devised a drama with Rabindranath as the main character but, more crucially, with all the ordinary people he wrote of in these letters—Gofur Mian, Gagan Harkara, the members of the Sunītisancāriṇī Sabhā, the village postmaster, the boatmen, the revenue collectors—as the other characters who speak in their own distinctive dialects.[15]

The ordinary women of village Bengal, especially, are a source of constant wonder—not just their shyness or their beauty but also their strength and combativeness, as he observes how, although 'hidden behind her veil', one woman has a 'voice like bell metal' that emerges without a 'trace of fear or anxiety', and that in this she is representative of most of the others of her sex and class. The rich complexity of these letters resides also, then, as the playwright has seen, in the range of people who make an appearance in them and in the involvement of the writer observing them go about their daily lives.

The presence of water has an overwhelming charisma in the countryside described in these letters. Writing on the East Bengal landscape of his youth—the early twentieth century—in *Bāṅgāli jībane ramaṇī*, Nirad Chaudhuri comments that its beauty has a certain 'vastness, glory and majesty' about it that he puts down to Bengal's waters. Eight of Rabindranath's 'greatest' short stories, according to him, are written in close proximity to Bengal's waters at this time, and the writing here, he feels, is as 'generous and tender' as the teardrop Rabindranath had envisaged as a metaphor for literary creativity in these environs. The life of the Bengali, according to Chaudhuri, resided in that landscape of 'river, water, a free, generous and blue sky, in clouds as dark as kohl or as white as the swan, in rice fields stretching up to the horizon and dense green forests'.[16] With Partition, that landscape has been lost, and with it the Indian Bengali has lost not only his natural wealth but also his heartbeat. For Rabindranath in these letters, however, that heartbeat of the water and the land in close conjunction with each other still resonates as he traverses 'this shadowy Bengal, encircled by the embrace of its affectionate rivers'. Smaller rivers, huge awe-inspiring rivers, rivers that wind their way through the sleepy countryside, rivers made dangerous by strong currents or stupefied by the lack of any, quite still and without movement— the Ichamoti, the Gorai, the Yamuna, the Padma—make repeated

appearances here. The river Padma is eulogized again and again—
she is a beloved presence, a living presence, sometimes calm, as in
the winter, but often angry and swollen and magnificent in the
poet's favourite season, the monsoon. The scenes on the shores of
these rivers of domestic rituals, children's play, women's chatter,
farmer's work, ferries plying, all find a mention as Rabindranath's
boat moves through their everyday lives and practices, forward on
a journey called life.

Nature is a living presence here; it is vibrant and perceptible, a third
who walks beside him. While strolling along the moonlit sandbanks
of the Padma by night, he resents the company of two acquaintances:

> The three of us are walking together, but for a while I am not
> in their presence as they walk. My serious, silent, moonlight-
> drowned world suddenly lets me know in the momentary break
> of conversation,' 'Don't think you have only two companions,
> we too are by your side today as we have always been before—'

Such instances are not rare, but recur:

> After discussing the arrangements for the transfer of property to
> another name on the rent roll, etc., for a while, the moment he
> stopped speaking—I suddenly saw the eternal universe standing
> silently in front of me that evening.

'I have a certain human domestic relationship with nature
here, a certain intimate familial feeling—which no one knows
but me,' he says one evening in August 1894 from his boat on the
Padma. Intimacy with nature is fervently expressed and deeply felt;
nature is often personified: as a veiled bride, as his *grhalakshmī*, as
companionate partner and lifelong friend—someone who strokes
his hair, touches his body, embraces him, gives him refuge. His
attachment to this earth is palpable:

This enormous world that is lying quietly over there—I love it so much—I feel like clutching its trees, rivers, meadows, noise, silence, dawn, dusk, all of it to me with both hands. I think: the treasures of this world that the world has given us—could any heaven have given us this?

What is the meaning of such desire? In a different letter, he realizes he doesn't have an answer: 'I don't quite understand what the desire entwined in it is—it's like a pulsating attachment with this vast earth—at a time when I was one with this world, when the green grass rose on top of me, the śaraṯ sunlight fell over me, when every pore of my green body—spread across enormous distances—let off the fragrance and heat of youth . . .' A sentiment Rabindranath expresses time and time again in his songs is recorded here as fact: 'This world is constantly new to me, like someone I have loved for a very long time and over many lives; there is a very deep and far-reaching relationship between the two of us.'

Ranajit Guha calls the connection between Rabindranath and nature expressed in his letters and songs 'antaraṅga ātmiẏatā', an intimate relationship. The perception of nature as an 'autochthonous entity' has a 'particular local impulse', and is felt most keenly by Rabindranath, he thinks, in the evenings and afternoons of certain seasons—that feeling of the revealed character of nature is related to a feeling of immediacy.[17] In a famous letter (Letter 142), Rabindranath had compared the 'world of the day' to 'European music' and 'the world of the night' to 'our Indian music, a pure, tender, serious, unmixed rāginī'. But if evening and night have an immediate existence here as companionate presences, dwarfing the humans in his proximity with their living presence, in these pages in particular, it is the afternoons that reappear most often with a felt intensity. The 'intense attraction' that the 'afternoons here' in Shahjadpur hold for him is described: 'The sun's heat, the silence, the solitude, the call of birds, especially the crow, and the

long, beautiful leisure—all of it entangled together makes me very
detached and yet emotional.' This immersion of self in the torpor
of still afternoon sunlight has affected him, he says, 'right from his
childhood', and here it seems that 'I want to write about the same
thing every day—the afternoons over here. Because I just cannot
surmount the attraction they hold for me. This light, this air, this
silence enters my pores and mixes with my blood—this is newly
intoxicating for me each day, I cannot say enough to exhaust the
tender intensity of it.'

Light, and space, and air are like an addiction in the pages of
these letters. Again and again, he speaks of these things being as
essential to him as the oxygen in one's lungs. 'The sky, the light,
the air and song have come together from every direction and
loosened me up and absorbed me within themselves', he writes
from Shilaidaha in 1892. Writing from the boat on the way to
Boalia in the śarat sunlight of September 1894, he exults:

How I love the light and the air! Perhaps because of the
appropriateness of my name. Goethe had said before he died:
More light!—if I had to express a wish at a time like that I would
say: *More light and more space!*

Goethe is mentioned often, and another quotation is given
twice in the original German in the same letter (*Entbehren sollst du,
sollst entbehren*), as though the music of the words was important
enough for the line to be quoted in German alongside the English
translation. He speculates:

If you want to keep the heart's faculties of sight, sound, touch
and thought vigilant, if you want the ability to receive all that
you can receive to remain sharp, you must keep the heart always
hungry—you have to deprive yourself of abundance. I have kept
something Goethe said always in mind—it sounds simple, but to
me it seems very deep—

Entbehren sollst du, sollst entbehren.
Thou must do without, must do without.

. . . That's why the relative comfort of Calcutta begins to prick me after a short while, as if its small pleasures and enjoyments were making it difficult for me to breathe.

Frugality of habit and extravagance of feeling, inner emotion and outer delight, leisure and work, land and water, the everyday and the eternal—each mode of being is contradicted and complimented by its opposite in the pages of this book of letters. Such a correspondence is a form of literary extravagance possible only when a surplus of thought and emotion accumulates. Other forms of literature remain the author's and are made public for his good; letters such as these that have been given to a private individual once and for all become the reader's with an intimacy that is therefore characterized by a more generous abandonment. What they do, above all else, is allow us to savour with some immediacy the plangent feeling of being in the presence of a young poet within the radiant particularity of time and place inhabited so intensely by him here.

1

Darjeeling
September 1887

We've only just reached Darjeeling. Beli *behave*d very well on the way.* Didn't cry a great deal, although she did holler and create a commotion, and ululated as well, and turned her hands around and called out to the birds, though one couldn't see where the birds were. There was a great fuss while boarding the steamer at Sārā ghat. Ten o'clock at night—thousands of things, very few coolies, five women, and only one man. After crossing the river we managed to get on to a small train which had four sleepers while we (including Makhan) were six human beings. The women and all the extra things were loaded on to the *ladies' compartment*—the statement is brief, but the doing of it wasn't quite so simple. There was a huge amount of calling and shouting and running around involved—still, Na-didi says I didn't do a thing.† That is, a full-

---

* Beli (Bela): Rabindranath's firstborn, daughter Madhurilata, born 25 October 1886.
† Na-didi: Swarnakumari Debi (1855–1932), fourth daughter of Debendranath Tagore and Rabindranath's older sister (*didi*). She was an accomplished writer, editor of *Bhāratī* and *Bālak*, famous nationalist and activist for women's rights.

grown man like me, accompanying five women, should have done a great deal more of calling and shouting and running around, and should have sometimes got off here or there on the *platform* to stride around spouting Hindustani. That is, it would have been much more appropriate for me to have become the image of what happens when one whole man gets wholly incensed—that would have been more befitting of a real man. Na-didi was utterly *disappointed* with my cool demeanour. But in these two days I have opened so many boxes and closed them again and shoved them underneath benches and then pulled them out again from the same place, and I have chased after so many boxes and bundles, and so many of these boxes and bundles have followed me around like a curse, so many have been lost and so many found again, and so many not found again and then so much effort expended in trying and continuing to try for their retrieval, in a way that no twenty-six-year-old son of polite parents has had fated to happen to him. I'm sure I've developed box-*phobia*—when I see a box, my teeth start chattering. When I look all around me and all I see are boxes, only boxes, small, big, medium, light and heavy, wooden and tin and leather and cloth—one on top, one below, one on the side, one behind—then all my ordinary strength to call and shout and run around ebbs away—and then if you see my vacant gaze, drawn face and poor aspect you'll think me a downright coward—therefore Na-didi's opinion of me is quite correct—trapped in the midst of this variety and multiplicity of boxes, I was not myself. Tell Suren to draw a picture of me in this state. Anyway. After that I got into another compartment and lay down. That compartment had two other Bengalis in it. They had come from Dhaka—the moment you saw them you thought of them somehow as being from Dhaka [*dhākāi*]—one of the two had a head that was almost completely bald and speech that was extremely at an angle—he asked me, 'Was your father on Darjeeling?' If Lakhhi had been there she would have had an appropriate answer; perhaps she would have said: 'He was on Darjeeling, but Darjeeling was feeling cold then, so he has gone home now.' My reflexes couldn't supply me with such Bengali.

From Siliguri to Darjeeling, Sarala's continuous wonderstruck *exclamations*: 'O my, how wonderful', 'how amazing', 'how beautiful'—she kept nudging me and saying, 'Rabi-mama, look, look!'* What to do, I must look at whatever she shows me—sometimes trees, sometimes clouds, sometimes an invincible blunt-nosed mountain girl, or sometimes so many things at the same time that the train leaves it all behind in an instant and Sarala is unhappy that Rabi-mama didn't get to see it, although Rabi-mama is quite unrepentant. The train kept on going. Beli kept on sleeping. Forests, hilltops, mountains, streams, clouds and a vast number of flat noses and slant eyes began to be seen. Progressively it became wintry, and then there were clouds, and then Na-didi developed a cold, and then Baṛ-didi began to sneeze, and then shawls, blankets, quilts, thick socks, frozen feet, cold hands, blue faces, sore throats and, right after, Darjeeling.† Again those boxes, those bags, that bedding, the same bundles. Luggage piled on luggage, bearer upon bearer. Checking all the things kept in the *brake*, identifying them, loading them on to the heads of the bearers, showing the receipt to the *saheb*, arguing with the saheb, not finding things, and then making various arrangements to find those lost things—all this took me about two hours, by which time Na-didi and company had got into their conveyance, gone home, wrapped themselves up in shawls and were reclining on sofas, resting, thinking to themselves that Rabi was not really fully a man yet.

* Sarala: Rabindranath's niece and Swarnakumari's daughter, Saraladebi Chaudhurani, who was best known for her militant nationalism and, later, her friendship with Mahatma Gandhi.

† Baṛ-didi: Saudamini Debi, first daughter of Debendranath Tagore and Rabindranath's eldest sister.

2

Darjeeling
1887

You will get all the news about my back from Suri's letter.* Never
again shall I think of the back as merely a place to tuck in the
ends of one's *dhuti*—man's humanity is sheltered in his back. If
today's letter is *dull*, that is, if it has no *movement*—if my pen does
not move fluidly from subject to subject, feeling to feeling, news
to news—then you will know that it is the fault of my broken
back—one cannot blame anything else. In addition, occasionally
there is a disastrous sneeze released—and it seems as if the upper
half of the body shall hurtle away from the broken back. But that's
it. I shall not write of my back any more. I swear that I shall not
write of my back again! Worthless waist, and it too has a tale!
Firstly it neglected every law of *aesthetics* and gradually increased
its girth in serial increments; over and above that, it has a thousand
different demands. Whoever I speak to about this back laughs; it
attracts nobody's pity; as if breaking one's back is in any respect
any less than breaking one's heart! But I will not speak of it—I do
not ask for pity—

>   My back is mine alone,
>   I have not sold it to anybody else!
>   It may be broken, but whatever it is
>   My back remains mine alone!

But however proud I try to be in my verse—the truth is I really
wish my back was somebody else's back! I have heard of the phrase
that tells you that it is always best to oil one's own mill, and I've
always agreed, but if you are speaking of the back then I'll freely

---

* Suri: Surendranath Tagore, Indira's brother.

say that rather than massage hot mustard oil into my own back, I would much rather *prefer* to knead oil into somebody else's back. On this subject, my *sentiments* are entirely *unselfish*, in fact *almost Christian*! But let it be; when I have promised not to speak of my back let us not speak of it. Because, apart from the back, man has many other parts to his body; he has a mind, a heart, a soul—but whatever you say, he also has a back—very much so—

> I have immersed my mind in enjoyment
> Yet   why does my back ache so!
> All around me people move around,
> My   back, why does it ache so!

When one is heartbroken, one comes to the hills to be comforted, but if one's back is broken, then level ground is the best place. I was thinking of those bolsters in Park Street, and at the same time, a few other memories came to mind—but that's it—I shall not speak of anything to do with my back any more—I shall forget everything about the time I last suffered from backache; but the ache in my back right now—how do I forget that?—

> Keep aside your *bīṇā*,   do not sing your song,
>   How will my pain be gone?

Na-didi said there's a way out—'*Rus Tox 6th dilution* every two hours.' I too think so. Sarala is waiting to read my letter and *contradict* me. But the poor thing will be extremely disappointed—there's no way she can look into what is happening inside my back, her womanly *prying instinct* cannot enter there, for there is *no admittance* there for anything *except* mustard-oil *ointment*. But still, it doesn't seem as if Sarala will give up. She will not tolerate my receiving any sympathy from all of you in this foreign land. This time, though, you will have to concede that as far as my back is concerned, I remain the most trustworthy informant, even Sarala is not a *better authority* on this subject. But, Bob, don't worry about this back of mine at all—I shall silently suffer this back of mine all on my own. But 'silently' is the wrong word, because the manner in which I've been shouting out loud from time to time when compelled to move about cannot exactly be called silent. And this letter I've written to you today can hardly be called silent either. I had thought at first that you would come to know all about my back from Suren's letter—that I would not speak of or raise the subject of my back with you, that I would not awaken those old memories of oil massages—but look where we've ended up! Instead—

> All of that, all of that,   that lamentation
>   Those flowing tears, the backache.

But I shall not speak about my back any more—mainly because I'm running out of space. If there were space enough, I could continue to speak of it from now up until *Doomsday*. But would I have been able to stand up on *Doomsday* with this back? The trumpet would sound, everybody would stand, and I would be moaning with my hand on my back. But that's not something to make light of; you might just get a little annoyed. In any case, both my letter and talk of my back end here.

3

Calcutta
June 1889

When the train started, Beli sat gravely, looking all around her, thinking, where did my sisters go, where am I going—in this world, where do we come from and where do we go, what is the purpose of life—and as she thought, gradually I saw her yawning repeatedly and, a little later, she put her head down on the ayah's lap, stretched her legs, and began to doze. My mind too was weighed down by many worries about the joys and sorrows of our existence, but I couldn't sleep. So I began to sing the Bhairabī *ālāp* to myself. You know, perhaps, when you hear the embellishments in Bhairabī, a strange feeling towards the world rises in you—it is as if the hand of habit is endlessly turning the handle of an organ and the pain of that friction is making a deep, sorrowful, piteous *rāginī* well up from the entire universe's innermost being—all the morning light of the sun pales, the trees stand silently as if listening to something, and the world over the sky seems overcast with misty tears—that is, if you look at the distant sky, it seems as if an unblinking blue eye, swimming with tears, is looking at you. Near Khirkee station I could see those sugar-cane fields of ours, the rows of trees, the tennis courts, the glass window–covered house; seeing these my mind suddenly filled with emptiness and despair. How surprising! When I used to live there, it wasn't as if I was particularly fond of this house—even when I left it to go to Solapur with all of you I can't say that I was very distressed—yet when I glimpsed it for an instant from the speeding train window—that solitary house, standing with its playing fields and empty rooms—then it was as if my entire heart leapt upon that house at lightning pace, and it began to seem to me that if we could somehow all sit down in that house again in a group, temporarily life would somehow be fulfilled and the emptiness of this world somehow banished. . . . As soon as I saw the house, it struck my heart with a thump—from the left side to the right a thudding sound—while the train went whistling past, whoosh—the sugar-cane fields dissolved—that's all, it's all over—only, because of the sudden attack, two or three strings in my heart descended by a few scales. But the train's engine doesn't think very much on all these issues, it keeps going single-mindedly on the steel tracks, it doesn't have the time to think about who is going where and in what way—it only glugs down water, lets out steam in spurts, shouts out loud and rolls on. It might have been possible to use this as a metaphor for the course of life, but that would be so stale and unnecessary that one can only hint at it and stop. Near Khandala there was cloud and rain. Clouds had congealed at the top of all those hills and obscured them—exactly as if somebody had drawn hills and then rubbed an eraser over them—a few *outlines* were visible and in some the pencil lines had been smudged. . . . Finally the train bell rang—its red, wakeful eye could be seen from a distance; the earth began to tremble; the station officers began to come out of their many rooms wearing their sandals, buttoned official dress and liveried round caps over their tufts—their enormous handheld lanterns scattering light in all directions; the startled ranks of khansamas alertly guarded each one's luggage; Beli continued to sleep; my heart began to beat very fast. . . . I said to the ayah, 'Hurry, pick Beli up and bring her with you.' As soon as Beli arrived a pair of *memsahebs* overtook me at great speed and made for the empty carriage. I thought to myself 'Whatever happens, I *will* get into that coach.' The memsahebs went and stood in front of the empty coach and I too stood there; the guard arrived, I asked him, 'Is this a ladies' compartment?' Immediately the *mem* said to him, 'Of course, if necessary it can always be *reserved* for ladies.' The guard made no reply and inquired after my destination; I said, Calcutta. He said, *'You may get in sir!'* The mem too began to try and get into the coach; her husband told her not to. Suddenly the guard asked me where my 'lady' was. I said I had no lady with me, but was accompanied by a *maid servant*, upon which the woman went a little distance away and began to laugh loudly, saying to the saheb, *His maid servant!* In other words, the woman this black man was calling his *maid servant might be his wife as well!* . . . At any rate, I said to myself, you can laugh, but I have the empty compartment. But one funny thing was that I saw that the saheb did not want to cause me any inconvenience. If he had not been there, the woman would have got into the carriage out of *spite* and occupied it—yet there was space in the other cars. I firmly believe that if these beauteous English women with their turned-up noses had never come to India then the English would have behaved much better with us; it is they who are at the bottom of *Anglo-Indian* attitudes. They are supposed to be terribly *delicate*, their heads ache very easily and they are easily *shocked*, that's why they cannot feel any empathy for the black races. Alas! After having undertaken such a lot of soap scrubbing, intake of khana, and emptying of so many bottles of *Cherry Blossom*, the tips of their white noses continue to remain crinkled. One feels like cursing, 'May you be born in your next birth as women in the South and may your husbands pierce the tips of those noses of yours.' . . . Beli pointlessly began to whimper a little. The day wore on, and although there was no sun, it began to feel hot. . . . Time refused to pass. Every minute seemed to have to be physically pushed forward. . . . Began to read *Anna Karenina*, but it was so dreadful that I couldn't—what is the point of reading these sorts of *sickly* books, I don't understand. I want writing that is quite simple, beautiful, sweet and generous—a strange mess of a situation full of convoluted turns doesn't suit me for very long. Thankfully, it began to rain heavily after a while. It felt good to shut everything on all sides and sit down by the glass window to watch the clouds and the rain. At one place the sight of a monsoon river was quite amazing. It had become swollen and enlarged, frothing, twisting, muddied, racing, banging its head against the stones upon which it flung itself, hitting and falling over them, leaping over and whirling around them, behaving most terribly. I've never seen such madness anywhere else. By the time we got to Sohagpur in the evening and had our dinner, the rain had stopped; when the train started I noticed the sun setting brilliantly among the clouds. I was thinking often of all of you, that for you time was passing unnoticed while you ate, played, studied and conversed—time was flowing over you and you hadn't even noticed its presence—and I was swimming through time, the entire expanse of time was hitting my face, my heart, my whole body. . . .

[In] due course the train reached Howrah. At first the house sweeper, after that Jogini, then Satya, all emerged into my field of vision one by one. And then with the bedding on the second-class roof, the ayah's battered tin trunk, and the bathing tub (which had a feeding bottle, *lotā*, *hāṅṛi*, tin pot, bundle, etc.) loaded, we managed to reach home. A commotion and a hubbub, a crowd of people, *dāroẏān*'s salaam, servants' *praṇām*, managers' namaskar, the absolute difference of opinion among people generally on who has become fat and who thin, Swayamprabha and co.* tumbling about with Bela, everybody gathered around the tea table, a bath, food, etc.—all of this you can well imagine. Suddenly Dada arrived and began a tremendous lecture on common sense—a huge commotion ensued.[†] Khoka looked very novel to me when I saw him.[‡] A big round head, an absolute simpleton [*nitānta hāṅdā*], quite dark, shaven head, chubby cheeks, the constantly wavering look on his face and eyes one of absolute brainlessness, plump hands curled into fat fists—if you make a movement or a sound of any sort to draw his attention, he smiles, if you give him a squeeze or a shake, he expresses his gratification with a loud *ho-ho* laugh. These are his *general characteristics*, but in all these departments I don't see much difference between him and the rest of the children of the human race. . . .

4

Shilaidaha
29 November 1889

[Our] boat is moored to the front of a sandbank on the other side of Shilaidaha. It's a vast sandbank—utterly desolate—its limits

* Swayamprabha was the daughter of Sharatkumari Debi, and a niece of Rabindranath's.

† *Dada*: Bengali term for elder brother; also used as a suffix. It is unclear in this instance which older brother is being referred to.

‡ Khoka: Rathindranath Tagore, Rabindranath's second child and elder son, born on 27 November 1888.

cannot be seen—just sometimes, in some places, the river's lines are visible—while again, sometimes you could mistake the sand for the river—no villages, no people, no trees, no grass—for variety occasionally cracked wet earth, and in some places dry white sand—if you turn your face towards the east you can see endless blue above and endless white below, empty sky and empty earth; a wretched, dry, hard emptiness underneath and a spirit-like, generous emptiness above. Such *desolation* isn't to be seen anywhere else. If you suddenly turn your face towards the west, you see the lap of a still, small river, tall banks on the other side, trees and bushes, huts, all looking like an amazing dream in the light of the setting sun. Exactly as if on the one side you have creation and on the other annihilation. The reason for mentioning the light of the evening sun is that we normally go out for a stroll in the evening, and therefore it is that picture that remains etched on the mind. When one is living in Calcutta one forgets how astonishingly beautiful this world is. It is only when you live here that you comprehend that this sun that sets every day among these peaceful trees by the side of this little river, and the hundred thousand stars that silently rise every night above this endless, ashen, lonely, silent sandbank—what a surprisingly noble event this is. The sun, as it rises slowly in the east at dawn, opens a page in some tremendous book, and the evening gradually turns another enormous page in the sky from the west—what an amazing script that too is— and this barely flowing river and this sandbank spread across the horizon and the other shore like a picture—this neglected bit at the edge of the world—what sort of large, silent, deserted school is this! Anyway. These words may sound very much like 'poetry' in capital letters, but here they are not out of place at all. Anyhow, as a family we experience the pure joy of separation for some time in the evenings in this huge sandy expanse—the boys go with their attendant in one direction, Bolu goes in another direction, I go my own way and the two women go their way. . . . In the meantime, the sun sets entirely, the golden hue fades from the sky, the surroundings become unclear in the dark; gradually, from the faint shadow by my side I realize that the bent, thin moon's light is slowly beginning to blossom—the white moonlight upon the white sand seems to increase the illusion for one's eyes—which is sand and which water, which is earth and which sky, one needs to guess at which is which. As a result, it all merges into one another and begins to feel like an unreal mirage-world. . . . Yesterday, after loitering on this magic coast for a long time, I went back to the boat and saw that except for the boys, nobody else from our group had returned. For a moment I thought, let me send for them, but both selfishness and pity together disarmed me. In other words, keeping both my own happiness and theirs in mind, I drew up an *easy chair* and began to read a book upon an extremely obscure *subject*—*Animal Magnetism*—in the equally obscure light of just one lamp. But still nobody returned. . . . Keeping the book face down on the bed I ventured out. Looking out from upstairs I could see no sign of any dark heads anywhere—everything around faded into a pale emptiness. I shouted out Bolu's name once at the top of my voice—its sound ran eerily past me in ten different directions—but there was no response; then my heart suddenly seemed to stop on every side, as happens when you suddenly close a big open umbrella. Gofur took a light and went out, Prasun went, the oarsmen of the boat went, everybody went in different directions—I went one way, shouting, 'Bolu', 'Bolu'—Prasun on another side calling 'Choto-ma'—occasionally, one could hear the sound of the boatmen's faint 'Babu', 'Babu'.* In that desert, on that silent night, several shouts could be heard rising. Not a sound anywhere. Once or twice from a far distance Gofur called out, 'I see them,' but almost immediately corrected himself, 'No, no'— just try and imagine the state I was in! If you must imagine it you have to picture all of it—the silent night, the weak moonlight, the

---

* Choto-ma: Rabindranath's wife, Mrinalini Debi. Later referred to as 'Choto-bau': wife of the youngest son in a joint family.

lonely, quiet, empty sands; far away, the moving light from Gofur's lantern—sometimes, from a certain side, a distressed call in the form of a question could be heard, and from every other side, its indifferent echo—occasionally, a flicker of hope, and in the next moment, deep despair. All sorts of the most impossible anxieties started to arise in my mind. Perhaps they have fallen into quicksand; perhaps Bolu has suddenly had a fainting fit or something; all sorts of frightful hallucinations of carnivorous animals began to come to mind. I began to think: 'Those unfit to protect themselves are those who unthinkingly bring danger to others.' I became firm against women's liberation—I could quite see that Bolu, poor thing, was a complete innocent; he had been compromised because he was at the mercy of the two free women. After about an hour, a cry arose that the entire lot had climbed up on the dunes and were marooned on the other side, unable to return. Then I ran towards the *boat*—it took a long time to reach it. The *boat* went to the other side; the *boat's* goddess returned to the boat—Bolu began to say, 'I'm never going out with you lot again.' Everybody was penitent, tired, distressed, so all my well-chosen and impressive remonstrances remained in my heart—waking up in the morning the next day, I still found myself incapable of getting angry. So we all dismissed this enormously serious affair by laughing about it, as if it was all greatly amusing. Anyway, writing about it in detail to you over the course of the last three days has certainly made my mind feel much lighter.

Oh no! The *maulabī* saheb has arrived with a crowd of peasants★ and has salaamed—I feel like saying to him—

Fie on you, these peasants and these estates—
Let the estate go to nothing, and take the maulabī with it!

★ The word *prajā* literally means subject or the people, and here refers to the poor tenanted farmers who tilled the estates. The word 'peasant' or 'tenant' has been used throughout in place of prajā.

5

Shahjadpur
January 1890

The students of the Entrance School here have formed a
Sunītisancāriṇī Sabhā [Society for the Dissemination of Good
Morals] in which they deliver lectures on ethics, and their *masters*
had come to catch hold of me so I could light up the face of
their proceedings. When they all got into action about my poetic
ability and a variety of other great talents—when they reached top
gear on the subject of my gifts in comparison to every *master* and
every *pundit* ever, with one person taking off at the point at which
another had stopped—if one says poet, another says great poet and
yet another says that the language and the feeling both equal each
other, a fourth says everything is new, Bengali literature has not
seen the like of it until now—what the fifth said cannot be declared
publicly, hearing what the sixth had to say the tips of my ears became
quite red—before the seventh could speak I hurriedly agreed to be
present at their Society for the Dissemination of Good Morals. The
second master of the school here is a particular fan of my *Heṅyāli
nāṭya*.* He said my '*Heiṅli nāṭya*' was completely new in the Bengali
language—'Reading this, we are falling about laughing!' The next
day, we managed to arrive at the Society for the Dissemination of
Good Morals. Boys and old men included, there must have been
about five or six hundred people there—some quite thin, with no
shoes, sitting upon benches swinging their feet and coughing; some
others were quite fancy, with watch chains over massive new black
alpaca robes [*cāpkān*], that is, our *munsef*s, lawyers, etc.† I was sitting

---

  * *Heṅyāli nāṭya* was the title of a number of charades composed by Rabindranath
and published in the periodicals *Bālak* and *Bhāratī* between 1885 and 1886.
  † A *munsef* was an officer trying suits at the lowest civil court. The *cāpkān* was
a long and loose robe that was usually part of the official dress.

there quite dejected, my hands and feet quite cold, face getting quite red, when suddenly somebody announced that the revered Sri Rabindranath Thakur Esquire should take his seat as chairman. The munsef-babu said, 'I second that.' Without a word, I ascended the seat of the chairman. The students are supposed to speak on the subject of modesty today. I wait expectantly . . . And then a large, sleek boy from amongst them got up and began to deliver a lecture on *modesty* in the English language. He said:

> Modesty is an ornament of mind. Modest men are praised and immodest men blamed by all. Every man is pleased to see a modest man, but a proud man is very much disliked. Newton was a modest man. When his dog upset an ink bottle on his papers Newton said to his dog, 'My friend, you do not know what harm you did to me'—such was his modesty. Brethren, let us all be like Newton. One day Chaitanya was walking in the street—a dog was lying on his way—Chaitanya said, 'My friend, please move a little'—the dog moved away at once—such was the force of his modesty. The dog required no beating. We should treat every man like this dog.

He gave everybody a lot of good advice in this way. A second student stood up, and in melodious Bengali began to say:

> Once upon a time my travelling companions and I were all sojourning together. Afflicted by the summer heat we entered a pleasant, birdsong-filled forest glade. (A very long description) At one place we saw some men employing manly words while engaged in the fiercest argumentation. We did not know who they were—our companions had fallen behind, so they too could not be asked. After going a little further, we arrived at a flower-bedecked, becalmed poolside upon which swans floated peacefully. (Long description) Upon seeing some beauteous maidens sporting upon the waves, we surmised these must be the daughters of gods.

Later we came to know that those aforementioned men were
pride and arrogance, and these beauties were modesty. Modesty
has endless virtues. Of all the virtues with which God has blessed
mankind, modesty is the most valuable virtue of all. Oh, when
you see modesty in men then the eyes fill up with tears of joy
and the heart is flooded with delight. Etc.

After this another boy immediately got up and began—

There is no virtue anywhere that can compare with modesty.
Everybody everywhere is appreciative of the modest person.
Be obedient to your mother and father and everybody—
Only then will everyone call you a modest person.

                                                            Etcetera

Another boy began with modesty and ended with true love
and God's endless mercy. After every speech, there was ringing
applause for some time. I sat there, quite clueless. Suddenly the
Headmaster came and said, 'There are many more compositions,
but everybody is eager to hear your speech.' Face drawn, hands
and feet cold, ears ringing, hemming and hawing, I stood up and
started. I said, 'Before I start to speak on the subject of modesty, I
should humbly say that I am not sure I will be able to speak very
much about the subject. I completely agree with the speakers
preceding me, the students who have proved that modesty is among
one of our chief virtues: undoubtedly, Newton was very modest,
nobody can doubt that any more.'—This was the way things went.
Gradually, as I spoke, one or two thoughts made an appearance.
After I sat down, two by two they went up and began to praise my
qualities and those of my ancestors. The first to rise was the *head
pundit*. He said he didn't have the power to speak, but after having
heard my speech he was so charmed that he was unable to help
himself—that the powers of poetry, oratory and, on top of these,
singing, could not be found combined anywhere but in me. Having

said this, he sat down with a thud. The *second master* rose and said, 'I do not think what the master pundit has said is enough, more needs to be said on the subject. The person who is present before us today is no ordinary person; who does not know the name of the revered mahatma (at this point he forgot the name he needed, until somebody nearby prompted him) Dwarakanath Thakur— whose name, it would not be an exaggeration to maintain, is well known all over the world—who is his grandfather, and his father, the great saint, or you could say great king, Debendranath Thakur.' This was followed by 'poetic prowess' and 'Heiṅli nātya'. I was completely taken aback. Then he said, what is the need for a lecture on modesty—*Example is better than precept*—he is himself the best example of modesty. Etc. Etc. Everyone clapped. Then the meeting broke up.

6

Shahjadpur
January 1890

So it was that in the afternoon I put on my turban, wrote my name on a card, got into my palanquin and set off as the *jamidār-bābu*. The saheb was dispensing justice from the veranda of his tent, the police spies to his right. Those seeking justice were waiting around on the grounds, the fields, under the trees—the palanquin was put down right under his nose, so the saheb politely seated me on a chair. A young lad, a hint of a moustache, very blonde hair with occasional black patches in between—so that it had turned out very strange; one might suddenly think him an old man, yet the face was very immature. Exchanged a vast amount of felicitations with the saheb; said to him, 'Come and have dinner with me tomorrow evening.' He said, 'I'm leaving for somewhere else today itself to arrange for *pig-sticking*' (I was secretly pleased). Said I'm very sorry to hear that. The saheb said, 'I return on Monday' (which made me very gloomy). I said, 'Then make it on Monday.' He was instantly agreeable. Anyway, I sighed and reminded myself that Monday was still some distance away, and reached home. Terrible clouds darkened the sky—an immense storm, pounding rain. Didn't feel like touching a book, it was impossible to write, the mind became terribly restless, what in poetic language one would say is a feeling of something missing, some desired one absent and not to be found anywhere near, etc. I paced through this room and that—it had become dark, thunder rolled, lightning struck repeatedly, gusts of wind whistled though the air and seemed to take hold of the low tree in front of our veranda and shake it by its beard—in no time at all our dry canal filled up almost completely . . . I feel like writing another like that, but perhaps there is nothing more to write. Anyway, while wandering around in this manner, it suddenly struck me that it was my duty to ask the *magistrate* to shelter in my house in this storm. Dashed off a letter, 'Saheb, you shouldn't leave for *pig-sticking* in this weather—although you are the son of a saheb, it is impossible for the species who live on land to reside in tents, therefore if you think dry land is a good thing, then do come and take shelter with me.' After sending off the letter, when I went to inspect the room I saw that it had two bamboo hammocks with mattresses, pillows and dirty quilts hanging from them—the servants' tobacco, two wooden chests, also theirs, a worn-out quilt, also theirs, a coverless oily pillow and a blackened cane mat, also theirs, a piece of torn jute with a variety of worn-out faded marks—some . . . boxes with the remnants of broken things—such as the rusted lid of a kettle, a bottomless broken iron oven, a very dirty zinc sheet, the bottom of some glass tumblers, shards of glass from a broken lamp, a dirty candlestick, two *filters*, a *meat safe*, some thin liquid gur in a *soup-plate* that had become thick with layers of dust, many broken and whole plates, a few dirty, wet, black dusters—in one corner, a bucket to wash plates in, Gofur Mian's dirty kurta and old velvet *skull cap*, a weather-beaten, ant-eaten, mirror-less *dressing table* adorned with

water marks, oil marks, milk marks, gur marks, black marks, *brown*
marks, white marks and mixed-colour marks—its frameless broken
mirror kept leaning somewhere else against a wall, its cavities filled
with dust, toothpicks, *napkins*, old locks, bottoms of broken glass
tumblers and *soda water bottle* wires, some bed stands, rods and rice,
one broken-legged *washhand stand*, a terrible smell, the walls stained
and with nails driven in here and there—seeing this state of affairs, I
was completely astounded.—'Call everybody, bring the *nāÿeb*,* call
the *khājāñci*,† find some coolies—bring the broom, bring water, set
up the ladder, untie the cord and the bamboo sticks, pull down the
pillows, the quilt, the covers, pick up the pieces of broken glass bit
by bit, dislodge the nails one by one . . .' 'Hey, what are all of you
doing standing there open-mouthed, take, take these things away
one by one—O my God, broken, they've broken everything—bang,
crash, smash—three glass lamps broken to bits—pick them up
piece by piece.' I pulled down and threw away the broken baskets
full of accumulated dust and torn mats with my own hands—five
or six cockroaches emerged from under them with their families
and scattered all over the place. They had been residing with me
as part of my joint family—living off my gur, my bread, and the
varnish off my very own *burnished* new shoes. The saheb wrote, 'I'm
coming right now, am in grave danger.' '*Ore*, he's here, he's almost
here—hurry, quickly.' And then—there comes the saheb! Quickly
dusting off my hair and beard, I become quite the bhadralok, sitting
with him in the hall as if I had no work at all at hand, as if I had
been sitting around relaxing the entire day. With the occasional little
smile and much waving of hands I begin to chat with the saheb
in a most carefree way. The thought of what had become of the
saheb's bedroom kept pushing its way into my mind from time to
time. Went and saw that it had somehow managed to pass muster.
Perhaps the night might even pass peacefully, unless those homeless

---

* *Nāÿeb*: administrator and rent collector of the estate.
† *Khājāñci*: treasurer or paymaster of the estate.

cockroaches tickle the soles of his feet at night. The saheb said, 'I'll
leave tomorrow morning for shikar.' I didn't object. In the evening,
the saheb's broken-down *pāik* came and reported that his tent had
been torn to pieces in the storm. His *kāchāri* tent too was destroyed
in the rain, so the plan to hunt animals had to be put on hold, and
he has had to remain stationary at the jamidār-babu's for now.*

7

London
3 October 1890

When I come to this country I really, truly think of that wretched,
unfortunate Bhāratbhūmi of ours as my mother. She does not have
the power this country has, the wealth it has, but she loves us. All
the love I have felt since I was born, all the happiness, is in her
lap. The attractive spit and polish of this place will never be able
to lure me—it'll be such a relief to return to her. If I could sit in
one corner of that land and like a honeybee accumulate love in
my own hive, remaining unknown to all of civilized society, then
there is nothing more I could want.

8

London
10 October 1890

Is man an iron machine that he shall always run on schedule? Man's
mind is a thing that functions in so many diverse ways—it moves in

---

* *Pāik*: footman, guard or messenger. *Kāchāri*: landlord's, or in this case the
district magistrate's, court of justice.

so many directions—and it has so many claims, that it must lean in one direction or the other. That is its life's aim, its sign of humanity, its protest against inertia. A person who does not have this hesitation, this weakness, is terribly narrow and hard and lifeless. Our life force is that which we call propensity [*prabrtti*], which we are always criticizing in harsh language—through our many joys and sorrows, good deeds and sins, this is what allows us to blossom towards the cosmic. If we completely disbelieve our inclination, we would make the same mistake as the river if it were to wonder at every step, 'Why, where is the ocean, there is only desert, forest and sandbank to be seen, perhaps the power that pushes me onward is taking me in the wrong direction.' We too are flowing every day through many apprehensions, we cannot see our end, but He who has given us, in this limitless life, the tremendous force called our propensity, He alone knows how to use that force to direct us. We always make the enormous mistake of thinking that we shall perhaps be abandoned in this place to which our propensity has brought us; we cannot know then that we shall be drawn out of that situation. The power that brings the river to the desert is the same power that takes it to the sea. What pushes us into our mistakes is the very thing that pulls us out again. This is how we move on. The person who doesn't have this propensity of his, or the plenitude of this life force, whose mind does not manifest its mystery and variety, that person may be happy, or good, and people may call that narrowness mental strength, but he has an inadequate stipend for this limitless life. Here I am . . .

9

Kaligram
17 January 1891

This sort of morning is for laziness. Apart from the fact that there is nobody here to tell you to hurry up, a crowd of peasants and

responsibilities have not smothered one yet. As a result I'm feeling
sort of loose and slack and lonesome. As if there's no work in the
world that's really necessary, to the extent that one could have a
bath or perhaps not have a bath, and the habit of eating one's meals
at the right time seems to be an ancient superstition prevalent
among the people of Calcutta. The atmosphere around here too
is like that. There's a small river here all right, but it's bankrupt of
any flow. It seems to have become stupefied by its own moss and
watercress, and spreading out its body it lies there and thinks: if it's
quite okay to go on without moving, then why move? The long
grass and water plants that have grown in many places in the water
would not have moved at all the entire day unless the fishermen
came to throw their nets. Six or seven large boats are tied in a
row; on the roof of one of them, a boatman has wrapped himself
in a sheet from head to foot and sleeps in the sun—on another,
someone sits and twines cord while sunning himself; near its oars,
a middle-aged man sits bare-chested and stares at our boat for no
reason at all. On the shore, many different sorts of people come
and go in the most slow and sedate manner; why they come, why
they go, why one sits hunched with his arms wrapped around his
knees pulled up to his chest, why they stare surprised at nothing
in particular—one cannot be sure what any of this means. Only a
few ducks display an air of being busy in the midst of this—they
make a lot of noise, frequently, excitedly dunking their heads in
the water and immediately raising them again with a vigorous
shake. Exactly as if they were sticking out their necks each time
to investigate the deep mysteries under the water, then forcefully
shaking their heads to say, 'No, nothing, nothing at all!' The
days over here keep lying there, sunning themselves in this way
for twelve hours, and in the remaining twelve hours they wrap
themselves up in the deepest darkness and go silently to sleep.
Here one feels like looking outside all the time in order to sit and
be rocked by the feelings in one's own mind; at the same time,
one could hum a little tune; sometimes your eyelids droop with

sleepiness. Just like a mother who sits with her son and rocks him on her lap with her back to the afternoon sun in the winter, in the same way . . .

10

Patisahr Katchari [Patishar Kachari]
via Atrai
Sunday, 18 January 1891

I have brought my boat quite a distance away from the kāchāri and tied it at an isolated spot. There's no commotion anywhere in the vicinity; you won't get it even if you want it, unless perhaps on sale along with a variety of other goods in the market. You can't see too many human faces in the place I've come to now. All around, the fields stretch for miles—the crops have been cut and taken away, only the yellow stubble of the cut rice covers the expanse of the fields. Yesterday, at the end of a long day, I went for a walk in those fields at sunset . . . The sun slowly grew redder until it disappeared behind the absolutely last line of the earth's horizon. How can I describe how beautiful everything all around became! Very far away, at the absolute end of the horizon, there was a border of trees, that place turned so magical—the blues and the reds mixed together and became shadowy—it seemed as if the evening had its home there; it spreads out its bright *āncal**★** once it goes there, carefully lights its evening star, dresses its hair with sindoor in the privacy of solitude like a bride sitting and waiting for someone, and while waiting it stretches out its legs and weaves a garland of stars and composes dreams while humming a melody. A shadow has fallen over the entire never-ending field—a tender melancholy—not exactly tears—like a deep trembling

★ *Āncal*: The end of a sari flung over a woman's shoulder.

under the long eyelashes of an unblinking eye. One could imagine that mother earth lives with her own children and clamour and household work in the midst of society—but where there's a little space, a little silence, a little bit of open sky, that's where her vast heart's hidden sadness and melancholy can appear; there, one can hear her deepest sigh. It is doubtful whether you'll find the sort of unobstructed clear sky and flat land spread out over such distances as we have in India anywhere in Europe. That is perhaps why our race has been able to discover the limitless melancholy of this vast world. That is why our Pūrbī and Toṛi ragas seem to express the inner lament of the entire vast world, not someone's domestic story. One part of this world is efficient, affectionate, limited—that part hasn't found the time to influence us a great deal. But that part of the world which is unpeopled, empty and endless, that part has made us melancholy. That is why, when the sitar strings are pulled to sound the *miṛ*, our Indian hearts experience a pull too.* Yesterday in the evening Pūrbī could be heard playing in the empty field; I was the only living thing walking there within ten or twelve miles, while one other living creature with a turban tied on his head was standing in a disciplined way by the boat with a staff in hand. The small river on my left wound its way through the high banks on both sides to disappear from sight not very far away; the water had not a trace of a wave on it, only the colours of the evening stayed upon it for a little while like an extremely wan smile. The silence was as tremendous as the field itself. There was only a sort of bird that builds its nest on the ground—that bird, watching me constantly come and go near its isolated nest, began to call out with a *tee-tee* of anxious suspicion. Gradually, the rays of the current Kṛshnapaksha moon† became a bit brighter—

---

* The *miṛ* can most approximately be translated as glissando—a glide from one pitch to another, a bending of the strings on a stringed instrument or of the notes in a vocal performance.

† The waning moon during the dark fortnight is referred to as the Kṛshnapaksha moon.

there is a narrow path going all along the riverbank at the edge of the field—I was walking along there with my head bowed, thinking.

11

Patisahr Katchari [Patishar Kachari]
via Atrai
Monday, 19 January 1891

This small river has curved a little and created a little bit of a corner, a little like a lap, over here—I stay quite hidden away in this corner, shielded by the high banks on either side, so we cannot be seen from even a little distance away—the boat-wallahs approach us from the north, drawing out their measure, when they are suddenly surprised by the sight of a large boat tied unnecessarily by the side of these deserted fields. 'Hey there, whose houseboat?' 'The jamidār-bābu's.' 'Why here? Why not in front of the kāchāri?' 'He's here to take the air.'—I have come for something much harder to find than air. Anyway, such questions and answers are frequently to be heard. I've just had lunch and sat down—it is now one-thirty in the afternoon. The boat has been untied; it proceeds slowly towards the kāchāri. There is quite a stiff breeze. It's not too cold—the afternoon sun's rays have made it a bit warmer. Occasionally there's a *khas-khas* sound as the boat goes through the dense watercress. On that watercress are many small turtles sunning themselves with their necks fully stretched towards the sun. At a great distance from each other, occasional small villages appear. A few straw huts, some mud walls bereft of a roof, one or two bundles of hay, *kul* trees, mango trees, banyan trees and bamboo clumps, two or three goats grazing, a handful of naked boys and girls—an unstructured ghat extending till the river where a few are washing clothes, a few are bathing, a few washing utensils; a shy young wife looks curiously through the two-inch gap of her veil at the jamidār-bābu, her pitcher at her waist; by her side, holding her āncal, a small, naked, just-bathed infant, gleaming with oil, stares unblinkingly at the present letter-writer to quench his curiosity—a number of boats are tied to the shore and one half-submerged, ancient, abandoned dinghy awaits resurrection. This is followed again by an expanse of fields empty of crops—from time to time one sees a few cowherd boys, and one or two cows that have come to the banks of the river for the succulent grass there. The solitude and silence of the afternoons here are not to be found anywhere else.

12

Kaligram
January 1891

At the time when I began writing this letter to you, an office clerk of this place was going on and on about his limited means, prospects of a pay rise, and necessity of getting married—he went on chattering and I went on writing, until at one point I explained to him briefly that when a sensible man grants a wish, he does so because the cause is a good one, and not because the same thing has been reiterated five times over. I thought such a wonderful piece of wisdom would absolutely silence the man, but the result turned out to be quite the opposite. Turning the tables, he asked, if a son cannot go to his mother and father and tell them everything on his mind, whom should he go to? I was unable to find an adequate reply immediately at hand. Following which he continued to jabber and I continued to write. Out of the blue, suddenly the tremendous obligation to turn into somebody's parents!—Yesterday at the kāchāri around five or six boys suddenly came and stood in front of me in the most disciplined way, and the moment I asked some question or the other, one began, in the most exquisite Bengali, 'O Father, it is by the great good fortune of these unfortunate children of yours, and by the blessings of the Lord, that your lordship's auspicious arrival in this country has been accomplished.' He continued in this vein for about half an hour, occasionally forgetting his lines, looking up at the sky, and correcting himself before resuming. The subject was that their school needed stools and benches, and faced a lack of these wooden seats—'Where do we accommodate ourselves, where do we accommodate our revered teacher, and when the inspector arrives, what seat are we to grant him either?' To suddenly hear this speech rattled off by such a small boy really made me feel like laughing! Particularly in this jamidār's kāchāri, where the illiterate peasants express their very real sorrows of scarcity in the most rural of dialects—where one hears of stomachs remaining empty in famines caused by excessive rain even after selling off cows, calves, ploughs, where they use the word 'raharaha' when they mean 'aharaha', and 'atikraẏ' in place of 'atikram'—in such a place, to hear of the absence of stools and benches in a Sanskrit speech sounded so odd to the ear. All the other office clerks and peasants were amazed at the boy's grasp of the language and must have been ruminating to themselves—'If only our parents had taken greater care with our education, we too could have stood in front of the jamidār and pleaded our case in such chaste language.' I heard one person nudge the other and say, with some scorn, 'Who has taught him?' The moment his speech came to an end I stopped him and said, 'All right, I will arrange for stools and benches for your school.' But even that didn't impede the urchin; he began his speech again from the point at which he had broken off—although it was completely unnecessary, he continued till he had delivered the last word and touched my feet, and then returned home. The poor thing had taken a lot of trouble to learn it by heart and come here; he might not have minded if I had not granted him his stools and benches, but if I had snatched away his speech, it would perhaps have been intolerable. That's why, although I had a lot of vital jobs to get done, I sat and listened to him very seriously from beginning to end. If there had been one other appreciative person around, perhaps I would have run into another room to have a good laugh, but the jamidāri is no place to express a love of laughter—here all is gravity and wisdom.

13

Kaligram
January 1891

This enormous world that is lying quietly over there—I love it so much—I feel like clutching its trees, rivers, meadows, noise, silence, dawn, dusk, all of it to me with both hands. I think: the treasures of this world that the world has given us—could any heaven have given us this? I don't know what else heaven might have given us, but from where would it have given us such a wealth of affection as is there in these tender, anxious, immature human beings, so full of gentleness and frailty, so full of pitiful anxiety? It has brought in its lap all the poor mortal heart's tearful treasures—this clay mother of ours, this earth that is our own, its fields of golden crops by the side of these affection-giving rivers, its localities full of a love that is sometimes happy and sometimes sad. We wretched people cannot keep these, we cannot save them, many invisible forceful powers come and tear these away from near our hearts, but the poor earth, she has done as much as she could. I really love this world so much. Her face has a very beautiful melancholy spread over it—as if she thinks to herself, 'I am the daughter of a god, but I do not have the power of a god. I love, but I cannot protect. I start things, but I cannot complete them. I give birth, but I cannot save from death!' That is why I quarrel with paradise and love my poor mother's home even more—because she is so helpless, ineffective, incomplete, always beset by the thousand anxieties of love. . . .

14

Not too far from Shahjadpur
Saturday, 24 January 1891

I'm still on the way. We've been continuously afloat from dawn till about seven or eight in the evening. Motion, by itself, has an attraction of its own—the shore on both sides continuously keeps sliding away from in front of one's eyes; that's why I've been looking the whole day, I can't turn my eyes from it—I don't feel like reading, don't feel like writing, there's no work, I just sit silently here and look. It's not for the variety of scenery alone—there may be nothing on either side, only the bare line of the treeless shore—it's the continuity of motion that's the chief attraction. I'm not putting in any effort or work, yet the tireless motion outside envelops the mind in quite a slow, pleasant sort of way. It's the sort of feeling when the mind has no work, but no rest either. It's like sitting on a chair and absent-mindedly swinging one's legs; on the whole the body is at rest, yet its extra energy, which never wants to sit still for a moment, has been given some monotonous work and kept unmindful. . . . We left behind Kaligram's slow-moving river, which flows like a faint pulse, very long ago yesterday. I used to think that that river has absolutely no current at all, but dependable sources have told me that it does have a bit of very faint current, which only those who have always lived by its banks can know. From that river, we came gradually on to a fast-flowing river. Crossing it, we came to a place where the land and the water had become one. The difference between the character and appearance of the river and its banks had been erased, like two young siblings, brother and sister. The bank and the water were at exactly the same height—there was no border. Gradually, the river loses its slim-and-trim shape and divides and spreads out everywhere in many different directions and in many different ways. Here you have some green grass, there you have some clear water, everywhere, as far as you can see, there's some land and some water. It makes one think of the earth's childhood—when the land had just raised its head above the limitless waters—when the rights of water and land had not been fixed as yet. On every side, fishermen have planted their bamboo poles—the kites fly overhead to snatch fish from the fishermen's nets, the harmless crane stands in the mud, many waterbirds, moss floating on the water releasing a particular sort of smell, sometimes in the middle of the muddy fields untidily sprung rice plants, hordes of mosquitoes flying over the still water . . . The boat set off at dawn and we arrived at the *kāñcikāṭhā*.* The kāñcikāṭhā is like a twelve- or thirteen-foot-wide narrow canal, continuously winding this way and that, through which all the marsh's waters are being expelled at a tremendous rate—in the middle of this our huge *boat* is a real problem—the force of the water pulls the *boat* along at lightning speed, while the oarsmen try to manage things with their punt-poles in case the *boat* is flung on to the land and broken. On the other hand, a showery wind is blowing furiously—there are heavy clouds, it's raining occasionally, we're all shivering with the cold—once

---

* As Rabindranath explains in the next sentence, *kāñcikāṭhā* is the word for a narrow passage that lets out the water from large marshes (*bil*) into a river.

or twice, in spite of all efforts, the boat hits land with a tearing sound, preparing to turn completely on its side—in this way, shouting 'We're finished', 'It's all over' all the while, we reach the open river. Cloudy, wet days feel awful in the winter. That's why I was feeling particularly listless in the morning. The sun appeared around two in the afternoon. After that, everything was marvellous. Very high banks—all along on either side trees, people, localities—so peaceful, so beautiful, so secluded—the river distributing affection and beauty on both sides as it goes winding along—an unknown, unseen river of our Bengal. Full of only love and softness and sweetness. No restlessness, yet it has no rest. The village woman who comes to it to draw water every day and sits by it to clean her body with a piece of cloth with so much care—it seems to have a daily conversation with her about what's on her mind and about her domestic duties. . . .

This evening they have moored the boat in a lovely isolated spot at the turn of the river. The full moon is up, there's no other boat here—the moonlight is glittering on the water—it's a clear night—lonely shore—surrounded by dense woods, a village sleeps in the far distance—only the cricket's sound—no other sound to be heard.

15

Shahjadpur
Sunday, 1 February 1891

This morning I was sitting around for ages dilly-dallying and writing that diary—I'd written about a page and a half in a couple of hours—when suddenly at about ten my royal duties became manifest—the chief minister came and said in a low voice that I was needed at the royal court. What to do—hearing Lakshmi's summons I had to leave Saraswati and quickly get up and go. I've only just returned after having dealt with abstruse royal work there for about an hour. Inwardly, I feel like laughing when I think of my own endless solemnity and deeply intelligent appearance—the whole thing feels like a farce. When the peasants present their case so respectfully and sorrowfully, and the clerks stand humbly with folded hands, looking at them I wonder how I'm a greater man than any of them, such that at my slightest hint their lives may be saved or at my slightest aversion, destroyed. What could be stranger than that I sit on this chair and pretend that I am somehow different from all these people, that I am their lord and master! Within myself I too am just like them, a poor man, affected by joy and sorrow; I too have so many small demands from the world, so many heartfelt tears for the smallest of reasons, so dependent in my life upon the grace of so many people! How mistaken they are in me, these simple-hearted peasants, with their children—cows—ploughs—households! They don't realize that I'm one of their own kind. And to keep this misrecognition alive, we deploy so much ceremony and use so much paraphernalia. I had suggested I walk from the boat to the kāchāri, but the nāyeb shook his head wisely and said—better not! What if the image suffers a blow? *Prestige* means one man misunderstanding another! In the fear that the peasants here might recognize me for what I am, and see that I am actually one of them, I need to wear a mask at all times. I don't use my legs to walk upon this low earth like the common low people: an armed footman walks in front of me with his rifle upon his shoulder shooing everybody from my path with his stentorian voice—as if it's a great offence for anyone to walk ahead of me. But in spite of the disguise, I'm quite convinced that I don't look like anybody but myself—and that just as I am acting, they, too, are merely acting. They're saying, 'Oh, what's the point of objecting! Let him dress up as a king.' But it's only me who keeps saying to myself, '*I* know the extent of your achievements!'—

16

Shahjadpur
February 1891

There are a variety of village scenes in front of me that I quite enjoy observing. Right in front of my window, on the other side of the pond, a group of *bede* [gypsies] have hung up some bamboo and cloth sheeting on some poles and taken shelter there. Two or three really small awnings—nobody could even stand inside one of them. Their domestic life is undertaken entirely in the outdoor—only at night they all somehow bundle up in that small space and go to sleep. The bede race is like that. A bit like the *gypsies*. No homes anywhere, no taxes paid to any jamidār. They roam around, here and there, with a herd of pigs, a couple of dogs and some children. The police keep a strict eye on them. I often stand at my window and observe the goings-on of the ones who are here. They aren't bad-looking; the Hindustani type. Dark, yes, but graceful; they have strong, well-formed bodies. The women too are quite good-looking. Quite slim and tall—compact bodies, with free movements like English girls. That is, their actions are unconstrained, there is a simple, easy flow in their quick movements—I do think they are just like dark English girls. The man has put a pot to cook on the fire and sits and makes rattan baskets, wicker baskets and winnowing platters by splitting bamboo into strips—the woman sits with a small mirror on her lap and parts her hair and combs it with utmost care. After the hairstyling is done, she wets a piece of cloth and wipes her face very carefully two or three times with special care, then hesitantly tugs and pulls at her āncal, etc., to rearrange her clothes, and, thus smartened up, she goes and sits on her haunches near the man; then she puts her hand to some bit of work or the other. I'm very entertained when I see this. These people, who are completely the sons of the soil, who are so absolutely attached to the body of this earth—even they are attracted to beauty and make an effort to please each other. They are born at any which place, reared on the streets, and die anywhere—I really feel like knowing their exact situation, their exact feelings. Days and nights under the open sky, in the free wind, on the unclothed earth—this is a sort of new way of life; yet, in the midst of this, there is work and love and children and domesticity, everything. I don't see anybody standing around for a moment being lazy; there is always some work or the other. The moment they finish what they were doing, one woman sits down behind another and deftly unwinds her hair and begins to carefully sort out lice while jabbering on—no doubt about domestic affairs—under those three bamboo awnings—I cannot say for sure, but it certainly seems like it from a distance. This morning, tremendous trouble arrived uninvited in this peaceful bede family. It must have been about eight-thirty or nine in the morning—they had brought out the old sheets and torn rags they sleep on at night and hung these out on the bamboo-sheet roof to sun them. The pigs and piglets, all stuck together, had immersed themselves in a sort of hole they had made in the ground, lying there like an enormous mound of mud—after the winter night, they must have been feeling quite relaxed in the morning sun—when a couple of dogs belonging to one of their families began barking, rousing them. Expressing their irritation audibly, they went off in various directions in search of a colonial breakfast [*choṭā hājrī*]. I was sitting and writing my diary, occasionally looking out unmindfully at the road outside, when suddenly an enormous commotion could be heard. I went to the window and saw that a crowd had collected in front of the bede ashram, in the middle of which an educated type was brandishing a staff and handing out terrific abuse—the head bede was shivering with fear and trying his best to answer him. I surmised that something must have aroused suspicion, and the police *dārogā* had decided to create a ruckus. The woman was sitting by herself and stripping a bamboo pole as though she were quite alone and there was no commotion anywhere at all. Suddenly she stood up and, waving her arms around, began to fearlessly deliver a lecture at the top of her voice right in the dāroga's face. In a trice his forcefulness declined to almost a quarter of what it had been—he tried mildly to get in a word or two, but didn't stand a chance. He began to slowly retreat, changing the attitude with which he had come quite substantially—after reaching a fair distance he shouted to them, 'I'm telling you now, the lot of you will have to get out of here.' I thought my bede neighbours would now perhaps begin to pick up their bamboo sheeting and poles, tie up their bundles, gather their kids, chase up their pigs and make their exit from here. But there's no sign of that—they're still sitting around, quite relaxed, splitting their bamboo, cooking, serving, picking lice.

In my durbar too, I've seen that when a woman comes with a complaint, she may be hidden behind her veil, but the voice like bell metal that emerges from under it has no trace of fear or anxiety or a pleading tone at all. Just total insistence and pure argument. Quite plainly she says, 'The nāyeb maśāi is not fair in his dealings with me!' It's impossible to get her to understand what's fair or unfair, just or unjust; she just keeps saying, 'I'm a widow, I have small children.' There's no answer to that. How should I argue with her! I feel like laughing. She too turns her face halfway towards me and keeps a covert eye on my expression from behind her veil. The day a woman arrives at the durbar, everything becomes quite lively: the bailiff becomes less ostentatious; other men who have come with requests do not find time to present their case.

Anyway, I get to see all sorts of scenes from my open window. Taken all together, I quite like it. But sometimes you see something that's really upsetting. When they pile the cart high with an impossible load and keep hitting or thrusting a pointed wooden stick into the cows, I find it absolutely unbearable. This morning I was watching a woman who had brought her small boy—thin, dark, naked—to bathe in the canal water. It's very cold today—when she was pouring water over his body, he was crying miserably and shivering, his throat racked by the most violent coughing. The woman suddenly gave him such a slap across his face that I could hear its sound from my room. . . . The boy bent over and, putting his hands upon his knees, began to whimper and cry, his tears getting caught in his cough. Then she caught hold of that naked, still-wet, shivering boy by the arm and dragged him homeward. This incident seemed so monstrously cruel! The boy was really young, about my son's age. When you see something like this, man's *ideal* suddenly suffers a blow, like stumbling awfully in the middle of a confident stride. How helpless small boys are! If you behave unfairly with them, they cry helplessly and manage only to irritate a hard heart even more; they cannot even express their complaint properly. The woman was well wrapped-up against the cold, and the boy had not a stitch on him—on top of that he had a dreadful cough, and then a beating at the hands of this witch!

17

Shahjadpur
February 1891

On some days, the postmaster of this place comes over in the evenings and begins to chat with me, telling me many stories about the letters that come and go in the mail. The post office is on the ground floor of this bungalow of ours—it's very convenient, we get our letters the moment they arrive. I really enjoy the postmaster's stories. He tells a huge number of the most impossible tales with complete seriousness. Yesterday he was saying that the people in this part of the country have such an extreme faith in the Ganga that when a relative dies, they grind the bones and keep them, and when they meet someone who has drunk Ganga water, they feed him those ground bones mixed in a paan, and think that some part of their relative has at last found the Ganga. I began to laugh, and

said, 'That's a story, surely?' He thought over it very gravely and
admitted, 'Sir, perhaps it is.'

18

Shilaidaha
February 1891

The maulabī and the clerks having left, and with the boat moored
to a secluded sandbank at the other shore of the kāchāri, I'm feeling
quite relaxed. I can't tell you how beautiful the day and everything
all around seem to me. It's as if one is renewing one's acquaintance
with this vast world again after a long time. It too said, 'Hey there!'
I too replied, 'Hey there!' And then we've both been sitting next
to each other—no further conversation, the water lapping and
the sunlight aglitter on it, the sandbank stretching on and on with
small wild *jhāu* trees growing along it. The sound of water, the
hum of the afternoon silence all around, and from the jhāu bushes
the *cik-cik* sound of one or two birds—taken all together it's a
dreamlike feeling. . . . I feel like writing on—but of nothing else,
this sound of water, this sunny day, this bank of sand. It seems I'll
have to come back to writing of these same things to you every
day—because when I get intoxicated I keep going on about the
same thing. . . . Our boat has crossed the bigger rivers and entered
the mouth of a smaller river now. On either side women bathe,
wash clothes, and walk home with their water pitchers in their wet
clothes, their heads veiled, the left hand swinging free—the boys,
smeared with mud, splash water at each other wildly, and one boy
sings tunelessly, 'Call me brother once, O Lakkhan!' Above the
high banks one can see the straw roofs and the tips of the bamboo
groves of the village nearby. Today the clouds have gone and the
sun is out. The clouds that are still left in one corner of the sky
look like a heap of cotton wool. The breeze is slightly warmer.

The small river doesn't have too many boats—one or two small
dinghies loaded with dry branches and sticks ply tiredly by, their
oars making a slapping sound—on the shore, fishermen's nets
dry on bamboo poles—the world's work this morning has been
temporarily suspended—

19

Chuhali. On the waterway.
16 June 1891

We have now unfurled our sails and are coursing over the Yamuna.
On my left are cows grazing on a field, to the south we cannot see
the bank at all. The fierce river current makes the soil from the
bank fall continuously into the water with a plopping sound. The
astonishing thing is that there is no other boat to be seen on this
enormous river save ours—all around, the moving water makes
a slapping, slipping sound, and one can hear the wind whistling.
. . . Last evening we had moored our boat to a sandbank—the
river was a small one, a tributary of the Yamuna; on one side, the
white empty sands stretched far into the distance—no relationship
with men or mankind—and on the other, green fields of crops
and in the far distance, a village. How many more times shall
I tell you—the evening as it falls on this river, these fields, this
village, is so incredible, so vast, so peaceful, so immeasurable that
it can only be felt silently; the moment you try to express it, you
become restless. Slowly, as everything began to become indistinct
in the dark, only the line of the water and the line of the land
could be demarcated any differently, and the trees and bushes and
huts had all merged into one another, spread out in front of one's
eyes like an obscure world, it felt exactly as though all of this was
the fairy-tale world of childhood—when this scientific world had
not yet completely come into being, when creation had only just

begun, when the whole world was enveloped in the darkness of evening and in a thrilling silence full of fear and wonder—when the beautiful princess was still asleep for ever in a fairyland across the seven seas and thirteen rivers, when the prince and the courtier's son were wandering around in the wilderness on some impossible mission—this seemed to be a certain silent riverside in that half-conscious, forgotten, enchanted and tender world of long ago and far away—and perhaps one could even imagine that I was that prince, roaming that evening world in search of some impossible expectation—that this small river was one among those thirteen mythical rivers, and the seven seas were still to come—that far distances, many events and much searching was yet to happen—so many nights lit by the faintest moonlight yet to come, waiting for me by unknown riverbanks or unacquainted seashores—followed perhaps by many journeys, many tears, much pain, until at last suddenly one day the story ends—'āmār kathāṭi phurolo, naṭe śākṭi muṛolo'*—suddenly it will seem as if there was a story happening all this while, that I was laughing and crying in turn at the fairy tale's joys and sorrows, that now the story has ended, now it is late night, now it is time for small boys to go to sleep.

20

Chuhali
19 June 1891

Yesterday, I had barely sat down outside for fifteen minutes or so when the sky was overcast with terrible clouds—very deep black, loose sort of clouds coloured by a hidden light falling in their midst—exactly like in the pictures one sees of storms sometimes.

* A colloquial phrase indicating that a story has ended; literally: 'my words have come to an end, the naṭe shrub is shorn of its leaves'.

One or two boats quickly made their way from the Yamuna into this little river, set down anchor and rope, and, holding on tightly to land, settled down unworriedly—those who had come to the fields to cut grain ran homeward with a load on each head—the cows too ran, and the calves, waving their tails in the air, tried to run alongside. After some time a roar of rage was heard—a number of ragged scattered clouds arrived from the far west like breathless messengers of bad news—and then thunder and lightning and rain and storm all arrived together and began a tremendous Turkish dance.* The bamboo trees, moaning loudly, began to sway and prostrate themselves this way and that, and the storm began to blow like a snake charmer's wailing flute. And the waves in the water lifted up their crests like three hundred thousand snakes and began to rhythmically dance along. The whole affair yesterday—how do I describe it to you! The sound of thunder refused to stop—as if an entire world was being broken into pieces in some part of the sky. I was sitting with my face upon the open window of the boat and letting my mind swing to the rhythm of the furious force of nature. Everything within me was leaping like a schoolboy suddenly on holiday. Finally, when the driving rain had quite soaked me, I shut both the window and the poetical, and sat down quietly in the darkness like a bird in a cage.

21

On the waterway. Shahjadpur.
20 June 1891

After receiving a reply from you all by telegram yesterday, we finished our work and set the boat off in the evening. There were no clouds in the sky, the moon was up, there was a slight

---

* *Khūb ektā turkinācan*: probably referring to the whirling dervish.

breeze—with the oars making a slapping sound, we sailed down the tributary in the face of the current. We seemed to be surrounded by fairyland. At that time all the other boats had tied their cables to the shore, furled their sails, and were lying fast asleep, silent in the moonlight. Eventually the boat reached a safe place nearby where the tributary joined the Yamuna and was tied there. But a safe place has many disadvantages—there's no breeze, it's a bit enclosed, near the other boats, smells of the jungle, etc. I said to the boatman, 'There's no breeze on this bank, let us go to the other side.' The other side did not have a high bank—the land and the water were at the same level; in fact, the rice fields were immersed in knee-deep water. At the royal command, the boatman tied the boat where he had been ordered. At the time small flashes of lightning had begun to appear in the sky behind us. I had just got into bed and was looking out at the fields with my face at the window when suddenly a commotion arose—a storm coming. Even as we heard: 'throw the ropes', 'weigh anchor', 'do this', 'do that', a tremendously destructive storm hurtled down upon us. The boatman began to repeatedly say, 'Don't be afraid, brothers, take the name of Allah, Allah is the master.' Everybody repeated after him, 'Allah, Allah.' Hit by the wind, the curtains on both sides of the boat began to make a flapping sound; our boat was like a chained bird flapping its wings—the storm was making a high-pitched sound like a predatory kite suddenly bearing down to snatch its prey by the tuft and tear it away, and the boat responded by shuddering and trembling noisily. After a long time, the rain began and the storm ended. I had wanted a bit of breeze—I was given it a bit excessively, beyond all expectation. As though someone were joking, 'Have your fill of the breeze now, and then, when you're full, I'll give you some water to drink—this will fill you up to such an extent that you wouldn't feel like eating anything in the future.' We have the status of nature's grandchildren, that's why she jokes with us in this way from time to time. I've constantly said that life is very seriously sarcastic; it's difficult to follow its sense of humour—because the person being made fun of cannot always appreciate the fun of it all. Think about it—you're lying in bed late at night, when suddenly the earth gives you such a sound shaking that there's no place for anybody to run to. The intention is very novel and entertaining, no doubt about that, quite befitting a first-of-April trick. What fun it is to make important and respected gentlemen run from their beds in the middle of the night, dishevelled and breathless! And is it any less of a joke to wreck an entire roof upon the heads of one or two helpless, witless, just-awakened people! How that prankster nature must have laughed when the poor man was writing a *cheque* at the *bank* that day to settle the mason's *bill*!

22

Shahjadpur
22 June 1891

Nowadays the nights here are full of such marvellous moonlight, what can I say! Of course, I don't mean to say that you too don't have moonlit nights at your place—it has to be admitted that at your place the moonlight slowly spreads its silent authority over the meadow you have, that church spire, the silent trees and bushes. But you have many other things besides the moonlight—you have your *harmony* and *discord*, your *tennis*, your *marble tables*, the song and music sessions in the *drawing room*—but I have nothing except this silent night. Sitting here alone, I cannot begin to express the boundless peace and beauty I see within all of this. There is one lot that becomes restless thinking, 'Why can't I know everything about the world?' and there is another lot that is frustrated wondering, 'Why can't we say everything that's on our minds?'—in between, what the world has to say stays within the world and the inner thought stays within. . . . I rest my head upon the window—like the affectionate hand of nature, the breeze slowly runs its fingers through my hair, the water flows past with a rippling sound, the moonlight shimmers, and sometimes 'the eyes spontaneously overflow with tears'. Often, when you're deeply hurt inside, tears well up as soon as you hear the sound of an affectionate voice. The lifelong hurt that we feel against nature for this unfulfilled life turns into tears and flows silently the moment nature turns sweetly affectionate. Then nature caresses you all the more and you hide your face in her breast with even more fervour, and you attain a sort of melancholic peace that comes from 'disinterested wisdom'. Such are my evenings.

23

Shahjadpur
23 June 1891

These days I really enjoy the afternoons, Bob. All around it's very quiet in the sun, the mind becomes very capricious—I pick up a book, but don't feel like reading. A kind of grassy smell emanates from the riverbank where the boat is tied, and from time to time, you feel the hot, steamy breath of the earth upon your body—it's as if this living, heated-up earth is breathing very near you; perhaps my breath too grazes its body. The short stalks of the rice plants tremble continuously in the breeze—the ducks descend into the water and incessantly dip their heads in and clean the feathers on their backs with their beaks. There is no other sound, except when the *boat*, pushed by the water, slowly leans over so that the *boat's* steps and cable keep making a sort of tender, faint sound. Not very far away there is a ferry ghat. All sorts of people have gathered under the banyan tree to wait for the ferry; the moment the boat arrives, they quickly board it—I like to watch this coming and going of boats over a length of time. There's a village market on the other bank, that's why there's such a crowd on the ferry boats. They go to the market and return from the market, somebody carrying a load of grass, someone a basket, and some a sack on their shoulders; this small river, and on either side these two small villages, and, between them, on this silent afternoon, this little bit of business, this little current of human life flowing very slowly. I was sitting and thinking, why are our country's fields, riverbanks, sky and sun bathed in such a deep melancholy? The reason might be that in our country, it is nature one notices the most—skies free of clouds, fields without any end, the sun beating down—in the midst of this man seems very insignificant—men come and go like the ferry boat from this side to that, one hears their faint, indistinct murmur, one sees their little bit of coming and going in life's marketplace in the hope of small joys and sorrows—but how small, how brief, how utterly futile those indistinct murmurs, the snatches of song, that constant activity and work seem in this vast, expansive, endless, indifferent natural world. One sees such a large, beautiful, careless and generous peace in this idle, drowsy, peaceful, aimless world of nature and, in comparison, one can see such a persistently trying, belaboured, harassed, minute and constant disquiet within one's self that, gazing at the shadowy blue line of the trees on the distant shore, one becomes quite inattentive. 'Chāyāte basiyā sārā dinamān tarumarmar pabane' [Sitting all day in the shade with the rustle of the trees in the breeze], etc. Where nature is cowering and shrouded in cloud and mist and snow and darkness, there man is very lordly—there man thinks that all his wishes, all his efforts will be permanent, adding his signature to all his work, he looks towards posterity, builds monuments, writes autobiographies and even builds stone houses over dead bodies for everlasting remembrance—many of these signs are broken later and many names forgotten, but nobody notices because nobody has the time.

24

Shahjadpur
June 1891

In the evening I moor my boat at the ghat in the village here.
Lots of boys play here together; I sit and watch them. But the foot
soldiers who are stuck to me day and night give me no peace. They
consider the boys' play impudence; they think it is disrespectful
towards the raja if the boatmen laugh and chat among themselves
freely and openly; if the farmers bring their cows to the water to
let them drink they immediately run towards them, stick in hand,
to protect the raja's prestige. In other words, they think the raja's
status is preserved only if the entire space around him is turned
into a terrible desert devoid of laughter, play, sound or people—
on the other hand, the miserable raja's heart cries out for some
relief. Yesterday too they had begun to chase the boys away when
I abandoned my raja's status and made them desist. The incident
was as follows—

There was a mast from an enormous boat lying on the ground—a
group of small, naked boys decided, after much discussion, that if
they could all roll it along by pushing it together with the help of
an appropriate amount of noise, they would have invented a most
novel and enjoyable game. The moment they thought of it, they
began work. 'Well done, soldier, hey ho!' 'Push it again, hey ho!'
All of them began to shout and push. The moment the mast rolls
around once, everybody laughs out loud with delight. But the
one or two girls who accompany these boys have a different air
about them. They've been forced to play with the boys because of
a lack of companions, but this bizarre and strenuous sort of game
doesn't connect with them. One little girl, without a word, went
and sat down quite calmly and seriously upon the mast. The boys'
wonderful game was ruined. One or two of them decided that
in this case, it might be better to concede defeat. Moving away

a bit, they stood around with wan faces and contemplated the unshakeable seriousness of the girl. One of them came up to the girl and began to experimentally push the girl a little. But she continued to sit there quite silently and peacefully. The oldest boy came up to her and showed her a different spot at which she could have her rest, but at that she vigorously shook her head and, folding both her hands upon her lap, settled down even more compactly. Then the boy began to use physical force and was immediately successful. Their joyous celebrations rent the sky once more, the mast began to roll again—in fact, after a while, the girl too abandoned her womanly pride and noble and natural independence to join the boys at their meaningless game with artificial enthusiasm. But it was quite obvious she was thinking, boys don't know how to play, they just know how to behave absolutely childishly. If only she had at hand a yellow clay doll with its hair in a bun, would she ever join these immature, childish boys in this stupid game of pushing the mast! Suddenly they thought of another sort of game, that too was great fun. Two boys would catch hold of another and swing him to and fro by his arms and legs. There was obviously some great mystery in this, because the boys were very excited by it. The girl found it completely intolerable. She scornfully left the playing field and went home. But there was a mishap. The boy being swung fell down. Miffed, he abandoned his companions and went and lay down on the grass some distance away with his head on his hands. His air proclaimed—he wasn't going to keep any further connection with this cruel, heartless world any more, he would just lie flat on the ground by himself and count the stars, he was going to spend his life with his head upon his hands, watching the clouds at play, and 'for the rest of my life I will not play with anybody else'. Seeing such an untimely disaffection in him, the oldest boy ran quickly to him, took his head upon his lap and began to say, in a tone of repentance and regret, 'Come, brother, get up brother! Are you hurt, brother?' In a few moments, like two puppies, the two began a game of arm wrestling and within a minute or two that boy had begun to be swung again! Such are man's vows! This is his mental strength! Such is his resolve! He leaves his playing to go and lie down at a distance and then again he allows himself to be caught and to be smilingly swung again in the swing of intoxication! How will such a man ever be free! There are some boys who leave their playroom and keep lying down with their head in their hands—there's a home being built in paradise for all those good boys.

25

Shahjadpur
June 1891

Last night I had a very strange dream. All of Calcutta city seemed enveloped in a great, terrible and yet surprising feeling—the houses could all be seen through a dark black mist—and within it there was some enormous commotion going on. I was travelling through Park Street in a hired carriage—as I went I saw that St Xavier's College was growing exponentially to an enormous size—in that dark mist, it had become impossibly high. Then gradually I came to know that a group of strange people had arrived who could use some sort of trickery to perform these astonishing feats for money. Reaching the Jorasanko house, I saw they had reached there too—awful-looking, with somewhat Mongolian features—thin moustaches, scraggly beards pointing this way and that on either side of their faces. They could make humans grow in size too. That's why all the women of our house were out on the porch—applicants for more height—those people were sprinkling some sort of powder on their heads and whoosh, they were all growing taller. I kept saying—how astonishing, this is just like a dream. Then, somebody proposed that our house be made to grow higher. They agreed and began to break a part of

the house. After smashing up a portion, they said, 'Now you have
to pay us a certain amount of money, or we shall not work on
the house any more.' Kunja Sarkar said, 'How's that possible, the
work can't be paid for until it has been completed!' Immediately
they became very angry—the whole house then sort of bent out
of shape and became horrible, and in some places you could see
that half a person was embedded in its walls, with the other half
hanging out. Overall it seemed as if all of it was the work of the
devil. I said to Baṛ-dada, 'Baṛ-da, do you see what's happening?
Come, let us sit and pray.'★ We went to the inner courtyard and
sat down to fervent meditation. Emerging from there, I thought
I would reprimand them in the name of god—but although my
heart felt as if it would burst, I couldn't speak. After that I'm not
sure when I woke up. What a strange dream, don't you think? All
of Calcutta under the devil's spell—everybody trying to grow with
his help and the whole city enveloped in this hellish, dark mist,
horribly growing all the while. But there was a bit of farce in it as
well—in the entire world, why was the devil so particularly well
disposed towards the Jesuits?

After that the teachers at the English school here in Shahjadpur
arrived with expectations of an audience with the lordship. They
just didn't want to leave, yet I had really nothing very much to
say to them—every five minutes or so I asked them one or two
questions, to which they gave me an answer or half, and then I
sat there like a fool, fiddling with my pen, scratching my head—I
ask them what the crops have been like this season over here. The
schoolmasters know nothing of crops, and whatever there was to
be known about the students has already been said at the start.
So I go back to the beginning and start again; I ask, 'How many
students in your school?' One of them says, 'Eighty.' Another
says, 'No, a hundred and seventy-five!' I think, now these two
are going to have a tremendous argument. But instead, both

★ Baṛ-dada: Dvijendranath Tagore, eldest brother of Rabindranath.

immediately agree with each other. One and a half hours after that, it's difficult to know exactly why, they suddenly remembered to say, 'We'll take your leave now.' They could have said so an hour earlier, or they might have remembered to say so twelve hours later—it seems that there's no rule for this sort of thing—just a blind faith in miracles.

26

Shahjadpur
Saturday, 4 July 1891

There is a boat moored to our ghat, and many 'common women' from the village are standing in front of it in a crowd . . . Perhaps one of them is going somewhere and everybody else has come to say goodbye. Lots of little boys, lots of veiled heads and lots of grey heads have got together. But there is one girl among them who attracts my attention more than anybody else. She must be about twelve or thirteen, but looks about fourteen–fifteen because she's well built. Her face is superlative. She's quite dark, yet quite good-looking. Her hair is cut like a boy's, and it suits her face. She has such an intelligent, self-aware, clear and simple look. She stood there with a boy on her hip, staring at me unabashedly with such unalloyed curiosity . . . Really, her face and figure were very attractive, but she was neither stupid nor lacking in simplicity nor deficient in any way. Her half-boy, half-girl look especially attracted my attention. A boy's complete unselfconsciousness had been mixed with sweetness to create an entirely new kind of girl. I had never expected to see this type of village girl in Bengal. I see that their entire clan is quite un-shy. One of the women is standing on the riverbank in the sun, running her fingers through her hair to disentangle it, while talking to another woman on the boat about domestic affairs at the top of her voice. I heard she had just one

'gal' [*māiẏyā*], no other 'kids' [*chāoẏāl nāi*]—but the daughter's not
sensible at all—'says anything to anyone, does anything at any time,
has no consciousness of "them" and "us"'. . . . I further learnt that
Gopal Sha's son-in-law wasn't that great and the daughter didn't
want to go to him. Finally, when it was time to go, I saw that they
were trying very hard to get my short-haired, round-limbed girl
with a bangle on her arm and her bright simple face on to the
boat, but she just didn't want to go—eventually, they got her on
to the boat after a lot of pushing and pulling. I realized that the
poor thing was probably being taken from her parental home to
her husband's home—after the boat sailed away, the women stood
on the shore, looking out, while one or two slowly wiped their
faces and eyes with their āncals. A small girl with tightly tied hair
climbed up on to an older girl's lap and, putting her arms around
her neck and her head on her shoulder, began to cry silently.
The one who left was probably the poor thing's elder sister and
playmate, who had sometimes joined in when she played with
her dolls, maybe giving her a push sometimes if she were naughty.
The morning sun and the riverbank and everything seemed to fill
up with such deep melancholy! Like the deep sigh of a piteous
rāginī of the morning, it seemed that the world was so beautiful,
but so full of pain. . . . The history of this unknown little girl
seemed to become very familiar to me. When it's time to leave,
to leave upon a boat on this flowing river seems to be even more
moving. A little like death—to float away from the shore—those
left standing wipe their eyes and turn to leave; the one who floats
away, disappears. I know that this deep sorrow shall be forgotten by
both those who remain and those who leave, perhaps it is already
lost to some extent. The hurt is temporary, while the forgetting is
permanent. But if you think about it, it is the pain that is real, not
the forgetting. At the time of certain partings and certain deaths,
man suddenly realizes how terribly true this pain is. He realizes
that man is quite mistaken to live serenely; it is this grief and this
anxiety that is the inner truth of the world. Nothing remains,

nobody remains; that's so true that we don't even remember it, and grief departs—and realizing that it is not only that we shall not be here, but that nobody will even remember, man becomes even more desperate. One shall disappear without a trace from both within and without. Truly, with the exception of our country's tender rāginīs, no other song is possible for all of mankind, for mankind throughout the ages.

27

On the waterway towards Cuttack
August 1891

A gentleman's self-respect is completely lost if he is preoccupied night and day with the fact that his clothes are becoming progressively shabby and unbearable, and his bag of clothes is missing. I cannot now stride around purposefully in society with my head held high in the manner in which I could have if I had had the bag. My only wish is to somehow keep myself concealed and out of sight. I've slept in these clothes at night and am revealed in the same attire in the morning. On top of that the steamer is full of coal dust and shabbiness, and my entire body is steaming in the mid-afternoon heat. Thinking of this state of affairs, coupled with my utterly meek character, you must be trying to hold your laughter in check. Besides which, what's the point of writing to you about the joys on board this *steamer*! There's no end to the variety and number of companions I've found. There's somebody called Aghor-babu here, who insists on referring to every conscious and unconscious object upon this earth as his mother-in-law's brother's nephew.* Another man with a musical knack

* *Māmāśvaśurer bhāgne*: The relationship referred to is brother-in-law or *śālā*, a common Indian expletive.

began to practise the Bhaiṅro ālāp in the middle of the night.*
For various reasons, this appeared to be entirely untimely. We've
managed to spend from last evening to about nine o'clock today
with our ship stuck in a narrow canal. I was lying down, dejected
and lifeless, surrounded by a crowd of passengers in one corner
of the deck. I had requested the khansamaji to prepare *luci* for the
evening meal—he made some fried floury stuff without shape or
substance and presented it without a trace of any accompanying
vegetables, fried or curried. I expressed some amount of surprise
and regret on seeing this. This person then anxiously said, '*Hum
abhi bana deta*.'† Seeing that it was very late in the night, I disagreed,
and, having eaten the dry luci as well as I could, lay down in the
light in the midst of all those people in my *pantaloons*—mosquitoes
in the air and cockroaches roaming all around—another person
sleeping right at my feet, whose body my legs were touching
from time to time, four or five noses snoring continuously, a
few mosquito-bitten, wretched, sleepless souls pulling at their
tobacco, and through it all, the Bhaiṅro rāginī. At around 3.30
a.m., some overenthusiastic people began to wake each other up
to encourage them to begin their morning ablutions. Hopelessly
tired, I quit my rest and went and sat down, leaning back on my
chair, waiting for dawn. The night passed like a strange curse.
One of the ship's crew informed me that the steamer was stuck
in such a way that it would not be able to move the entire day
today. I asked a worker whether it would be possible to board a
ship going to Calcutta. He smiled and said, this ship would be
returning to Calcutta once it had reached its destination, so if I
wanted to, I could always return on the same ship. Fortunately,
after a lot of pulling and pushing, around ten o'clock the ship
began to move again.

* Bhaiṅro: colloquial Hindustani for Bhairav, a morning raga; meant to be
played or performed in the morning.
† Hindi for 'I'll make some right now'.

28

Chandni Chowk, Cuttack
3 September 1891

Our lawyer, Hariballabh-babu, is a man of rounded and expansive proportions—his air is one of a very tall and large Krishna-Vishnu. He's getting on in years. A pleated shawl on his shoulder, very well turned out, the smell of essence on his body, two layers of chin, a proportionate moustache, rolling forehead, big swimming eyes half shut with self-conceit, the pupils of the eyes rising up towards the sky when he speaks—he speaks in a deep rumbling tone in a very mild, slow, and smiling way—time seems to stand like an obedient servant silently by his side, waiting for him—not the tiniest hurry about anything at all. He turned up his eyes and asked me at one point, 'Where is Jyoti now?'* My insides petrifying with respect at the unflappable seriousness of the questioner, I replied in low and modest tones, letting him know that my brother was in the capital. He said, 'I was a fellow student of Birendra's.'† Hearing which my soul was even more overcome. After this, when he suggested that my sudden and untimely arrival here without waiting for anybody's advice was childish and an ill-thought-out move, you can image how wan and taken aback I became. I hung my head and kept repeating—I didn't know anything about the actual situation, I've never come before, this is my first visit. Subsequently we began to argue about 'when did Jyoti visit last'. Calculating this led to complete disagreement between Baṛ-dā and him. He said, '74–'75, Baṛ-dā said, earlier. This will give you some idea how difficult history-writing is. That's why I think I'd better start putting a date to my letters from now on.

* Jyoti: Jyotirindranath Tagore, fifth son of Debendranath.
† Birendra: Birendranath Tagore, fourth son of Debendranath.

29

Tiron
7 September 1891

The ghat at Baliya is quite pleasant to look at. Tall trees on either side—taken all in all, the canal brings that small river in Poona to mind. . . . I thought about it quite a bit and decided that if I had known this canal to be a river then I would have liked it much more. Both banks have tall coconut trees, mango trees and all sorts of other shady trees, a clean sloping bank covered with lovely green grass and innumerable blue *lajjābatīlatā* flowers; sometimes a screw-pine forest; at places where the trees thin out a bit you can see an endless field stretching out beyond the high banks of the canal; the fields are such an intense green in the rains that the eyes seem to simply drown in them; occasionally, a small village encircled by date and coconut trees; and the entire scene shaded and dark under the cool shade of the stooping, cloud-covered monsoon sky. The canal bends and winds its way gracefully through the middle of its two clean, green, tender, grassy banks. A slow current; at places where it becomes very narrow there are red and white lotuses and tall grasses to be seen at the edge of the water; all in all, very much like an English *stream*. But still one regrets the fact that this is nothing more than an irrigation canal—the sound of its flowing water has no primeval ancientness, it doesn't know the mystery of a distant, lonely mountain cave—not named after some old feminine name, it has not breastfed the villages on either side of its banks from time immemorial—it can never babble—

> Men may come and men may go
> But I go on forever.

Even large lakes that belong to ancient times have attained greater glory. From this you can quite make out why an old and great lineage commands so much respect even if it is, in many respects, poor. It is as though there is an aura of the wealth and beauty of many ages upon it. A gold trader suddenly grown big may obtain a lot of gold, but doesn't find the lustre of that gold very quickly. In any case, a hundred years later, when the trees on the shore are much larger than they are now, when the sparkling-white milestones will have become worn and moss-covered, when the 1871 carved into the lock will seem very far away, if I could travel on this boat on this canal to look into our estates at Pandua with my great-grandson, undoubtedly my mind would be labouring under a completely different set of feelings. But alas for my great-grandson! God knows what fate holds for him! Perhaps an obscure and undistinguished clerkship. A fragment of the Tagore family, torn from it and flung far away, like a dark, extinguished splinter of a meteorite. But I have so many troubles in the present that there's absolutely no need to lament for my great-grandson. . . . We reached Tarpur at four o'clock. Our journey by palanquin began here. I had thought the road was about twelve miles and that we would reach our bungalow by eight in the evening. Field after field, village after village, mile upon mile passed—the twelve miles seemed endless. At about seven-thirty I asked the bearers how much further, they said—not much more, a little more than six miles. Hearing this, I tried to rearrange myself within the palanquin. Not more than half of me fits into a palanquin—my back aches, my feet go numb, my head starts feeling knocked-about—it might have been more convenient within the palanquin if only there was some way to tuck myself up three or four times and keep myself folded. The road was absolutely terrible. Knee-deep mud everywhere—in some places the bearers were treading very warily, step by step, for fear of slipping. They lost their footing three or four times, but managed to regain balance. Occasionally, there was no road—the rice fields were full of water—we moved ahead, splashing through all of it. The night was very dark because of the clouds, it was drizzling, and the flame of the torch kept going out from time to time for

lack of oil—and had to be lit again by a lot of blowing on it; the
bearers began to quarrel about the lack of light. After having
advanced in this manner for some distance the *barakandāj* [armed
footman] folded his hands and submitted that we had arrived at a
river and now needed to convey the palanquin on a boat, except
the boats hadn't reached yet, but would very soon—so now the
palanquins would have to be set down for some time. So down
went the palanquins. But then there was simply no sign of the boats.
Slowly the torch went out. In that dark night on the riverbank, the
footmen began to call out in their hoarse voices to the boatmen
as loudly as they could—the other bank of the river echoed their
call, but no boatmen answered. 'Mukunda-a–a–a–a!' 'Balkrishna-
a–a–a–a!' 'Neelkantha-a–a–a–a!' Such was the desperation in those
voices that Mukunda [Vishnu] and Neelkantha [Shiva] might well
have descended from their respective abodes in heaven—but our
helmsman had stopped his ears and was resting unperturbed in
his abode. There was nothing on that isolated shore, not even a
hut, only an empty bullock cart lying by the roadside sans driver
or passenger—our bearers sat down upon it and began to chatter
among themselves in their foreign tongue. The night resonated
with the sound of frogs chattering and crickets calling. I thought
to myself that we would perhaps have to stay the night here itself,
mangled and crushed and squeezed in the palanquin—perhaps
Mukunda and Neelkantha might arrive tomorrow morning. I
began to sing to myself—

> Oh,   if you come to me smiling at the end of the night
>   Will my smile remain?
> This   tarnished body, weary with waking,
>   What will you say when you see me?

Well, whatever will be said will be in the Oriya language, I wouldn't
understand a thing. But there's no doubt about the fact that there
will be no smile on my face. A long time passed in this manner.

Then suddenly, with a rhythmic *hñui-hñai, hñui-hñai* sound, Baṛ-dā's palanquin appeared. Seeing that there was no prospect of any boats arriving, Baṛ-dā ordered that the river had to be crossed with the palanquins carried on their heads. Hearing this, the bearers began to hesitate, and some hesitation and pity made an appearance in my mind as well. Anyway, after a lot of argument they took the name of god and descended into the river with the palanquins on their heads. They crossed the river with a lot of difficulty. It was half past ten in the night then. I curled up and lay down as best I could. I had just begun to nod off when suddenly one of the bearers slipped and the whole palanquin was given a good shake—waking up all of a sudden, my heart began to thud loudly in my ears. After that, half asleep and half awake, we reached the bungalow at Pandua in the late hours of the night.

30

Tiron
9 September 1891

Yesterday, after a long time, the cloud and rain cleared and golden *śaraṭ* sunlight appeared.* It was as if I'd completely forgotten that there was such a thing as sunlight in the world; yesterday, when the sun suddenly broke out at about ten or eleven in the morning, I was filled with amazement—as if I'd seen something completely new. It turned out to be a beautiful day. In the afternoon I was sitting in the front of the veranda after my bath and lunch, with my legs stretched out on the easy chair, half lying down, daydreaming. In front of me I could see some coconut trees of the *compound* of our house—beyond that, as far as the eye could see, only fields of grain,

---

* *śaraṭ*: Rabindranath's favourite season, and one that will recur many times in the course of these letters. Corresponds to the time of year in Bengal after the rains when the skies clear in autumn.

and right at the end of the fields just an indication of some trees in faint blue. The doves were cooing and occasionally the sound of the bells the cows wore could be heard. The squirrel sits upon its tail and looks up all of a sudden, turning its head this way and that, and then in an instant climbs up the tree trunk to disappear among the branches with its tail lifted upon its back. There's a very still, silent, and secluded feeling. The wind, unobstructed, blows freely through—the leaves of the coconut fronds quiver with a trembling sound. Three or four farmers are grouped together at one place in the field, uprooting the small saplings of grain and tying them up in bundles. That's the only work to be seen being done anywhere.

31

Shilaidaha
1 October 1891

Woke up late to see marvellous sunlight and the river's śarat waters full to the brim and spilling over. The banks and the river waters were almost at the same level—the fields of grain a beautiful green and the village trees dense and alive at the end of the rains. How can I tell you how lovely it looked! There was a sharp shower of heavy rain in the afternoon. After that, in the evening, the sun set by the Padma in our coconut groves. I had climbed up on the riverbank and was strolling slowly along. In front of me, in the distance, the evening shadows were lengthening in the mango orchards, and on my way back, the sky behind the coconut trees was turning golden with gold. Unless you come here you forget how amazingly beautiful the world is and what a large heart she has and how full of a deep fulfilment she is. In the evening when I sit quietly on the *boat*, the waters silent, the riverbank growing hazy, the sun's rays slowly losing their light on the margins of the sky, my whole body and mind feel such a touch—strangely generous, large, and incommunicable—of silent nature with her downcast eyes! What peace, what affection, what greatness, what limitless tender melancholy! From these inhabited fields of crops to that desolate world of the stars, the sky fills to the brim from end to end with such a stunned heartfelt feeling, and I sit alone, immersed in this limitless mindscape—only the maulabī stands next to me and jabbers on and on, making me disconsolate.

32

Shilaidaha
Tuesday, 6 October 1891

It's quite a lovely day today, Bob. One or two boats have come up to the ghat—those who live abroad are returning home in the Puja holidays with bundles, boxes and wicker baskets full of all sorts of gifts and things after an entire calendar year. I saw a babu who, the moment the boat approached the ghat, changed from his old clothes into a new pleated dhuti, putting on a white silk China coat on top of his gear, and, with a twisted scarf hung with great care over one shoulder and an umbrella on his back, then set off towards his village. The fields, full of grain, quiver with a shivering sound—piles of white clouds in the sky—the heads of mango and coconut trees can be seen above that—the coconut fronds are trembling in the breeze—one or two *kāś* flowers are preparing to bloom upon the sandbank—all together, it's a very happy scene. The feelings of the man who has just returned to his village from foreign lands, his eagerness to meet his family, and the sky in this śarat season, this earth, this cool, light breeze of the morning and the dense, ceaseless shudder within all of the trees, grass, flowers and river's waves, all this mixed together had

completely overcome this lonely youth by the window in joy and
sorrow. In this world, if you sit alone by the window and simply
open your eyes and look, new desires are born in your heart—not
exactly new—the old desires begin to take all sorts of new forms.
Day before yesterday I was sitting in the same way quietly by the
window, when a boatman passed by on a *dinghy*, singing a song—
not that he had a very good voice—suddenly I remembered how
many years ago, when I was a boy, I had travelled with Bābāmaśāẏ
[Father] on a boat to the Padma—one night, waking up around
two o'clock, I had opened the window and, looking out, I saw
the still river lit brilliantly by the moonlight and a boy rowing
alone on a small *dinghy* singing a song in such a sweet voice—I
had never heard a sweeter song till then. Suddenly I thought, what
if my life could be returned to me from that day onward! Then
I could test it once more and see—this time round I wouldn't
leave it lying thirsty and dry and unfulfilled—I would take the
poet's song and set out with the evening tide on a slender *dinghy*
to float upon the world; to sing and to captivate and to go and
see what the world contains; for once, to let myself be known and
to know others; carried enthusiastically along by life, by youth,
to travel around the world like the blowing wind, and then to
return to spend a fulfilled and happy old age at home as a poet.
It's not as if it's a very high *ideal*. To do good for mankind and to
die like Christ may be a much greater *ideal*—but being the sort
of person I am overall, I've never even contemplated that, nor do
I wish to wither and die like that. . . . I don't want to sacrifice
this precious life to a self-inflicted lack by starving, looking at
the sky, not sleeping, continuously quarrelling with myself and
constantly depriving both this world and my humanity at every
step. Instead of thinking that the creator of this world has cheated
us and that it's the devil's trap, if I can trust it and love it and,
if fate is willing, be loved in turn; if I could live like a man and
die like one, then that is enough—it is not my work to try and
disappear into air like a god.

33

Shilaidaha
15 October 1891

Last evening I was strolling around the riverbank towards a golden sunset in the west and back again towards a silver moon rising in the east, twirling my moustache as I walked—nature looking at me with the deep, silent and tender melancholy of a mother looking at a sick child—the river water as still as the sky, and our two tied boats lying like sleeping waterbirds with their faces hidden in their wings. All at once the maulabī came up and informed me in a scared whisper, 'Calcutta's Bhojiya has come.' . . . I can't tell you how many impossible anxieties sprang up instantly in my mind. . . . Anyway, suppressing my inward agitation, I went and sat down upon the royal chair in a grave and serious manner and sent for Bhojiya—the moment she entered the room, Bhojiya began to whine and fell at my feet, and I realized at once that if there was any disaster that had occurred, then it had happened to Bhojiya herself. After that she began to narrate a serial tale of disconnected misfortunes in her angular Bengali, howling and snivelling all the while. With great perseverance, we managed to get to the root of her story, which was this: Bhojiya and her mother used to quarrel quite frequently—nothing surprising about that—after all, they are both from a race of heroic women in western Aryavarta—not known for being soft-hearted. One evening, the mother and daughter got into a fight that went from the verbal domain to the physical—not the sort of embrace that comes from affectionate conversation but the fisticuffs that ensue from abusive language. It was the mother who lost that bout of wrestling—and she was also grievously wounded in the process. Bhojiya maintains her mother chased after her aiming a brass bowl at her head, and while she was trying to protect herself her bangle hit her mother on the head or somewhere and there was bloodshed. Anyway, all this resulted in Choto-bau immediately banishing her from the second floor to the lower reaches. Since then, she absolutely refuses to forgive her. Just look at that, Bob, a whining domestic warfront from the second floor in Calcutta has opened up in the middle of all the official work of this place. This happened about three or four days ago now, but I hadn't been informed— and then a sudden thunder-strike without *notice* in the form of Bhojiya [*binā noṭise bhajiẏāghāt*].

34

Shilaidaha
18 October 1891

I feel that the moment you travel outside Calcutta, man's belief in his own permanence and greatness recedes to a great extent. Here, man is less and the earth is more—all around, you can see the sort of things that cannot be made today, repaired tomorrow, and sold off the day after, things that have always been standing firmly through man's birth, death, actions and deeds—that travel in the same way every day and flow without rest through all time. When I come to the countryside, I don't see man as an individual any more—just as the river flows through many countries, so too man flows, chattering and winding, through woods and villages and cities forever—this does not end. *Men may come and men may go but I go on forever*—that's not quite the right way to put it. Man too goes on like a river does, through many tributaries and branches, one end of which lies in the fountainhead of birth and the other in the sea of death—two dark mysteries on both sides and a varied *līlā** of work and play and

* *Līlā* can be roughly translated as god's sport.

chatter in between—this has no end in any age. There, listen, the farmer is singing in his field, the fisherman's *dinghy* floats by, the morning lengthens, the sun grows warmer—at the ghat some bathe and some draw water—in this way, on both sides of this peaceful river, hundreds and hundreds of years rush by with a murmuring sound through the villages and the shade of the trees—and a tender sound rises from it all: *I go on forever!* In the still silence of the afternoon, when some cowherd boy calls out to his companion at the top of his voice, and a boat returns homeward with a smacking sound of the oars, and the women push at the water with their pitchers and that itself makes a gurgling sound, and alongside that the many unintentional sounds of nature in mid-afternoon—one or two birds calling, bees humming, the boat bending slowly in the wind, creating its own compassionate sound—all together it's such a tender lullaby—as if a mother has been trying the entire afternoon to comfort her hurt son by lulling him to sleep, saying: don't worry now, don't cry now, no more hitting and punching, don't fight and argue, forget about it for a little while, try and sleep a little! Saying this, she slowly pats a hot forehead.

35

Shilaidaha
Monday, 19 October 1891

Today is the day of the Kojāgar full moon.* . . . I was walking slowly by the riverside and conversing with myself—one can't exactly call it a 'conversation'—perhaps I was ranting on all by

* The Kojāgar Pūrṇimā is the full-moon night when Hindus worship Lakshmi, the goddess of wealth.

myself and that imaginary companion of mine had no option but to listen quietly; the poor thing didn't have a chance to put in a word in his own defence—even if I'd given him a completely inappropriate speech, he couldn't have done anything about it. But how marvellous it was! What more can I say! I've said it so many times, but it can never be told in its entirety. The river had not a single line upon it—there, on the other shore of the sandbank where the Padma's waters had reached their last horizon, from there to here, a wide line of moonlight was shimmering—not a single human being, not a single boat—not a tree to be seen on the new sandbank on the other side, not a blade of grass—it seems as if a melancholy moon is rising over a desolate earth—an aimless river flowing through the middle of an unpopulated world, a lengthy old story has come to an end over an abandoned world; today there is nothing left of all those kings and princesses and bridegrooms and their friends and golden cities, only the 'boundless fields' [*tepāntarer māṭh*] and the 'seven seas and thirteen rivers' of those stories stretch out in the wan moonlight. . . . I was walking as if I was the one and only last-remaining pulse of a dying world. And all of you were on another shore, on the banks of life—where there's the *British government* and the nineteenth century and tea and *cheroots*. If I could lift somebody out of there on a small boat and bring him here to this uninhabited moonlight, we would stand on this high bank and look out at the endless water and sand, and the fathomless night would shimmer and hum all around us! So many others have over the years stood here like me, alone, and felt this way, and so many poets have tried to express this, but oh, it is ineffable—what is it, what is it for, what impulse is it, what does one call this lost peace, what does it mean—when will that tune emerge, splitting open the heart precisely through the middle, which will exactly express this musicality!

36

Shilaidaha
Saturday, 21 November 1891

Received a letter from Sholli.* She has written analysing my work in *Bhagnahṛdaẏ* and *Rudracanḍa*. Previously, she had taken the side of *Bhagnahṛdaẏ* and argued with me frequently—now she has come around to my point of view. That is, she has criticized it extensively. She said its poets, Murala, Chapala, etc., are inhabitants of an imaginary grove. . . .

37

Shilaidaha
Monday, 4 January 1892

Just a short while ago, the engineer from Pabna turned up with his mem and kids. You know, Bob, I don't find it easy to be a host—my head gets completely muddled—besides which, I never knew he was going to bring a couple of kids along. This time I was supposed to be living on my own, so I haven't even brought too many provisions. Anyway, I'm trying to shut my eyes and ears and get through this somehow. Additionally, the mem drinks tea, and I don't have any tea; the mem can't stand dal right from her childhood, and due to the absence of other food, I have ordered for dal to be made; the mem doesn't touch fish from *year's end to year's end*, and I have quite happily ordered catfish curry to be cooked. Thank goodness she loves *country sweets*, that's why she managed with great difficulty to cut into a hard, dry *sandeś* with her fork and eat it. There's a

* Sholli may presumably be short for Sarala, his niece.

tin of biscuits left over from last time's rations that's going to come in handy. To top it all, I went and put my foot in it—I said to the saheb, your mem drinks tea, but unfortunately I don't have any tea, I have cocoa. He said, 'My mem loves cocoa even more than tea.' I rummaged through the cupboard and found that there was no cocoa—it had all been sent back to Calcutta. Now I'll have to tell him again: there's no tea and no cocoa, only the Padma's water and a kettle—let's see what his face looks like then. I can't tell you how mischievous and naughty the sahebs's two sons look! The mem isn't as awful-looking and short-haired as I thought she was—she's sort of medium-looking. From time to time, the saheb and mem are getting into the most tremendous fights which I can hear from this boat. The boys crying, the servants shouting, the couple arguing—it's driving me completely insane. I don't see any chance of being able to read or write or get any work done (the mem is scolding her son: *What a little śuẏār [pig] you are!*). Tell me, why has all this trouble descended on my shoulders? And then again, the mem has said she wants to go for a walk this evening and she's asking me to go with her—I'm sitting here in such a stunned state that if you saw me you would fall about laughing—I'm smiling a wry smile of sorrow myself, thinking about the state I'm in. I'd never dreamt I'd have to wander around the estates with a mem clasped under my arm. No doubt the tenants will be very surprised. If I can bid goodbye to them tomorrow morning then I might just survive; if they say they're going to stay one more day then I'm going to die, Bob.

38

Shilaidaha
Wednesday, 6 January 1892

Evening has fallen. When I was on the *boat* in the summer, at this time I would sit by the boat's window with my light out and lie there quietly; the sound of the river, the evening breeze and the silence of the star-filled sky would give the sweetest of forms to my imagination and surround me on all sides; the evening would pass till very late in the night immersed in a sort of intense, lonely sorrow and joy. In the winter the doors and windows are closed, shutting out all of nature, and my mind cannot run free in the *boat's* tiny wooden cave of a room with one lamp burning—it's as if one has to live in too close a proximity with one's self, brushing up and knocking against yourself all the time. In this situation, it's very difficult to live with one's own mind. . . . Speaking of literature, I had brought just two storybooks with me, but such is my wretched fate that today, while taking her leave, the engineer saheb's mem has taken both with her, and I have no idea when she's going to return them. She picked up both the books, and in a shy, pleading tone, began: '*Mr Tagore would you*'—even before she could finish, I nodded vigorously and said, '*Certainly.*' I'm not sure what one can make of this exchange. Actually, they were saying their goodbyes then, and I could have given them half my kingdom in my enthusiasm (not that the recipients would have profited greatly). Anyway, they've gone today, Bob—these last two days were a complete muddle—and it shall take me another two days to regain my equilibrium—I'm in such a foul mood that I'm afraid I might bark at someone unfairly without rhyme or reason—I'm being so careful that I'm speaking very diffidently to somebody I might have been sharp with in normal circumstances—this opposite outcome happens with me sometimes when I'm in a temper so that at this time if the boys are near me I'm afraid I might take them severely to task for the smallest of mistakes, so I don't punish them at all, cultivating stoicism with great determination.

39

Shilaidaha
Thursday, 14 January 1892

For the last one or two days nature here has been vacillating between winter and spring—in the morning it could be the north wind blowing cold, making land and water shiver—in the evening, a south wind might stir up everything under bright moonlight. It's quite apparent that spring is approaching and is quite near. After a long time, a cuckoo has begun calling nowadays from the garden on the other side. Human minds too are becoming slightly restless. These days in the evenings one can hear the sound of music and song from the village on that side—evidence that people are no longer that keen to close their doors and windows and go to sleep huddled under quilts. Tonight is full-moon night—exactly to my left, an enormous moon has risen above the open window and looks at my face—perhaps to see whether I'm criticizing him at all in my letter. Perhaps he feels that the people of this world gossip about the marks on his face far more than they talk about the light. A lone partridge calls out from the silent sandbank—the river is still—there are no boats—the dense woods on the other side, stunned, throw unmoving shadows upon the water—the full-moon night looks slightly hazy, like sleeping eyes do when they are open. Tomorrow, once again, it will slowly begin to get dark in the evening—tomorrow, once the kāchāri's work is done, when I begin to cross this small river, I will see that my beloved in these foreign lands has separated herself from me a little—she who had opened her mysterious, endless heart to me yesterday—as if she suspects today that she should not have revealed so much of herself last evening all at once, and so she begins to close her heart again, very slowly. Really, nature comes very close to one in the loneliness of foreign lands—I really have thought to myself these past few days—I will not get as much moonlight any more from the day after the full-moon night—as if I'll go from a foreign land further into foreign territory; that the peaceful, familiar beauty that awaited me by the riverbank every evening after work shall not be there any more—I shall have to return to the boat in darkness. . . . But today is a full-moon night, the first full moon of spring this year, I'm writing it down here—perhaps many years later I'll recall this silent night again—along with the cry of that partridge as well as the light that burns on the boat tied to the other side—this small bit of the brilliant line of the river, the coating of that little piece of dark forest there—and this aloof, disinterested, pale sky—

40

Shilaidaha
Friday, 12 February 1892

The other day I read a *sloka* from Kalidasa in a paper that I was quite surprised to read—

> *ramyāṇi bīkshya madhurāṅgaśca niśamya śabdān*
> *parayutsukī bhabati yaṭ sukhitohapi jantuḥ.*
> *taccetsā smarati nūnambodhpūrbaṃ*
> *bhābsthirāṇi jananāntarasauhrdāni.*

Meaning: 'Why is even the soul of a happy man rendered restless upon seeing a beautiful thing or hearing a sweet sound? It must be that he remembers, unbeknownst to himself, some friend from another life.' It's pretty apparent that Kalidasa's mind would sometimes be weighed down quite without reason. In the *Meghdūt* too, the poet has said '*meghāloke bhabati sukhinohapyanyathābrtti cetaḥ*'—seeing clouds, even the happy person turns absent-minded. Beauty awakens in man the most deep and mysterious and limitless of desires, that attracts the mind and takes it from one birth to the next—it gave me great pleasure to read of this feeling in Kalidasa's poetry. . . .

41

A lovely breeze has been blowing since morning. I'm not feeling like doing any work. It must be about eleven or eleven-thirty in the morning, yet I haven't put my hand to any reading or writing till now. I've been sitting still on a chair since morning. There are so many fragments of lines and unfinished feelings coming and going in my head, but I don't have the strength to tie them together or to give expression to them. I remembered that song of yours, '*Pāyeriyā bāje jhanaka jhanaka jhana jhana–nana nana nana*'— on this beautiful morning, in the sweet breeze in the middle of the river, my head resonates with that sort of *jhana-nana* sound of anklets, but only from this side or that—hidden—not letting itself be caught or seen. So I've been sitting quietly. Do you know what sort of place I'm at? Most of the river's water has dried up, there's no water anywhere that's more than waist-deep, so it hasn't been difficult to tie the boat almost in the middle of the river. To my right, farmers plough the fields upon the sandbank and sometimes bring their cows to drink from the water. To my left are Shilaidaha's coconut and mango groves, women at the ghat washing their clothes, drawing water, bathing, and talking loudly to each other in the East Bengali dialect—the younger girls play in the water endlessly—they finish bathing and come out and then jump into the water again with a splash—it's quite wonderful to hear their loud, carefree laughter. The men come seriously, immerse themselves once or twice, complete their daily ablutions and leave—but the women seem to have a special bond with the water. The two seem to be similar to and friendly with each other—both women and water have a simple, easy, bright way, a motion that's quite flowing and rhythmical, with melody and undulation—they can establish themselves in any vessel—they may slowly dry up in the withering heat of sorrow, but they will not irrevocably break into two at a blow. They encircle this hard earth from all sides in an embrace; the earth cannot understand the deep mystery of her inner heart; she does not produce grain herself, but if she is not there within, not a single blade of grass would grow. Comparing women with men, Tennyson said: *water unto wine*. It seems to me today: water *unto* land. That's why women get along so well with water—women are not suited to carrying many other sorts of loads, but to carry water—from the fountainhead, the well, the ghat—that has never been unsuitable when women do it. To wash their bodies, to bathe, to sit in waist-deep water at the riverside and talk to each other—all of this seems eminently suitable for women. I have seen that women love water, because both are of the same sort. Only water and women have this easy, endless flow and chatter, nothing else does. One could have shown many more similarities, but it's getting late, and one thought shouldn't be wrung excessively dry.

42

Shilaidaha
Friday, 8 April 1892

You must be quite surprised to hear that I'm reading so much of *Elements of Politics* and *Problems of the Future* after coming here. Actually, the thing is, I can never quite find a poem or a novel that's appropriate for this place. Whatever I open has the same English names, English society, the roads and *drawing rooms* of London, and all sorts of meaningless complications. I never come across anything that is quite easy, beautiful, free or generous, brightly tender, and rounded like a teardrop. Just complications upon complications, *analysis* upon *analysis*—just attempts at crumpling, wringing and scrunching up human nature to spin it around forcefully in order to prise out newer and newer *theories* or ethics. If I try to read that stuff, it shall completely muddy what I have here—the calm current of this small summer-worn river, the flow of the indifferent breeze, the undivided expanse of the sky, the continuous peace of both shores and the silence all around. I almost never have anything to read that is appropriate for here, except for the shorter verses of the Vaishnava poets. If I knew a few good womanly fairy tales of Bengal, and could write them down in a simple, rhythmic and beautiful way, replete with the homely memories of childhood, then it might have been appropriate for this place. Quite like the sound of this small river, like the loud laughter and sweet voices and inconsequential conversations of the women at the ghat, like the coconut fronds that shiver and tremble in the breeze and the deep shadows of the mango orchards and the smell of the full-blown mustard fields—quite simple yet beautiful and peaceful—full of a lot of sky, light, silence and tenderness! Fighting, arguing, jostling and crying—all that is not of this shadowy Bengal, encircled by the embrace of its affectionate rivers. Anyway, *Elements of Politics* flows over the silent peace of this place like oil upon water, it doesn't disturb or break it in any way. . . . I'm sitting here in the middle of the river, with the wind blowing through night and day, the banks on either side looking like two starting lines of the world, where life has only just suggested itself, has not yet assumed a clear, sharp shape—as if those who draw water, bathe, row boats, graze cows, and come and go across the field's footpaths are not completely, really, alive. In other places, people crowd around, they interrupt your flow of thought if they are in front of you, as if their very existence seems to nudge you; they are all, each and every one, a *positive* human being; but here they come and go and talk and work in front of you—yet they do not push against your mind. They stand and stare at you out of curiosity, but that simple curiosity does not crowd you or overwhelm you. Anyway, I'm really liking it here.

43

Bolpur
Saturday, 14 May 1892

The universe has many *paradoxes*, one among which is that where there's an extensive landscape, endless sky, dense clouds, a deep feeling, in other words in a place where the eternal is manifest, there its appropriate companion can be only one person—too many people make it too petty and messy. Infinity and one person are both evenly balanced in relation to one another—both deserve to sit on their individual thrones face-to-face. And if you have many people staying together, they tend to cut one another down to size—if a person wants to spread out his entire inner soul, he needs so much space that there's no room for five or six people near him. In my judgement, if you want a good fit, then in this wide world it is possible to fit only an intimate two—there's no space for more—the moment you gather a number in excess of that, you have to lessen yourself in order to accommodate one another's demands—you have to insert yourself into the available gaps. In the meantime, I am unable to receive—with hands cupped and arms extended in prayer—the blessings of nature's deep, limitless expanse that is given so generously.

44

Bolpur
15 May 1892

Beli maintains quite clearly that she loves Bolpur next only to England, and Khoka endorses her opinion *ditto*—Renuka is unable to express her opinions in articulated words.* She

---

* Renuka: the third child and second daughter of Rabindranath and Mrinalini, born 23 January 1891.

pronounces a variety of uncertain sounds day and night, and it's becoming difficult to manage her. She keeps pointing in every direction and then tries to follow her finger in the direction pointed at—the *regiment* of servants who have accompanied me here are frequently almost all of them occupied with this tiny godhead—they are responsible for putting a stop to all the wishes that she follows up with such unruly speed and so every moment resounds with her sharp protesting wails. My little son stands still in unblinking silence—it's impossible for anyone to say what he's thinking. . . .

When Khoka sits there immersed in his own thoughts, I feel like entering his mind. I want to see how, in that taciturn country of theirs, their feelings come and go as indistinct figures in the first light. I remember a few things from when I was very small, but those memories are so unclear that I cannot catch hold of them. But I recall very clearly that on some mornings I would suddenly, quite without reason, be filled with great joy in life. In those days, the world was shrouded in mystery on all sides. . . . I used to sit and dig the soil at Golabari every day with a piece of split bamboo, thinking I was about to uncover some mystery. I would gather a small pile of soil on the south veranda and, burying some custard apple seeds in it, would water it all the time, thinking that some amazing thing would happen when the seeds germinated! Everything in this world—its beauty, taste, smell, all its stirring and movement—the coconut trees in the garden within the house, the banyan tree by the pond, the world of shadows upon the water, the sound of the road, the cry of the kite, the smell of the garden at dawn, storms and gales—spread over all of this was the embrace of a large, half-known, living thing that kept me company in various forms. Just as a child has an inner resemblance of a sort with dogs, cats, sheep, calves or other animals, in the same way they have a connection in their hearts with this vast, spread-out, restless, dumb outer world.[1]

45

Bolpur
Tuesday, 17 May 1892

'*Jagate keha nāi, sabāi prāṇe mor*' [The world is empty, my heart is full]—that's the special feeling of a certain age. When the heart first wakes up and extends its arms, it's as if it wants the entire world. Just as Renuka feels about her newly grown teeth—that the entire world may be ingested—it's only gradually that the mind understands what it really wants and doesn't want. Then, that all-encompassing heart's vapour takes on a more limited, narrow aspect, it begins to burn and to make others burn. If you go and lay claim to the entire earth you don't get anything—finally, if you manage to immerse yourself heart and soul in some one thing, only then do you enter the infinite. *Prabhātsaṅgīt* was the first enthusiastic outward expression of my inner nature, that's why it has no discrimination or judgement at all. I still love the whole world in a way—but not with that wild enthusiasm—a ray from the lighted world of my love is reflected upon all mankind—in that light, on certain occasions, the world seems very beautiful and very intimate. The movement of your mind is not obstructed by those whom you love a great deal; in them, your heart can always roam—those whom you don't love so much aren't never-ending for you in that way. You see them partially, just the part that's visible to you, that's why if they brush up too close they enclose you from all sides like unclear walls of glass; if you want to let your thoughts have a free run, your thoughts stumble upon them at every step and return irritably again. That's why one doesn't like ordinary company all the time. When you're in a room, the walls seem like a good thing; in fact, it's impossible to get by without them. When you go out, if the walls accompany you, you don't like it. So if I've been complaining about crowds of people, don't think it's because I've become a complete *misanthrope*—I only want to say this much, that there are times when it's better not to have so many people around. . . . You see, I don't have an iota of patience, Bob. Perhaps that's the way men are—they want to fall upon things and devour them in an instant—they can't do anything with slow, silent finesse and beauty—they have been reduced to this state because they have worked as labourers in the world through the ages. Women are nowadays trying to lessen men's load of paid labour, and that wouldn't be such a bad thing for our race of dispirited fellow men—it might give us some time to practise a little finesse—but it doesn't seem as if these large-limbed wretched idiots are going to pay much attention to that aspect—perhaps if they have extra time on their hands they will eat like a python and sleep like a python instead. It seems that in the not-too-distant future men are going to face a time of great disgrace. Civilization is progressing so much in the direction of fineness and beauty that these big animals will be in a great deal of trouble. At the beginning of the world, large creatures like the mammoth and mastodon were plentiful—they had so much strength, their skins were so thick—they're all extinct now. Now the thin-skinned, three-and-a-half-cubit-high man is king of the world. But our time's almost up—now's the time for those even younger. . . .

46

Bolpur
Wednesday, 18 May 1892

The other evening, Bela and Khoka got into an argument on a subject that's worth citing. Khoka said, 'Bela, I'm feeling hungry for water' [*Jal kshide peẏeche*]. Bela said, 'Nonsense, gap-tooth

[*dhūr, phoklā*]! You don't say hungry for water! Thirsty for water.'
Khoka, very firmly—'No, hungry for water.' Bela—'*Āyei,*
Khoka, I'm three years older than you, you are two years younger
than me, do you know that? I know so much more than you!'
Khoka, suspiciously, 'You're that old?' Bela—'Okay, why don't
you ask Baba?' Khoka, suddenly excited, 'And what about the
fact that I drink milk and you don't?' Bela, scornfully, 'So what?
Ma doesn't drink milk, does that mean she isn't bigger than you?'
Khoka, completely silent, with head on pillow, thinking. Then
Bela began to say, '*O father*, I have a tremendous, tremendous
friendship with somebody! She's mad, she's so sweet! *Oh I can eat
her up!*' Saying this, she runs to Renu and hugs and kisses her
till she starts to cry.

Yesterday Bela came to me very upset. What happened
was—yesterday the Swayamprabhas had gone to the small
bungalow to cook fish. A madman had taken shelter there
with some mangoes—Choto-bau and the Swayamprabhas were
afraid, so they sent him off. I was lying down quietly in the
second-floor room. Bela returned from the small bungalow
and began to plead with me, 'Baba, there's a very poor man.
The poor fellow is very hungry, that's why he was sitting with
some mangoes in the lower bungalow. They chased him away
with a stick.' She kept repeating, 'The wretched fellow is very
poor, he has nothing, he's wearing only one little piece of cloth,
maybe he doesn't have anything to wear in the winter, and he
feels cold. It's not his fault. When they asked his name, he told
them. He said he lives in heaven. They chased him away, and he
didn't say a word! Just went off!'—I found this so sweet! Beli is
really very kind-hearted. Yesterday she pleaded with such real
anxiety—she found this needless cruelty so wanton! I was very
moved to hear her. When Beli grows up, she will be a very
affectionate, simple, good girl. Khoka too is very affectionate.
He loves Renu so much. He caresses her so gently and puts

up with all her tantrums with the sort of kindness that many mothers themselves may not show.

47

Bolpur
Friday, 20 May 1892

Witticisms are very dangerous things—if they arise spontaneously, with a pleasant and smiling face, they are first-rate; but if you pull and push at them then there is a chance of them misfiring completely. The comedic [*hāsyaras*] is like the ultimate weapon [*brahmāstra*] of old—those who know how to use it can deploy it to deadly effect in war—and the poor wretch who doesn't know how to throw it, yet wants to handle it, in his case, the weapon turns around like the brahmāstra and destroys the user, it turns the wit himself into a laughing stock. . . . When women try to be witty, but become garrulous instead, then that's a most unseemly sight. In fact, I think that it doesn't suit women to try to be '*comic*', whether they do it successfully or not. Because the '*comic*' is a very bulky and large thing. There's a relation between '*sublimity*' and '*comicality*'—that's why elephants are *comic*, camels are *comic*, giraffes are *comic*, largeness is *comic*. Beauty, in fact, is better displayed alongside sharpness, as the flower with the thorn—similarly, sharpness in speech is both very effective from, as well as very suitable in, women. But women should never tread anywhere near the sort of scornful witticism that has any trace of heaviness about it; that is for our *sublime* (in Chandranath-babu's language—'huge' [*birāṭ*]) sort. A male Falstaff will make us laugh till we split our sides, but a female Falstaff would have been very annoying.

48

Bolpur
Saturday, 21 May 1892

What a storm we had yesterday! I had just completed my daily
writing for *Sādhanā* and was proceeding upstairs for tea, when
suddenly a tremendous storm arrived. The sky became dark
with dust, and all the dried leaves in the garden came together
and began to whirl and dance around the garden like a spinning
top—as if every ghost in the forest had suddenly woken up and
begun a phantom dance. All the trees in the garden began to
shudder and shake like the tremendous mythical Jaṭāyu bird
flapping its wings and straining against its chained legs. What
roaring, what chaos, what a hectic affair! Looking at the storm
I was reminded of the descriptions I had read occasionally
of the *American ranch*—of six or seven hundred wild horses
suddenly breaking down a fence and running away at full speed
in a whirl of dust, followed by men on horses with lassos to
chase them down and bring them back—the sound of their
whips whistling through the air on whatever it finds—the
open skies and fields of Bolpur seemed to be witnessing a similar
wild outbreak and chase—a run and catch and flee and smash
and bang and crash sort of affair. All the servants here were
busy trying to save the temple—in case that coloured glass
bubble is broken and bursts. It has been covered with very large
curtains made of a strong material—but the storm cuts the
curtains to pieces, tears the ropes into bits, breaks the curtain
rails into sections and then those flap against the glass walls of
the temple and smash them into smithereens. Earlier, in another
storm, the temple keeper's head was split in two by a blow
from one of these curtain rails. Going upstairs, I see my son
standing on the north veranda in the middle of this tremendous

revolution with his small, immature nose inserted between the
gaps in the railing, silently taking in the smell and the taste
of this storm. It began to rain heavily and I said to Khoka,
'Khoka, you'll get wet in the rain. Come and sit here on this
chair.' Khoka called his mother and said, 'Ma, you sit on the
chair here and I'll sit in your lap.' Then he took possession of
his mother's lap and continued to feast upon the rainy scene in
silence. Sometimes one gets a hint as to what Khoka is thinking
about when he sits silently by himself and smiles to himself
and makes faces—one can see that he too is ruminating on the
handful of early memories of his very short life. I've seen that
he suddenly asks, out of the blue, 'Baba, there was a river in
Shilaidaha, wasn't there?' After much thought, he says to his
mother, 'Ma, we were very happy in Shilaidaha.' The other day
he asked Choto-bau, 'What day is it today?' Choto-bau said,
'Sunday.' Khoka said, 'Then today the steamers are not plying
in Shilaidaha.' But more than anything, I like to observe the
crazy affair going on between Khoka and Renu. The moment
Renu sees Khoka lying quietly somewhere, she will immediately
launch herself upon his shoulders, put her face upon his face,
kiss him, pull his hair, beat him and begin the most violent
demonstrations of her love for him—Khoka is so sweet and
kind, caressing her, calling her, 'Rani, Rani,' and putting up
with all of it. If Renu sees Khoka sleeping, she will promptly
push him, pull him, beat him—then Khoka pleads with her and
says, 'Rani, let me sleep a little.' But still when Renu will not
leave him alone he sits up and begins to play with her—doesn't
express the tiniest bit of irritation. But the two of them are
not really friends with Beli that much—Renu, in fact, is always
expressing her regal displeasure at Beli in very clear terms. It
seems as if they are temperamentally different from Beli—she's
outside their group.

49

Bolpur
Sunday, 22 May 1892

Yesterday in the evening there was tremendous storm and rain; however, that's not a matter of regret. In fact, good; let the trees and the earth and the grass cover become green and shining and luscious. Let the eyes find rest at the sight. Let the sky be covered from one end to the other with downy, vaporous clouds—let the forests turn dark and shadowy, the unceasing rain make veils with which to cover the horizon's brides, the woods resonate with the sound of pattering rain on the dense leaves, the still, immense land come alive with the childish restlessness of the sound and variety of the līlā of the many temporary big and small rivulets of water. And that is exactly what has happened. This morning, the sky seemed to be drooping with the weight of the clouds made heavy with water, and, all around, the shadow of the rain has made everything calm . . . Khoka cannot express himself well, so everything on his mind stays in his mind, and all his enthusiasm works gradually within it, that's why the lines of his thought cut very deep. Bela talks continuously and so doesn't find time to think about anything properly—all her energy is spent in her incessant speech. But she's extremely soft-hearted—she tried her utmost to stop Khoka from killing an ant the other day. I was very surprised to see this—I was like that when I was a child; I couldn't tolerate even insects and birds being hurt in any way. But I have become so much harder now on growing up. I remember feeling such a wrench of the heart at others' sorrows in those days. Where does that happen any more? Will Bela too become harder as she grows older? Maybe not—after all, she's a girl. In the first place, she will never have to do anything cruel by her own hand, besides which, women's minds have a sort of *elasticity*: they do not harden with ripeness. If I was as sensitive now to the pain of living things as I was in my childhood, it would become impossible to step out into the world; perhaps I would then be hurt by sorrow and death at every step and keep lamenting and regretting it like Pierre Loti.* That would have been a nuisance! Besides which, if you express your pain about something that most people ordinarily don't feel any distress about, then other people get very annoyed; they think—this fellow's trying to be superior. I remember that when my elders did not show pity towards the pitiable, I wanted to be able to say something, but embarrassment would hold me back—what if they thought, 'Oh, I see this righteous Yudhishthir has come to knock us down a peg!' It's most troublesome to have a greater sensitivity than others all around you. The logical and rational thing to do is to hide it at first, and eventually to lessen it. I remember I was once travelling with Jyoti-dada in the carriage when a Brahmin wayfarer stopped us on the road and said, 'Can you make some place for me in your carriage? I'll get off on the way.' Jyoti-dada got very angry and shooed him away. I was dreadfully upset by that incident—as it is the man was a weary traveller, on top of that he was insulted and shamed and had to go away hopelessly. But I found it very embarrassing to show any pity where Jyoti-dada had not—I couldn't say anything in spite of feeling very troubled, but my admiration for my brother suffered a grievous blow.

50

Bolpur
Tuesday, 24 May 1892

I've told you before, in the afternoon I wander around the terrace by myself, sunk in my own thoughts; yesterday in the evening

* Pierre Loti was the pseudonym of Julien Viaud (1850–1923), a French novelist and naval officer. Edmund Gosse said about his work in the *Encyclopaedia*

I set off with my two friends on either side, with Aghor as our guide, thinking it was my duty to show them the natural beauty of this place. The sun had set by then, but it was not yet dark. At the extreme end of the horizon, rows of trees were to be seen in shades of blue and, just above it, a deeper blue line of very dark blue clouds had made the scene very beautiful—in the midst of it all, I became a little poetic and said: just like the blue line of kohl on the eyelid above blue eyes. My companions did not all hear me, some did not understand me and others said briefly, 'Yes, looks great, doesn't it.' After that I did not venture into any poeticisms a second time round. After about a mile, there was a row of palm trees by a dam, and near the palm trees was a rustic waterfall in a field; we were standing and looking at that when suddenly we noticed that the blue clouds in the north had become extremely dense and swollen and were coming towards us with their lightning-teeth bared. We all decided unanimously that such natural beauty is best appreciated indoors—that it is the safest option. Just as we turned homeward, taking long steps over the vast field, an enormous storm fell upon our shoulders with an angry roar. While we were busy praising the kohl in her eyes we had not realized for a moment that nature's beauty would run up and attack us in this manner with a tremendous slap like an enraged housewife. It became so dark with dust that it was impossible to see beyond a distance of a few feet. The strength of the wind began to increase—the gravel, impelled by the wind, began to pierce us like shrapnel—it seemed as if the wind had caught hold of us by the nape of our necks and was propelling us forward—drops of rain too began to fall upon our faces and hurt us. Run, run! The field was uneven. In some places one needed to descend into the rifts [khoÿāi], where it's difficult to walk even

---

Britannica (1911): 'Many of his best books are long sobs of remorseful memory, so personal, so intimate, that an English reader is amazed to find such depth of feeling compatible with the power of minutely and publicly recording what is felt.'

in ordinary circumstances, and even more so in the middle of a storm. On the way a dry branch with thorns managed to impale itself on my foot—while trying to peel that off, the wind tries to push you from the back and make you fall flat on your face. When we had reached the vicinity of the house we came across three or four servants who fell noisily upon us like a second storm! One holds your hand, another commiserates, someone else wants to show you the way, another thinks that the babu might fly away in the wind and embraces you from behind. Getting past the tyranny of these servants somehow or the other, I finally got home, panting, with dishevelled hair, grimy body and wet clothes. Anyway, that's a lesson well learnt—perhaps one day I might have sat down to describe the hero of a novel or poem encountering a terrible storm in a field as he goes blithely towards his beloved, thinking of her sweet face—but now I will not be able to write such lies. It's impossible to remember anybody's sweet face in the middle of a storm; one is too preoccupied with keeping the gravel out of one's eyes. And then on top of that I had my *eye glasses* on. They kept getting swept away by the wind; I found it impossible to keep a hold on them. With spectacles clutched in one hand and the ends of the dhuti in the other, I had to walk avoiding both thorny bushes and holes in the ground. Imagine if I had a beloved in a house by the Kopai River here, would I have been busy with thoughts of her, or with keeping my spectacles and dhuti in order! After getting home, I thought about it for a while—the Vaishnava poets have written a great deal of very good and sweet poetry on Radhika's unwearied assignations on a stormy night, but they have not thought for a moment about what she would have looked like in this storm when she arrived in front of Krishna. You can well imagine what would have happened to her hair. Think about the state of her clothes! Grimy with dust, caked with the mud of rainwater—what a wonderful image she would have presented in the forest groves! Of course you don't think about these things when you're reading the Vaishnava poets—one just sees with the inner eye of one's imagination a beautiful woman on a dark night in the rainy season travelling, driven by love, through the flower-filled *kādamba* forests by the banks of the Yamuna through storm and rain, impervious to her surroundings as if she is walking in her dreams; she has tied her anklets so that she may not be heard, she has worn *nīlāmbarī* clothes in a shade of deepest blue so she may not be seen, but she has not brought an umbrella in case she gets wet, nor a light in case she stumbles and falls. Alas, the necessities of life are so necessary when we need them, yet so neglected in poetry! Poetry pretends with untruths so that we may be free of the thousand bonds of slavery with which we are tied to necessity. Umbrellas, shoes, clothes—these will last forever. In fact, it seems that with the progress of civilization, poetry shall slowly die out, but new *patents* on umbrellas and shoes will continue to appear.

51

Bolpur
Saturday, 28 May 1892

The cup of tea I had last evening was somewhat on the stronger side—on top of that, the letter I wrote you last night was also on a subject that had become somewhat inflamed with the heat of my thoughts, so it kept ringing in my head for a long time—as a result, after I went to bed I spent more than half the night completely sleepless. There are no church bells that sound at night over here—and because there is no human habitation anywhere nearby, the moment the birds stop singing the whole place is enveloped in the most complete silence from the evening onward—there's not much difference between the first hours of the night and the middle of the night. In Calcutta, a sleepless night is like a large, dark river—it keeps flowing very slowly—you can lie flat on your bed and calculate its

motion by its sounds—here, the night is like a vast motionless lake
that is dreadfully still—there is no movement anywhere. However
much I might turn on this side or that, a vast, humid want of sleep
hung over me which had no trace of any flow in it. This morning,
getting out of bed a little late, I sat in the downstairs room leaning
against a cushion with a slate on my chest and with my feet up,
one on top of the other, and began to try and write a poem in the
midst of the morning breeze and the call of the birds. It was all
just beginning to gel—pleased expression, eyes slightly closed, head
swaying frequently, and a rhythmic humming recitation growing
progressively clearer—when suddenly a letter from you, a copy of
Sādhanā, a proof of *Sādhanā* and a *Monist* paper presented themselves.
I read your letter and proceeded to race my eyes across the pages
of *Sādhanā* at a brisk gallop. Then, with a renewed nodding of the
head and an indistinct humming, I resumed my poetic occupation.
Other things could wait until it was done. I'm wondering why there
is so much more joy to be obtained from the completion of a single
poem than in the writing of a thousand pages of prose. In poetry,
one's thoughts attain a completion, almost as if one can pick it up
with one's hands. And prose is like a sack, full of separate things—if
you hold it in one place, all of it doesn't come up so easily—an
absolute specimen of a burden. If I could complete a poem every
day then life would pass so pleasantly! But I've been pursuing it for
such a long time now, and it still hasn't quite been tamed yet—it's
not the sort of Pegasus that will allow you to put a harness on it
every day. One of the chief joys of *art* is the joy of freedom—to
take one's self quite far away, and then even after one returns to the
prison house of the world, there's an echo in your ear, an elation
in your mind, which stays with you for a long time. I'm unable to
turn my hand to the play because these short poems keep coming
up spontaneously. Otherwise, there were a few messengers from
two or three future plays knocking at the door. I might not be able
to attend to them before winter, possibly. With the exception of
Citrāṅgadā, all my other plays are written in the winter. That is the

time when the passion of lyric poetry cools down a bit, and one can sit down calmly and quietly to write plays.

52

Bolpur
31 May 1892

It's not yet five o'clock—but it's already light, there's quite a breeze, and all the birds of the garden have woken up and started to sing. The cuckoo has outdone itself—nobody has yet been able to fathom why it calls so continuously—obviously it's not just for our pleasure, nor to make the beloved feel the pangs of separation even more—it must surely have a *personal* ambition of its own—but it's impossible to decide what that wretched ambition is! Nor does it let off—its *cooo-o, cooo-o*, goes on and on—and then, occasionally, as if its impatience had doubled, it coos more rapidly still. What does this mean? And again, a little further away, some other sort of bird is consistently repeating itself—*kuk-kuk*—in a very low tone, without the sting of the least bit of eagerness or enthusiasm—as if it were a man who was feeling quite despondent, all his hopes lost, but was still unable to give up the impulse to sit in the shade the entire day with its little bit of *kuk-kuk, kuk-kuk*. Really, these small, timid living things with wings, sitting in the shade of the trees with their intensely tender little necks and chests, running their individual households—we don't know anything of their actual story. We don't really understand why they need to call out in such a way. Some zoologists say it is to call out to their beloved. Their paramours too don't seem to be far behind humans, I see—making the gentleman quite maddened at this early hour—if the cuckoo lady wants to come to him, she might as well come at a call or two—why is she making the lovelorn admirer call so frantically in this way?

53

Shilaidaha
Sunday, 12 June 1892

What you wrote yesterday in your letter about the duties of life
is absolutely true. Our chief duty is to make the place where we
have somehow arrived happier, brighter and more peaceful to the
best of our ability. All of you do exactly that with your happy,
beautiful faces, your selfless service, love and affection—there is
nothing further to be done. Not everybody is able to do this. We
are cursed beings, we are born accompanied by such a tremendous
unhappiness that we are unable to make the world a happy, calm
place in a natural and easy way; we keep struggling and kicking
in the same place and we muddy everything around us—we don't
know how to make the world sweet—exactly the opposite. A
hundred thousand curses on the race of men—there is no greater
rubbish on the face of the earth.

54

Shilaidaha
Monday, 13 June 1892

I'm fed up with civilized behaviour—nowadays I often sit and
recite—'What if I were rather an Arab Bedouin!' What a healthy,
strong, free barbarism! Instead of allowing one's judgement,
behaviour, intelligence and thinking to make you decrepit in body
and mind before time, caught up day and night in an ancient,
worn-out set of rites, one could have enjoyed an intense, joyful
life with a heart free of worries or hesitation. All one's hopes and
desires, whether good or bad, could have been fearless, unhesitant
and commendable—no continual conflict between one's brain and

one's customs, between the brain and desire, between desire and work. This closed life—if I could just let it run on in the most wild and lawless way, I would have created a storm and sent the waves crashing everywhere, riding one's frivolity like a strong, untamed horse running with the joy of one's passions!

But I'm not a Bedouin, I'm a Bengali. I will sit in a corner and nitpick, I will judge, argue, turn my mind over once this way and then the other way—in the way one fries fish—you let one side splutter and sizzle in the boiling oil, then you turn it over to let the other side sputter. Anyway! When it's impossible to be completely uncivilized, it's politic to try and be absolutely civilized. No point setting up a fight between civilization and barbarism. . . .

As such by nature I'm uncivilized—I find the intimacy of people completely unbearable. Unless there's a lot of empty space all around, I cannot completely *unpack* my mind, spread out my hands and feet, and settle down. All my blessings are with the human race—I hope it prospers—but let them not come up too close against me. . . . I'm sure the general populace will get on completely fine without me and find themselves a lot of good friends. They will not lack consolation.

55

Shilaidaha
Wednesday, 15 June 1892

Yesterday, on the first day of Āshāṛh, the coronation of the rains was conducted with much pomp and ceremony. After a very hot day, dark clouds rolled in with a lot of fanfare towards evening. . . . Yesterday I thought: it's the first day of the rains, today it would be better to get drenched than spend the day inside a dark room—the year 1299 [Bengali Era] will not return a second time in my life—if you think about it, how many times will you experience the first

day of Āshāṛh in your entire life—if you collect them all together
and you have about thirty days, then you must concede that that's
a very long life. Ever since I wrote 'Meghdūt' the first day of Āshāṛh
has had a special significance—at least for me. I often think, these
days of my life that keep coming one after the other—some brilliant
with sunrise and sunset, some the calm blue of dense clouds, some
shining like white flowers on a full-moon night—how lucky I am
to have them! And how valuable they are! A thousand years ago,
Kalidasa, sitting in the royal court of nature, had welcomed the
first day of Āshāṛh by composing, in immortal rhyme, the song of
man's pain of separation from his beloved; in my life too, the same
first day of Āshāṛh rises every year with its entire sky of wealth—
that same first day of Āshāṛh of the ancient poet of ancient Ujjaini
with its men and women with their multitude of joys and sorrows,
separations and reunions, of many many ages ago! That first great
day of that very old Āshāṛh will be subtracted by a day every year
from my life, until a time will come when there will not be a single
day remaining in my life of this day of Kalidasa, this day of Meghdūt,
this first day of the rains in India for all of time past. When you
think about this deeply, you feel like looking once again at this world
very carefully—you want to greet the sunrise every day in your life
fully and consciously and say goodbye to every sunset like a familiar
friend. If I were a renunciate by nature I might have thought that life
is transient, so instead of spending my days uselessly I should engage
in good works and in taking the name of god. But that is not my
nature, that's why I sometimes think—such lovely days and nights are
going from my life every day, and I'm unable to take them in fully!
All these colours, this light and shade, this silent splendour spread
across the sky, this peace and beauty that fills the entire space between
earth and heaven—how much preparation all of this takes! Such a
vast field of celebration! Such a huge and amazing affair happening
every day outside, and we cannot find a proper response to it within
us! We live at such a far remove from the universe! The light of a
single star reaches us after travelling through the infinite darkness for

millions and millions of years, from millions and millions of miles away, and it cannot enter our hearts, as if our hearts were a further million miles away! The colourful mornings and evenings are falling from the torn necklace of the horizon's brides like so many gems into the ocean's water. Not one of them enters our thoughts! That time on the way to England the unearthly sunset I had seen upon the still waters of the ruby-red sea—where has it gone! But thank god I had seen it, thank god that that one evening of my life had not been rejected and wasted—in all our endless days and nights no other poet in the world had witnessed that one amazing sunset except me. Its colours remain in my life. Each day of that sort is like an individual legacy. The few days I spent in that garden of mine at Peneti,* a few nights on the second-floor terrace, a few rainy days in the western and southern verandas, a few evenings by the Ganga at Chandannagar, one sunset and moonrise on the mountain peak at Sinchal in Darjeeling—it's as if I have *filed* away a few brilliant, beautiful fragments of moments of this sort. Beauty, for me, is a real drug! It really and truly drives me mad. When I used to lie on the terrace on moonlit nights as a child, it was as though the moonlight was the white foam of liquor overflowing and drowning me in it. . . . The world in which I find myself is full of very strange human beings—they are all occupied night and day with rules and building walls; they carefully put up curtains just in case their eyes actually see anything—really, the creatures of this world are very strange! It's a wonder they don't cover up every flowering bush, or erect canopies to keep out the moonlight. These wilfully blind people, traversing the world in closed palanquins, what do they see as they go? If there is an afterlife in which one's wishes and desires are taken into account, then I want to get out of this wrapped-up world and be born again in an open, free, beautiful and heavenly place. Those who are unable to truly immerse themselves in beauty are the ones who scorn beauty as merely the wealth of the senses, but

* Peneti: colloquial term for Panihati.

those who have tasted it know that it has within it an unutterable depth—beauty is far beyond even the most powerful of the senses; forget about the eyes and ears, even if you enter it with your entire heart you will not reach the limit of its melancholy. Why do I come and go on the city streets dressed up like a gentleman? Why waste my life in polite conversation with neatly dressed gentlemen? I'm truly uncivilized, impolite—is there no beautiful anarchy for me anywhere? No festival of joy with a handful of madmen? But what's all this poeticism I'm engaging in—this is the sort of thing that heroes of poems say—pronouncing their opinions on *conventionality* over the course of three or four pages, thinking they are bigger than the rest of human society. Really, it's quite embarrassing to say such things. The truth within these thoughts has always been suppressed by talk over the ages. Everybody in this world talks a lot—and I'm foremost among them—I've suddenly realized this now after all this time. . . .

P.S. Let me finish telling you what I wanted to say to you at the start—don't worry, I won't take up another four pages—that is, it rained heavily in the evening on the first day of Āsharh. That's all.

56

Shilaidaha
Thursday, 16 June 1892

The more time you spend in open spaces on the river or in villages, the more you realize every day that there is no greater or more beautiful thing than to be able to accomplish one's everyday work with simplicity. Everything, from the grass on the field to the stars in the sky are doing precisely that; they're not trying to aggressively take over domains that are not their own, that's why nature is full of such deep peace and endless beauty—yet the little bit that each does is not a negligible amount at all—the grass expends all its energy to survive as grass, using its entire root up to the very tip to absorb nourishment. It is not trying in vain to exceed its own strength or neglect its own work in order to become a banyan tree—that's why the world is so beautiful and green. Really, it's not because of large schemes and boastful talk, but because human beings fulfil their small duties on a daily basis that human society has its share of ordered beauty and peace. Whether it is poetry you talk of, or bravery, none of these is complete in itself. But even the most minor duty done has a satisfaction and fulfilment about it. Nothing could be more ignoble than sitting and impatiently chafing, imagining things, thinking that no situation measures up to you and, in the meanwhile, watching time pass before you while all your big and small everyday duties flow by unnoticed. When you make a mental resolve that you will perform all your duties for the well-being and happiness of those around you truthfully and strongly, with all your heart, through all your joys and sorrows, only then does life fill up with joy, and all the small sorrows and pain are banished forever. Of course, every day and every moment of my life is not available in front of me, perhaps that's why I'm getting quite carried away by the excitement of my imaginary hopes from this distance, managing to draw a rough picture of my future life by ignoring all the little details and minor complications of danger and conflict, but that's not correct. . . .

57

Shilaidaha
Friday, 17 June 1892

Nowadays in the evenings I get up onto the land and stroll around for a long time—when I turn towards the east I see one sort of sight, and another sort in the west—it's as if there is peace dropping slow from the sky overhead, as if a golden stream of auspiciousness is entering my heart through my entranced pair of eyes. It's as if this breeze, this sky and this light makes new leaves grow in my mind, and I am fulfilled by new life and a new strength. It has become very easy for me to perform my duties in society and to interact with people. Actually, everything is easy—there is only one straight road and it's enough if you keep your eyes on that road and keep going; no point in looking for the clever *short cut*—there are joys and sorrows on every road—there's no way you can avoid them on any road—but peace reigns only on this main road.

58

On the way to Goalundo
21 June 1892

We have been floating on the river the entire day today. What I find surprising is that I have travelled this way so many times, traversing the waters on this *boat*—and I have enjoyed the particular pleasure of floating through the middle of the river—but the moment you spend a day or two on land, you don't quite remember it properly any more. This experience—this sitting quietly on one's own and looking—with villages, ghats, fields of grain, sandbanks, all appearing and disappearing on either side, the clouds floating in the sky and the different colours that bloom in the evenings—the boat moves on, the fishermen catch fish, the incessant liquid sound of the water full of such a strange affection—in the evenings the vast reaches of water become absolutely still like a tired sleeping child and all the stars in the open sky keep watch from above—deep into the night on sleepless nights I sit up and see the two shores asleep, covered in darkness—occasionally a jackal cries out in the village forests and the Padma's silent, strong current makes the banks fall into the water with a sloshing sound—as you keep looking at these ever-changing images, immediately a stream of imagination begins to flow in the mind and images of new desires manifest themselves on both its shores like distant scenery. Perhaps the scene in front of you is quite ordinary—a sort of yellow sandbank bereft of grass or trees stretching out before you and, tied to it, an empty boat, and the river, pale blue with the colour of the shadowy sky, flowing on—I cannot describe what the heart feels at this sight—perhaps that childhood experience of reading Arabian tales in which Sinbad ventures out to trade in many new countries, and I, confined by servants in the storeroom, roaming with Sinbad in the afternoons—it's as if the longing that had taken birth in me then is still alive now—as if that's what becomes restless once more at the sight of the boat tied to this sandbank. I can say with some certainty that if I had not read the *Arabian Nights* or *Robinson Crusoe* as a child, or heard fairy tales, then such a feeling would not have risen in my mind at the sight of that riverbank and the distant scene at the margins of the field—the whole world would have appeared differently to me. The imaginary and the real are entangled in such a strange web within the small minds of men! What gets embedded in which—everything gets entwined and knotted together—so many stories, pictures, events, the ordinary, the big—all of it gets entangled unconsciously every day—if you could open up the twists and knots in the net of a man's vast life and separate the small from the big—what a *heterogeneous* heap you would have!

59

Shilaidaha
Wednesday, 22 June 1892

Today, very early in the morning, I was lying in bed listening to the sound of women at the ghat ululating—this made me feel a bit depressed, but I really couldn't think why. Perhaps when you suddenly hear a sound so full of joy it reminds you that the world is a vast field of continuous activity, most of which has no connection of any sort with you—most people in the world are nobody to you, yet they are so busy with work and business, joys and sorrows, festivals and fairs—how vast the world is! How enormous human society! The sounds of life flow towards you from such a distance—you get a little bit of news from an entirely unknown family. When man realizes that however important I may be to myself, I alone cannot constitute the entire world—that most of the world is unknown to me, un-experienced, unrelated, empty of my presence—then in this vast, loose world he feels extremely small and unwanted and marginal—that is when the mind fills with this sort of spreading melancholy. Besides which, the sound of the ululation brought my own past and future, my entire life, in front of my eyes like a very long road, and it was as if this ululation was reaching the ear from its most distant and shadowy edges. This is how my day began. In a moment when the head rent collector, the office clerks and the people arrive, even the echo of this ululation will have fled from the precinct; the young and vigorous present will push aside the faint past and the future by their elbows and come and salaam in front of me—and I will have to concentrate on the collection of taxes. . . .

Yesterday I applied the last coat to my play and finished it. There are a few changes here and there—you cannot let the play out of harness too much—the work is a bit like driving a chaise and four—you have to take a number of horses along, tied to one carriage and on one road, and travel in one direction. So you cannot let one horse among the rest on too loose a rein, you have to make all of them run at the same speed. . . .

I don't disagree with you on the subject of keeping up a friendship with a foreign friend through letters—attempting to save the flame of friendship from dying into ashes by the solitary means of occasional letters is very trying and almost impossible. In this world, minor relationships come and go every day—we have no important lifelong ties with them—the centre of their world, where all their important joys and sorrows manifest themselves, is completely unknown to me. What's the huge necessity of overcoming so many sorts of obstacles for a tug of war with each other in these cases!

60

Shahjadpur
Monday, 27 June 1892

Last evening it became so terrifying that I was afraid. I don't think I've ever seen such ferocious-looking clouds—dark blue clouds had stacked themselves up in layers at the edge of the horizon in swollen ranks, like the anger-swollen moustaches of an enormous, murderous demon. Right next to that dark blue, at the extreme end of the horizon, a throbbing red hue had appeared from amidst the scattered clouds there—as if a giant unearthly *bison*, suddenly enraged, was spread across the sky, standing with its head lowered and bent, eyes glaring, blue hairs on its shoulders swelling up, ready to start attacking the earth with its horns, and, in the face of this impending danger, every field of grain and every leaf on the trees of the earth were trembling with fear, the upper surfaces of the water shivering, the crows wheeling about restlessly in the sky, crowing loudly.

61

Shahjadpur
28 June 1892

Today's letter from you had a small reference to Abhi's singing*—
the moment I read it my mind became suddenly so desolate—

* Abhi: Abhigyasundari, third daughter of Hemendranath Tagore and Rabindranath's niece.

many of life's small, uncared-for pleasures, which get no purchase from us in the confusion of city life, present their petitions to our hearts when we come away to foreign lands, sensing the moment is right. I love music and singing so much, yet, even in the city, where there are so many singers and musicians, so many days pass by one after another without my paying any attention to music and song even for a day. Although I don't always realize it myself, I can't tell you how starved I feel mentally! The moment I read your letter I felt such a desire to hear Abhi's sweet singing that I realized immediately that like many other sorrows, I had suppressed these tears of longing too within my inner self. We starve our lives to such an extent by running after the larger illusions at the expense of the small pleasures of life! When I was travelling to England, one of the imaginary scenes of pleasure in my mind was one of all of you in which somebody was playing the piano while the light and air came in through the open doors and windows, outside which were the distant sky and the trees, and me, listening, lying on a couch near an open window with my eyes on the scenery outside. I can't say that this is a particularly hard-to-obtain desire, but in three hundred and sixty five days, on how many days does fate ordain such happiness? The frustration of denying yourself such easily available pleasures in life accumulates in the account books, and later such a day may arrive when I will think that if I get back my entire life, I will not try and achieve the impossible, I'll just feast upon these small, gratuitous, everyday pleasures and savour them each day. Anyway, what I basically want to say is that when I return to Calcutta this time I want to listen to Abhi's singing sometimes and when any of you want to play your instruments, you must count me among your audience. This time when I return to Calcutta there are so many things I'm going to do—I shall work, sing, laugh, converse, love, sleep in the deep of the night and greet the ever-new sunrise every day in the morning and start my work—I shall bring my scattered life together to order and set it afloat upon a shaded, peaceful, musical little stream. It will be somewhat more difficult to do than it is to write of, but there's happiness because it will be hard.

62

Shahjadpur
29 June 1892

I had written to you that yesterday at 7 *pm* I would set up an *engagement* with the poet Kalidasa. Just when I had lit the light and pulled my armchair up to the table and was quite ready, instead of the poet Kalidasa, the *postmaster* of this place turned up. A living *postmaster* has far greater claim than a dead poet—I couldn't say to him, 'Why don't you leave now, I have some urgent work with Kalidasa'—even if I had said so, he would not have understood what I meant. Consequently, Kalidasa had to vacate his *chair* for the *postmaster* and slowly take his leave. I have a particular connection with this man. At the time when the *post office* was located on the ground floor of this bungalow itself, and I used to see him every day, that's when, one afternoon, sitting on this first floor, I had written that story about the *postmaster*, and when that story appeared in the *Hitabādī*, our *postmaster*-babu had referred to it with much half-embarrassed laughter. Anyway, I quite like the man. He chatters on with his stories, and I sit quietly and listen. He has quite a good sense of humour, so he can liven things up in a jiffy. After a whole day spent quietly by yourself, sometimes when you strike up against someone as alive as this, then life stirs and starts up again. . . . He was talking about our munsef-babu. Listening to the story and watching his mimicry I was laughing continuously till I was quite tired. The story is this—one day, all of a sudden, the munsef-babu saw Shiva in the trunk of a tree. On the first day it was Shiva, the next day Kali, after that Radha–Krishna, and so on—the entire pantheon of gods and goddesses had suddenly come down from their celestial abode to live under the banyan tree at Shahjadpur. He was catching hold of everybody and saying, 'Look! Look! Don't you see it! There are the eyes! There's the tongue!' All his clients or debtors were able to see it as required, while those who were not dependent on him in any way could see nothing at all. Our *postmaster* belonged to the latter group. On days when the goddess is worshipped with *kshīr* [sweet condensed cream] and jackfruit he can see it all—but the moment the kshīr is finished he asks the munsef, 'Which one are you calling the eyes, mister?' The munsef says, 'Can't you see? There they are, up there!' The *postmaster* says with great gravity, 'Is that so! That's the part I thought was the head!' Some days the munsef says to him, 'Tell me, mister, did you look at it closely? Today, during the ringing of bells at *ārati* [worship], something came and sat on the tree and two or three drops of water fell from above!' The *postmaster* replies, with a very innocent face, 'Oh yes, the tree was moving all right.' The ground around that tree has been paved—the munsef worships there day and night, the conch shell is blown, a *sannyāsī* sits there and smokes marijuana and closes his eyes and says, 'There she is—I can see Kali Māi.' Occasionally someone will go and faint there as well, and relay divine messages in that state. Various kinds of fraud have begun there. The *postmaster* was saying, 'When the magistrate comes to your jamidāri, you go and see him, and so many gods have found their way to rest under the banyan tree—you really should go and *pay a visit*.' I too think I should go and see the fun for myself. Anyway, if this entertainment continues for very long then Shahjadpur might turn into a pilgrimage site. We stand to profit from that. After the *postmaster* left, I sat down with the *Raghubaṃśa* once more the same night. I was reading about Indumati's *svayambar*. The rows of thrones in the court were occupied by well-dressed, good-looking rajas when Indumati came and stood in their midst to the sound of conch shells and the bugle horn, dressed in bridal clothes, holding Sunanda's hand. It's such a beautiful scene to imagine! After that Sunanda introduces them to her one by one, and Indumati touches each one's feet formally and moves on. This touching of feet is so beautiful! To touch the feet of those you are rejecting to show your respect and humility is so appropriate! It's much better than the proud Englishwoman's arrogance. Indumati is a mere slip of a girl, all the suitors are kings and much older than her—if she had not wiped away the obvious rudeness of the fact that she was leaving all of them behind with a graceful and humble praṇām, the scene would not have been beautiful. But I had to go to bed before she could put the garland around Aja's neck, as it was getting very late—that's why yesterday Indumati's wedding could not be concluded at the same time as Priyo's.

63

Shahjadpur
30 June 1892

It is difficult for a man to understand what it means for a woman to enter a new life—especially for precocious-to-the-bones old men like us. Perhaps there's a great intoxication about it—and its intensity is increased quite a bit by its being mixed with anxiety. . . . That freedom may be quite joyful and a little sorrowful too. It's impossible for me to try and imagine—how does one spend days and nights with an unknown man in an unknown place! To think of it is just unbearably wearying. That's because I am a man. Women have been doing this ever since they've been created. It has become entirely natural for them. Perhaps they quite enjoy taking a new husband in hand and, taking his joys and sorrows, wishes and taboos into consideration, indulging in some serious doll play— particularly when that is your only duty in life. Here we are in our old age, when one among our many renunciations includes sitting and philosophizing about life in a room—how do we properly understand how a young girl feels when she crosses the threshold, with her entire blossoming heart and mind, from one life to another one, and what sort of radiance fills her entire being with a kind of light! A young person's life, with its new hopes, is like a very faraway scene to someone like me—it's a place we have left behind a long time ago. But we too have a vast new life—occasionally we hear in front of us a very generous tune of hope, as if played upon an organ spread across the sky. Our new life happens when we leave happiness behind and enter the large kingdom of satisfaction—when we reject futile search and accept our duties unflinchingly. That too is an attainment of great freedom, to set out upon the road with one's entire load and sustenance upon one's shoulders. At this moment the tune that is being played in the *nahabat khānā* is not exactly the raga Sāhānā.* The musical elaborations of the Kānāṛā can be heard—the further the night deepens the sweeter it will sound. It's good to look back at the world at this stage—all of you are ready in this new age to set sail upon the stream of life and flow in many directions in many ways—there's a very sweet melody in all of that—it's as if I can hear, with a calm, peaceful and loving heart, that amazing joyous sound of your new life, and a beautiful glow of affection and pleasure seems to emanate from my life's horizon and fall upon your new lives like words of peace. May my blessings be reflected from my heart upon your heads.

64

Shahjadpur
3 July 1892

Last night I had quite a new sort of dream. It seemed as though the *Lieutenant Governor* had come to some place where they had arranged a function as a welcoming ceremony for him. Among the

---

* *Nahabat khānā*: The outdoor location for the performance of a group of musicians, usually on the *śānāi* (shehnai in Hindi or Urdu), which is a wooden wind instrument. The recital itself is referred to as the *nahabat*.

various amusements organized, there was a tent in which a famous old vocalist was singing. I wasn't inside the tent, but I could hear everything from outside. The singer had embarked upon quite a long song in Imankalyāṇ. While singing this, he suddenly forgot his lines at a certain place. He tried twice to remember it—then the third time he gave up and decided to forgo the words and continue with only the melody, when suddenly his singing was transformed into weeping—everybody had thought he was singing, but suddenly they saw that he was crying. On hearing him weep, Baṛ-dada immediately began to commiserate with him, saying, 'āhā, āhā', as if he could clearly understand how much such an incident might hurt a real artist—standing outside, I too began to feel dreadfully sorry for him when I heard the note of genuine sorrow—I felt like shielding him from the circumstances that might arise in case there were some in the audience who thought the singer's sudden outpouring of grief peculiar, and expressed their irritation and ridicule without understanding its real meaning. After that there was a great deal of chaos and confusion and the *Lieutenant Governor* of the realm of Bengal flew off I can't remember where. Anyway, I quite enjoyed the first part of the dream.

65

Shahjadpur
4 July 1892

Today I had to go to the Shahjadpur School students' function . . . I arrived at the function hall at about 4 p.m. I had to go and sit in the chair meant for the chief guest. Although my audience consisted almost entirely of smooth-cheeked adolescent village students, the thought of having to stand up and make a speech made my chest hurt all of the time—although I tried to shore up my mental strength, I just couldn't make it go away. The first student began to speak in very strange English about the benefits of good health; he said: '*Used key is not dirty. Great men always take care of their health. Take for instance Pundit Vidyasagar & Keshab Chandra Sen. They took great care of their health. If you do not take care of your health you get ill and you cannot study or do anything.*' We heard many more such knowledgeable sentences in English and Bengali. Finally there came a point when I too had to stand up—I completed my part as briefly as possible. In a serious tone, I said—'Students! The subject you have discussed is one in which I am entirely deficient and that, along with an incapacity for verbal discussion, prevents me from saying very much today—besides which, the subject is such that it is very difficult to say anything new about it. But I'm sure you've clearly understood the benefits of keeping yourself in good health, and the pain of suffering from ill health, so that even if I do not say anything new to you on the subject, you will surely try and keep yourself in good health—etc., etc.' As I spoke, there were a couple of other things too that cropped up, and the lecture was not too brief after all.

66

Shahjadpur
5 July 1892

Today is an auspicious day here. There's been music playing since last night. Yesterday in the evening suddenly a *Brass Band* arrived here from god knows where—they play Indian tunes in an English way, somewhat like at *theatre concerts*—*bhyãñppo bhyãñppo* they go, beating the *drum* with all their strength—one can't stand it for very long. But this morning the raga Bhairabī was being played upon a *śānāi*—how can I tell you how extremely sweet the sound was—the empty sky and air in front of my eyes seemed to fill with the passion of locked-up tears—very sorrowful but very beautiful—I don't understand why the same tone doesn't appear in vocal renditions in the same way. Why does the brass pipe manage to convey so much more feeling than the human voice? Right now they are playing Multān—it's made the mind so melancholy—it's drawn a cover of vaporous tears over the entire green of the world—the entire world can be seen through a curtain of the Multān rāginī. Wouldn't it be quite something to always be able to see the world through a particular rāginī? Nowadays I really feel like learning singing—quite a few tunes in Bhūpāli. . . . and the tender tunes of the rains—a few really good Hindustani songs—you could say that I hardly know any songs at all.

67

Shilaidaha
20 July 1892

We were just about to lose our lives a few moments ago. I'm not sure how exactly we managed to save ourselves. Anyway, I'm not unhappy to have been saved, certainly. We were travelling today from Panti to Shilaidaha—the sails were full and we were ripping along at a splendid pace—the monsoon river was full to the brim and the waves were coming up with a roaring sound—I was intermittently looking out and intermittently reading and writing. At about 10.30 in the morning we caught sight of the *bridge* on the river Gòrui. While the *boat* continued towards the *bridge*, the boatmen began to argue about whether the *boat's* mast would get stuck under it. The boatmen hoped that since we were travelling against the current, there was nothing to worry about, because we could lower the sails if we thought the mast might get caught in the *bridge*, even if we were quite close to it, and that would make the *boat* slow down. But upon nearing the *bridge* we found that the mast would indeed hit it and that there was a whirlpool there. As a result, because of the whirlpool, the current was moving in the opposite direction. That's when we realized we were facing disaster. But there wasn't much time to think—before we knew it, the *boat* crashed into the bridge. The mast began to slant sideways with a cracking sound—I kept saying to the stunned boatmen, 'Move away from there, the mast will fall on your heads'—when suddenly another boat quickly rowed up to us and picked me up and began to pull our *boat* with a rope. Topshi and another boatman swam to the shore with the rope between their teeth and began to pull from there. Many more people were gathered upon the shore—they all pulled the boat up. But nobody had any hope. The more the mast bent to one side, the more the *boat* listed sideways—if the other boat had not come up in time, it wouldn't have survived for long. Everybody crowding the shore then said, 'Allah has saved you, or you didn't have a chance.' After all, we are inanimate objects, you see! However distressed we were, or however much we might have shouted, when the wood hit the iron, and the water began to push upward from below, whatever had to happen would happen—the water didn't stop for a second, the mast didn't lower its head by even a hair's breadth, and the iron bridge too remained standing as before. When I reached the shore on the other boat, our *boat* was still on the verge of collapse—luckily we were so close to the shore that there was no possibility of anybody drowning. But the *boat* was a goner and, along with it, all my exercise books and other writing. The boatmen are saying this journey itself is not a good one—this is the third time this has happened. At the Kushtia ghat the rope snapped while the mast was being raised so that it fell, and Phulchand *mājhi* was lucky to escape with his life. Then again the mast got stuck in a banyan tree at the creek in Panti, and that too was quite a dangerous moment. The current there had been very strong. And then this *bridge* disaster. The only consolation I have is that even in the midst of utmost danger, I was warning the oarsmen of the danger to them, not howling or crying for my own safety; I kept a calm head. I was prepared at every moment for the terrible manner in which the mast would break—whatever I urged the oarsmen to do was quite in order—none of it was irrational. Ooh! How my heart quails to think of you all with me in this situation!

68

Shilaidaha
21 July 1892

Last evening we reached Shilaidaha, and this morning we have set out for Pabna. These days the river doesn't look as it did before—when all of you had come you had seen riverbanks as high as single-storey buildings, while now it has filled up entirely, leaving a margin of only a few feet. The spirit of the river! It's like a wild young horse with its tail waving, mane flying and head bent. Pride of speed makes the waves swell up and rise—we're riding this crazy river, swaying as we go. There's a great joy in this. How do I tell you about the sound of this full river! It gurgles and chatters as if it cannot stop itself—it has an air of intoxicated youth about it. And this is just the Gorui River. After this we reach the Padma—it will probably be impossible to form an idea of the margins of its banks. That woman has perhaps become completely insane, dancing and skipping crazily, refusing any confinement. When I think of her, I think of the image of Kali—dancing, destroying and running along with her open hair. The boatmen were saying that the Padma had become very 'sharp' [dhār haẏeche] with the new rains. 'Sharp' is the right word. The fast-moving current is like a shining scimitar, it cuts like a blade of thin steel. Like the hatchet that used to be tied to the wheels of the war chariots of ancient Britons, the Padma's fast-moving victorious chariot too has the sharp, cutting current tied like sharpened hatchets to both its wheels, cutting through both banks on either side with utter abandon. . . . One doesn't experience the joy of the river except at this time! We often come at the end of winter or the start of summer, when the emaciated river has become tame and placid—there's nothing wild about it then at all. Your mother had been so fearful even then; if she saw it now, she would probably be afraid even if she were on land. Not that there is anything to be afraid of. Rather, it was what happened yesterday that was quite serious. Yesterday we managed to say *how-do-you-do* to the god of death, Yamaraj, and come away. Unless one undergoes an experience of this sort, one doesn't really realize that death is our immediate *next door neighbour*. Even when it happens you don't remember it afterwards. The image of him that flashed suddenly before our eyes yesterday is difficult to recall today. We don't think about him very much unless he absolutely descends upon us unannounced like an unwanted, unneeded friend. But although he stays hidden, he's always taking note of how we are and what we're doing. Anyway, I bow low before him with a thousand salaams and inform him that I don't *care* a whit about him at all—whether he raises waves in the water or whistles from the sky—I've filled my sails and I'm on my way—everybody in the world knows exactly how far he can go—so what more can he do! Whatever happens, I will not howl and cry.

69

Shilaidaha
18 August 1892

Such a beautiful śarat morning! How can I describe the nectar that rains down upon the eye! There's a beautiful breeze and bird call. On the shore of this full river, looking at the śarat sunlight falling upon this new world made happy by the rain, it seems as if this young and beautiful earth goddess is having an affair with some god of light—that's why this light and this air, this half-melancholy, half-happy feeling, this continuous trembling in the leaves of trees and fields of grain—such an unlimited fulfilment in the water, such green beauty on the land, such a transparent blue in the sky. A vast, deep, endless love affair is being enacted between heaven and earth. Just as love has the virtue of finding the biggest events of the world quite insignificant, so too the sky here has such a feeling spread across it that it makes all the running around, the panting and the struggling, the rolling and the rumbling of Calcutta seem very small and extremely distant. The sky, the light, the air and song have come together from every direction and loosened me up and absorbed me within themselves—as if someone had picked my mind up on his brush and applied it like another coat of colour upon this vibrant śarat scene, so that there's another layer of intoxicating colour over this entire blue, green and gold. I'm enjoying this. '*Kī jani parān kī ye cāy*' ['I know not what the heart wants'] is something I feel shy saying, and if I were in the city, I wouldn't be saying it—but although it's a full sixteen annas of poeticism, there is no harm in saying it here. Many an old and withered poem that seems worthy of being burnt in the flames of ridicule in Calcutta comes into leaf and flower in no time at all the moment I come here. . . .

70

Shilaidaha
20 August 1892

Every day when I open my eyes in the morning I can see water to my left and to my right the riverbank flooded in sunlight. Often when you look at a picture and think—oh, if only I could be there—that's exactly the feeling that is satisfied over here. It seems as if I am living within a shining picture, as if the hardness of the real world is entirely absent here. When I was a child, the pictures of trees and oceans in books such as *Robinson Crusoe* or *Paul-Virginie* made me very melancholy—the sunlight here makes those childhood memories of gazing at pictures come alive.* I don't quite catch what the meaning of it is, I don't quite understand what the desire entwined in it is—it's like a pulsating attachment with this vast earth—at a time when I was one with this world, when the green grass rose on top of me, the śaraṯ sunlight fell over me, when every pore of my green body—spread across enormous distances—let off the fragrance and heat of youth, when I would lie silently under the bright sky, stretched over native and foreign lands, water, mountains, when in this śaraṯ sunlight my immense body would gather up, in a very unsaid, half-aware and large way, a particular flavour of joy and a life force—it's as if I can partly remember that time—this state of mind seems to be the feeling of that prehistoric world that was at every moment full of seed, flower, joy and the overlordship of sunlight. It's as if the stream of my consciousness is moving slowly through the veins of every blade of grass and root of tree, as if all the fields of grain are thrilling to the touch, and every leaf on the coconut trees is trembling with the passion of life. I want to properly express the heartfelt affection and kinship I feel towards this world, but perhaps most people wouldn't quite understand it correctly—they may think it very weird. That's why I don't feel like trying.

71

Boyalia
18 November 1892

Are you on a train right now? After the severe chill all night long, you have perhaps woken up and, having washed your face, sat down with a blanket over your legs. If you were travelling by the Jabalpur line I would have been well able to imagine the sort of scenery you're travelling through by now. At this time in the morning the sun rises

---

* *Paul et Virginie* (or Paul and Virginia) is a novel by Jacques-Henri Bernardin de Saint-Pierre, first published in 1787.

near Nowari on an undulating, hard-as-rock, treeless world. Possibly it might be the same on your Nagpur line too. Perhaps the new sun has made everything all around very bright, sometimes you can see a hint of blue mountains in the sky—not too many fields of grain around—suddenly at one or two places you see the churlish farmers of that region beginning to plough their fields with oxen—on either side, the cleft earth, black rocks, signs of dried-up waterfalls in gravel-strewn paths, small stunted *śāl* trees and, on the telegraph lines, black, long-tailed, restless *phiṅge* birds.* It's as if a large, wild thing of nature has been tamed by the bright, soft touch of a young godchild of light to lie down quietly, very calm and still. Do you know why I picture it like that? In Kalidasa you have read of how the young son of Dushyanta, Bharat, used to play with a lion cub. It's as if he were affectionately running his pale, soft fingers slowly through the lion cub's long mane, and that large animal were lying quietly by his side and occasionally glancing sideways at his man friend with a look of affection and complete dependence. And you know what those dried-up waterfalls with their gravel-strewn paths remind me of? In English fairy tales we read about a stepmother who sends her stepchildren into an unknown forest, and then the brother and sister use their intelligence to mark the way home by dropping one pebble after another to show them the way. The small streams seem like those little children, who have wandered out into this unknown vast earth when they were very young, which is why they drop small pebbles on the way as they go—when they return they'll find these paths to their way home once more. This morning from the moment I woke up I've been sitting with you next to the window of your train to try and watch with you the sunlit scenes on either side. I'm arranging my recollections of long-ago train journeys, the many memories and many fragmentary scenes, on either side of my mind, spacing them, ordering them, spreading them out in the winter morning sunlight and talking to you sometimes about them.

* *Phiṅge*: a species of fork-tailed passerine birds.

72

Natore
1 December 1892

So yesterday Loken and I managed to set out. You have to go a long
way by horse-drawn carriage. Twenty-eight miles ahead of us, and
only 'us two travellers'. Loken began with a cigarette and a book,
I started to hum '*Sundañ rādhe āoẏe bani*'; after we had travelled
about ten miles or so thus and the sun began to grow fainter the
closer it reached sunset, Loken suddenly began a quarrel with the
Vaishnava poets in the context of my song. I don't know if that
argument would ever have reached a conclusion, but fortunately a
lean and thin river suddenly appeared in the middle of it and drew
a long full stop [*dāṅṛi*] there. We had to get down from the carriage
on that riverbank and cross a bridge over the river on foot—on
the other side we suddenly discovered half a moon risen in the
sky and beautiful moonlight. We both agreed that we should try
and walk as far as we could. Then we stopped arguing and the
two of us began to walk slowly and silently upon the hushed road
engraved with the shadows of trees in the moonlight. Yesterday
was Wednesday, so it was market day in the nearby village, from
where at the end of the day a few villagers and village women were
returning home, talking to each other. A single empty bullock cart
pulled by two cows ambling slowly and absent-mindedly on, with a
watchman huddled in a *wrapper* fast asleep upon it, went towards the
rest house. Occasionally we came across a village hidden in dense
woods—layer upon layer of smoke from fires lit with straw in the
cowsheds hung low upon the bushes, heavy with dew, unable to
rise up in the still winter's night. After travelling for a mile or two
in this manner we got into the carriage again. . . . It was almost
one o'clock by the watch. After a lot of begging and pleading we
managed to persuade the Maharaja to take us for a drive and drop
us home. Everybody agreed: *Such a night was not meant for sleep!*

Really, it was a beautiful night. There were no people on the roads and the moonlight upon the large lakes of the royal palace and the shadows of the dense trees beside them were looking splendid. We went to bed after reaching home at about one-thirty at night.

73

Natore
2 December 1892

Yesterday we went to the Maharaja's place after *breakfast*, and in the evening we all went out together. I liked the road through the middle with the fields on either side. The vast, empty, desolate fields of Bengal with trees at their farthest margins in the light of the setting sun—I just can't describe how beautiful it is—such an enormous peace and soft pity—such a silent, wan embrace between this world of ours and that distant sky, modest with the weight of affection! The infinite has a sort of great un-fragmented sorrow of eternal separation that partially reveals itself in the evening light upon this abandoned earth—all the water, land and sky fill up with a particular spoken silence—if you gaze wide-eyed at it for a long time in silence, you think that if this complete silence stretched across everything cannot hold itself in any more and its self-born language bursts out into expression, then what a deep, serious, peaceful, beautiful, tender music would sound out from this earth to the starry skies! Actually that's what is happening. Because the trembling of the earth that comes and hurts our eyes is light, and the trembling that hurts our ears, sound. If we try to sit still and meditate we get a rough idea in our minds of the vast melody created with the *harmony* of all the light and colour of the world. If we could just try and be still and attentive, we would be able to partly translate in our minds the vast *harmony* created by all the earth's light and colour as it comes together into one enormous song. We only have to shut our eyes and listen with our inner hearing to the endless trembling sound of the flow of images over the world. But how many times will I write to you about this sunrise and this sunset! I experience it in a new way every day, but can I express it in a new way every time?

74

Shilaidaha
9 December 1892

Now I'm alone, settled by my *boat's* window, at peace after a very long time. The *boat* is moving with a favourable current; on top of that its sails are full—the winter day has warmed up a little in the afternoon sun, there are no boats on the Padma—the empty sandbanks' yellow colour is drawn like a line between the river's blue on one side and the sky's blue on the other—the water trembles and shimmers very slightly in the north wind; there are no waves. I'm sitting leaning by the open window; there's a gentle breeze that touches my head—it's very soothing. After a severe illness over many days, the body is in a slack, weak condition—at this time nature's slow, affectionate care and attendance feel very sweet—like this narrow winter river, my entire being seems to lie lazily in the mild sun and shimmer while I almost absent-mindedly go on writing this letter to you. Every time before I come to the Padma I fear that perhaps my Padma has become old. But as soon as the boat pushes off, and the sound of water is heard on all sides—a trembling, pulsating murmur in the light and the sky in every direction, a very soft, spread-out blue space, a very new green line—a continuous celebration then begins of colour and dance and song and beauty, and once more my heart is completely overwhelmed. This world is constantly new to me, like someone I have loved for a very long time and over many lives; there is a very deep and far-reaching relationship between the two of us. I can remember quite well, many ages ago when the earth was young, how she had raised her head above the sea water to greet the new sun, and I, a tree in the first flush of life then on this earth's new soil somewhere, had borne new leaves. There were no animals or living things in the world then, just the vast ocean swaying day and night, wildly embracing the earth from time to time like an ignorant mother, covering it completely. I had drunk the first sunlight on this earth with my entire body; like a newborn child stirred by the blind joy of life under the blue skies, I had embraced my mother earth with all my roots and drunk her breast milk. My flowers bloomed and new leaves grew with a dumb joy. When the dense monsoon clouds amassed, their deep blue shade would touch all my leaves like the palm of a familiar hand. Even after that have I been born on the soil of this earth in every new age. When the two of us sit alone, face-to-face, that old acquaintance comes back again to my memory little by little. My mother earth sits now by 'one sunlit yellow region of gold' by that riverbank's fields of grain—I fall at her feet, into her lap—just as many a son's mother remains absent-minded yet affectionate and calm, not paying much attention to their child's coming and going, so too my earth looks towards the horizon this afternoon and thinks of many ancient things, not paying much attention to what I do while I keep on talking endlessly. Time passes in this way. It's almost evening. It's winter, you see, and the sun falls away very quickly.

75

Shilaidaha
18 December 1892

Just as you hear thunder only after it has fallen, so too we don't hear anything at the right time if we're some distance apart; we can only discuss the event in a letter well after it's all over! Have you only just come to know about the pain in my teeth and ears? When I had obscured my head in layers of soft cotton to nurse it with the utmost tender care—covering and enclosing my face on every side like a sick child is wrapped up and protected—there were people in this world blithely assuming I was both healthy and happy. And now, when all that's left is only the faintest memory and the tiniest bit of inflammation of the molar tooth, one hears all sorts of expressions of fear, worry and advice! Now I feel like slapping that godforsaken forehead of mine and saying, 'You've wasted that precious pain of yours on Jadu-babu! Such a big calamity gone to "neither the gods nor religion"!' . . . There's no '*fun*' in falling ill these days, that's why nowadays I try to pay special attention to my health. But the mysteries of the body are exactly like the mysteries of the mind. I've made a sort of acquaintance with this wretched body of mine over the last thirty years—I've developed some understanding of what results in what and what doesn't. And after all that experience, I had just begun to function accordingly. Now suddenly at thirty-one I see that when I do something, what didn't happen before happens when I do it—once again there are new lessons to be learnt, new introductions to be made. And then again just when I've spent another thirty or thirty-five years stumbling around—figuring out these new discoveries of when I must wear *flannel*, when I must keep the doors and windows closed, when I must bathe in hot water, when to use hot bandages and when the *poultice*, when to have over-boiled soft rice and when to have *morolā* fish curry—there won't be too many days left to put that valuable experience gained over so many days to much use. . . . I ask you, this toothache, earache, throat ache—where was all of it all these days? If I'd been given some prior notice, why should such terrible things have happened in Natore, of all places? Man's mind, after all, is *unreasonable* enough and, if you think about it, the body is right after. Tell me, Bob, where is the thing called *reason*? Only in Sully's *psychology*?* Today after reading your letter I've been thinking about many such serious problems of this sort.

76

. . . We're ready to put up with mental torture, but cannot accept that the mind become inert. From this we may conclude that man does not want happiness but progress—he doesn't mind unhappiness as much as he does decline.

77

Cuttack
February 1893

In the first place, you know I can't stand the sight of these Englishmen in India. They habitually look down on us, they don't have an iota of *sympathy* for us, and, on top of that, to have to *exhibit* one's self to them is truly painful for me. So much so that I don't have the slightest inclination to enter even their theatres or shops (except for Thacker's†). Even a great big cow born in an English home feels he's superior to every person in our country—that always hits me hard. Until they concede that we have something in us, we have to approach them with servility every time or be humiliated. Sometimes I feel so unbearably angry with the people of our country! Not because they aren't getting rid of these Englishmen here, but because they don't do a thing

* James Sully (1842–1923) was an English psychologist; his books include *Sensation and Intuition* (1874), *Pessimism* (1877) and *Illusions* (1881; 4th ed. 1895).
† Thacker's refers to Thacker, Spink & Co., well-known publishers and booksellers in Calcutta in the nineteenth century.

about anything at all—they can't demonstrate their superiority
in any field. They don't even have that aim in mind—all they
do is pick up the peacock feathers the English have plucked and
tuck them into their tails and keep dancing around in this strange
fashion—they don't feel the slightest shame or humiliation in doing
so. They don't want to teach our countrymen anything, they look
down on our country's language, they're indifferent to anything
that the Englishman doesn't pay attention to—they think they're
going to become important people if they form the Congress and
raise their folded hands in supplication to the government. My
personal opinion is that until we can do something for ourselves
it is better for us to remain in exile. After all, since we really do
deserve such indignity, in the name of what do we plead for self-
respect in front of others? Will it suffice only to learn how to shake
our tails exactly like them? Only when we establish ourselves in
the world, when we can contribute to the work of the world,
shall we be able to smile and talk with them. Until then it's better
to hide away and shut up and keep doing our own work. The
people of our country think just the opposite—whatever work is
done out of sight, whatever has to be done privately, they dismiss
as unimportant, and that which is completely short-lived and
impermanent, mere gesture and ornament, that's what they lean
towards. Ours is the most wretched country. It's very difficult here
to keep one's strength of mind so one can work. There's no one
to really help you. You cannot find a single person within ten or
twenty miles with whom you can exchange a few words and feel
alive—nobody thinks, nobody feels, nobody works; nobody has any
experience of a great undertaking or a life worth living; you will
not be able to find an instance of mature humanity anywhere. All
these people seem to be wandering around like ghosts. They eat,
go to office, sleep, smoke, and chatter and chatter like complete
idiots. When they speak of feeling they become *sentimental*, and
when they speak of reason they become childish. Man thirsts to
be in the company of real men, one longs for a give and take, an

argumentation and quarrel of thoughts and ideas. But there are no real flesh-and-blood solid men to be found—all are phantoms, floating like vapour in a disconnected way in this world. I don't think there's anybody lonelier and more isolated in this country than the man who has one or two *ideas* in his head. I don't know how this train of thought has got going—but this is my most heartfelt complaint. Much of the disenchantment of life stems from this lack of real people.

78

Baliya
Tuesday, 7 February 1893

I don't feel like travelling any more—I really feel like creating a den in a corner so I can be alone. India has two sides to it—one of domesticity, the other of renunciation; there are some who don't move from the corner of the house, while some are absolutely homeless. I have both these sides of India in me. The corner of the home is attractive to me, and the outside too calls to me. I really feel like travelling and seeing, but then again the tired, frantic mind craves a nest. Like a bird, you know. A small nest to stay in and a vast sky to fly in. I love the corner only to give my mind a rest. My mind wants to keep working relentlessly in its interiority, but its enthusiasm for work keeps stumbling upon crowds of people at every step and is thwarted until it becomes frantic—then it seems to keep hurting me from within its cage. The moment it gets a little solitude it's able to quench its desires, to think, to look around on every side, to express its feelings in the most elaborately detailed way possible. It goes too far sometimes—it seems unable to even put up with the fact that . . . has accompanied me here. Day and night it wants complete, un-fragmented free time. It is happy only when I don't exchange a word with anybody the entire day. It wants to reign over its own kingdom of thoughts and feelings in the same way that the creator is alone amidst his creations. Otherwise it's as if all its power, all its being is frustrated. . . . Is this what is called *misanthropy*? Not exactly. It's not as if I want to stay at a distance from people because I don't like them, it's just that my mind wants a lot of space to move about and do its work.

79

Cuttack
10 February 1893

It is the lame man who finds the ditch. As it is I can't stand these *Anglo-Indian*s, and on top of that yesterday at the *dinner table* I had occasion once more to observe their crude behaviour. The *Principal* of the *college* here is an uncouth Englishman—huge nose, crafty eyes, one and a half foot of a jaw, clean-shaven, bass voice, a strangulated pronunciation that cannot articulate the letter 'r'—all in all a most complete and mature John Bull. He really had it in for the people of our country. You know, I think, of the intense objections everywhere against the *government's* attempt to change the *jury* system in our country. This man forced the subject upon us and began to argue with Bo——— babu. Said the *moral standard* in this country was *low*, people here did not have enough belief in the *sacredness of life*, so they're not fit to be in a *jury*. How do I describe to you what I was feeling! My blood boiled, but I couldn't find any words. So many things came to my mind as I lay in bed, but at that time I seemed to have become completely mute. Just think of it, Bob, to be invited to a Bengali's house, to sit among Bengalis and not to feel embarrassed to speak in this manner—what sort of opinion do they have of us! And why! Forget about *sympathy*, these are people who don't even think it necessary to behave politely with us—why do we even go anywhere near them—to smile and smile, and brush against them, and sacrifice our honour for a love affair with them, Bob? At the slightest handshake of favour on their part, why are our entire bodies and souls immediately transformed into a mass of *jelly*, trembling and wobbling from top to toe? Ooh, how proud they are, how scornful! And as for us, what poverty, what lowliness! It's bad enough to swallow the insults and keep quiet, but on top of that to go and sidle up to them and ask for their affection—I feel that's the lowest point one can reach. Let us draw this wretched, insulted, scorned Bhāratbarsha of ours to our hearts, let us try carefully to mend and to forgive all her faults, all her weaknesses, all her deficiency—let us not push her away from our hearts because all her thoughts and ways are not in tune with our minds! If our own country keeps us at a distance because of some mistaken orthodoxy, why do we instantly move away without a word, but when the sahebs openly beat us with brooms and kick us a hundred times, the diehards will still refuse to be evicted from under their feet or from their doorways. Where they do not allow us to wear shoes we take off our shoes and go, where they do not allow us to raise our heads high we bow our heads in salaam and enter, where our fellow people are not allowed entry we turn up disguised as sahebs. They don't want us to go and sit in their meetings, to participate in their amusements, to interfere in their work—but still we try, we hawk our wares, we find an opportunity, we flatter them, we keep our own people at a distance and join in when our race is criticized, we digest every insult to our country—we feel vindicated if we can just be near them in any way possible. I don't want to dress up as an *exception*, but if you have no respect at all for our race, I don't want to act civilized and be your pet. I will stay among my own people and do my duty with all the love in my heart—you will never hear of it or notice it. I don't have the slightest expectation for the scraps of your leftovers, for the fragments of your affection—I kick them away. Your affection is to me what the pig is to the Muslim. It makes me lose caste—really lose it—the degradation of the self is what really makes you lose caste—it destroys your standing in a moment—what pride can I retain after that! Let us not have any respect at all for those who buy outer pomp and ceremony after having destroyed their true worth within. I will not be ashamed to call the most miserable farmer in the most ramshackle hut in our country one of my own people, but if I ever feel tempted to keep the company of those who dress in tip-top style and go about in *dogcarts* and call us *niggers*, however civilized or high-up they may be, let me be beaten soundly on the head with a shoe. Yesterday my head and my heart were hurting so much that I could not sleep all night—I kept tossing and turning in my bed. When I had gone and sat down in one corner of that drawing room, it all appeared like a shadow in front of my eyes—it was as if I could see all of this great country spread out before me, as if I was sitting by the head of this humble, unhappy and wretched motherland—such a vast, disconsolate feeling overwhelmed my whole heart—what can I say? Yet in front of me were memsahebs in *evening dress* and the murmur of English conversation and laughter was in my ear—all together such discordance! How true our eternal Bhāratbarsha was to me, and this *dinner table*, with its sugary English smiles and polite English conversation, how empty, how false, how deeply untrue! When the mems were talking in their low, sweet, cultivated voices, I was thinking of you all, oh wealth of my country. After all, you are of this Bhāratbarsha.

80

Cuttack
15 February 1893

Then we read a few more of his poems. I find it impossible to praise falsely just in order to be polite, but, on the other hand, to quickly suppress the thorn of criticism and talk coherently is very difficult. One has to constantly hum and haw like an idiot. When he asked me, 'Should I continue to write poems?' I said, 'Why not? Poems are not written only for other people to hear them. They have a joy of their own. If other people don't appreciate them, I feel that that joy is enough reward in itself.' I don't think he was too excited by these encouraging words of mine. It's not that his poems are really bad, they're just okay, that's all. Some people pass in the first division, and others fail in the first division. But it's only those who pass who get sectioned into various divisions; we don't find it necessary to give those who fail different divisions— they all fall into the same group. If I had said to him, among all those unknown, unpublished writers of poetry who have failed, you are in the first or second division, would he have derived the slightest satisfaction from that? It's better to remain silent than to issue *certificates*. There are so many good students in the university who fail in maths; similarly, those who fail in poetry generally fail in music. They have feeling, they have words, they have a manner, there's no dearth of preparation, but they just don't have the music that would, in a moment, turn all of it into poetry. It's very difficult to show them that. There is wood, and there is the breath to kindle it, just the spark to make the whole thing catch fire is missing. You may have worked hard to bring that load of wood from many other places, but that tiny spark of flame is within your self—if that little bit is not there, then a pile as high as a mountain fails to accomplish anything. This is what I had said about Kamini Sen's poetry as well. There may be quite a lot in her writing that has a great deal of feeling and even a lot of new feeling, but none of it has caught fire. If somebody protests, 'No, no, it's very poetic,' who's going to argue with that? That's why I don't like to discuss poetry unless I can praise it. But, Bob, I've still not forgotten the audacity of that Englishman yesterday. He blithely said that we have no idea about the *sacredness of life*! These are the people who exterminated the *Red Indians* of *America*, who had no qualms in shooting down even helpless, weak *Australian* women like hunted animals for no reason and no fault of their own, who cannot be tried by one of our countrymen if they murder one of us; they come to the timid, pitiful Hindu and *preach sacredness of life* and *high standard of morals*? Anyway, what's the point of lamenting something of this sort?

81

Puri
14 February 1893

Some people have minds like the *wet plate* of a photograph. The picture you take has to be printed immediately on paper, or it spoils. My mind is of that kind. Whenever I see something picturesque, I think, I must write to Bob about this properly. After that, before I even realize it, new impressions keep getting stamped on it until it fades away. I travelled from Cuttack to Puri—there's so much to describe of this journey! If I had the time to write down what I'd seen on the day that I saw it, the picture could have come through much better—but a few days of confusion have gone by in between, and in the meantime the finer details of the images have been obscured. One of the main reasons for this is that ever since we've reached Puri I've spent every moment looking at the sea in front of us, it's captured my mind completely—I don't have the time to turn around and look back at our long journey. But I don't want to entirely leave out those few days from my letter to you. Instead of suddenly creating a gap in my daily descriptions, let me write down a brief history of the last few days for you.

On Saturday afternoon, after lunch, Bolu, Bihari-babu and I got into a hired *phaeton* carriage and spread out our blankets and bedding, and, with three pillows tucked behind three backs, and a *cāprāśi* [orderly] perched upon the *coachbox*, started our journey. . . . The rivers here dry up when the rains are over; Cuttack is situated by the side of two such rivers. One of these is called the

Mahanadi, and the other is called the Kathjuri. We had to cross the Kathjuri on our way. We had to get down from the carriage there and get into a palanquin. The white sands stretched for miles. In English they call it a riverbed, and it is a bed indeed. It is like the relinquished bed in the morning—it rises and falls in places whichever way the river current has turned on its side, or wherever it has applied some pressure—nobody has tried to carefully smooth down that dishevelled bed evenly, everything is still in disarray and scattered—at the other side of these vast sands a narrow little stream of clear water flows by faintly. In Kalidasa's *Meghdūt* we read a description of the separated loved one, the yaksha's wife, lying on her side like the lean outline of the new moon on the day of the Kṛshnapaksha fortnight in the east. Looking at this sliver of river at the end of the rains, another metaphor seems to come to mind for the pining woman. . . .

The road from Cuttack to Puri is a very good one. It has been maintained with such care that you don't see the marks of carriage wheels upon it anywhere. The road is on a higher level, with both sides falling off in either direction. It is shaded by large trees. Mostly mango trees. At this time of year, most of the mango trees are in flower, and their smell makes the whole road distraught. An attractive, saffron-coloured, neat and clean road has made its way between the dense, long rows of trees—ploughed farmland descends from it on either side. Occasionally, you see a village surrounded by mango, *aśvattha*, banyan and coconut trees. There are no jungles here, or ponds full of water hyacinth or bamboo groves like in our Bengal—the whole country seems to have been tidied up as if for a Brahmin's feast, altogether there's quite an air of pilgrimage about it. We were supposed to stop midway at a *ḍāk bungalow* in a place called Sardaipur. On the way there we had to cross two rivers again. One was called Baluhonta, and the other, Bhargavi. There wasn't much river in them—from time to time just a little clear water shining in some places in the dry sand. On the bank, a number of covered bullock carts stood upon the sand, sweet shops had been set up under roofs of round leaves—passengers ate on the roadside under the trees and inside small rows of huts, and teams of beggars began to whine in a variety of voices and languages the moment they saw new travellers and carriages or palanquins.

We reached the bungalow at Sardaipur in the evening. The bungalows here are pretty. Small, clean, hidden amidst trees and groves, secluded—one feels like spending a couple of days in these rest houses and really getting some rest. We all set out to look around after having our tea. The sun had just set at that time—in the evening twilight, the entire sky, vast fields, distant hills and a small broken-down temple on top of a hill appeared washed in a peaceful, beautiful exaltation. How do I say any more than this to you—you know how often I have written to you expressing the intense, deep love I have for this sort of evening scene. Not a single living creature was to be seen upon that long and silent road intersecting the rows of trees and the vast low-lying lands on either side; I wished that we too could be quiet and walk through the middle of this silence slowly, with our heads bent—but there was no let up in the conversation. . . .

We woke up on Sunday morning to a cloudy sky. We had our bread and tea, finished our morning bath and got into the carriage. The *phaeton*'s veil could be discarded because the sun was covered with clouds. The closer we got to Puri, the more travellers we saw on the road. Covered bullock carts were travelling together like a crowd of *misfortunes*. There were people sleeping, cooking, and gathered in groups by the road, under the trees, beside the ponds. Yet, until then we had barely come across any travellers. There are times when this long road absolutely fills up with people, and in the old days both sides of this road would be strewn with the bodies of travellers who had died of plague or starvation. Even today when it gets crowded a lot of people die of disease, starvation, and the travails of travel. . . .

The trees on both sides of the road began to decrease the nearer we got to Puri. Occasionally there were temples, and inns and large ponds began to be appear more and more frequently. We could also see plenty of *sannyāsīs*, beggars and travellers. Some of these beggars followed our carriage for almost half an hour at a time, running continuously while invoking the blessings of Lord Jagannath upon us all, panting as they begged. They're almost all of them quite healthy, well-built and strong Brahmins. Puri is near the sea, so there aren't that many trees near it. There is a sort of large lake on the right side of the road, and on the other side, above the tops of the trees to the west, the temple's spire can be seen. From the incremental density in the rows of temples and the crowds of travellers on the roadside I realized we were very near Puri. We were to stay in the *circuit house*, which was outside the town. Suddenly at one point the moment we emerged from the groves of trees we saw a spread-out shore of sand and a line of deep blue sea. On the shore two or three scattered white houses, a *chapel* and some wells. There were paved footpaths in the sand and occasionally a bench to sit on. I can't even begin to express how much I like the sea at Puri; perhaps it might suffice if I tell you that a poor person like me is thinking about borrowing some money to build a bungalow here. I kept thinking of Kalidasa's *Meghdūt* when I saw this road in Orissa. In the *Meghdūt* we read about the village Dasharna fenced with *keyā* trees, and here too there are many villages bordered with keyā trees. All along the horizon one can see blue mountains at the edges and what in the *Meghdūt* is called the *nagnadī*, or the mountainous streams, those that flow with water only in the rainy season, and are full of sand and gravel in the summer—there are many rivers of that sort over here. And on top of that our journey to Puri this time has been conducted almost entirely in cloudy weather, with the dark shadows of the clouds falling upon the large coconut groves, temples, and farmer's fields, and the lines of the mountains on

the horizon and the lines of the clouds had come together as
one. And then tonight we are going to see the ruins of the Sun
Temple at Konarak.

82

Cuttack
25 February 1893

You'll see that my writing will progress in leaps and bounds
today—today I shall surely finish the Diary I had begun to write
for the Caitra issue of *Sādhanā*, which, like a heavily loaded
bullock cart on a broken road, hadn't been making any progress
at all. When my mind is a little unhappy, *Sādhanā* seems like an
unbearable load. When I'm happy, I feel I can lift up the entire load
on my own. Then I think, I'm going to work for my country, and
I will be successful. The encouragement of others or favourable
circumstances don't seem necessary, and I feel that for my own
work I alone am enough. But sometimes I see a vision of myself
in the distant future—I see that I have become white-haired
and old, and I have almost reached the end of a large, disorderly
forest through which I have carved a long, straight road, and at
the other end of the forest the travellers who have come after me
have begun to enter that road, one or two of whom can be seen
in the evening light. I know for sure that 'my efforts shall never
be in vain'. Very slowly, little by little, I shall capture the heart of
my country—at least some of my words shall find a place in its
heart. When I think like this, the attraction of *Sādhanā* increases
for me. Then I think *Sādhanā* is like an axe in my hand which
will cut through the large societal wilderness of my country—I
won't let it lie neglected to gather rust—I shall always keep it in
my grasp. If I can find helpers, well and good; if I don't, then I
must work alone.

83

Cuttack
27 February 1893

But the person called M——— who was sitting on the stage had given such a long speech that the audience had become very impatient. If you have to listen continuously to so many words the mind becomes quite frantic—it's just the opposite effect of meditation. One is happier sitting at home playing cards or dice. This is why I don't feel like going to the weekly sermon at the Brahmo Samaj. Everything has a good and a bad side, an appropriate and an inappropriate side. You really can't say that it's my duty to go every week and patiently sit and listen to any old person who is going to speak in any which way he likes about religion. Instead, it makes me feel dissatisfied and rebellious. The person who speaks well should speak, and I will hear what he says—that's the rule. The nobler the subject matter, the better the speaker should be. But it's become the case that a religious speech is frequently assigned to an incapable person. That's because people think a good deed is done the moment they hear anything religious—that's why anybody can climb up on a rock and speak anyhow and people listen silently and do their duty and leave. That's why nobody judges the capability of a man making a religious speech. I think this is completely wrong. A person with a finer appreciation for a particular subject cannot tolerate fraudulence in that subject. I cannot comprehend how those who have any appreciation of religion or literature can tolerate this pallid and tasteless flow of old nonsense. And I don't see how such a sermon can make those without it develop any sense of appreciation either. Actually, what George Eliot calls *otherworldliness* is how many people think unconsciously of religion—they think that the time you spend in any religion-related activity is like an *investment* entered into some ledger where the interest rates keeps increasing. But I think it's a great loss if a worthy subject is not spoken about well enough. Not only is your mental equilibrium ruined, your innate conscious ability to understand is also destroyed. Just as listening regularly to songs that are not sung in tune is bad education, so too listening regularly to unsuitable religious sermons is a very harmful thing for mankind. That's why I don't want to get onto the stage myself to speak either: I know I don't have a natural ability for it, nor is there an irresistible urge in me to do it—and I don't consider it my duty to go every Wednesday to listen to ———'s sermons—rather, when Baṛ-dada speaks then my heart is wholly absorbed and I benefit from it. When incompetent people begin to speak, my mind fills with an unbearable impatience and irritation which is detrimental.

84

Cuttack
Tuesday, 28 February 1893

I'm in complete agreement with what you've said. I don't remember what I wrote to you; perhaps, in my frustration, I'd said too much. But, in my opinion, we need to be unknown and operate in private for a long time to come now. This is the time for us to get ready, not the time to dance around in front of others unprepared. The time when one is building something is a very secret time. Very small boys and girls who are allowed to participate all the time in the amusements and meetings of adults don't progress any further—if they speak a few *clever* words and imitate their elders' amusing ways and are applauded for it, they think, 'We're perfect now, quite equal to our older brothers'— similarly at this stage in our national childhood if we too hanker after a bit of applause and a seat at the side of the meeting by displaying our outer polish and a couple of brisk English mannerisms, we will make the mistake of thinking that we have accomplished everything. All those hard tasks without immediate reward, difficult duties, the complete dedication of heart and mind without which the national character cannot be formed—those will seem unnecessary and insignificant. Take a look at just one example—all those *patriots* who make good speeches in English, how they look down on Bengali language and literature! And the temporary benefit from that one good English speech is so slight in comparison with all that is lost because of that scorn! Once somebody has been honoured with a seat at the India or Bengal Council, how little that person comparatively values working from within society! Someone who has dressed up as an Englishman and been allowed to sit briefly at one side of an English table doesn't care an iota about winning the hearts of his countrymen any more! This is entirely natural. But we need to be extra careful exactly because it's natural. I know that if the Governor saheb spends two days on the second floor of our house reclining upon that easy chair of mine and calls me 'my dear' while puffing on his cheroot, then this Rabi that I am, who has assumed an aspect like a ball of fire in the mid-afternoon sun, I too may be swallowed up whole in a single ring of smoke expelled from those outcaste lips of Lansdowne. What a satisfied smile would spread over my entire face then, and what sticky sweetness drip from my speech! That's the chief worry! That's why the second-floor terrace needs to be locked (just in case our Governor saheb comes by to smoke a cheroot with his dearest friend *Tagore* under that tin roof)! The Pandavas spent one year in hiding when they were preparing for the Kurukshetra war—Guru Govind spent many years out of sight, making himself ready in solitude, before he accepted the status of Guru. That is the time for us now. If we don't keep ourselves secluded at our lonely workplace to work for our own people and our own society in the deepest, most serious and completely engaged way, if we once let our hearts be distracted, if we desire constant applause for the small incomplete tasks that we have accomplished long before we are really done—then nothing will be attained. Trees derive nourishment from the sun, but seeds shrivel up and die in it—similarly, the initial stages of work should not be exposed to outside praise or blame, criticism or scorn—it's only when it becomes a little older and pushes out of the soil that it can accept the sun and the rain and use them to become strong. Let the English criticize us, praise us, whatever—let them be unhappy with us or happy—we must not spare a single glance in that direction but continue to dedicate our lives to working for our neglected country, our neglected language, our humiliated people. It's not an easy thing to enter a doorway so low and dark, so full of insult, rejection and ignominy! Once you are used to the luxury of fame and honour, how will you survive in poverty! You constantly think—how do I get the English to read my book, how to get a slap on the back from the English, how to ensure that my detestable countrymen don't mistake me for one of their own, and how to see to it that the English accept me as a great *exception* to the rule in my country. I don't blame those who have once tasted the honour of English company thinking it's an invaluable thing—it's a tremendous attraction and temptation, no doubt about it. But that is exactly why I want to hide inside my hole. ——'s raja prefers to go to Simla and play tennis with the sahebs and dance with the mems rather than sit in his own country and govern it—and the sahebs and mems praise him much more than they do the Raja of Darbhanga, saying there is no difference between him and an Englishman—how difficult it must be for him now to be in —— and rule his kingdom! Perhaps I too might have been exactly like that—after all, I too am a Bengali, I too lack a fierce independence of my own. That's why I must store it secretly and nurture it with a lot of care—and until it becomes strong and able to protect itself I must keep it hidden and supply it with fuel and straw. After that I shall not be afraid of anybody, after that I won't be ashamed of myself—but for now I cannot trust myself.

85

Baliya
Friday, 3 March 1893

We are still on the *boat*. It's a small *boat*. This *boat*'s been made by building a roof on a large *jolly boat*—I see now that its chief ambition seems to be to humble the pride of tall people like me—the moment I make the mistake of raising my head a little, an enormous slap from a plank of wood hits me hard on the head—it takes the wind out of you completely—that's why I've been going around with my head bowed since yesterday. There's no need to tell you, of course, that I manage to knock my head on things, stumble, get cuts on my hands or legs, and suffer similar mishaps quite effortlessly even in the safest of places; in that context, it's not difficult to imagine the misery of an absent-minded six-foot-tall man in this four-and-a-half-foot boat. All the sorrow and pain that was written on this forehead now increases anew every time I try to stand up. Even that I really don't mind so much—but last night I couldn't sleep the entire night because of mosquitoes—and that I find extremely unfair. I'm used to putting up with all sorts of discomfort, but lack of sleep is something I find difficult to get used to. That's why all the joints of my body seem to have become loose today—I'm lying flat on the bed, resting on my left elbow with the *portfolio* spread out on the pillow, writing to you in the laziest way. And then over here winter's gone and summer is at hand—the sun has become warmer and a slow, cool, damp breeze comes and touches my back from the window beside me. Today neither the winter nor civilization has any purchase with me—the cāpkān and *cogā* [outer garment] hang from the hook in an extreme embrace—I'm blithely spending the morning in a blue-and-red striped *jin* night suit, the bell isn't ringing, the uniformed khansama isn't coming in to salaam—I'm enjoying the untidy, relaxed state of the half-civilized. The birds are calling, and on the shore the two big banyan trees' leaves make a shivering sound in the breeze, the sun on the surface of the trembling water flashes and shines when it comes inside our *boat*, and the morning proceeds in this loose sort of way. In Cuttack, watching the hurrying of the boys going to school and Bihari-babu going to court, one really felt that time was expensive and civilized society very busy. Here time is not divided into small well-defined sections—only into the two large divisions of night and day.

86

Teertal
Friday, 3 March 1893

This cloud and rain is all very well in a concrete building, but not very congenial for two imprisoned souls in a small *boat*. In the first place, the moment you stand up or move about you get a knock on the head, but on top of that if you have water falling on your head, it might alleviate the pain a little, but it completely fills up my 'cup of woes'. I had thought that the rain and storm had finished in a way, and that the freshly bathed earth-beauty would now dry her loose wet hair with her back to the sun, that she would put her wet green sari to dry upon the branches of the trees, spread it out upon the fields—and her vernal orange āncal would dry up and flutter lightly in the air. But it's not quite like that yet—there's no let-up in the rains. I had the forethought to borrow a copy of *Meghdūt* from somebody in Cuttack at the end of this Phālgun—the day the skies above the endless fields of grain in front of our small house in Pandua are a wet, calm, deep blue, like the tear-filled, adoring eyes of love, I will sit on the veranda and recite from it. Unfortunately, I can never memorize anything—I don't have the great luxury of being able to recite the appropriate verse at the appropriate time. When I need to, by the time I fumble around trying to find the book to read from, the moment is gone. Just imagine how difficult it would be if you felt like crying because you've been hurt, but you have to send the doorman to the house at Bathgate to bring back a bottle of tears! That's why each time I set out for the *mofussil* [district] I have to take a great number of books with me—not that I read all of them every time, but you never know beforehand when you might feel the need for a particular book, that's why you have to keep all the arrangements at hand. It would be much easier if men's minds had particular seasons—just as we travel with only winter clothes in the winter and there's no need to take the ulster* with us in the summer, so too, if only we knew when winter or spring would arrive in our minds, we could take the appropriate poetry or prose along with us in advance. But then the mind doesn't have six seasons, it has a full fifty-two—like a *packet* of cards—you never know which one you'll pick—and I don't know the name of the whimsical player who sits inside and *deals* out the cards for this whimsical card game. That's why there's no end to man's preparations—there's no accounting for the kinds of and number of things that need to be kept at hand. That's why I have an entire range of books with me, from '*Nepalese Buddhistic Literature*' to Shakespeare. I'm not going to touch most of these, but there's no saying when I might need which one. On other trips I have always brought along my Vaishnava poets and Sanskrit books; this time I didn't, which is why I feel I need them the most. If I had had the *Meghdūt* with me when I had travelled in Puri and Khandagiri, I would have been very happy. But I didn't have the *Meghdūt*, I had Caird's *Philosophical Essays* with me instead—that's what one calls '*her-pher*' [this for that].

---

* A long, loose overcoat of rough cloth, frequently with a belt and a detachable hood or shoulder cape.

87

Cuttack
Monday, 6 March 1893

You've asked me if I'm happy to have been praised by the magistrate
of Puri. The question arises in your mind because I haven't told you
the whole story. So let me give you a detailed account. At first when
Bihari-babu had asked me to *call* upon the magistrate of Puri, I had
hesitated a great deal, but when they reassured me and said they
wanted me to do it, I went ahead in spite of my reservations. Writing
my name down upon a couple of cards, I set out with Bihari-babu
and the others. They didn't have cards with them—they just sent
word and at the same time sent up my two cards. After five minutes
we received the news that we could meet the saheb the next day
in the morning. Bihari-babu and Mrs Gupta were very surprised.
We all proceeded to sidle out of the magistrate's front door and
leave. Bihari-babu was very annoyed. Then in the evening a letter
arrived to say that Mrs Walsh (the magistrate's called Walsh) was
very sorry. Her cāprāsi had not informed her that the judge saheb
and his memsaheb had sent word. I too had thought so. But the fact
of the matter is that the magistrate does not want to disregard the
judge saheb, but if any '*native*' gentleman presents himself, then he
is told to come back the next day to meet him. Perhaps he thinks
it very forward to have cards sent to Mrs Magistrate. Of course
he can always say he doesn't have time that day, but to tell me to
come back at a time of his own choosing to salaam him—which
nawab's son does he think he is? The fault, though, lies with our
own countrymen—they go and solicit for jobs, and salaam and
wait at their doors at the appointed time because they're thinking
of their daily bread and butter—so it's inconceivable that a person
like me, with a Bengali name, should show off my sense of social
duty and 'call' upon the magistrate and Mrs Magistrate. So it's a
bit much to go and get upset with the magistrate over this matter.

But this is something I've been thinking about quite a lot—that it's really the ultimate botheration trying to lovingly establish a social relationship with them. I may be a bhadralok, and a well-respected one at that, but that has absolutely no value for them. They don't give us any purchase until we've extinguished our distinctive national characteristics and worn an artificial honour given out by them. Take a look at the barristers in our country, for example—however anglicized they might be, or fond of English society, when they return to this country they can never establish a relationship with the sahebs. Even in the bar library, like a dark spot on a full moon, they exist in a separate, limited dark space, naturally segregated. What's the point of it, really, what's the great need for it! Are we so sick of our own homes? However dark our dark relatives may be, they are not, after all, darker than us. As long as the English honour me separately from my countrymen, that honour is insulting and inconsequential. When the Puri magistrate met me the next day and invited me over—do you think I was very happy about that? Don't even think that. Ignoring the invitation would have been too explicit a way of showing I was upset and would have belittled the nature of my real distress—besides which it would have meant upsetting Bihari-babu a great deal. So I went to dinner, shook hands with the magistrate's sister-in-law and smiled and sat down to dinner, agreed with the lady next to me on the beauty of the seaside scenery, and expressed my happiness at the fact that the sea breezes of Puri made the summers more bearable. Then I listened to some singing, sang myself, applauded, and received applause. This little bit of appreciation that one gets—does it really enter the heart? Isn't it a bit like satisfying one's curiosity? Isn't it like testing to see which sort of food from our cuisine is palatable to the taste buds of a species entirely different from us? Do they really like everything that I like? And is everything they don't like really not good? If that's not the case, then why should I be so happy with the applause from those white hands? If we begin to attach disproportionate importance to English applause, we shall have to neglect many a good thing of our country and accept many awful things of theirs. Then it could be that I'd be ashamed to step out without my socks on, but I wouldn't shy from donning evening dress for their dances. Then I won't be anxious about completely abandoning the civilized manners of our country and blithely taking up some common uncivilized custom of their country. I'll abandon our country's *āckān* [short coat] because it's not exactly to my liking, but I'll put their country's hat upon my head even if it looks dreadful. Applause and handshakes from white hands are very terrible things for us; they give us the minimum of superficial respect, but underneath, they destroy our self-respect. Consciously or unconsciously, we begin to structure our lives according to the dictates of that applause, and that makes us very small indeed. I address myself and say, 'Oh vessel of clay, stay away from that vessel of brass: you will crumble to pieces if it gets angry and strikes you, and if it is friendly with you and gives you a slap on the back, then too you'll get a hole in your side and drown in the depths'—so listen to the advice of the aged Aesop and stay away—that's the basic moral. Let it stay in the big house, and I, a small vessel, in a small house with minor jobs to do, but if it manages to break you then you have neither the small house nor big—you will become the same as the earth from which you were made. Then maybe the owner of the big house might pick you up as a clay fragment and display you on one side of his *drawing-room cabinet* like a *curiosity*—it is better to be firmly ensconced by the waist of a housewife in a small village—there's more honour there.

88

Cuttack
Tuesday, 7 March 1893

Poor Suri wasn't created to pass examinations. He should have sidestepped all that and become '*literary*' like me. But the problem for him is that just as he himself is quite comfortably sunk in the depths of his *easychair*, his mind too is quite comfortably settled within its inner quarters—its vast peace is difficult to disturb. We may be unsociable, inefficient, and unsuccessful in worldly affairs, and yet our mind is not confined to a corner but constantly taking off in flight—it's difficult to tie it down even for a moment. That's the chief sign of craziness. There's no craziness in Suri, he's very calm. He has the sort of deep, unworried, unhurried feeling that the face of nature displays. For a constantly restless person like me, the seclusion of nature and the still, calm company of a person like Suri is very essential. When he embraces me in his characteristically peaceable and calm manner, putting both his arms around me, it is as if he's raised a dam against all my restiveness. There are some people who, without doing anything at all, achieve unlooked-for results; Suri belongs to that group. It's almost as if it's really not necessary for him to pass a lot of exams, get prizes, write, do something big or have a good job—one feels that he has accomplished something even without having done anything. For most people, being useless doesn't look good, that only accentuates their incompetence. But even if Su doesn't do anything at all, nobody will be able to look down on him as incompetent. The busyness of work is like a cover for most people. It's very necessary for *commonplace* people, it covers up their poverty and their thinness. But those who are the naturally fulfilled type can retain their dignity and good appearance even when they are without any cover of work. If you saw that type of sixteen-to-the-anna laxness in any other boy except Suri, I'm sure it would have been unbearable, but Suri's laziness has a sort of sweetness about it. That's not because I love him—the main reason for that is because sitting quietly by himself, he's become quite mature, and he's not the slightest bit indifferent to his relatives. It's when laziness is inflated with stupidity and neglect of others to become greasy and plump that it's really an object of scorn. Suri saheb seems to be soaked in a sweet juice of laziness that is full of empathy and good sense. The tree that blooms with fragrant flowers need not also bear edible fruit. I often think to myself that if I had not had a couple of natural strengths such as poetic and other talents then it would have been difficult to find someone as unbearable, prickly and fruitless as me in this world. I too am unemployable by birth, but I've managed to get by somehow on this journey because I had a natural talent for writing. Otherwise none of you would have been able to love me at all, Bob. I know that for sure. Everybody loves Suri—not because of his work, or his ability, or his effort—but because of the harmony and beauty integral to his character. But society demands work of a man regardless of his character—that's why sometimes I wish someone would give Suri a shake so that he becomes more self-aware and tries harder—not for us, but for outsiders. When others ask 'What do you do', why should Suren reply 'I don't do anything'! After all, they wouldn't know his worth. There's a simple and easy nobility in him because of which he attracts the love and respect of all his relatives and friends, which is why he functions as an example for those who know him. But until a man establishes himself in society he remains unsuccessful. Then what's to be done? Everybody doesn't have the strength to be everything. I'm completely satisfied with the way Suri is. To have had all of you as close relatives after I was born in this world is something I feel grateful about. Only I know how much all of you have helped me. Those who are good don't know how valuable their love is. Suri and you love me—and although I expect it, it also seems very surprising to me. If I think about it properly, I don't feel I deserve anything good, everything seems like a special favour—I get so much so easily that I don't understand properly how immeasurable and unlimited that getting is, but even so, if perhaps I get a little less, I feel that it's very unfair neglect. The most important sign of the fact that man is undeserving is his—ingratitude.

89

Calcutta
16 March 1893

A little bit of sun is out today after a long time—what a relief—all
this while the cloudy days seemed to be lying there huddled in a wet,
black blanket, but today the day has appeared wearing the yellow
garb of spring and a happy, healthy countenance. Just think, it's the
start of Caitra, but this time it's still not hot at all—I wear a cāpkān
and *jobbā* [long coat] during the day, and at night I wrap myself in a
shawl and blanket—to lie under the stars on the open terrace in the
south wind, all of us crowded together on the cotton mat, is beyond
imagining. Everybody is saying that such an unprecedented affair's
never happened in the country before. One has heard of no rain
in the rainy season, or that it wasn't cold enough in the winter, but
managing to cheat the Bengali summer is a very surprising thing. . . .

Su—— was conducting the conversation in the most
accomplished *style*. Brushing up close and bending over, he was
conducting a conversation in English with a slight smile on his face,
head inclined, showing the pictures in the album and making all
the right moves. He didn't show the slightest bit of discomfort or
the sort of constraint or shyness that a boy from a Bengali home
would normally display in such a situation.

I was very amused and surprised to see this. I don't think I'd
be able to conduct a conversation with the weaker sex with such
absolute ease and sweetness and confidence even now that I'm
almost thirty-two years old. I stumble when I walk, stutter when I
must speak, can't decide where to keep my hands, feel it's my duty
to arrange my long legs somehow, but always fail to do anything
about them—by the time I've decided whether to keep them tucked
away under me, or in front, or behind, I'm unable to match the
correct answers to the appropriate questions. In the presence of three
gas lamps and a roomful of people, to establish one's self solidly by

the side of some young woman in an instant, without hesitation, like a piece of iron attracted to a magnet, is impossible for timid, anxious creatures such as myself. . . . Our boys with the looks of the god Kārtik keep standing respectfully in the wings, their fair faces growing redder with shyness all the time—they don't have the skill to elbow through the crowd and find a nice soft spot and warmly cosy up. What could be more regrettable than that!

90

Calcutta
6 April 1893

Nowadays I sometimes have conversations with Mo—— about all manner of things—I like that a great deal. My mind continually hungers for these sort of discussions. It's as if my mind is starved all day and night in this wretched, desolate country—it keeps feeding upon itself from within. There's nobody here who's alive, who thinks, who speaks—who protests, who encourages, who listens to you, who understands you—who tries to look beneath the surface into your heart! Some are busy amusing themselves, some are lazy, some go to office—nobody has the slightest headache about the fact that the living thing that is a man's mind is drying up until it is half-dead. I went to Priya-babu's house this morning; it was as if I'd consumed a lot of food and drink there.

91

Calcutta
16 April 1893

I have my doubts about how you'll feel reading this sitting in a hotel in the midst of the chaos of your journey. How far apart that sea in Puri and your hotel in Agra are from one another! The deep, ancient relationship we have with this earth, this sea—unless we sit down alone in nature, face-to-face with it, how do we ever understand it or feel it within our hearts? When there was no soil on this earth and the oceans were completely alone, my restless heart of today would have rocked silently upon the waves of that desolate sea; one seems to understand that when gazing at the ocean and hearing its concerted sound. Sitting here alone, my inner ocean too is being rocked in the same way—deep within it something is being created—so many uncertain hopes, unnecessary fears, so many kinds of creation and destruction, heaven and hell, trust and suspicion, so many feelings and conjectures based upon that which is beyond man, or experience, or evidence—the endless mystery of beauty, the fathomless frustration of love—all sorts of amazing, immeasurable things entwined and entangled in the mind of man. Unless one sits down alone under a free sky or on the shore of a vast ocean, one cannot experience one's own hidden inner mystery properly. But there's no point in my worrying myself to bits regarding all this—I have said what came to my mind and that's all—after that, let the ocean's waves keep pulsating in the same way and let men continue to huff and puff and run around in circles.

92

Calcutta
30 April 1893

That's why I was able to keep lying on the terrace till ten at night yesterday.

A Caturdaśī moon* had risen in the sky—there was a wonderful

* Caturdaśī: the fourteenth day of the lunar fortnight.

breeze—there was no one else on the terrace. I was lying there
on my own and thinking about my entire life. This second-
floor terrace, this moonlight, this south wind is mixed up in
my life's memories in so many ways. The leaves of the *śisu* trees
in the south garden were making a shivering sound, and I was
trying to bring my childhood feelings to mind with my eyes
half shut. Old memories are like wine—the longer they stay
stored in your heart, the sweeter their colour and taste and
intoxication. These bottles of our memories should be kept
cooled for our old age '*in deep delved earth*'—to be tasted then
a drop at a time on moonlit nights on the terrace—I'm sure
we'd like that. When we're young we aren't satisfied with
only imagination and memory; because then our blood is
strong, our bodies energetic—we want to engage in some sort
of work. But in old age, when we are naturally unable to work
and the excessive energy of our youth is not bearing down
upon us, then perhaps only memories are enough—our past
memories then fall upon our calm minds like moonlight upon
still waters with such clarity that they are difficult to distinguish
from present affairs.

93

Shilaidaha
Tuesday, 2 May 1893

I'm on the *boat* now. This seems like my own home. Here I alone
am master—no one else has any authority over me or my time.
This *boat* is like my old *dressing gown*—entering it one can enter a
time of looseness and leisure—I think as I please, imagine what I
please, read as much as I want, write as much as I want, and I can
put both my legs up on the *table* and stare absent-mindedly out at

the river and immerse myself as much as I wish in these days full of sky and light and laziness . . .

The first few days now will be spent getting past the hesitant feeling of being reacquainted with someone you knew before. Then, as I routinely read and write and stroll on the riverbank, our old friendship will become quite easy once again. Really, I do love the Padma a great deal. Just as Indra had his Airābat [winged elephant] I have my Padma—my ideal mount—not too tame, somewhat wild—but I feel like stroking her back and shoulders and petting her. The waters of the Padma have receded quite a bit now—they've become quite transparent and thin—like a pale-complexioned, slender girl, her soft sari clinging to her body. She's going along in a graceful way, and her sari bends with her movement as she goes. When I live on my boat in Shilaidaha, the Padma is like a real separate human being for me. So if I write about her a bit excessively, don't think that what I say is unfit to be written in a letter. Over here, that's like *personal* news.

How differently one feels from Calcutta in the space of only one day! Last evening I was sitting there on the terrace—that was one thing, and this afternoon I'm sitting on the boat—this is another. What is *sentimental* or *poetical* in Calcutta—how real and true that is over here! One no longer feels like dancing upon a *gas*-lit *stage* called the *public*—one feels like hiding away in the transparent daylight and secluded leisure of this place and doing one's work privately. The mind's tiredness does not go away unless one can retire offstage and wash and wipe away all the make-up. Then it seems quite unnecessary to run *Sādhanā*, to help *Sādhanā*, and die huffing and puffing—there are many things in it that are not real gold but base metal—and, if I can continue working single-mindedly under this endless sky and within this vast peace, doing my own work immersed in my own deep joy, only then will any real work be done.

94

Shilaidaha
8 May 1893

Poetry is an old love of mine. She was engaged to me perhaps from
the time I was Rathi's age—from that time onward our pond's
banks, the space under the banyan tree, the garden within the
house, the undiscovered ground-floor rooms inside our house, and
the entire outside world and all the stories and rhymes heard from
the maidservants were creating an intense wonderland within my
mind—it's very difficult to express the shadowy, wonderful state
of mind of that time—but this much I can say quite clearly—that
I had exchanged wedding garlands with *kalpanā* [the imagination]
at that time itself. But one has to admit that that girl does not
bring good luck—whatever else she brings, she does not bring
good fortune. I wouldn't say she doesn't give happiness, but she
has no relation with contentment. To those whom she welcomes,
she gives intense pleasure, but at times her hard embrace wrings
the heart and draws blood. The wretched man she chooses finds
it completely impossible to be a householder and sit still and enjoy
himself at leisure after establishing himself in the social world. But
it is to her that I have pledged my true life. Whether I'm writing
for *Sādhanā* or looking after the jamidāri estates, the moment I
begin to write poetry, I immediately enter my own eternal, genuine
self—and I can quite understand that this is my place. In life, one
may consciously or unconsciously lie or dissimulate, but I have
never lied in my poetry—that space is the only shelter of all the
deepest truths of my life. . . .

The whole morning passed looking at Ravi Varma's paintings.
I really like them. Whatever else, we realize from looking at
these pictures how much our indigenous subject matter and our
indigenous forms and feelings mean to us. The proportions of

the bodies and the hands and legs are a bit awry in some of the paintings, but taken altogether they do make an impression on you. The main reason for that is that our mind keeps cooperating with the painter all the time. We understand in advance what he is trying to say—when we see what he's trying to do we can complete the rest of it ourselves. It's easy to nitpick, one doesn't need any special talent to do that, but when you think about it you realize how difficult it is to imagine any subject very clearly—the pictures that arise in our imagination are almost always half-baked, somewhat made-up—but once you embark upon painting a picture, every line counts, the important and the unimportant—everything has to be thought out carefully, you have to pour an ever-changing substance like the imagination into the hard, fixed mould of the tangible—that's not a small thing!

95

Shilaidaha
10 May 1893

Meanwhile, I can see that a number of big, swollen clouds have come crowding around from all sides and congealed—like a thick *blotting pad* they have soaked up the raw golden sunlight completely from the scenery all around me. After this if it begins to rain now, then shame on the god Indra! The clouds don't have an empty or impoverished look about them any more . . . instead, like the babus they're nicely luscious and dark, with a rotund, roly-poly-boy look. It's going to rain any moment now—the breeze too seems to feel teary and wet. Sitting on your towering mountain top, you can't quite imagine how important this business of sunshine and cloud is over here, or how many people sit and gape open-mouthed at the sky. I feel very sorry when I see my poor peasant subjects—they are like the children of the gods—helpless—unless He puts food into their mouth with His own hands, they have no way out. They can only cry when the earth's breast milk runs dry; the moment they manage to satiate their hunger, they forget everything. I don't know whether it is possible or impossible to divide up the earth's wealth as the *socialists* do—but if it is completely impossible, then fate is very cruel and man is very wretched! There may be unhappiness in the world, and that's all right, but there should be the smallest gap, the smallest possibility always, so that man's higher instincts can work without rest to put an end to that sorrow, and he is able to nurture hope. Those who say that it is an absolutely impossible unfounded dream to think that in some future age all the people of the world will be provided with at least the basic necessities of life, that most of the world's people will always remain malnourished, that there's no way out—it is a very hard thing they say. But social issues such as these are so difficult! God has given us such a small, worn-out and poor garment to wear that when one part of the world is covered the other side is exposed—if you want to do away with poverty you lose your wealth and if you lose your wealth then so much of society's loveliness and beauty and reasons for progress also disappear that there's no end to it.

But the sun is reappearing from time to time, while quite a few clouds are also amassed in the west. It will certainly rain if there are clouds in the west—that's what the proverb says.

96

Shilaidaha
11 May 1893

The clouds amassed darkly last evening, and then it rained for a while, after which everything cleared up again. Today a few clouds, scattered and separated from the group and made white by the sunlight, are wandering around in the most innocent and harmless way on the margins of the sky, looking as if they have not the slightest intention of rain in them—but Chanakya, in his famous śloka where he warns us against trusting in a number of things, should have included the gods in that list. Yet the morning today has become quite beautiful—the sky is a clear blue, there are no lines on the water at all, and the drops from yesterday's rain on the grass which has grown on the rolling slope near the shore are shining. Taken all together in the sunlight, nature today has taken on the appearance of the glorious goddess Maheśvarī dressed completely in white. The morning is so completely quiet—I don't know why there is not a single boat on the river; nobody has come to the ghat near our *boat* to bathe or draw water; the nāyeb has completed his work and left early—if you listen carefully for a while you can hear a sort of buzz, and this sunlight and sky slowly enter your head and absolutely fill it up, colouring all the thoughts and feelings there with a blue and golden hue. I've brought a curved *couch* up to one side of the *boat*; on mornings like these, one feels like spreading out one's entire body on it and forgetting all about work to lie there quietly; one thinks—

'I have no before or after
As if I have blossomed forth in one day
Like an orphaned flower of the forest.'

It is as if I am of this sky, this river, this old, green earth. This is how my time passes on the *boat*. I lie here and keep looking at the countless changing moods of this familiar landscape. There's another pleasure that I have here. Occasionally some simple, old, devoted subject will come to see me whose devotion is so genuine that my eyes fill with tears. Just a moment ago an old peasant and his son had come from Kaligram to see me—it was as if he wiped both my feet with all of his simple, brimming heart and left. In the Bhāgabat Krishna has said, 'My devotee is greater than me'— one understands the meaning of that a little bit. Truly, this man is so much greater than me in his beautiful simplicity and sincere devotion! I am the one who seems unworthy of this devotion, but this devotion is no small thing, after all. Their peasant dialect, their affectionate greeting, all of it is so sweet! It is like the love one feels for small boys—the affection one feels for these old boys—but there are some differences. These men are even younger than the boys. Because small boys will grow up one day, but these men will never grow up—there is such a simple, soft and pure mind in their worn, emaciated, wrinkled, creased old bodies! Children have only simplicity, but they don't have such a fixed, trustful and single-minded devotion. And am I worthy of being this old man's raja! If there really is a spiritual connection between one man and another, then my inner good wishes for him may perhaps be useful to him one day—besides which, of course, I shall do everything I can as his landlord. But not all one's subjects are this sort, and one shouldn't expect them to be. The best is always the most rare—but in god's world that shouldn't have been the case.

97

Shilaidaha
Saturday, 13 May 1893

Today I received a *telegram* from you which said: *Missing gown lying Post Office*. This can mean two things. One: that a lost garment is lying down in the post office. Another—that the *gown* is *missing* and the *post office* is *lying*. Both meanings may be possible, but until I hear anyone protest, I'll take it to be the first. But the fun is in the fact that the letter accompanying the telegram clearly states that there's no doubt a *gown* could not be found. . . .

Poor letter! All it possesses are a few words that have been shoved into an envelope which it carries on its shoulders all the long way as it staggers along—in the meanwhile it has no knowledge of all the things that have happened in the world, and neither can it contradict the short and rude summary that its younger brother has presented by jumping over him in one big leap; it says, like a simple-hearted person, 'I really don't know anything, you know, I've only brought what I've been told to you.' And really, that's what it has brought. Not a single word has been displaced this way or that—walking the entire way, it has come at the correct time with so many signs of the road stamped upon its front and back. Well then, let its news be wrong, I still love it. And the *telegraph* arrives riding on the cable in the blink of an eye—no sign of the weariness of the road, the envelope absolutely fresh and red—saying the two things it had to say in a great hurry, with at least eight or ten words missing in between—it has no grammar, no manners, nothing—not a single word of greeting, nor the politeness of a leave-taking—as if it has not the slightest friendliness towards me, as if all it wants is to hurriedly deliver its message in any which way possible and leave as quickly as it can. Anyway, although it took a long time to know that the *gown* has spent so many winter days in the *post office*, it would have taken even longer if there were no *telegraph*, so thanks are due to it.

98

Shilaidaha
16 May 1893

In the evenings, after six-thirty, I have a bath, and then, neat and clean and cool, I walk by the riverside on the sandbank for about an hour, after which I drag our new *jolly boat* into the river, and,

spreading out my bedding on it, lie down in the cool breeze in
the dark of the evening in complete silence.

Shai——— sits by me and chatters away. The sky above my eyes
is inlaid with stars—I think to myself almost every day—will I ever
be born again under this starry sky? If I am, then will I ever again
be able to make my bed on the *jolly boat* and lie down upon it on
the silent Gorai River in this beautiful corner of Bengal in such a
peaceful, entranced state of mind on such a tranquil evening? I shall
perhaps never find another evening like this one in another birth.
One doesn't know how the scenery will change, or even what sort
of mind one will be born with! Perhaps I may be given many such
evenings, but those evenings may not rest upon my breast with
loosened hair and with such deep love. And will I remain exactly
the same man I am now! Amazingly, my deepest fear is that I may
be reborn in Europe. Because there's no way one can expose one's
entire heart, bring it up so close to the surface and lie around in
this way over there, besides which, it's considered a great sin to just
lie around like this. One has to work very hard in a factory or a
bank or in *Parliament*, with all one's body and soul—the mind and
its habits are paved and made appropriate for running a *business* in
the same way that the city's roads are laid with bricks and made
hard for business and commerce and carriages and horses to use—
there are no cracks there for a soft blade of grass or an unnecessary
tendril to grow. It is a very well-trimmed, beaten-and-moulded,
tied-down-with-laws and sturdy sort of system. God knows, but I
don't think my imagination-loving, useless, self-absorbed, spread-
out-like-the-sky manner of mind is in any way a thing of shame.
Lying here on the *jolly boat* I don't think I am the slightest bit
smaller than those men of business in the world. Rather, if I too
had tightened my belt and got down to work, I might have felt
terribly diminished in comparison with those strong men capable
of cutting down big *oak* trees. But, on the other hand, does that
mean that this entranced youth lying flat upon a *jolly boat* is really
a bigger man than Rammohun Roy?

99

Calcutta
21 June 1893

The *diary* this time is not exactly a eulogy to nature—it's a discussion on the subject of the turmoil created by the wild, restless thing called the mind when it enters our body. Actually the deal was that we should eat, be clothed, live—there was absolutely no crying need to try to investigate the original reason for the existence of the world; to wilfully create a very difficult metre and then try and express a very difficult thought within it and then again want the rhyme to scan at every step; to be drowning in a sea of debts and yet spend money from our own coffers every month to publish *Sādhanā*—and, on the other hand, look at Narayan Singh, how he makes thick *ruti* with wheat and *ghī* and adds some curd and happily indulges in a pleasurable meal, and, having first had a smoke in advance, falls easily into an undisturbed sleep in the afternoon; he does a few odd jobs for Loken in the morning and evening, and rests comfortably all night; he never even dreams that his life is in vain, or that it has not mattered—he doesn't think it is his responsibility to see that the world is progressing as rapidly as it should. The word 'success' does not mean anything in life—nature has ordained only one thing, and that is 'keep living'. Narayan Singh obeys that commandment and is at peace—and the wretched man who has allowed a living thing called the mind to dig a hole and build a nest in his heart has no rest, no end to his duties, no peace; for him, nothing is enough—he has lost all sense of proportion vis-à-vis the situation surrounding him; when he is on water, he wants to be on land, when he is on land, he is full of an 'endless desire' to swim in the water. What I want to say is—it would be a great relief to be able to take this dissatisfied, restless mind and drown it in the fathomless peace of nature so that one could sit and be still for a moment.

100

Calcutta
22 June 1893

You took a dig at me the other day in your letter, saying we look at things like marriage, etc., in an excessively *theoretical* way—and I've thought about what you said a great deal, after which I have no doubt in my mind that what you've said is true. Really, people like me do tend to look at most things from a distance—the tendency is to want to look at every single thing analytically. The mind is like a *bull's eye lantern*. The light cast by its thoughts falls upon one thing at a time so that you cannot see the next thing—in fact, it tends to make the first object twice as dark and light up the adjacent thing with an excessive brightness. This way of looking has many faults. If you look at things in the context of everything that surrounds it, then the eye and the mind tolerate almost anything—if you see one part of this vast world as a constituent of the entire world, it will not seem so important to you any more. All my *philosophising* with regard to Sw——'s marriage is quite useless. Joy and sorrow exist in every situation, neither is present in absolute excess—on the whole a man and a woman who have pledged their lives to each other are meant to live in harmony and happiness—if you keep in mind the fact that the world is not greater than what it is and compare all its aspects, you'll find that it all adds up. Just see how the Sw——s are quite happy—of course the force of this happiness will become lesser with time, and life, tied to the bonds of routine and affection, will flow slowly along on its course. Wretched, 'thinking' people like me don't seem to understand this fully. Even with regard to ourselves, we have made ourselves unsuccessful and unproductive by constantly thinking and imagining things—every single section of a situation assumes far too much importance with us. So happiness becomes excessive happiness and sorrow turns intensely powerful, but the chief happiness and peace of life, a proportionate harmony and unity in our totality, are missing—that's why, walking for such a long time with these fragmentary, scattered joys and sorrows, life becomes absolutely exhausting—one feels that one doesn't want happiness or unhappiness or anything any more, but to just lie down forever, calmly and peacefully, in this generous, open, beautiful, tranquil countryside and bask in the sunlight—what a relief that would be. But those who are not in the least bit disturbed by the thing called the mind have no particular worries about anything at all in the world—they will be happy, they will make others happy, and it will be very easy for them to fulfil all of life's obligations. It's tremendously unfair of me to express these unhealthy thoughts of my worn heart and make you unduly anxious about the world. For you, the world will hold plentiful happiness, and life will unfold in many new scenes with many changes—and you will be able to enjoy all of it with a happy mind and full heart.

101

Shilaidaha
Sunday, 2 July 1893

If you want to properly enjoy something, you must build a fence of leisure on every side of it—and you will enjoy it to the full sixteen annas only when you can spread it out to dry, let it loose, stretch it out in all directions. One of the principal reasons that one likes to receive letters in the mofussils is because here one has the time to drink in every drop of every word to the dregs; the imagination can twine around, wind around, and get entangled in every word—one can feel a certain motion in one's imagination for quite a while. If you become greedy and hurry, you are deprived of that joy. The desire for happiness hurries along at such a speed that there are times when it leapfrogs over happiness itself, and then it's all over in the blink of an eye. No letter is quite enough in the midst of all this work to do with land records and landholdings and litigation and clerks—it's as if one has not found food sufficient for one's hunger. But the older I become, I see that what you get is often dependent on your own ability to receive. It's wrong to file a complaint or a lawsuit about how much you are entitled to receive from others; the real thing is, how much can you take? To be able to possess entirely what comes to hand is accomplished only with a lot of education, practice and self-discipline. Almost three quarters of one's life is spent in acquiring that education, and there's not much time left after that to enjoy the fruits of that education. Thus goes the first chapter of the *śāstra* on how to live happily.

102

Shilaidaha
Monday, 3 July 1893

Yesterday the wind howled all night like a street dog—and the rain, too, was unending. The water on the field was flowing through it from every direction like small waterfalls and entering the river with a gurgling sound. The farmers were getting wet as they crossed over on the ferry to cut the rice on the sandbank on the other shore, some with *togās* [hats] and some holding a broad *kacu* leaf over their heads—the boatman sitting at the helm of these large, fully loaded boats, getting drenched, and the oarsmen towing the boat along from the shore, getting soaked as they walked. Such a calamity, yet the world's business cannot come to a stop; the birds sit dejectedly in their nests, but the sons of men have left their homes and come out. Two cowherd boys have brought a herd of cows to graze in front of my *boat*; the cows wander around, chewing on the luscious, green, rain-freshened wet grass with a munching sound, their mouths full and their tails swishing to drive away the flies from their backs, their eyes calm and peaceful as they eat—the rain and the cowherd boys' sticks come down ceaselessly upon their backs, both equally irrationally, unfairly and unnecessarily, and they're putting up with both without comment, with the utmost patience, continuing to chew noisily on the grass. The look in the eyes of these cows is strangely melancholy, calm, deep and affectionate—why do these large animals have to be burdened with the load of man's work in the middle of all this? The river's water rises every day. One can see from the window of the *boat* today almost as much as could be seen day before yesterday from the top of the *boat*—every morning I wake up and see that the landscape is gradually getting extended. All these days I could see the heads of the trees of that distant village like so many clouds of green leaves; today, the entire forest presents itself in front of me from end to end—land and water approach each other slowly like two shy lovers—their timidity has almost overflowed, they are almost in an embrace now. It will be wonderful to travel on this full river during the full monsoons on this boat—I'm impatient to untie the *boat*'s mooring and take off.

103

Shilaidaha
Tuesday, 4 July 1893

This morning there is a hint of sun. The rain is on hold from last evening onward, but there are so many clouds stacked in so many layers by the sides of the sky that there's not much hope—it's exactly as if the dark *carpet* of clouds has been rolled up and kept piled in one corner of the sky. A busybody wind will come right now and scatter the clouds all over the sky again, and then there will be no sign of the blue sky and golden sunlight. The amount of water the sky had in it this time! The river water has entered our sandbank.

The farmers are bringing back their unripe grain, cut and piled high on the boats—their boats pass by mine, and I can constantly hear the sounds of lament. You can quite understand how terribly cruel it is that they have had to cut down unripe grain when the grain would have ripened in another four days' time. They can only hope that some ears of rice might hold a couple of grains that have hardened a little. Nature's way of functioning must have mercy in it somewhere I'm sure, or else where did we get it from, but it's difficult to know where to find it. The complaints of these hundreds and thousands of wretched innocents is not reaching anywhere—the rain continues to fall as it must, the river rises as it must, one cannot obtain an audience with anybody concerning all this in the whole universe. One has to make one's self understand that nothing is understandable. But if man has been endowed with so much intelligence, he should have also been given the brains to realize that there is pity and justice in the world, because it is imperative that he understands that much at least. But all this is just unnecessary nitpicking—because creation can never be a happy experience. As long as there is incompleteness, there will be want and there will be sorrow. If the world had not been the world but had been God, then there would have been no imperfections anywhere—but one doesn't have the courage to ask for that much. If you think about it, everything goes back to the fundamental problem—why was the world created? But if you don't have any complaints on that score, then to raise the complaint that there is unhappiness in the world is quite bogus. That's why the Buddhists deal with it by treating the fundamental issue—they say that as long as there is existence, there is sorrow, so they want nirvana. The Christians say that sorrow is a noble thing; that God himself was born as man in order to share in our suffering. One must obtain whatever consolation one can from that. But philosophical sorrow is one thing, and the sorrow of ripening grain getting submerged is quite another. I say that whatever happens is good; this fact that I have happened, that this amazing universe has happened, is a huge gift—such a thing should not be spoiled. Buddhadeb says in reply, if you want to keep this thing, then you must put up with sorrow. A wretched man like me replies, if it is necessary to suffer in order to protect whatever is good or dear to you, then I will suffer—let me live, and let my world exist. Occasionally, I will have to put up with a lack of food or clothing, with unhappiness, with despair; but if I love existence more than suffering, and if I put up with that suffering in order to exist, then it does not behove me to say anything further.

104

Ichamoti
Thursday, 6 July 1893

Yesterday it was quite clear the entire day. After a long time, the clouds had gone and the new sunlight had brightened up each and everything; nature seemed to have had a bath and was sitting happily drying her wet hair in the desultory breeze with a pleased, contented air, wearing freshly washed clothes of yellow—but my mind was very anxious. Exactly as if it were in solitary confinement. But in the busyness of all the work that needed to be done today, I didn't find the time to nurse that frame of mind. After finishing work at about four or five in the evening, when we set off on the *boat*, a very dark bank of clouds had risen in the east. Gradually we also had some wind and rain. The rain stopped when we entered this tributary. The sandbanks have been flooded—the *boat* had to be towed with a scraping sound through grass as tall as men between forests of jhāu. Further on, there was a favourable wind. I told them to raise the sails; the sails were raised. The *boat* went proudly on, cutting through the waves with a gurgling sound. I sat outside on a chair. I won't even attempt to describe how beautiful the sunset was behind the dense blue clouds and the half-submerged, desolate sandbanks and the full river spread out up to the horizon. Particularly, at the far end of the sky, right above the Padma's waterline where there was a break in the clouds, it had an appearance so excessively fine and golden and distant, and upon that golden picture, rows of tall, dark trees had been etched with such soft blue lines—it seemed that nature had reached its ultimate apotheosis and turned into an imaginary land. The boatman asked, 'Should I moor it on the sandbank of the kāchāri ghat?' I said, 'No, let us cross the Padma.' The boatman set off—the breeze picked up, the Padma began to dance, the sails puffed up, the daylight began to fade, the clouds at the side of the sky gradually amassed themselves densely in the middle of it, the wildly restless waters of the Padma began to applaud from every side—in front of us we could see the blue line of the forests on the shore of the Padma under a pile of distant blue clouds—there were no other boats in the middle of the river but ours—near the shore, two or three fishermen's boats have raised their small sails and are heading home—I'm sitting here as if I were the king of nature, carried along at a great speed in a dancing motion by its restless, foaming-at-the-mouth royal horses.

105

Shahjadpur
7 July 1893

Yesterday we reached Shahjadpur in the evening after winding our way continuously through small villages, broken-down ghats, tin-roofed bazaars, granaries fenced with wooden planking, bamboo groves, jungles full of mango, jackfruit, berry, date, cotton, banana and ākanda trees, castor oil, arum and kacu plants, an aggregation of creepers, shrubs and grass, a group of large boats with their masts raised tied to the ghat, and nearly submerged fields of rice and jute. Now we shall be stationary here for the next few days. After a long time on the *boat* I quite like the house at Shahjadpur—it's as if one has found a new independence—one suddenly discovers what a vital element of man's happiness is dependent on the ability to move about as much as he wants and to find space to stretch his body. This morning, quite a bit of sun has appeared intermittently, the wind is blowing briskly, the jhāu and *licu* trees are swaying with a creaking, scraping sound, many different kinds of birds have been calling in many voices and many tunes, making the morning concert in the woods hum with excitement—I'm sitting here in this large, empty, secluded, bright and open first-floor room, quite happily watching from my window the rows of boats on the water, the village amongst the trees on the other side, and the slow flow of work in the inhabited regions nearby on this side of the bank. The flow of work in a village is not too rapid, yet not entirely lifeless and comatose either. It's as if work and leisure are both walking side by side in unison, holding hands. The ferries cross the river, travellers with umbrellas in hand walk by the road next to the canal, women immerse their wicker baskets and wash rice, the farmers come to market with bundles of tied jute on their heads—two men have flung a tree trunk on the ground and are splitting its wood with an axe, making a *thak-thak* sound, a carpenter works upon an upturned fisherman's boat under an *aśvattha* tree, repairing it with a chisel in hand, the village dog roams around aimlessly by the canal, a few cows lie lazily on the ground in the sun, swishing away flies with a languid movement of their ears and tails before they feed upon excessive amounts of fresh grass, and when the crows sitting on their backs irritate them beyond endurance, they shake their heads at them and express their annoyance. The few monotonous *thak-thak thuk-thāk* sounds of this place, the cries of the naked children playing, the high-pitched tender songs of the cowherds, the *jhup-jhāp* noise of the oars, the sharp, sad sound of the oil mill hitting the *nikhād* note, all of these sounds of work come together and are in a sort of proportion to the bird call and the sound of the leaves—all of it seems to be some part of a long dreamlike *sonata* full of peace and enveloped in pity, somewhat in the mould of Chopin, but composed and bound to a very vast, spread-out, yet restrained metre. The sunlight and all these sounds seem to have filled my head to the brim, so let me stop writing this letter and just lie back for a while.

106

Shahjadpur
10 July 1893

You've received my songs. The tune for the song '*baṛa bedanār mata*' might not be quite appropriate for a performative drawing-room gathering. . . . This sort of song should be sung in seclusion. I don't believe the tune is bad; in fact, it would not be too much of an exaggeration to say it's good. I had composed that song over many days in the bathing room, little by little, along with its tune—there are a great number of advantages to composing a song in the bathing room. Firstly, the seclusion; secondly, no other duty may claim you—if you pour a *tin* of water over your head and spend the next five minutes humming, your sense of duty doesn't suffer too much—and the greatest advantage is that since there's no possibility of an audience one can freely contort one's face as much as one wants. One really can't attain the state of mind in which one composes songs without contorting the face. It's not exactly something that requires logic or argumentation, you see, it's pure excitability. I'm still constantly singing this song—I hummed it for quite some time this morning too, and as you keep singing it a certain intoxication comes over you. So I have no doubt at all about the fact that this song is quite a favourite of mine. . . . Here, I sing alone, with an entranced and liberated heart, my eyes half shut, and the world and this life appear to me touched by the sun's bright hands, swathed in the finest layer of tears, coloured like a seven-layered rainbow—one can translate everyday truths into eternal beauty, and sorrow and suffering too become radiant. In no time at all, the khājāñci appears with the accounts for two eggs, one sliver of butter, a quarter litre of ghī and six paisa's worth mustard oil. My history here is like this. . . .

107

Shahjadpur
13 July 1893

Nowadays writing poetry seems to have become like a secret, forbidden pleasure for me—on the one hand, I still haven't written a single line for next month's *Sādhanā*, and on the other, I've been receiving reminders from the editor from time to time; not too far in the distance, the joint Āśvin–Kārtik issue of *Sādhanā* has been standing empty-handed in front of me and rebuking me, and I've been running away into the inner quarters of my poetry to seek refuge. Every day I think to myself—today is only one day, after all—so many days have gone by in this way. I really don't quite know what my real work is. Sometimes I think I can write lots of short stories and not too badly at that—it's also quite a pleasure to write them. At other times I think—there are certain thoughts that come to me that are not exactly appropriate for poetry, but which might work if published as a diary or in some other form and preserved, perhaps that will be both fruitful and pleasurable. Sometimes it's very necessary to fight with our countrymen on social issues—when nobody else is doing so, then it behoves me to fulfil this unpleasant duty. And then again I think, what the hell, let the world take care of itself—I'm quite fluent at composing short rhyming poems set to metre—let me forget about everything else and sit in my own corner and write these. I've become something like the insanely proud young woman with many lovers who doesn't want to let go of any one of them. I don't want to disappoint any one of the *Muses*—but that multiplies the workload, and in the 'long run' I might not be doing full justice to any of them. A sense of duty is important even in literary matters, but there is a difference between it and doing your duty in other departments. When you fulfil your literary duties you don't need to think about what will be the most useful for the world, what you need to judge is what you can accomplish the best. Perhaps all the departments of life function the same way. In my own evaluation, it is poetry that I have the most grasp over. But my hunger wants to spread its flame everywhere, over the kingdom of the world as well as the kingdom of the mind. When I begin to compose songs I think it wouldn't be half-bad to continue with just this work alone. Again, when I get involved with some performance, I get so intoxicated with it that I think if one wants then one can spend one's entire life on this too. But then, when one gets involved with issues such as 'child marriage' or 'whither education' then that seems to be the most valuable work in one's life. What an impasse I'm at, Bob! And then again, if one swallows one's pride and tells the absolute truth, then I have to admit that that thing called painting—I'm always looking towards it with the lustful glances of unrequited love—but there's no hope of winning it, the age for wooing it is past me now. Unlike the other knowledges, one cannot hope to acquire it easily—to attain it is like breaking the mythical bow; you cannot win its favour until you exhaust yourself with repeated strokes of the paintbrush. The state I'm in is something like Draupadi's—she thought to herself, well, if I am to have five husbands at one time in any case, then why not a sixth, including Karna—that would be great. I'm sure if she had got Karna, she wouldn't have wanted to let Duryodhana or Duhshasana go either. Because you can have either one or an infinite number—there's no natural resting place in between the two extremes. If you say five, then six comes forward on its own accord, and then after six, seven, eight, nine, ten, etc., are all standing in a line looking at you with unblinking eyes, waiting. So I think it's most convenient if I confine myself to poetry alone—for she is perhaps the one who is under my spell the most—my childhood love, my beloved companion of such a long time. . . .

You have asked me a question about the silent poet, about which what I have to say is that the silent poet and the poet who expresses himself may feel the same amount, but the really poetic is an independent thing. Not only because of the power of language but also the ability to put it all together. Feelings acquire many different forms in the hands of a poet by the power of an invisible, unconscious talent. That power to create is at the root of the poetic. Language, feeling and expression are merely its tools. Some have language, some have expression, somebody may have both language and expression, but there is somebody else who has language, expression and also the power to create—you can call this last person a poet. The first three types of people may be silent or vocal, but they are not poets. The correct word to describe some of these types might be thinkers. They too are very rare in this world and the poet's thirsty heart is always yearning for them.

After reading the preface I've provided above, it might be easier to understand my poem 'Jāl phelā' [Casting the Net]— you've asked me its meaning. If I had it in front of me, I might have been able to look at its meaning properly myself and then tried to explain it to you—still, I have a vague memory of it. Imagine a person standing by the sea at the start of his life and watching the sunrise—that sea is his own mind or the outside world or an ocean of feeling somewhere between the two—that has not been made very clear. Anyway, standing there looking at that amazingly beautiful fathomless sea, the person thinks, let me see what I might get if I throw my net into this sea of mystery. So saying, he throws his net into the sea with a circular motion. Many amazing things begin to come up—some white as a smile, some bright as tears, some coloured like shame. In his excitement, he continues with this work all day long—he keeps bringing up the beautiful mysteries from the depths of the sea until he has a pile on the shore. This is how he spends the entire day that was his life. In the evening, he thinks, I have enough, let me go and give these now. To whom has not been made perfectly clear—perhaps to his beloved, perhaps to his country. But she has never seen all these amazing things before. She might wonder, what are these things, what is the need for them, will they banish poverty, how much would they be worth if I take them to a shopkeeper for valuation? In other words, this is not science, philosophy, history, geography, economics, sociology, theology or data of any kind—these are merely many-coloured feelings, and we don't even know their nomenclature or description very well. As a result, the person given all the gems collected by throwing your net into the endless ocean says: What on earth are these? The fisherman too then feels remorse, 'True enough, this is nothing much, just something I dredged up by throwing my net into the water—I didn't go to the market, and I haven't spent any money, I didn't have to pay a paisa in tax or duty on it!' He then picks it all up with a dejected and shameful face and, sitting at the door of his house, throws it all on the road one by one. The next day in the morning, passers-by pick up these hugely valuable things and take them away to their own homes in this country and abroad. It seems that the person who has written this poem thinks that his country, busy with domestic duties in the inner quarters, and his contemporary readers cannot quite comprehend the meaning of his poems—they don't understand their value—so for now, it is all being discarded on the road, 'you neglect them and I too neglect them', but when this night is over, then '*posterity*' will pick them up and take them away to other parts of this country and abroad. But will that help mitigate that fisherman's regret? Anyway, hopefully nobody will have any objection to the happy thoughts of the poet as he dreams of *posterity* coming slowly towards him through the long night like a lover on an assignation—perhaps she might just reach him by the time the night has come to an end.

I can't quite recall what the exact meaning of the poem about the temple is. Perhaps it's about an actual temple. That is, when you sit in a corner and swathe your god in a lot of artificial ideas, thereby taking your mind too to an unnatural and very sharp level, and then a lightning bolt of doubt breaks down those artificial barriers of so many ages, so that suddenly your place of chanting and ritual and incense and smoke is exposed to nature's beauty, sunlight, and the song of the world, and then you see that *this* is real worship and this is god's satisfaction. Perhaps it was the temples of Orissa that put me in this sort of mood. Inside one of the temples at Bhubaneshwar, the place where the god was placed was terribly dark, closed, and with a suffocating smell of incense—the floor wet with water used to bathe the image of the god, bats flying around—the moment you came out of there into the beautiful light outside you knew exactly where god really was.

108

Patishar
13 August 1893

We had to travel through a number of large marshes on our way. These marshes are very strange—they have no shape or size, water and land everywhere—as the world was when it first woke from the womb of the ocean. There is no limit to anything—there's water, some half-submerged fields of rice, some algae and some water-plants floating—cormorants swimming, large bamboo staffs planted in the water to secure fishing nets with a few large pale kites sitting on top—all together a very monotonous and analogous sort of scenery. In the distance, the outlines of villages can be seen like islands—as you go on, suddenly again a bit of river, villages on both sides, jute fields and bamboo groves, and then again there's no way of telling when all of that disappears into the vast marshes. . . .

Exactly around sunset when we were crossing by a village, a number of boys rowing a longboat were singing in a dialect, in rhythm with the slapping of the oars—

   '*yobafī, kyān bā kara man bhañ?*
     pābnā thākye ānye deba
       tyākā dāmer motori'
   (Young girl, why do you feel sad?
   From Pabna I will bring for you
   A rupee worth of motor.)

The mode adopted by the local poet in composing his song is one that we too deploy, but there are some basic differences. When our young girl is depressed, we are immediately ready to give our lives or bring her the *parijāt* flower from the mythical woods of *nandankānan*, but I must say the people of this region are very fortunate—a little sacrifice is enough for their young women. It's not for me to speculate on what exactly this '*motori*' thing is, but its price is mentioned in the very same breath—which makes it clear that it doesn't cost the earth and need not be brought from too inaccessible a place. It was fun to hear the song. One was reminded again even at the margins of these marshes that the sadness of young women agitates the world. This song may be laughed at elsewhere, but in this particular context it has considerable beauty. The compositions of my rural brother poets are absolutely integral to the joys and sorrows of the village folk; my own songs would not be any less laughable to them.

109

Patishar
13 August 1893

This time, as I travelled through the marshes to Kaligram, one thought came to me with great clarity. It's not a new thought, I've known it for many days now, but still, sometimes one can re-experience an old thought in a new way. The water is not beautiful until it is bound on both sides by the banks—uncertain, unregulated marshes are monotonous and unattractive. In language, the work of the banks is done by the ties of metre, which gives language a particular form and a particular beauty; a beautiful picture is created. Just as rivers that are bound by their shores have a particular character, so that they seem to have individual personalities like certain men, metre enables poetry to stand on its own like an individual existence. Prose does not have the same beautiful, well-thought-out independence; it is like a vast, characterless marsh. Again, the moment the river is closed off by the shoreline, it has a speed and a motion, but the marsh is without flow, it just lies there spread out, engulfing all sides. In language too, if you want to give it a passion, a motion, you have to tie it down within the narrowness of metre; otherwise it simply spreads itself out, it cannot flow with all its force in one direction. The water in the marshes is called 'dumb water' by the village people—it has no language, it cannot express itself. In a river you can always hear a gurgling sound; words too, if you tie them in metre, clash and strike against one another and create a music of their own. That's why language in rhyme is not dumb language; it is always speaking and singing. Staying tied up makes motion, sound and form beautiful. There is as much beauty in being bound as there is strength. Poetry reveals itself very slowly and naturally through the metre within which it is captured, not because it is catering to an artificial pleasure created by force of habit—it is a deep, natural happiness. There are many idiots who think that to enclose a poem in rhyme is merely done to show off, that it is only to evoke wonder in ordinary people, that it is merely an exercise in language. But that's completely wrong. The rules that give birth to metre in poetry are the same rules that create all the beauty in the universe. Beauty has such an amazing strength only because it travels at speed through well-directed ties to strike the mind. And, the moment that you exceed those graceful bonds, everything spills out and it does not have the strength to strike any more. As I travelled from the marshes into rivers and crossed from the rivers into marshes, this thought woke in my mind like a bright flame.

110

Patishar
18 August 1893

Haven't you understood the Diary for the month of Śrābaṇ, Bob? If I begin to explain I might have to write an entire book. . . . I've been thinking for a long time now that men are somewhat disjointed and women are quite nicely complete. There is a wholeness and proportion to women's conversations, attire, behaviour and life's duties. As if all of it is one *organic whole*. The main reason for that is that nature has given them their duties herself many aeons ago and has built them according to that intention from top to toe—no change, no national revolution, no creation or destruction of a civilization has so far split that accord; they have always looked after, loved, given affection and not done anything else. The skill they have developed at these tasks has merged and become one with their limbs and parts, their language and gestures. Their nature and their work have combined together like flowers and the fragrance of flowers, which is why they have no hesitation, no doubts at all within themselves. Men's characters are very uneven; the different types of jobs they've done, their different strengths, the changes that they've come through in the process of their formation—their bodies and their habits seem to bear those marks. Quite unexpectedly, their foreheads may be terribly broad, or their nose might push outward suddenly in such a fashion that it would be impossible for anybody to keep it down, or their jaws might follow no rules of grace at all. If men had been driven by the same thoughts and learnt the same lessons from the beginning of time, then perhaps their faces and manners too might have been more in harmony with each other—a mould could have been created a long time ago—then there would have been no need for them to use their strength and think so much in order to do their work. All their work would have been accomplished easily and beautifully—then a simple law too would have established itself for them. That is, their minds would have become habituated to the work they had been doing without interruption for many ages, and no lesser force would have been able to remove them from that familiar duty. Nature, by making them mothers, has poured women's natures into a mould. Man has no natural ancient bond of that sort, that's why he has not been built in an all-round way in the shelter of a single lode star. He has always been wrenched apart in every direction, his wild and scattered inclinations have not allowed him to build up a beautiful completeness. Remember I wrote a lot to you in a letter that day about being bounded as a cause for the creation of beauty—well, women too are like that—they have been made complete and beautiful by the ties of a natural rhythm. And men are like prose—without ties or beauty, there is no particular mould within which they have been entirely formed. I'm not sure if I've managed to explain myself very well, but in my mind it's very clear. That's the reason why women have always been compared to music, poetry, flowers, tendrils and rivers—nobody ever dreams of applying these similes

to men. Just as all the attractive things in nature are beautifully
related, complete, organized and restrained, so too are women.
No hesitation or doubt or thought enters their mind to interrupt
their rhythm, no discord destroys the scansion—they are each
of them like individual sweet and slender poems. They are as
Chandra described them in *Goṛāy galad*.* I don't think this letter
is turning out to be any clearer than the Diary, but there's no way
I can use any clear and evident proof here.

111

Calcutta
21 August 1893

Today I received some newspaper cuttings from you. Where's the
wild intoxication of the *artist* community in Paris and where my
simple peasants of Kaligram who bring their sorrow and their
poverty to me! Alas, I have never seen such peasants anywhere—
their genuine love and their unbearable suffering bring tears to
my eyes. To me these wretched peasants, full of an unwavering
faith and adoration, have such a soft sweetness on their faces that
my heart really does melt with affection when I look at them.
Really, it's as if they are a large family of mine whose members
fill the countryside. There's a great happiness in thinking of these
helpless, powerless, completely dependent, simple farmers and
peasants as my own people. I find listening to their language
so sweet—it has such a mix of affection and tenderness within
it! When they speak to me of some injustice, my eyes begin to
fill up, and I have to maintain my composure by dissembling in
various ways. They put up with so much sorrow with so much

---

* *Goṛāy galad* [The Initial Mistake]: Rabindranath's first prose comedy,
published in 1892.

patience, but still their love never pales. Today someone came and said, 'That year the crops failed so I went to my old father in Chunchura to come to a settlement with him. So he said, I'm giving you all a portion, in return you too should give me some food. The supervising land surveyor here got annoyed because I went to him for help and put me in jail for three months on a false charge. Then I salaamed the land you own and went off to a different region.' But still, such was his devotion that when he discovered that the jamidār of that different region had stolen some of our land and was profiting from it, he told our *serestā* [office of the record-office superintendent] about it and as a result, the new jamidār in his anger took away all his land and crops. He said, 'I can't even look out for the welfare of those whose land I have been brought up on and grown old on and tell them anything!' So saying, he wiped away tears from his eyes. If you could see him and hear what he was saying, how simply he put it without any cleverness of any sort, as if he was giving us a bit of news, then you would have understood the actual depth of it all. They don't know how much I respect them, how much better than myself I think them to be. But still, what a difference from civilization in Paris! That is so much harder, brighter and better composed than this! But the people here have something that is not to be looked down on. Until this clear simplicity is established at the centre of civilization it will never be complete or beautiful. It is the absence of these qualities that seems to be making European civilization increasingly *morbid*. An unhealthiness, a worm seems to be gradually eating away at its insides, wearing it away. Simplicity is the only resource that will make man healthy—it is like the Ganga, one can rid one's self of many of life's afflictions by bathing in it. And Europe seems to be nurturing all afflictions, and on top of that, its nights and days are artificially heated with a thousand different intoxicants. Each and every piece of the newspaper cuttings you have sent proves this.

112

Karmathar
Saturday, 9 September 1893

The garden is overrun with roses. There's a rain tree [*śiṅśh*] that is full of flowers from top to bottom, its fragrance fills the air. The rain-tree flower is as beautiful to look at as it is fragrant. . . . There are a couple of them lying entangled on the table in front of me, like soft, sweet kisses, like sleepy eyes. . . . The rain-tree flower was a favourite of Kalidasa's. In Kalidasa's books, the rain-tree flower was a metaphor for youthful good looks. . . .

In an earlier letter you had asked me why I don't like the company of others. One reason could be that if there is an interruption of any kind when you're thinking or feeling something, then the frustration due to this obstacle and the thwarted, unsuccessful efforts within yourself bring about a great weariness—trying to pay attention to others and trying to think one's own thoughts both at the same time seem to make the mind intensely irritated. But if the other person is the sort who can push away all your other thoughts and efforts and attract your entire mind towards himself, then it is very relaxing. The real thing is that unless I can completely immerse myself in something I cannot be still; those things that don't absorb my entire attention are very wearying for me at this age—it is as if one cannot find the space to set down the weight of one's thoughts anywhere, and so one keeps hanging in mid-air. . . . —— wrote me a letter—asking if I could be a close friend and write frequently. I've written back saying, in not so many words, that I have no time for friendship as a sort of luxury. At this age, one has to work, and protect and enjoy all that is old deeply in one's heart. Nowadays one doesn't feel like indulging whimsical hobbies any more.

113

Patishar
Monday, 19 February 1894

The bank on which we have moored the boat is very isolated—no villages, no dwellings, the ploughed fields stretching desolately, just some buffaloes tearing up the dry grass by the riverside as they graze. And, we have a couple of elephants who also come to graze on this side of the river. It's great fun to watch them. They raise one leg and kick gently at the grass roots, then they pull at them with their trunks, and immediately large chunks of soil and grass come up together. They use their trunks to wave the chunks in the air till all the soil falls off, and then they stuff it into their mouths and eat it up. And then again, sometimes they suddenly feel like doing something else, so they take some dust in their trunks and blow it all over their backs and stomachs with a whoosh—such are the ways in which elephants accomplish their toilette. Large bodies, enormous strength, ungraceful proportions, extreme placidity—I quite like watching these enormous beasts. It's as if you feel a special affection for them exactly because of their largeness and their ugliness—its *awkwardness* of body makes it seem like a huge baby—and one feels more tenderness towards it than for the cat, dog or horse. Besides which, the creature has a very generous nature, like the simpleton god Shiva Bholanath—when it gets crazy, it gets really crazy; when it's calm, there is a bottomless peace. At times I was thinking that the sort of affectionate, compassionate feeling I have towards the elephant is perhaps similar to what women think of the male sex. The ungracefulness that accompanies largeness is not repulsive to the heart, but rather attracts it. If you compare the portrait of Beethoven I have in my room to many other beautiful faces, it may well seem not worth looking at, but when I look at it, a strange attraction draws me to it—what a large, silent universe of sound existed within that dishevelled head! And what a strange, boundless pain whirled constantly within that man like an enclosed storm. When I look at B—— a similar sort of respectful pity rises up in me—all his untidy distractedness expresses a restless, incomplete, troubled talent. All men are not Beethoven or B——, and it's not as if Beethoven or B—— have a woman's love, but I can see a great beauty in them. Men usually have a certain *awkward* helplessness along with their strength, and a large quantity of oafishness mixed with brains, which makes women feel partially respectful, and to a large degree motherly, with regard to them. I think boys can attract more motherly love towards themselves than girls do. Anyway, all this talk is a bit vague—based largely on the feminine side of one's own character.

114

Patishar
Monday, 26 February 1894

Sometimes it becomes cloudy, sometimes it clears up—from time to time, suddenly a strong wind comes and rattles my boat to its joints, so that it lets out strange groaning and grunting and moaning sounds—the afternoon today has been passing in this way. . . .

It's now one in the afternoon—all of you must have routinely lunched and looked at accounts and retired behind the closed doors of your bedrooms to sleep. The village afternoon's quacking of ducks, calling of birds, sounds of clothes being washed, the lapping sound of water on which boats ply, the distant noise of the crossing of herds of cows, and the melancholy, lazy soliloquy of song within one's own heart here is unimaginable in Calcutta's *chair-table*-infested, monotonous, colourless everyday routine. Calcutta is very polite and very heavy, like a *government office*.

Every day of one's life seems to emerge in the same shape, with the same stamp, freshly cut one after another in the mint—dead, lifeless days, but very civilized, and all of the same weight. Here I am an outsider, and every day here is my own day—it has no relation with the wound-up machine of everyday routine. I take my own mind's thoughts and all my leisure in hand and go out in the fields to walk—there are no impediments of time and place here. The evening grows dense on the land and water and sky; I keep walking slowly, my head lowered.

115

Patishar
Saturday, 17 March 1894

The moonlight has been blossoming every night little by little. So nowadays I walk outside for quite a while even after dark. The fields on this side of the river have no trees, no horizon marked anywhere—the ploughed fields don't have a single blade of grass, the only grass by the river has turned yellow and dried up in the intense sun. The desolate, empty field looks quite amazing in the moonlight—the sea looks endless in the same way, but it has a ceaseless motion and sound—this sea of soil has no motion, no sound, no variety, no life anywhere—just a very melancholy, dead emptiness—among things that walk I am the lone living being walking around on one side, and, near my feet, a shadow walks with me. Far away in some places fires have been lit by the farmers where the remnants of the dried roots of last year's crops were, and occasionally the only thing to be seen are the rows of fires they form. When the faint light of the moon comes and falls upon such a vast, spread-out lifelessness, a sorrow of separation as large as the universe fills the mind—as

if an almost fainting woman clad in white lies silently, her face
hidden, upon a vast desert grave.

116

Patishar
21 March 1894

My affection for the peasants of this place is really overwhelming—
one doesn't want to give them any sort of trouble at all—when
you hear their simple childlike demands, made with such genuine
affection and pleading, the mind really softens with empathy.
When they address me familiarly, slipping from the formal *tumi*
to the informal *tui*, when they give me a telling-off, it feels very
sweet. Sometimes I laugh when I hear what they have to say,
and when they see that, they too start to laugh. The other day
during my evening walk one of them came up to me and said,
'Just stand still for a second'—I was somewhat surprised, but I
stood quietly as he said. He took the dust from my feet, put it
upon his head and heart, and said, 'My life is fulfilled now.' He
said he had been suffering from a cough and cold, so had not eaten
for three days, and now, after arranging for a meal, had come to
touch my feet in obeisance. I can't say if his simple faith may make
the dust of my feet perform any miracles. When love, devotion
and affection fall upon even the most undeserving recipient in
unwarranted quantities they have such an astonishing beauty—my
peasants here are made beautiful by the complete simplicity of
their devotion. There is a childish look of youthfulness even on
their worn and lined old faces. But I've told you all this plenty
of times before in my previous letters—so from afar all of this
will seem very repetitive to you. But to me it seems new every
time and every day. In this ancient world, it is only beauty and
the things of men's hearts that never become old in any way, that

is why the world is still fresh and the poet's poetry will never disappear from it entirely.

117

Patishar
Thursday, 22 March 1894

I spent the entire morning today with an essay called 'Love of Animals' that Bolu had sent me. Yesterday I was sitting in the *boat* by the window looking out towards the river when I suddenly saw some sort of bird frantically swimming to the other shore, and behind it, a massive catch-catch-kill-kill hue and cry. Finally I saw that it was a hen—it had escaped from approaching death in the boat that serves as my kitchen and, managing to free itself somehow, had jumped into the water and was trying to flee, but just as it reached the shore the human messengers of death chasing it managed to grab hold of it by the neck and bring it back to the boat. I called Phatik and said that I didn't want chicken today. Just then, Bolu's 'Love of Animals' essay arrived by post; I was not a little surprised at that. You know, I don't feel like eating meat any more, Bob. It's because we don't think about how wrong and how cruel we are being that we can shove meat down our gullets. There are many things in the world that have been polluted by man alone, and the positive or negative aspect of those things depends upon the rites and habits and customs of a particular society—but cruelty is not one of those. This is an absolutely ancient wrong—about that you cannot argue or have any doubt; if our hearts are not hardened, if we do not tie up our hearts with blindfolds and make them blind, then we can hear the order forbidding us to be cruel with a crystal clarity. Yet we are all very easily cruel—all of us are casually and blithely so; in fact, we think those of us who are not cruel to be a little strange. Man has such an amazing artificial notion of good and evil. I think that the greatest dharma of all is that which enjoins us to have pity for all living things. Love is the foundation upon which all religions are built. Let me not create unhappiness in this world, but give happiness. I must understand the joys and sorrows and pain of all living creatures and not hurt anything for my own selfish motives—this is the true dharma—this is what making yourself in the image of god means. The other day I read in an English newspaper that fifty thousand pounds of meat had been sent from England to some army establishment in Africa—the meat had spoiled so it was sent back—and then that meat was auctioned off at Portsmouth for five or six hundred rupees. Just think about it, Bob, what a colossal waste of life, and how cheap life is! When we host a dinner, think of how many living things sacrifice their lives just in order to fill up our *dishes*; and quite possibly those dishes may make the rounds and return, nobody takes them. As long as we are unconscious of it and commit cruelty unconsciously, nobody can blame us. But when we feel pity, and then strangle that pity by the neck and continue with our cruelty along with ten others, that really is an insult to our better selves. I've been thinking, Bob, of trying to become vegetarian once again. . . .

I've found a good friend in this solitude—I had borrowed a copy of *Amiel's Journal* from Loken—now whenever I find the time I sit and turn over its pages.* It's exactly as if I'm sitting face-to-face with him and talking—I've very rarely found such a close friend in any other printed book. Many other books are better written than this and it may have many faults, but this book is after my own heart. There are times when one touches upon book after book but discards them all; none of them seem to give any comfort—just as often, when one is ill, it is difficult to find a comfortable position upon the bed, and one has to keep turning over in order to test

* Henri-Frédéric Amiel (1821–1881) was a Swiss philosopher, poet and critic. His most famous book is the *Journal Intime* (Private Journal), which, published after his death in 1882, became widely popular in Europe, and was almost immediately translated into English by Mary Ward or Mrs Humphrey Ward.

every position, sometimes piling pillow upon pillow, sometimes throwing all the pillows away—in that sort of mental framework, whichever part of *Amiel* I open to, the head finds the right position, the body finds some rest. That close friend Amiel has written about the cruelty of men towards animals in one place—I've added it all as a note on Bolu's piece. Taken all in all, I didn't really like this particular piece of Bolu's—it seems to have been stretched and padded while being written. It's as if he hasn't written it with his full attention—he's drawn it out and overextended the argument, making it up as he's gone along—it's not sounding a note of truthful simplicity, of empathy without exaggeration. . . . Made-up things are not always wrong in all places, but if this sort of thing is not genuinely felt, one becomes both averse to it and angry with it. I've told Bolu to translate from *Kādambañ* the portion describing the hunt. Birds are a bit like us—there is a place where there is no difference between them and us—their soft-hearted love for their children is like ours—Banabhatta has felt and expressed this with his own sympathetic imaginative powers—that *touch of nature makes the whole world kin!*

118

Patishar
24 March 1894

Nowadays I've been missing my lone companion on my evening walks, none other than our Śuklapaksha [the bright fortnight] moon. It's disappeared since yesterday. It's most inconvenient, it gets dark very quickly and then it becomes difficult to walk. . . . Nowadays at dawn I can see the Venus star from my open window the moment I open my eyes; I find her very sweet—she too keeps looking at me, exactly like one of you, like someone I've known all my life. I remember that in Shilaidaha, after a day's work when

I crossed the river on the boat in the evening, seeing the evening star in the sky every day would provide me with a feeling of great comfort—it used to seem exactly as if the river was my home and that the evening star was the gṛhalakshmī [presiding deity of one's home], dressed up brightly to wait for me to return home from work. She had such a look in her eyes, such an affectionate touch! The river used to be silent then, the breeze cool, no sound anywhere, my peaceful home full of a deep intimacy. I often recall that crossing of the river at Shilaidaha every evening in the silent darkness with great clarity. Every morning at dawn when I see the lone Venus the moment I open my eyes, I can't help but think of her as a very familiar and pleasant companion—she seems to radiate pleasure and affection upon my sleeping face like an ever-wakeful well-wisher.

Today when I returned to the *boat* after my walk I saw that there were so many light insects around the lamp that it was impossible to sit at the table. That's why I put out the light and sat outside in the dark on my easy chair—the entire lit-up sky and all the world and its beyond seemed to be looking at me like groups of women from behind the wooden shutters of the upper floors—I knew nothing about them, and wasn't sure that I would ever know anything about them—yet what an eternal history of variegated life flows through that constellation of light. I couldn't get down to writing to you in the evening, therefore I'm writing now. What time of the night do you think it is now—eleven. You must be in bed and fast asleep—when you get the letter in the stark light of day, you will be alert and restless, busy with lots of work—then where will this sleeping silent night have gone, with its silent message of light from the endless universe! Such a sharp difference! It's difficult to recall the way it was exactly—so limited are man's abilities. When you close your eyes you can't remember every line of the image of even those closest to you—that which is the most important for you at one time becomes difficult to access with your memory at another. During the day we forget about the night, at night we

forget the day. You'll realize the moment you read this letter that
it has been written in the middle of the night. . . .

A fragment of the moon has risen a while ago—it is absolutely
silent and sound asleep all around—only a couple of village dogs
bark from the opposite shore—there is just one light burning on
my *boat*, all other lights have been put out everywhere. There's
no motion in the river at all, which makes me feel that the fish
must sleep at night. The village sleeps by the water and the water
reflects the shadow of the sleeping village.

119

Patishar
Wednesday, 28 March 1894

It's getting quite hot here as well. But I don't pay much attention
to the heat of the sun—I think you know that. The hot wind
howls and runs along, making the sandy dust and bits of straw
fly—suddenly somewhere a queer whirling wind stands in one
place sucking up dried leaves, and a veil of dust whirls round
and round in a dance until it disappears—it's quite interesting
to watch. The birds call out very sweetly from the garden next
to the river—it feels like spring indeed, but served up piping
hot after peeling its skin. Except, it's a bit too hot; there would
have been no harm done if it had been allowed to cool down a
bit before serving. This morning, though, it was suddenly quite
cool—in fact, almost like winter—one didn't feel too enthused
about taking a bath. It's difficult to gauge exactly what's happening
when in this large affair called nature—something happens in some
remote corner of it somewhere and suddenly the feel of everything
around you changes. I was thinking yesterday that man's mind too
is mysterious—exactly like the immense natural world. There's a
ceaseless jugglery going on in all directions within the veins and

arteries, nerves and brains and marrow—the flow of blood rushes
along furiously, the nerves tremble, the heart beats with a rising
and falling motion, and the seasons change within the mysterious
character of man. We never know from which direction the wind
will blow and when. One day I think I'll be able to cope with life
quite well—I have quite a bit of strength, I'll leap right over all the
sorrow and suffering of life. So I get a *programme* of life printed and
bound in hardback and sit back calmly with it in my pocket—when
the next day I see that some other wind is blowing from some
unknown underworld and the entire intention of the sky seems to
have changed, and then I don't feel at all that I'll ever be able to
tide over such inclement weather. Where does all of this originate?
There's been some sort of movement within some vein or nerve,
and I'm caught in the middle, unable to cope with it despite all my
strength and intelligence. One feels very apprehensive when one
thinks about the boundless mystery that is within one's self—one
can't speak with any conviction about what one might do or not
do—and one thinks, what is this enormous burden that I carry
around on my shoulders every day without understanding any of
it—I cannot control it, yet I cannot avoid its reach—I don't know
where it will take me, or where I will take it—was it really necessary
to add this enormous weight to my shoulders in this way? What
happens in the heart, what runs in the veins, what moves inside
the head—so many thousands of things ceaselessly obscure my
view that I can't see, and they don't consult me either, yet I take
all of it and stand up straight like a masterful personality and think
that I am what I am! '"You", what do you know of "you"—you
hardly know anything about yourself.' After a lot of thought I've
come to the conclusion that I don't know myself at all. I'm like a
living piano, with lots of wires and mechanical bits inside me in
the dark; I never know who comes and plays it, and it is difficult
to completely comprehend why as well, I can only know what is
playing—whether it's happiness or sorrow, soft note or sharp, in
rhythm or not—just that much. And I know how far up or down

my *octave* will extend. No, do I know even that much? I'm not even sure if I'm a *sympathetic grand piano* or a *cottage piano*.

120

Patishar
Friday, 30 March 1894

What a lot of unnecessary anxiety and suffering there is in man's fate! Our happiness and peace are dependent upon so many thousands of big and small things! Yesterday, for a long time I suffered a lot of unnecessary grief in the most helpless manner. There's so much unhappiness that is self-created which I feel is my duty to suffer with humility and fortitude; but when I don't get a letter and worry about calamity or illness then I cannot find any *philosophy* near at hand to calm down those fears. Then one's intelligence too stops working. Yesterday while I was walking up and down I imagined so many sorts of impossible and unreasonable things—to any of which my brain too did not object—that today I feel both amused and ashamed of myself when I think of it. Yet I know for sure that once again in a few days when something like this will happen again, I'll have exactly the same reaction. I've told you lots of times, you know, that the brain doesn't belong to a man completely, it still hasn't been totally *naturalized* in our minds. . . .

When I remember that life's path is long, and that the reasons for sorrow and suffering are innumerable and inevitable, it becomes difficult to preserve one's strength of mind however much one tries. When you become so extremely impatient upon not having received a letter for two days, then it's difficult to keep faith in one's self. Sometimes, sitting alone in the evenings, staring fixedly at the light on the table, I think to myself, I shall face life like a brave—steadfastly, silently, and without complaining—and the thought makes me feel reassured for that moment, and I promptly make the mistake of thinking myself a mighty brave man. And after that, when a thorn pierces my foot while walking and I leap up in pain, I feel terribly doubtful about the future, and once again life seems very long and I feel completely unworthy. But perhaps the logic is faulty—really, perhaps a sharp thorn of grass is actually more unbearable. The mind has a tidy domesticity about it—it spends only according to its need, it doesn't want to waste its energies on trifling matters. It seems to be saving all its strength carefully like a miser for the really big dangers and sacrifices. The thousands of tears you shed at the smallest of wounds do not warrant its help. But where your sorrow is deepest, it is never lazy. That's why one sees that one of life's frequent *paradoxes* is that the smaller sorrows are more unbearable than the larger ones. That's because the place where the heart is torn asunder by a larger sorrow is also the fountainhead of a certain consolation that keeps rising up, and all the resources of one's mind, all one's patience, work together—the greatness of the sorrow is what enables you to have the strength to put up with it. Just as one side of man's heart is full of the desire for happiness, so too there is also a desire for self-sacrifice on the other side; when the desire for happiness is in vain, the wish for self-sacrifice becomes strong, and the mind, getting the opportunity to work towards accomplishing that wish, is filled with a generous enthusiasm. We are cowards when faced with the smaller sorrows, but the larger tragedies turn us into brave-hearts by awakening our genuine humanity. There is a happiness in that—it is the happiness of finding one's self completely. There's an old saying about the happiness of unhappiness which is not merely a clever turn of phrase—and what they say about the dissatisfactions of happiness too is quite true. The meaning is not difficult to understand. When we do nothing else but enjoy ourselves, one part of our minds remains dissatisfied, wanting something for which to suffer and sacrifice, or we feel unworthy of enjoying our happiness—that is the reason why the happiness which is mixed with sorrow is the one which is permanent and deep, and that is what helps our character accomplish its goals.

But the *philosophy* on joy and sorrow keeps on growing. If one counts the living of one's life with grace and beauty to be an *art* then there is a particular necessity for this *philosophy*, but there is an *art* to letter-writing as well, which one shouldn't ignore completely. There are many things indispensable to one's self; if I am able to tie up the entire discourse on joy and sorrow once and for all it would be of great help to me, which is why I'm using this letter as an opportunity to make my own feelings more articulate and clear—but that task is not always accomplished reasonably.

But if one begins to account for one's hopes with such accuracy it's very likely to result in mishap—so I've decided that I won't be receiving a letter tomorrow. If I don't get one tomorrow, I *will* get one the day after—but that '*will*' isn't too good a word, it's a word that gave me a terrible drubbing yesterday. It is one's duty to cautiously and with great care remove that word from all the balance sheets of one's life—that's one of the principal rules of living your life as an *art*. But it's very difficult to escape from it—it attaches itself to you like a leech and sucks your blood.

121

Shilaidaha
24 June 1894

It's only been about four days since I arrived, but it seems as if I've been here forever—it feels as though if I go to Calcutta today, I'll see that it has changed in so many ways. . . . it is as if I'm alone in a place outside of the flow of time, quite still, while unknown to me, the whole world is changing its position little by little.

Actually, when you come here from Calcutta, time stretches to about four times its length—one has to live only in one's own mental world—the watch doesn't work properly here. Mental time is measured according to the intensity of one's feelings—an occasional fleeting moment of happiness or unhappiness seems to last for a very long time. In a place where the outer flow of people and events and the daily work schedule don't keep us occupied always calculating the time, there, as in a dream, the short-lived moments turn into long periods and the long into the short all the time; that's why I think that fragmented time and a fragmented sky are both delusions of the mind. Every atom is endless and every moment is eternal. I'd read a story about this in my childhood in a Persian narrative which I had liked very much—and though I was very young then, I had understood its inner meaning to some extent. In order to show that time cannot be quantified, a certain fakir filled a *tub* with magic water and asked a *badshah* to dive into it and have a bath. The moment the badshah dived in, he saw that he had arrived in a new country by the sea; there he spent a lifetime, experiencing many events and situations and many joys and sorrows in the process. He got married, and one by one he had many sons; the sons died, the wife died, all his money was lost, and when he had been driven to his wits' end with grief he suddenly saw that he was sitting in a *tub* full of water in his own royal court. He became very angry with the fakir, but all his courtiers assured him that he had only immersed himself in the water for a moment before raising his head.

Our entire lives and all the joys and sorrows of our lives are enclosed in a moment such as this—however long and however intense we may think it is, the moment we raise our heads from the *tub* of this existence, immediately all of it will become very small, like a moment's dream. Time is not lengthy or brief—it is we who are big or small. It is not just the anticipation of a letter from you that brought so many thoughts to my mind—this is something that keeps coming up in my mind from time to time, and the fact that even the most intense of life's joys, sorrows and desires are not permanent is something I cannot find an answer to, and it vexes me greatly. One answer to this could be that even if happiness or unhappiness is impermanent, their results can be permanent. But then why does it delude me, tricking me into enjoying its fruits? Why does it say to me 'The wealth of love is eternal'? Who has given man the false reassurance that love conquers death—the reassurance that has driven man to make up stories such as that of Savitri and Satyavan to comfort himself? Etc., etc., etc.

Yesterday the day was very fine. The sun and the clouds were playing a new game from moment to moment—on the lines etched on my river, on the sandbanks, and on the forest scenery on the other bank—whichever direction I looked towards from the open window, it was so beautiful! Like a dream! I don't quite know why we always compare what's beautiful to a dream, perhaps in order to express the sheer extraordinariness of it, that is, as if it doesn't bear the slightest trace of the weight of *reality*—that our food comes from these fields of grain, that the river is the path through which boatloads of jute travel, that these sandbanks need to be rented from the jamidār in lieu of taxes; it's when these, and many other thousands of things like these, are removed far from the mind so that we may enjoy a picture of unaccounted-for, unnecessary and pure beauty and happiness alone, that we say 'like a dream'. At other times, we take it for granted that the world is true, and later as beautiful or otherwise. But when we see it chiefly for its beauty, and don't notice whether it is true or not, that's when we say it's 'like a dream'! . . . Sometimes men separate out truth from beauty—*science* leaves out beauty from truth and poetry does not respect beauty as truth. The beauty that is to be found in *science* is a beauty inseparable from truth, while the truth found in poetry is the truth of beauty. There's no space for more, so this time round you've escaped a lengthy disquisition.

122

Shilaidaha
26 June 1894

Getting out of bed this morning, I saw the sky was dark and
stooping under the weight of livid clouds, a damp storm wind
was blowing, there was a ceaseless drizzle, there weren't too many
boats on the river, the farmers, scythes in hand to cut grain, were
crossing the river on ferry boats with bamboo hats on their heads
and bodies covered with jute bags, no cows grazed on the fields and
no chorus of women bathing at the ghat—on other days by now
I would have heard their loud voices from this side of the river—
today, all that cacophony and the song of the birds was missing.
I had shut the window and drawn the curtain on the side from
which I expected the spray of rain and opened the window on the
other side, and was waiting all this time for work to commence.
I'm gradually realizing now with increasing certainty that the
clerks will not leave their homes today in this weather—alas, I
am not Shyam, and they are not Radhika—such a marvellous
opportunity for a rendezvous in the rain has been nipped in the
bud. Besides which, even if I did play the flute, if Radhika had
the slightest understanding of melody she wouldn't have been too
'thrilled'. Anyway, given that the situation is such that Radhika
will not be coming, and the clerks aren't coming either, and my
'Muse' too has of late left me to visit her father's house, I may as
well sit and write a bunch of letters. Actually what has happened
is, since I didn't have any work, I'd been sitting looking out at the
river and humming, trying to construct a morning rāginī that was
a mix of Bhairabī, Ṭoṛi and Rāmkeli, absorbedly practising the
ālāp, and this suddenly gave rise to such a sweet yet sharp feeling
of restlessness, such an indescribable, forceful feeling of yearning
in me, that, in a moment, this real life and the real world appeared
to me in another aspect entirely; such a song-filled and emotional,

yet wordless, meaningless and diffuse answer to all the intractable problems of our existence sounded in my ear, and through that portal of song, the liquid sound of water falling ceaselessly upon the river created such a wellspring of joy, such tear-filled, dense, dark clouds of Āshāṛh—joyous and sad—came crowding around this solitary, companionless soul at one end of the world, that suddenly there was a point at which I had to say, 'Let it be, there's no point in this, let's sit down to read *Criticisms on Contemporary Thought and Thinkers* now.' But to exhibit such extreme bravery on a rainy day like this is not for a weak person like me. Which is why, sighing, I've decided to sit down with inkpot and pen to write a letter. . . .

Nowadays I think to myself very often that I wish I could return somehow to a lonely, silent place without fame. Or at least, that as long as I am alive, all the fame and accomplishment of my life stays shut up within itself. Then I can be quite comfortable. Of course, depending on your individual preferences, all of you may not like everything I write—in fact, a lot of good writing too may remain unappreciated—but still, one doesn't feel like venturing out beyond that space.

123

Shilaidaha
Wednesday, 27 June 1894

Since yesterday, a *happy thought* has suddenly occurred to me. I've been thinking that even when one wants to do something that will help the world, one is not always successful, so instead, if one just does what one can do, then often the world derives some benefit from it, and at least the work too gets done. Nowadays I've been thinking that if I don't do anything else other than write short stories, then I'll be happy, and if I'm successful, then some of my readers too will be happy. No doubt it is a very noble task to

write essays on elevated subjects in *Sādhanā* and thus propel Bengal
towards progress, but of late I have not been happy doing it, nor
have I been able to do very much. One of the pleasures of writing
stories is that those I write about completely occupy my entire free
time; they are the companions of my solitary mind—during the
rains they drive away the sorrow of separation in my closed room,
and when it is sunny, they roam around in front of my eyes like
the bright scene on the shores of the Padma. That is why I have
managed to make a small, proud, wheat-complexioned girl called
Giribala descend into the world of my imagination this morning.
I had only just written about five lines, and in those five lines only
just said that it had rained yesterday, and today at the end of the
rains the restless clouds and restless sunshine were hunting each
other, when along the village path, below the trees from which
drops of water collected from yesterday's rain were falling, down
which the said Giribala should have been coming, came instead
the entire group of my *boat*'s clerks, as a result of which Giribala
has at present had to wait for a little while. Even so, she is still there
in my mind. Today I tried out another experiment with how to
spend one's days. Today I sat down and tried to bring my childhood
memories and my state of mind then very clearly and perceptibly
to my mind. When I was in the garden at Peneti, when I first went
to the Bolpur gardens with Bābāmaśāy̆, my head shaved for my
paite ceremony, when the farthest room on the western veranda
housed our schoolroom, and I used to draw crooked lines upon a
torn exercise book of blue paper and write down descriptions of
nature in it in large uneven letters—when the *toshākhānā** used to
be in Sej-dada's rooms and in the winter a servant called Chinta,
humming a tune in a low tone, used to toast bread with butter
for Jyoti-dada on the coal fire—we had no warm clothes then,
we used to wear a single *kāmij* and sit in front of that fire to drive
away the cold, staring with lustful, despairing eyes at the fragrant

* In his reminiscences, *Chelebelā*, Rabindranath says: 'In the *nabābi* style, the
servants' quarters in those days used to be called the *toshākhānā*.'

piece of melting cream crackling on the bread while sitting quietly, listening to Chinta's song (I can even remember the tune, it's called the *Madhukān* tune)—I was watching all those days exactly as if they were in the present, and all those days were dissolving into the sunlit Padma and the Padma's sandbanks so beautifully, exactly as if I were sitting by that open window of my childhood and watching a fragment of a scene from this Padma. Then I thought of how powerful I was—I could write stories if I wanted to, I could transport myself away from the present to experience the farthest countries and the farthest times if I wanted to, that I could make myself quite happy without the help of any real thing. Immediately, I remembered the saying: *nothing succeeds like success*. 'Money begets money', so happiness begets happiness. When we're happy, we think we have an endless ability to be happy—then at unhappy times we see that none of those powers are working, nothing is available near at hand, all the mechanics of it have gone completely awry. Yesterday perhaps some small thing had created a happiness that reverberated in the mind, which is why all its instruments started up simultaneously—life's past memories and the present beauty of nature came alive at the same time, that's why the moment I woke up this morning I thought to myself, I am a poet—there's no end to my powers, I can flood the world with my compositions, my imagination, my joy. Whatever my poetic talent, however proud I might be of my abilities, man is terribly unfree. These starving souls roam the world: tall, rigid, emaciated—they want an entire heaven, and then they try to satisfy their hunger with whatever bits and pieces they get, until their beggarly, upward-stretched bodies fall to the dust and they pretend that death is the attainment of heaven. If we can hold on to the little happiness that is required for all the instruments of life to keep working, then all our strength can be deployed and all our work completed before we go. Today Miss Giribala has arrived uninvited; tomorrow when I need her the most, not even the tip of her swinging plait will perhaps be visible to me any more. But there's no need to get agitated about that today. If there's a possibility that Miss Giribala may disappear tomorrow, so be it, but there's no doubt about the fact that her arrival today is something to be celebrated. . . .

Your letter this time informs me that the tiniest occupant of my home has learnt to pout her little lips to show her hurt pride. I can quite imagine it. My face, my nose, my eyes are thirsty for the scratches of her soft fists. She would clutch at me anywhere with her fists, head wobbling, to come eat me with a big bite, and, twining the cord of my spectacles in her small little fingers, would stare at me, cheeks puffed out, in the most unconscious, calm and serious way. Her fat little hands feel so sweet on my body!

124

Shilaidaha
28 June 1894

I still get very worked up if there's any problem with my letters. Perhaps there's a pleasure even in that . . . there's a certain happiness in imagining that my scoldings are reaching you at regular intervals. If that flow is suddenly interrupted, one feels very restless. For me, all unhappiness perhaps stems from this cause. If the easy flow of life is obstructed at any place the hurt foams up and divides within itself and turns into tears. Just as the river, as it keeps flowing, cuts a path that is accessible and deep, so too the hundreds and thousands of routine habits of our lives create their own broad path as they repeat themselves, and suffer if they are suddenly faced with an obstacle on that road. My home, my friends, my dear ones—they are all part of the easy and familiar path of my life's familiar flow. My wishes, my dreams, my work, all flow over them in a hundred thousand streams. Every path in life may not have been made out of habit, there are natural paths as well. The waterfall, for instance, flows towards the valley, but the valley has not been created by it.

So too each individual's life's waterfall has a particular valley—and his entire strength and entire motion propels it in that direction—if it cannot do so, if it is obstructed anywhere, then all its motion, strength and life are frustrated. I'm expanding on the issue because you've raised the question of happiness and unhappiness in your last letter. In life, it is the development of all one's strengths and the force of all one's parts that's called happiness and success. Whether it's love, devotion to god, or social work—different people use different means to give meaning to their lives; people use whatever is nearest at hand, is easily accomplished, or that which gives them the greatest pleasure in life—there's no point delivering a lecture on this subject. There may be many ways to be happy in the world, but not all of them are available to everybody. What's the point of chanting edicts on ethics in the ears of a fate that has not managed to grant one's barricaded life a modicum of freedom? I cannot bring flowing water to the marshes of Kaligram just because the Gangotri exists on the peaks of the Himalayas. One cannot but accept the fact that there are many unhappy people in the world. To say happiness lies in doing one's duty is a deception propagated by life's law books, like what we learnt as children—

> Lekhāparā kare yei
> gāṛi ghoṛā chaṛe sei

(He who learns his reading and writing
Is the one who will ride a horse and carriage)

Now I know that even after having learnt reading and writing, there are many who have to beg or borrow for the money to ride a *tram*-car; so too many wretched souls have to continue to do their duty without being happy, in fact while being positively unhappy. And then later on habit begins to wear down the path—the path of unhappiness too is made somewhat bearable by habit as it cuts an easy road through life—the lines of habit fall upon even the most adverse of paths—and, subsequently, one's life may be sucked dry halfway in the desert instead of finding its way successfully to the sea. This is quite a common occurrence—that's a *fact*. You cannot prove this to be untrue however much you try and however many verses you may extract from the Vedas, Puranas, Koran or Bible—sorrow will remain sorrow. Hundreds and hundreds of flowers in this world begin as buds but fall to the ground instead of bearing fruit because of the worms that attack them and shrivel them up—just because one doesn't get an answer if one asks why, one cannot deny the fact. There are so many hundreds and hundreds of unsuccessful lives in the world that are ruined because of terrible sorrow—I don't know where they find any consolation. Men have created many consolations for themselves from ancient times—there's no limit to the number and variety of conjectures and fancies they've piled up. I was sitting on the *boat* one day and thinking—man is a creature oppressed by the weight of things, all the things essential to him have a certain weight; even if you publish a book in which you have expressed all your inner feelings, you have to exhaust yourself paying a charge to send it by parcel post—clothes, housing, food, etc., are all like heavy loads to be borne. That is why one of man's chief concerns is to find a way to bear all these loads but at the same time to make them easier to bear. The wheels of a carriage are an important means; one can put a heavy load upon wheels and bear it along quite easily. On water, the boat turns out to be a great help; one can load the heaviest of things upon the tide and travel to other countries. Our laws, ethical principles and social norms perform a similar function. Want, separation or death will always weigh down on man and make him unhappy; that is why men try to structure their society and religion in such a way as to make the load as light as possible so it can float. If we allow the weight to settle down on ourselves it becomes unbearable; but if we allow religion or social duty to bear the load then one can get some rest. The chief value of any large *idea* is—that like a large river, it has the ability to bear loads and convey loads; the moment we cast ourselves in them we become lighter, we don't have to bear our sorrow and our suffering upon our own shoulders any more. There's no end to this subject on which we've begun, but it's getting late in the night and the letter too keeps getting longer. And it seems to me that man prefers to keep unresolved issues suppressed, for if you try to explain them too much the audience is liable to feel irritated.

125

Shilaidaha
Saturday, 30 June 1894

I had thought it might be best to deal with all the problems in a single day. With time, a *programme* for solitude gets gradually firmed up, and then one doesn't feel like breaking into its complete wholeness from time to time—because once you break into it even for a single day it becomes very difficult to gather all its threads together again. On the other hand, it is in the first few days when the mind cannot make a place for itself in its new nest and cannot settle down that one can tolerate the company of friends. But now I have filled up my free time with my imagination—if human beings suddenly arrive in that space there will be a problem. The imagination is as fearful as a doe; at first it takes some time to tame it and make it one's own, and then if men intrude on the grounds in which it roams then of course you'll never catch another glimpse of it for quite a while. That's why, when I'm in this uninhabited kingdom in which my mind occupies far more space than my body, I want people here who are dearer to me than my imagination, or people to whom I have not the slightest obligation to pay any attention. The difficulty begins when it is something between the two. This tiny bit of solitude is like my mind's *work-shop* for me, with all its invisible machinery and finished and unfinished work spread all around—when a friend arrives, he doesn't notice all of it, and there's no saying where he'll step next; he sits blithely there, unconsciously and happily discussing the news of the world, breaking off one by one all the fine threads wound so carefully upon the loom of my leisure—when I accompany him to the station and return alone to my workroom I can see how much I have lost. How will other people know in what ways exactly I'm engaged in composing my life! When we live with another person we each compose the other—we keep enough space for each other, in fact so much so that there's very little left for one's self. But when I'm completely alone—my complete 'me' doesn't leave a *margin* for anybody else but spreads itself out in its own compositions, fearlessly laying out a number of fine, beautiful things all around—those then constitute a major problem. . . . There are many types of conversations, many kinds of work and many discussions that are unimportant for others and quite natural in public—but very wounding for my life of solitude. That's because when we are alone the secret, deep and scattered parts of ourselves all come together and awaken—it's a bit like we are ourselves, so it's strange and wild—in that situation, the self has become unfit for human company and its entire nature attains a certain unity, so that whatever breaks that unity hurts it terribly. . . .

One of the best things about the external world is that it does not come forward on its own to oppose you; since it doesn't have a mind of its own, it's quite willing to concede all the space available to my mind—like a companion that gives me company it occupies endless space yet doesn't take up an inch of mine—it doesn't yap like an idiot or argue like an intellectual; it sleeps in the lap of the sky like my Meera, it's sweet when it's quiet and it's sweet even when it flings its hands and feet about and roars—especially when there are such excellent arrangements for its bathing, eating and dressing, for which I bear no responsibility—then that large, healthy, beautiful child without language or mind is quite ideal for my solitude. Men of words, intellect and experience are pleasant only in society. One shouldn't give expression to such asocial thoughts, but if you are receptive to the feeling with which I say it then perhaps it will not seem so reprehensible.

126

Shilaidaha
5 July 1894

There is nothing at all that is more impermanent than the new. Fortunately, man's heart is so fluid that it manages to adjust its measure to almost any vessel it finds itself in—only some small containers are unable to hold it and some big ones hold it somewhat loosely. And, occasionally, one or two hearts turn up that are congealed solidly in the old—if they are to be transferred to a new container, they have to be broken.

127

Shilaidaha
Thursday, 5 July 1894

Yesterday in the afternoon I had just sat down to some solid writing when, after I had barely five lines or so written, the maulabi suddenly turned up. Seeing that I was writing, he assured me that he would leave after just a couple of words ['*dotho kathā*']—after which he proceeded to spend two hours [*dotho ghantā*] on those two words. Just as he was about to leave somebody cried out from the shore—'Maharaj, I've been seeking an audience for about a week now, but the doorkeepers [*doubārikgan*] have been forbidding my entry.' Just the language made it evident that this was not just anybody. I forbade the 'doorkeepers' to forbid. Then a bearded, balding Brahmin with a high forehead and a pleasant

aspect, wearing saffron robes and a tilak, came and stood in front
of me and took out an enormous piece of paper. I thought it
might be an application. But then he began to read it out himself
very loudly. From the very first line it became clear that this was
a poem. In it the Brahmin was praising the qualities of god [Sri
Hari] in his heaven. I sat there gravely and listened. As long as god
was in his heaven the poem was proceeding in the *tripadī* metre, but
then I suddenly realized that god had descended into the 'world-
famous capital Calcutta' in order to preserve the surname Tagore
as Dwarakanath—the poem too descended accordingly from the
tripadī to the *payār* metre. When the payār eulogy was done with
Debendranath and approached Rabindranath, I privately began
to become fretful. My poetry and my generosity were shown to
be spreading through the world like the sun's rays and dispelling
the darkness of ignorance and poverty in the process—however
wonderful the comparison might have been, this was news to me.
In any case, spreading the news of how charitable I am means
nothing. I said to him, 'You go to the kāchāri, I have other
work to do.' The man said, 'Why don't you do your own work,
let me stand here and watch your moon-face for a while'—and
then he took up a posture of wonderment and stood quite still
in front of me, staring unblinkingly at my face all the while like
a dumb animal; my alarmed inner self seemed to writhe within
my entire body. I told him repeatedly to go. Then he said, 'Give
me whatever you want to give—write it down on this piece of
paper and I will take it to the accounts officer and read the poem
out to him as well.' I thought to myself, this is my profession too,
I too read out poems for a living. But I too have to return from
many a door empty-handed—the Brahmin too had to do so. Sri
Hari's four hands hold the conch shell, the disc, the mace and the
lotus. This avatar of Sri Hari used only the hand that holds the
mace and showed the Brahmin the door. Within moments of his
leaving the *boat*, a famous orator here in Birahimpur called Dwari
Majumdar arrived. I imprisoned both my hands upon my chest and

leaned back on the chair, sitting as stiffly as a solid stone statue. He began immediately—'Maharaj, many people disbelieve the *hysteria* (*history*) of Yudhishthir in the olden times; they ask, is it possible to achieve so much, but after so many ages, seeing you with their own eyes, their doubts about Yudhishthir's accomplishments have been laid to rest'—and so on and so forth. When I said to him, 'Why don't you go and get some rest in the kāchāri now,' he said, 'Why talk of rest today! Today I have obtained an audience with you after so many days, today I have finally been able to see your lordship after waiting for seven, eight, nine months—had I ever hoped that I would be able to see you!' As he spoke his voice began to tremble and he caught his breath, wiping his dry eyes with his shawl repeatedly; increasingly, he began to become more and more emotional at the thought of his former lordship Jyoti-dada's endless affection and trust for him. . . . He then began to tell me in minute detail, without leaving out a thing, exactly what work he had done, which events had occurred, what his employers had said, and how he had answered them. The sun went down, evening came; the birds returned to their nests, cows to their cowsheds, farmers to their huts—but Dwari Majumdar refused to budge from the *boat*. At this time, when another audience seeker arrived from Kushtia, he finally left, consoling me that he would be back tomorrow morning to tell me the rest. He hasn't arrived yet, but somebody quite equal to him in speechifying has come and is sitting on the *bench* next to me waiting for my leisure so as to begin his speech.

128

On the way to Shahjadpur
Friday, 6 July 1894

I'm en route now. Yesterday in the afternoon, just as we were about to untie the boat, a clerk came up with folded hands and pleaded,

'Your lordship, it would be better if you set out tomorrow morning rather than today.' When I asked why, he said it is the conjunction of three lunar days today, and therefore very inauspicious for travel. I said I would prove that the day was an auspicious one for travel—I would reach Shahjadpur quite safely. So saying, I snapped my fingers in the face of all the planets, stars, and days of ritual and set off. On the way the Padma was flowing terribly fast in places—the swollen water whirled around and crashed on the shore; the *boat* didn't want to move forward at all, all its joints began to shiver and tremble; those towing the boat found it impossible to keep their feet steady despite stooping low and pulling with all their strength; I thought to myself, now I suppose it's the turn of all the planets, stars, and days of ritual to snap their fingers under my nose. After a while, once we had crossed the Gorui and reached the real Padma, it was possible to raise the sails—then we proudly and forcefully cut our way across the chest of the opposing current and proceeded to make our way dancing over the waves. At five or six in the evening we managed to enter the Ichamoti River. . . .

In the evening, we tied our boat to a ferry ghat near Pabna town. On the shore there were some people singing to the accompaniment of the tabla, a mixture of sounds entered the ear, men and women walked down the road with a busy air, the lamplit houses were visible through the trees, there was a crowd of people of all classes at the ferry ghat. The sky had a very dark cloud of a single colour, the evening too was darkening, lights came on in the row of usurers' boats tied to the other shore and brass bells began to sound from the temple for evening prayers—sitting by the *boat's* window with the light extinguished, my mind was filled with the force of a most wonderful feeling. A living, pulsating beat from this human habitation seemed to pierce through the cover of darkness and strike my breast. Under this cloudy sky on this intense evening, how many people, how many desires, occupations, jobs, homes— and so many mysteries of life contained within those homes—so many people so near each other, brushing up against one another, resulting in so many thousands of sorts of collisions and reactions! This vast population, with all their good and bad, all their joy and sorrow, had become like one to enter my heart from either shore of the tree-lined, small, rainy river like a tender, beautiful rāginī. I think I had tried to express something of this feeling in my poem 'Śaiśabsandhyā' [Childhood Evenings]. What it means, in brief, is perhaps this, that man is small and transient, yet the stream of life—full of the good and the bad, of joys and sorrows—will flow on with its ancient, deep murmur as it always has and always will—one can hear that eternal hubbub at the margins of a town in the darkness of evening. Then the impermanent and individual daily life of man dissolves in that entire undifferentiated melody and enters the heart's silence like the single tone of a great ocean—a very vast, spread-out, melancholic, mysterious sound without beginning or end, without questions or answers. I don't think I can quite explain or describe the state of my mind last evening. There are times when the larger currents of the world enter our hearts through some tear or rent somewhere, and then they resound in a way that is impossible to translate into words. That is why I've noticed that I have not managed to write poetry about many of the deepest and most intense feelings of my heart, which may have occasionally found expression in my writing only as the merest hint.

129

On the way to Shahjadpur
7 July 1894

I spent the day reading a *Polish novel* called *The Jew*. Fate had ordained that the novel be an unreadable one—I managed to somehow desperately finish it only because I had started it. It's difficult to understand the dutiful compulsion to complete something only because one has started it. It's not exactly a sense of duty—Loken is partly correct when he says that all our mental faculties have a certain pride. Our minds don't ever want to easily admit that we are inconsequential or impermanent or defeated by the smallest of obstacles—that's why they often keep themselves awake with the utmost effort. Our resolve too has a certain pride—it has started something, so it wants to take it through to the end, even if it means going against itself. That stubborn and wasteful pride has made me sit the entire long rainy day in a closed room and finish a huge, unreadable book full of disjointed argumentation—it gave me no satisfaction other than the satisfaction of having finished it. I had wanted to write, but you can't write in this damp and closed situation. I was thinking that I've written to you every day every time I have travelled down this narrow, winding Ichamoti River—and I'm writing to you this time as well. My letters from the provinces are all written from the same places, the same scenery and the same situations every time—if you look at them all together I've no doubt they'll be full of numberless repetitions. Perhaps I've used the exact same language again and again. When you're in Calcutta it is easy to say something novel at every moment—but in the rural outback there are only two subjects, nature and my own self—both subjects give me immense joy—and there's no dearth of variety in these two subjects too—but man's '*point of view*' and the language and powers with which he expresses himself are limited—so there's nothing to do but repeat one's self thousands of times. Having heard the same things over and over again you must have my state of mind and daily life in the provinces more or less by heart—perhaps you could forge one of my letters from the provinces quite easily. This time if it had not rained and been sunny instead and I had been able to sit by the window and look at the scenery outside all day, perhaps I would have written the sorts of things to you about this winding river that I have already written at least four times; and I would've thought that I was writing it all down for the first time. Not only that—I would think that the indescribable feelings and thoughts that arise in me when I see the banks of the Ichamoti River are as huge and important news to you as they are to me—and that expressing them appropriately and completely after gathering them up by their roots from the inaccessible parts of my mind and sending them to you in their entirety—is a desperately urgent task. Nowadays it has been proven that those who are writers by race are a sort of madmen. That seems to be substantially true to me. To feel sad if you're unable to express your thoughts is certainly a kind of madness.

Bar-dada isn't satisfied until he has written his *boxometry*. Birendra writes on every wall and on every flowerpot on the second floor, drawing the sun and writing in the middle: 'sun'—one can't describe how painstakingly slowly he writes, rubbing it out so many times, and with so much care. God alone knows what particular happiness resides in the correct expression of that sun both for him and for the world. I too suffer from a similar madness, only the subject and the form are different. Those who are completely and entirely mad don't know how mad they are. I know that I am crazy in one part—however much I want to or I try, I will not be able to tie that part down in this life; whatever my intelligible part pledges, my madness does not protect but destroys.

130

Shahjadpur
10 July 1894

One doesn't want to lose sight of any part of the lives of those who are close to us and those whom we would always want to keep near us—but if you think about it properly, it's funny in what little measure two people, even if they are very close, remain conjoined together in every line in this life. A person we have known for ten years—what a great part of those ten years have been spent

not knowing him—perhaps if we do our accounts for a lifelong
relationship we will find that we're not left with very much in hand
at the end. And that is only the knowing that comes of seeing;
beyond that there's the knowing of the mind. If you think about it
like that then everybody appears unknown to you, and we realize
that there is not much chance of getting to know anybody really
well—because after a couple of days we will have to be completely
separated, and that before us, countless millions of people have lived
their lives under this sun and blue sky and met in rest houses and
separated again and been forgotten and then removed. Thinking
in this vein may make some of us want to renounce the world,
and one may feel, 'then why'—but in me, it's just the opposite. I
want to see more, know more, get more. Sometimes I think, here
we are, just a few self-conscious living things who have raised their
heads like bubbles floating in the ocean of life and have bumped
into one another in a sudden coming together—and it is doubtful
if the quantity of wonder, love and joy that has been created by
this coming together will ever be built up again in all time. In one
place in Basanta Ray's poetry there is a line—

In a moment we lose hundreds of centuries

It's quite true that man may experience the conjunction and
disjunction of a hundred centuries in a moment. That is why
one feels every moment is invaluable. The words aren't new,
but to me they seem so astonishingly new sometimes! This time
before I left, on the day that S——— had come to Park Street in
the afternoon, you were sitting at the piano, I was preparing
to sing, when suddenly looking at you all I thought, here you
were in the afternoon, your hair tied, wearing fresh clothes,
on a particular cloudy day in front of an open window at the
piano, and a person called me, standing, leaning upon the piano
lid, S——— sitting and waiting to hear the songs—just a bit of
astonishing business in the endless flow of events through time.

It seemed that whatever beauty, whatever joy this contained was limitless, and that the light emanating on this cloudy afternoon was an amazing gain. I don't know why the routine materiality of the everyday is sometimes suddenly torn a little for just a moment; then it seems to me that with my newborn heart I can see the scene in front of me and the present event reflected on the canvas of eternal time. Then the fact that you all are who you are and I am who I am—and that I'm looking at you and listening to you and thinking of you all as my own and you too are thinking of me as your own—comes to me again as an amazing thing that I can see in a new and vast way. Who knows if such an amazing occurrence will ever happen again! I quite frequently see life and this world in a certain way so that the mind is filled with limitless wonder—I may not be able to quite explain that to anybody else. That's why a lot of things become so much for me that someone else may think it to be unnatural and excessive: 'overreacting to every little thing'. One of the virtues of habit is that it manages to lighten and thereby lessen many things, protecting the mind from outside impact like a shield, but habit cannot ever completely envelop my mind—to me, the old seems to be new every day. That's why my *perspective* gradually becomes different from other people's, and I have to test with trepidation anew where each one of us is situated.

131

On the way to Calcutta
13 July 1894

We managed to enter the Ichamoti River. What a lovely, bright day it was! You couldn't turn your eyes away from the scene on either side of the small river. There were hardly any clouds in the sky—the forests at the edge of the river and the dark green fields of crop happy in the sunshine, the breeze sweet—I sat like a king reclining comfortably on five or six pillows piled high on the bed next to the window—somebody had spun a dream upon my eyelids—the fishermen caught fish, women washed clothes, boys falling in the water created a rumpus, cows grazed, storks sat upon fields submerged in water, all of it looked like a picture. It's impossible to try and describe exactly why all of it was feeling so wonderful to me. We say that a beautiful thing is like a dream for exactly the reasons that we say it is like a picture. Otherwise the saying is actually a bit strange—it wouldn't be wrong to say that a picture was like a thing, but to say that something was like a picture is in one sense saying it the wrong way around. But the real meaning of it is that in a picture we see only one part of a thing that is held up before our eyes, so what becomes most intense in our minds is the pleasure we feel in partaking of the beauty of the scene. I feel that the function of *Art* is to carefully separate out that part of the world that we love from the rest to hold it up in its brightness, undiluted and on its own. The *artist's* job is to strain that part out from the surface of truth and then put it on view. That's why I feel that pure *art* is in pictures and music—not in literature. Man's language is far more voluble than man's paintbrush or his voice, which is why in literature we mix in too many things—in order to express beauty we give information or advice, and say many other things. Anyway, we use phrases such as 'like a picture', 'like a song', 'like a dream' very frequently—but that's not the important thing. We think of beauty as more heavenly than truth, delight more heavenly than knowledge. . . .

But over here my *boat* is not advancing any further. We had come this way trusting that the wind that had obstructed us on the Yamuna would be favourable for us on the Ichamoti. But to trust in the wind is not a very intelligent thing to do. People have divided madness into forty-nine classes and named them the forty-nine winds. And, truly, among the five elements, wind contains a level of madness in excess of almost any other.

132

Calcutta
15 July 1894

How shall I describe the beauty of what I saw when the steamer left
the Ichamoti behind and came upon the Padma towards evening?
You couldn't see the ends of the horizon anywhere—there were no
waves, everything was full of a calm seriousness. When that which
can whimsically create a storm right now takes on a beautiful and
pleased aspect, when it hides its huge force and power in a form full
of sweetness and dignity, then its beauty and glory come together
to create the most amazing and generous wholeness! Slowly as the
twilight gathered density and the moon rose, all the chords seemed
to begin to resound in my entranced heart.

133

Calcutta
16 July 1894

Going up to the just-waking second-floor room, I saw my youngest
hatchling lying on the bamboo mat on the floor trying to call out.
The thing is almost exactly as it was before, its cheeks as plump, eyes
gawking in the same silly way, head nodding and bobbing up and
down on the shoulders all the while. All in all, the tiny person was
like a dewdrop trembling upon the lotus of the vast world. I picked
her up on my lap. At first for a while she seemed to be trying to
recall her previous acquaintance with me—a thorough review was
conducted while looking me up and down in a significant way.
Sometimes, for no particular reason, an occasional sweet smile
appeared. Gradually, in no time at all, she began to lay her soft fat
hands with their sharp nails upon my nose, face, eyes, hair, moustache

and beard—in fact, on whatever she could find in front of her, and not only that, she then began to roar and try to put my nose and eyes into her mouth to eat it all up. After that, lying flat on her stomach on the bed, fat hands and legs waving and head bobbing about, she began to swim enthusiastically for a while. Among the changes I observed, it seemed that she has managed, with a lot of effort, to start pronouncing the consonants in the 'p' group nowadays, and that a little bit of intelligence has found expression in her eyes. She recognizes the sound of her own name and manages to recognize some of her friends and relatives as well. The smell of her body too has the same baby-baby feeling. Most of my time after returning to Calcutta has been spent in laughter-filled conversations with her.

134

Calcutta
19 July 1894

It's impossible to get any work done because of Meera, Bob. . . . When this tiny personality lies flat on the bed and raises both her legs up to the sky as if they were the most precious commodities and then tries to put them into her own mouth, shouting out—*aah baah baah baah*—in the loudest voice, then it is absolutely impossible for me to get any reading or writing or any work done at all. I lie down flat on my stomach next to her somewhere, and she stretches out both her arms, flailing around, and begins a great commotion with my moustache, beard, hair, nose, ears, spectacles and watch-chain, getting increasingly excited and starting to yell. So my time passes in this way. Some days in the night I can hear her wake up and start to make all sorts of sounds—the moment I go near her, she gives me a bit of a smile; the thought is: now I've got someone to play with. Then there's no sleep for a long time, as she lies flat on her stomach and keeps swimming around on the bed.

135

Calcutta
21 July 1894

I have a great desire to have somebody who can sing or play an instrument live near my room. If Beli becomes a maestro in both Indian and English music then perhaps my desire will be fulfilled to some extent. But by the time she becomes a maestro, she will leave my house. The other day when Abhi was singing I thought to myself that man's happiness is constituted of materials that are not all that inaccessible—a sweet voice for singing is not an absolutely impossible *ideal* in the world, yet the pleasure it gives is very deep. But however easily available it might be, finding the appropriate amount of time for it is very hard. The world is not made up only of those who wish to sing and those who wish to listen; the maximum number of people all around us are those who will never sing and never listen to any singing. That's why, taken all in all, it's something that never happens; day after day passes, one's soul becomes increasingly thirsty, the world seems to turn into worn skin and bone. I often think that it's true that we're sorry when our larger desires remain unfulfilled, but the dissatisfaction of our smaller needs and desires remaining unfulfilled all the time makes our inner selves, unbeknownst to ourselves, become gradually shrivelled and dry—we don't always count those losses, but they're not a negligible amount. When the soul is denied nourishment and remains neglected and starved, it becomes really difficult for it to bear our sorrows. I know that the way I am makes me want song, art, beauty, the company of thinkers, literary discussion—but in this country these are futile desires, futile striving on my part. People here cannot even begin to believe that things like these are absolutely essential for anybody. I too slowly begin to forget that almost none of the roots that feed my self are getting any nutrition. In the end, when suddenly one day some little source of nourishment becomes available, and I feel the intensity of my eager heart, I remember that all these days I was starving, and that this is an essential requirement for my temperament to continue to live.

136

Calcutta
1 August 1894

Somebody called Sharatchandra Ray had come to meet me, but I refused to see him. Once you let a Bengali's son into your rooms, it becomes near impossible to oust him. But the Bengali daughter Meera is also no less than anybody—she too, once she enters my rooms with a clamour, doesn't leave in a hurry. She mauls me with her paws and dances on my breast, and then, having messed up my beard, moustache, the parting of my hair, my writing notebooks, the plots of my stories and the continuity of my thoughts with her two tiny hands, is expelled from my room leaving me completely defeated. And the problem is that if she doesn't come to me then I have to go to her—she begins to shout from the next room— anybody nearby who hears the loud shouting abandons all their work and rushes towards the sound—and once they are there, they see this plump, fat figure lying on her stomach in the middle of the huge bed thumping the pillows and hollering with unnecessary joy. The moment she sees the newly arrived person, her face is illuminated with a smile; sometimes she opens her mouth as wide as she can to try to express some unknown thought, but fails. At the end of it all, I stretch my large body out by her tiny one and spend a long time in completely meaningless, disjointed polite conversation, and only then can I go back to concentrating on my work. If you try to have a conversation with a grown-up you run out of subjects, so you may soon be free to go, but where there's no subject at all but there is conversation, one can't think of where to stop—in all the *tête-à-têtes* that I always have with Meera one can't find a break in the flow of thought anywhere, so if you must stop, you stop by asserting all your bodily strength.

137

Calcutta
2 August 1894

My visits to Priya-babu are of great help to me in one thing—I can then tangibly see that literature has a huge contribution to make to the history of man, and that there is a significant connection between it and this insignificant personality's insignificant life. Then I feel confident in my ability to preserve myself and complete my work—then in my imagination I can see a wonderful picture of my future life. I see that at the centre-point of my everyday life and all that happens—its joys and sorrows—there is an extremely lonely and silent spot where I sit immersed, forgetting everything, in order to undertake my work of creation—where I am happy. All our important thoughts have a generous renunciation about them. When we study *astronomy* and so go and stand in the sphere of the stars and creation's mystery, how much lighter all the small burdens of life seem! Similarly, if one can make a great sacrifice or involve one's self with some large world affair, immediately the burden of one's own existence seems easily bearable. Unfortunately, even among the educated people of our country, the winds of thought do not blow freely, the connection between life and thought is really very little, and it's impossible to feel, when you're in the company of our countrymen, that literature is an important force for humankind—one feels eternally hungry to find one's own ideals reflected in other people.

138

Shilaidaha
4 August 1894

There's been a change of scene. Where is that Calcutta, that second-floor terrace, the daily routine of life in the disorganized clutter of bed, bedstead and chair, that *practising* of *scales* on the piano in the next room—that Meera, who although very tiny, occupies such a large space in my world! Suddenly, like a dream, all the towering mansions all around piercing the sky have been transformed into green fields swaying in the wind, the main road of Chitpur flows in the form of an immense, spread-out stream of liquid sound and song, the dust-filled heavy air is clear and transparent, bringing joyful life all over the vast, free sky—in a boat by an open window, at the head of a *camp-table* upon a cane chair is the chief protagonist, Sri Rabindranath, occupied in writing a letter this morning, and opposite him in another cane chair, his friend Sri —— is concentrating completely on writing a story for *Sādhanā*. This is how today's scene has begun. In a moment the nāyeb will enter with the *peśkār's* [bench clerk's] notebook and tied-up *bundles* of papers in hand, and then the manner in which the *dialogue* will begin is such as could never have been composed in this day and age by any human playwright, and even if it were, it would have been roundly criticized by the reviewers' faction. But the poet of our providence who divides our lives into new and newer acts and scenes every day, propelling us forward to the denouement of the fifth act, is not the least concerned with synchronizing context and character, or with clever composition, or with the arrangement of events; he allows clerks to gather in this dearest of boats upon the stream of the wave-rocked Padma, causes grammatical and rhetorical faults to crop up·in the conversation between hero and heroine, and if by any chance or good fortune the hero receives a poetic love letter written correctly according to the rules of aesthetics, then the letter-writer turns out to be a man.

Today the scenery is beautiful, the light is beautiful and the breeze is beautiful. Immersed in this sweetness, I feel like writing something or composing a song while humming to myself, or reading a storybook without too much variety or too much analysis—to lean back comfortably upon the *chair* and forget about the world, and, as I read, to have the shore's green line gradually pass by the corner of my eye and for the liquid sound of water to ceaselessly enter my ears. But I don't see any possibility that all these relatively easily attained desires will be satisfied at the moment. Because even as I write the nāyeb and the maulabī have come in. The nāyeb has begun to explain the modalities of the traditional account-keeping of our jamidāri to Sri —— babu; as a result, the sort of revolution in jamidāri language that has been unleashed is such that if I extract even a particle of it in one corner of this letter, you will perhaps not forgive me for the rest of this life—so I shall stop now.

139

Shilaidaha
5 August 1894

It rained very heavily all of last night—this morning when I woke up at dawn it was still raining continuously and it was grey on every side. Coming out of the bathing room just this moment, I saw layer upon layer, stack upon stack of dense, dark, low cloud amassed in the west above the autumn rice fields, and on the south-east side the clouds had separated a little and the sun was trying to come out, as if a temporary truce had been called between sun and rain. The scene on the other side of the Padma, where the morning light was trying to appear from behind torn clouds, was very beautiful—a freshly bathed, spiritual figure of light seemed to be rising from the mysterious depths of the water to stand in quiet beauty, and on the shore, black clouds that looked like a lion with waving manes were sitting quietly, frowning, paws stretched out over the rice fields, as if conceding victory to the beautiful celestial power, but not yet tamed—sitting in one corner of the horizon with all its anger and pride coiled up. It's going to rain again right now, one can see signs of that, preparations are on for a proper Śrābaṇ shower—the open door before which the just-awakened smiling rays of light had come and stood is closing again very slowly—the muddy waters of the Padma are getting covered in shadow, from one side of the river to the other, the clouds have joined up with other clouds to occupy the entire sky—its entire set-up is very dark and dense. . . .

By now the autumn rice and jute fields should have been almost empty, but this time the gods have ensured that the grain is still swaying on the fields. It's very beautiful to look at—the monsoon sky is tranquil with rain-filled clouds and the entire world is made tender by waving, luscious, green grain—the colour above is deep, and there is a coating of dark colour below as well—the soil is covered everywhere, and the actual colour of the soil can only be seen in the middle of this muddy river water. The river is very muddy. The Padma is carrying along an entire country and many districts; its waters contain so many landowners' estates dissolved in it. The Padma in its terrible mischievousness takes away one raja's kingdom hidden in its deep saffron āncal and deposits it overnight at the door of another—and ultimately, a great fight ensues in the morning between the rajas.

140

Shilaidaha
8 August 1894

Today the entire day —— babu has been away; today the entire day I have heard the sounds of the river. No unnecessary replies have had to be made to incoherent questions. If just one person is present in front of you, you immediately cannot hear half of what nature is saying. I've noticed that nothing is more draining than piecemeal conversation. If you need to keep your strength of thought and strength of imagination alive preceding an act of creation, it is necessary to maintain absolute silence for quite some time. Your own talk completely distracts you. None of you have perhaps ever experienced spending day after day without speaking at all. If you had, you would have understood that in that situation one's ability to be receptive towards what is all around you and the power to enjoy it increases exponentially—for then suddenly one realizes that there are conversations happening on every side, and that we can hear that variety of speech only when we stop our own endless blabbering; today every liquid consonant of the gurgling river seems to be showering the softest affection on every part of my body—my mind today is very solitary and completely silent, and within me, a secret silence reigns stilly, so as to be fit to sit respectfully and affectionately face-to-face with this cloudless, light-filled, crop-swayed, gurgling-watered, generous countryside—I know that when in the evening I pull up the easy chair to the roof of the *boat* to sit there alone, that evening star of mine in my sky will appear before me like a member of my family! This evening of mine on the Padma is a very old acquaintance—when I used to come here in the winter and it would get very late returning from the kāchāri and my *boat* would be tied to the sandbank on the other side, I would cross the silent river on a small fisherman's *dinghy*, and this same evening would wait for me with a serious yet pleased expression; the entire sky would be ready, spread out with a particular peace, benevolence and repose; the still silence of the Padma in the evening would seem to me exactly like my own inner quarters at home. I have a certain human domestic relationship with nature here, a certain intimate familial feeling—which no one knows but me. How true that is cannot be felt by anybody even if I try to tell them. The deepest part of life which is always silent and always secret—that part slowly come out of itself and goes around in the naked evening and naked afternoons here in silence and without fear. Those ancient footsteps seem to leave their mark on the days over here.

We have two lives—one is in the world of men, and the other in the world of thought. Many pages of the life story of that world of thought have I written upon the sky above the Padma. I can see that writing whenever I come here, and whenever I can be alone. When I come here I understand I have not been able to accomplish anything in my poems. I have not been able to express what I have felt. That's because language doesn't belong to me alone—it belongs to everybody, but what I experience with my entire temperament isn't experienced by everybody, so their language therefore cannot express my experience with any clarity.

141

Shilaidaha
9 August 1894

The river is absolutely full to the brim. One can barely see the shore on the other side. The water is bubbling up and boiling in some places, and again in some others somebody seems to be pressing down on the restless water with both hands and ironing out the creases to hang it up to dry. Nowadays I often see the dead bodies of small birds come floating down the current—the history of their deaths is quite clear. They had their nests in the branches of the mango trees in some mango orchard at the edge of a village. They had returned to their nests in the evening and were sleeping, their soft, warm wings gathered together, their bodies tired; suddenly at night the Padma turned over on her side and immediately the soil at the base of the tree crumbled, and the tree fell into the water with all its anxious spread-out roots; the birds, expelled from their nests, woke suddenly in the night for just a moment—and then there was no need to wake any more. The sight of the floating dead bodies of these birds suddenly strikes the heart quite hard. One realizes that the life that we love more than anything has very little value for nature. I've noticed that when I'm in the districts, animals and birds and other living things come very close to me—one doesn't think of one's self as very much different or of a higher status than them. The difference between me and other living things feels trifling in the face of a vast, all-enveloping, mysterious natural world. The deaths of these birds that float by in such neglect don't seem any less important than my own death. In the cities, human society is so complex and human endeavour so bright that man becomes extremely important there—so, cruelly, he does not consider any other life even worth equating with his own. In Europe too, man is so complex and so important that animals are considered to be only animals. Indians don't think twice about the fact that one is a man in this birth and an animal in the next, and then from animal to man again—they feel very strongly that even insects by virtue of being living things are on an equal level with you—that is why in our śāstras pity for all living things has not been discarded as an impossible excess of feeling. When I come to this generous mofussil, and an intimate relationship develops between our bodies, the Indian part of my personality awakens—I can enter into the happiness and sorrow of all living things. If one has to eat the meat of birds simply in order to quell one's hunger, then I'm reminded of our own young ones. Then I cannot unconsciously disregard how keenly the small beating breast of a bird, covered in the softest of feathers, feels the happiness of life. That's why every time I come to the mofussil I feel a real repugnance towards meat-eating, and later when I enter Calcutta society again I turn non-vegetarian once more. There all living things except man become inanimate objects. In the villages, I am an Indian, and when I go to Calcutta, I am a European. Who knows which one is my actual character?

142

Shilaidaha
10 August 1894

Last night, not very late, I was woken by the sound of water. A great tumult and powerful restlessness had suddenly come to the river. Perhaps all of a sudden a new current of water had entered it. This sort of thing happens almost every day. You've been sitting for some time when suddenly you see that with a gurgling, splashing sound, the river has awoken and there is a great celebration all around. If you put your foot on the planks of the boat you can clearly feel what a variety of forces run untiringly underneath it—at different times it either trembles or wavers or swells up or falls with a thud. Exactly as if you're feeling the pulse of the land. Last night at midnight a sudden surge of restless joy came and quickened the dance of this pulse rate quite a bit. I sat for a long time on the *bench* by the window. There was a very misty light, which made the entire wild river seem éven madder. Occasional clouds in the sky. The shadow of a great big flickering star lengthened upon the water for quite a distance, shivering like a shuddering, piercing sorrow. Both banks of the river lay unconscious, shrouded in indistinct light and deep sleep. In the middle, a sleepless mad restlessness flowed on in full force and disappeared. If you wake up and sit like this in the middle of the night, in the midst of such a scene, you feel as if you and the world are somehow in some way made anew, as if the world of daylight and commerce with men had become utterly untrue. Again, waking up this morning, how faraway and indistinct that world of my night seems to have become. For man, both are true, yet both are terribly independent of one another. It seems to me as if the world of the day is European music—in tune and out of tune, in part and in the whole—coming together like a huge, forceful tangle of *harmony*, and the world of the night is our Indian music, a pure, tender, serious, unmixed rāginī. Both move us, yet both are opposed to each other. There's a hesitation and a tremendous opposition right at the root of nature, where everything is divided between king and queen—there's nothing we can do about it: day and night, variety and wholeness, the expressive and the eternal. We Indians live in that kingdom of night. We are entranced by that which is timeless and whole. Ours is the song of personal solitude, Europe's is that of social accompaniment. Our music takes the listener outside of the limits of man's everyday vicissitudes to that lonely land of renunciation that is at the root of the entire universe, while Europe's music dances in different ways to the endless rise and fall of man's joys and sorrows.

143

Shilaidaha
12 August 1894

Are you enjoying Goethe's biography? You will have noticed one thing—that although Goethe was in some respects a very aloof personality, he still had a connection with men, he was absorbed in man. The royal court he inhabited had a living affection for literature; Germany was stirred at the time by certain forceful currents of thought—important thinkers and intellectuals like Herder, Schlegel, Humboldt, Schiller and Kant had arisen in different corners of the country, and both the company of the men of those times and the revolution in thought countrywide were very alive. We wretched Bengali writers feel that lack of man's inner life very keenly—we cannot always keep our imagination alive by supplying it with the provision of truth; our minds do not impact upon other minds and so our compositions remain joyless to a large extent. The people of our country have read so much English literature, but the pressure of thought has not spread corporeally in their bones—there is no hunger for thought in them, no mental substance has taken shape yet within their material bodies, that's why the need for a life of the mind is absolutely minimal in them—yet there's no way one can make that out from their conversation, because they've learnt all the mannerisms of the English language. They feel very little, think very little and do very little work—that is why their company brings no pleasure. If even Goethe needed a friend like Schiller, how do I explain how absolutely indispensable the life-giving company of one real, genuine thinker is to people like us! It is necessary to feel a loving touch, a sort of constant warmth from the presence of human company upon the place where our entire life's achievements stand—otherwise its flowers and fruits do not accumulate enough colour, smell or taste.

144

Shilaidaha
13 August 1894

Although some of my published writing is insignificant, such as what I write only in order to fill up the spaces of *Sādhanā*, still, even there I try my utmost to take as much care as possible. I try to express my inner truth in my writing with an appropriate respect and genuineness—I can never neglect my Saraswati under any circumstance. Recently . . . I read an English article written by . . . a famous *artist*. I disagreed with him on a number of subjects, but I saw that we were alike in two respects. First, that one has to make one's ideal of beauty and one's talent succeed despite the incompleteness of the material world, and second, a fierce desire to express one's self. That doesn't mean wanting to talk about yourself because of conceit; but all that I really think, really feel or really have has to be expressed as truly as possible—that's the only true end—this feeling is absolutely integral to my character—a restless inner force works constantly in that direction. Yet I don't feel that that force is mine alone, it seems that it is an energy spread over the world that works through me. Almost everything I write seems to me to be beyond my own powers—in fact, even my minor prose pieces. Something outside of my own abilities comes naturally and does its own work even in all the logical argumentation that I've prepared beforehand and turns the whole thing into something unthought-of by me. My greatest joy in life is in dedicating myself, enchanted, to that force. Not only does it allow me to express myself, it also makes me feel, makes me love. That's why my own feelings are new and surprising to me each time. The sorts of feelings that arise in my mind when I am in the midst of nature seem to be beyond my own powers, my own character. That's why I feel that I will never be able to explain it to anybody or make them believe it. All my feelings have that ingredient of something that is more than me. In my fondness for Meera I feel the presence of such a limitless mystery that she does not remain just my daughter Meera any more—she becomes a part of the fundamental mystery and beauty of this world, and my affectionate enthusiasm becomes like a meditative prayer. I believe that all our affection, all our love is like a mysterious prayer—only, unconsciously so. Love means the awakened appearance of the inner force of the universe within us—it is a momentary experience of the joy that is at the root of the constant joy of the universe. Otherwise it has no meaning at all. The omniscient power of attraction that ties the entire rotating world together by a single thread is the same force that makes the apple fall from the tree to the ground. That force in the material world is similar to the force of world-enveloping joy in the mind—and we feel love within our hearts and beauty in the world because of that force—the endless activity of joy within the world is what works within my mind as well. If we see the two separately then it has no real meaning any more. There is only one proper answer to the question of why we feel such joy in nature and in man (however minute or restless that joy may be): *ānandāddhyeba khalvimāni bhūtāni jāyante, ānanden jātāni jībanti, ānandaṃ prayantyabisaṃbiśanti.* If you don't understand what this means yourself there's no way you can explain it to anyone else.

145

Shilaidaha
16 August 1894

It's the Śuklapaksha fortnight now, you see, so I get bright moonlight during my walks—then I return to the *boat* and sit down on the easy chair with my legs stretched out. After that little bit of bodily exertion, that chair, that moonlight, that sound of the water, are all bearers of the joys of heaven to me. The river has swollen to the point where its line merges with the shore, so that sitting on the *boat* it is possible to see the entire landscape of shore and river spread out right in front of my eyes. To my south is the expanse of a large field with autumnal rice crops in some places—most of it is green grass, on one side is a narrow path composed by the signs of treading feet, in front of me to the east is the bazaar's barn in front of which hay is piled up in heaps— that worn-out hut and the heaps of hay look very beautiful in the moonlight. The evening—above my head, in front of my eyes, under my feet, all around me—rises with such a beautiful, peaceful, solitary yet full silence, standing close to me like a person with such human intensity, that the entire scene, from the stars in the sky to the distant shadows of the Padma's shores, surrounds me on all sides like a small secret room made for my own secluded comfort—and the two living things within me, me and my inner

---

* A line from the Bhāgabat Gītā, which may roughly be translated to mean: 'God's creation has not its source in any necessity, it comes from his fullness of delight, and then it is his love that creates, therefore in creation is God revealed.' Or, to summarize: 'Joy springs from creation itself, it has no external cause.'

soul, we occupy the entire room and sit there—and all the animals, birds and living things in this scene are incorporated into the two of us—the murmuring sound of the water reaches the ears all the time, the bright hands of the moonlight keep stroking the face, the head, with its affectionate touch, the *cakor* bird in the sky calls out and leaves, the fisherman's boat slips easily through the middle of the Padma on a strong current without any effort, the softly spread-out sky enters my every pore and ever so slowly cools down my heated body—I lie there with my eyes shut, my ears pricked, my body extended, as though I'm the one and only thing that nature cares for: all her hundreds of handmaidens look after me. The imagination too has no boundaries, she too decorates a ceremonial plate with both her hands and comes and stands by my side encircled by a host of shadowy, magical servant girls—I feel the soft touch of her fingers along with the slow breeze running through my hair.

146

Shilaidaha
19 August 1894

This time I have brought the Bengali works of Rammohun Roy with me—it has about three Sanskrit Vedanta books and their translations; I've found them very helpful. Many people are quite convinced by the account of the world and its origins that's found in the Vedantas. As important and highly intelligent a person as Rammohun Roy was a Vedantic, and Doyson saheb too has praised the Vedantas throughout, but none of my doubts have been dispelled. In some respects, what the Vedanta says is simple compared to many other opinions; because one is simpler than two. The words 'creation' and the 'lord of creation' may sound quite consistent and simple, but there's no problem more complex than that for the mind of man. The Vedanta sits there having torn through the *Gordian knot* and brought the two together; whatever else it has achieved, it has certainly reduced the problem by half. There is no creation at all, and we are not there either—there is only one Brahma and perhaps we too are there. The surprising thing is that man can make room in his mind for such a thought— even more strange is the fact that this thought is not actually as odd as it sounds. In fact, it is very hard to prove that anything exists. That Vedantic opinion is nowadays spreading in Europe too, but it's doubtful if it will survive in the water and air of that place. Or maybe it will assume a new incarnation there. Whatever it is, nowadays in the evenings when the moon rises and I sit outside on the *boat* on my easy chair with my legs stretched out and my eyes half shut, and the soft evening breeze keeps touching my overwrought, heated forehead, then this water, land and sky, this murmuring river, the occasional wayfarer upon the shore and the coming and going of the occasional fisherman's *dinghy* on the water, the obscure edges of the field in the moonlight and the distant, almost asleep villages surrounded by rows of trees—all of it appears like a shadow, like *māyā*, yet that *māyā* embraces life and the mind more truly than truth itself—and then it seems that it cannot be that the salvation of the human soul lies in freedom from the hands of this *māyā*. The philosopher may say, the measure in which the world seems to be experienced as *māyā* at twilight is the measure of freedom, and the fact that I continue to derive pleasure from it is actually the pleasure of freedom—that is, that the ties that bind me during the day because I perceive of this world as real become very loose in the evenings when everything becomes shadowy; it is only when I'll be convinced from within that this world is completely and absolutely false that I'll attain a full independence and within that independence attain *brahmmatva*. This is something I understand and feel only very fractionally; maybe one day, before I've reached old age, I'll see that I've achieved freedom from this world.

147

On the way to Kushtia
24 August 1894

Over here the river waters have increased until they've reached the limit—in fact, crossed it by about half a foot—land and water are almost on the same level. The Padma is looking very grand now, absolutely strutting onward, chest extended—the other shore is visible like a single blue line of kohl. Looking out of the window on my right I see dense green fields of crop extending as far as the eye can see, from the window on my left, an endless, generous expanse of water. There is a gentle swaying in the fields of grain on my right, and on my left, from top to bottom, a tremendous, vast, flowing motion. I look at the water and think quite often that if one wants to experience movement as motion alone, separated from its material manifestation, one can find it in the river current. In the movement of humans, animals or plants, there is some movement and some rest, movement in some parts and rest in others. But the river moves from top to bottom—that's why it's possible to compare it to the movement of our minds, our consciousness. Our bodies move partially—the legs move the body—but our minds habitually move in their entirety. That's why the Padma in this month of Bhādra seems like a strong current of mental energy—it moves, builds and breaks like mind's desire; like it, it tries to express itself in a myriad ways through the breaking of the waves and an indistinct sound of song. The fast-flowing, single-minded river is like the desires of our minds—and the still, calm, outspread, diversely green and pleasant land is like the thing of our desires. I am in the middle with my boat; dividing the strong current and lament of desire on my left and the calm beauty of fruition and its gentle rustle to the south. Our *boat* has started off. It runs upon the face of the current. The shore is on the left now—how shall I tell you how beautiful it looks! Very dark blue vaporous rows of clouds bend, with motherly affection, over a very dense quantity of luscious green. Occasionally the clouds rumble with a *guru-guru* sound. One is reminded of the description of the Jamuna in the rainy season in the *Baishnabpadābalī*—many scenes of nature bring the Vaishnava poets' resonant rhymes to my mind— mainly because all this beauty all around is not an empty beauty for me—it is full of the ancient songs of love and togetherness in the history of mankind, as if the līlā of an everlasting heart were being enacted there, as if the eternal Vrindavan of the Vaishnava poets were still extant in this beauty. Those who have internalized the true meaning of the Vaishnava poems will hear the resonance of those poems within all of nature. But most readers do not read the Vaishnava verses in that way—they analyse each verse and each line from the outside in the most critical way, that's why they find fault with them all the time. Those are things that should never attract our attention—the *stranger* sees many things that the close relative does not, so too what the relative sees is not discernible to the keen eye of the *stranger*.

148

Calcutta
29 August 1894

This morning I was sitting and composing a tune for a new song of mine—it's not as if the tune is a very new one, it's a sort of *kīrtan*-type Bhairabī. But still, singing along to a particular rhythm, the intoxication of song slowly infuses all the blood of one's body—the entire body and the entire mind from end to end seem to vibrate and hum like a musical instrument and the beat of the tune seems to travel from my body and mind towards the outer world into which it spreads, and a connection of sound is established between me and the universe. Just as the vibrating string of the bīṇā is a blur when you look at it while it is being played, so too the melody of song fills the whole world with vapour and musical resonance. But as I continued to sing in this way, the time for work passed by, the proofs remained lying there, the clock struck afternoon, the sun's heat and light began to get sharper and penetrate the head—nothing else was accomplished today. On the other side I can hear Renu and Khoka playing on the west veranda with a reverberating toy that makes a cracking, creaking sound, the sound of the crows and sparrows and many other birds are getting mixed together into a directionless sound in the sky, on Madan-babu's lane the hawkers are peddling their wares with a plaintive cry—an unhurried south wind enters and touches me on my back—the myriad different melodies and sounds of Calcutta express a deep melancholy and peace in the afternoon sun. I don't know why my rice hasn't arrived yet—who knows whether the Brahmin cook had discarded the rice ladle this morning to compose a tune—but I can't hear anybody anywhere—it seems as though the servants, their masters and the entire universe have all taken a holiday today.

149

Shahjadpur
5 September 1894

After a long time spent living on the boat, it feels quite wonderful to suddenly alight at the house in Shahjadpur. Large doors and windows, and the light and air entering unrestrained from every side—in whichever direction I look I see the green branches of trees and hear the sound of birds—the moment you step out into the south veranda the smell of *kāminī* flowers overwhelms you, filling every pore in your head. I suddenly realize that all these days there was a thirst inside me for a vast expanse of sky which I have quenched to my heart's content after coming here. I am the sole owner of four large rooms here—I keep all the doors open. The desire to write and the mood for writing come to me here in a way that they don't anywhere else. The outside world seems to enter freely through these open doors like a living influence—the light, the sky, the breeze, the sounds, the smells, the undulating green and my intoxicated mind all come together to keep creating many different kinds of stories. The afternoons here, particularly, are full of a very intense attraction. The sun's heat, the silence, the solitude, the call of birds, especially the crow, and the long, beautiful leisure—all of it entangled together makes me very detached and yet emotional. I don't know why, but it seems as if the *Arabian Nights* had been created on afternoons filled with golden sunlight such as these—that is, those Persian and Arabian countries, Damascus, Samarkand, Bukhara—the bunches of grapes, the groves of roses, the song of the bulbul, the wine of Shiraz—the desert paths, rows of camels, travellers on horseback, the sources of clear water in the shade of dense date palms—towns, sometimes narrow roads hung with awnings, shopkeepers by the road in turbans and loose clothing selling watermelons and pomegranates—a large royal palace by the road, inside, the smell of incense, a large bolster and a brocade throw next to a window—Amina Zubaidi Sufi in puffed pyjamas, gold-embroidered slippers and coloured bodice, a wound-up hookah's pipe rolling on the floor near her feet, a dark eunuch in gaudy clothes guarding the door—and in this mysterious, unknown, far-off land, this rich, beautiful, yet terrible palace, so many thousands of possible and impossible stories about human joys and sorrows and hopes and fears taking shape. These afternoons of mine in Shahjadpur are afternoons for stories—I remember writing the story 'Postmaster' on exactly one such afternoon, on this very table at this exact time, completely absorbed in my own self. I wrote, and as I wrote, the light, the breeze, the trembling branches of the trees all around me, all added their language to it. There are very few pleasures in the world that compare with the happiness of being able to suspend one's self entirely in one's surroundings and to sit and write something after your own liking. This morning I sat down to write a piece on '*charā*' [children's rhymes]—I was able to immerse myself in it quite completely—and it felt good. Children's rhymes exist in an independent kingdom of their own where there are no rules and regulations—like a kingdom of clouds. Unfortunately, that material domain which has an excess of edicts and laws always follows not far behind. As I was writing, suddenly in the middle, a delegation of clerks and officials arrived like a calamity, making my cloud kingdom fly off in a storm. By the time all their business was dealt with, it was time to eat. There's nothing more inertia-inducing than eating one's fill in the afternoon, it completely overpowers man's powers of imagination and all his heart's propensity towards the higher arts. It is because Bengalis eat so much at lunchtime that they cannot enjoy the intense feel of the beauty of the afternoons—all they do is close their doors, puff on their tobacco and chew on their paan while making satisfying and substantial arrangements for a siesta. With that they grow quite unctuously smooth and plump in the process. But nowhere else in the world does the desolate, tired afternoon spread itself out more silently and immensely upon the monotonous, endless, level fields of crop as in Bengal. These afternoons have made me fervent with feeling from my very childhood. In those days there would be no one about outside on the second floor, and I would lie there quite alone by the open door in the hot wind upon the curved *couch*—and in what imaginings, what unspoken anxieties would the entire day pass!

150

Shahjadpur
7 September 1894

I receive letters in the evenings, and I write them in the afternoons. I want to write about the same thing every day—the afternoons over here. Because I just cannot surmount the attraction they hold for me. This light, this air, this silence enters my pores and mixes with my blood—this is newly intoxicating for me each day, I cannot say enough to exhaust the tender intensity of it. Each śaraṯ afternoon rises up in the same way for me every day—the old appears newly to me every day, and exactly the same feeling I had yesterday wakes in me again today. Nature does not feel the slightest embarrassment in repeating itself every day. It is we who feel embarrassed; we think our language does not have the endless generosity that will allow it to express the same feeling in a new way each time. Yet every poet has always said the same thing in different ways and it is the same thing that has assumed a thousand different forms. Some minor poets have occasionally tried forcibly to be novel—all that proves is that their tiny imaginations cannot experience the everlasting newness that exists within the old, that's why they wander around in search of an outlandish novelty. There are many undiscerning readers who like novelty merely for being new. But real thinkers despise such tricks of novelty for being worthless deceptions. They know for certain that what we really feel can never become old in any age. But the moment a thing is separated from our feeling and comes to us only as knowledge— then and there it becomes inert. Then nobody can rescue it from the hands of certain death. That's why those who say something is beautiful from the vantage point of knowledge, without actually feeling it completely, are wont to exaggerate, and use a lot of force or a lot of novelty when they try to say something—but what they say isn't really new or really forceful. I don't see the need to discuss whether I am a major or minor poet—but I've repeatedly seen that there is nothing in the world that I've been able to put aside. Whatever I once find attractive seems so always, and its newness is intensely surprising to me every day. Nothing is worn out for me if I touch it repeatedly; instead, its brightness keeps increasing each time, yet there is nothing imaginary or unreal about that brightness—I despise artificial imaginings terribly. I see the materiality of all things quite clearly; yet, within that, within all its smallness and its self-dividedness, I see the hint of an indescribable heavenly mystery. With age and experience, the wonder and joy of that mystery increases rather than diminishes for me—it is what makes me realize every day that that which gives me joy is not false in any part, it is not at all negligible, it has an endless truth and joy. If I say this clearly then most people are surprised, but how am I to explain this in words to those who haven't felt these things in their own lives the way I have! They have built small fences of hard and fast rules and sit there quite happily thinking that the little bit of land enclosed by those fences is the entire universe, the light of eternity has never made a dent on their unimportant arrogance. No doubt they're happy, but if there is anything called a soul, then surely such happiness is not desirable, and when I perceive that that rigid worldly happiness is insignificant and I see that sorrow has a certain genuine freedom, I realize that there is such a thing as a soul, separate from all other things.

151

Shahjadpur
7 September 1894

When my writing grows in this way as I keep writing, and when the moment I get out of bed in the mornings I think of the point at which I had left off writing yesterday and from where I should begin again today, then I feel really good—the days seem like an earthenware pitcher full to the brim with my writing that I take home every evening to keep, and that writing's resonating sounds and their echoes linger and keep playing in my entire body and mind. Nowadays, as I journey in the land of children's rhymes, there's no end to the number of scenes and the different joys, sorrows and other emotions that I touch upon as I go. So much so that as I write, sometimes my eyes fill up with tears, and then again sometimes I find myself smiling. Today as I walked I thought to myself: why is there so much joy in this for me? The real thing is that it is when we feel that we express our heart's powers—when I feel a pain in my heart at some old memory, the pleasure in that pain comes from this much, that I can experience that memory, that it comes to me—my heart's ability to grasp is extended from the real to the immaterial, from the present to the past. In fact, we feel able to understand more when we are unhappy than when we are happy, the thought that hurts us appears in front of us more clearly and deeply—that is why it is sorrow that is more prevalent in the domain of *art*. Pity, the appreciation of beauty, love—these are the faculties of our hearts that enable us to attract others; that's why any sorrow or suffering they might embody too has a certain joy; but becoming distressed due to imagined contempt or cruelty makes us hostile, obstructing the free motion of our hearts, that's why those emotions bring no pleasure to us. It is the little bit of tenderness in Othello that attracts us, but towards the end, his barbaric cruelty creates an aversion towards him—it seems to almost exceed the boundaries of *art*. But just as dissonance may sometimes be inserted into the *harmony* of a large musical composition to make it more bright and give it variety, so too in the larger works of poetry there are portions that may be unpoetic; as a result, on the whole perhaps the poetic part may derive more energy—that's why you cannot base your comments on a section of that sort. But still, speaking of myself, I can say that in the higher echelons of literature, I simply cannot make myself want to reread *Othello* or *Kenilworth*.★ The question arises here about whether the joys and sorrows of the material world and the joys and sorrows and pleasures of the poetic world are very different from each other, and if so, why? That's because—the joys and sorrows of the real world are very complex and mixed up. Many things, such as self-interest, physical effort, etc., are entangled with it. The joys and sorrows of the

★ *Kenilworth*: a historical romance by Sir Walter Scott, first published in 1821.

poetic world are purely cerebral; they bear no other responsibilities, self-interest, material obstacles, no bodily satisfaction or tiredness. Here our hearts are able to find the time to feel independently, completely, unadulteratedly—our pleasure in poetry is absolutely immediate; we don't have to arrange an interview with it because we want something or because of our sensuality—although we are subjugated humans imprisoned within our bodies, with the help of our hearts alone we can roam freely in the world of the mind. That's why the pleasure of poetry doesn't take us to the limits of our pleasure in order to return rebuffed, but imparts an un-tired, unsatiated and endless flavour to every pleasure. . . .

Our own thoughts too are very ambiguous for us—we never come to know exactly what we are thinking, half of what we think only god can know. It is when I've tried to express my own thoughts that I've learnt from myself—most of my education has been of this sort; the moment I stop expressing myself, my school closes too. That's why I sit down, impelled by my own need, to keep talking away every day with you.

152

Patishar
10 September 1894

I've been on the waterway since yesterday morning. There are only marshes on every side—the raised tips of rice stalks—the villages, with their few densely packed huts, float in the distance—a mildly fragrant green lichen extends, congealed, up to quite a distance, so that one suddenly mistakes it for land; on that itself, a variety of waterbirds gather. It's a Bhādra day, there's not much of a breeze, and the slack sails of the *boat* hang limply; the boat has moved sluggishly throughout the day, proceeding in the most indifferent manner. The bright sun of śaraṭ falls on this lichen-diffused extensive water-

world, and I sit on a chair near the window with my feet up on
another chair humming to myself the whole day. All the morning
melodies such as Rāmkeli, which seem so absolutely routine and
lifeless in Calcutta, come completely alive in their wholeness
over here the moment you evoke them even fractionally. Such an
amazing truth and new beauty appear in them, such a universal
deep tenderness melts into the air all around, making everything
misty, that it seems as if this rāginī is the song of the entire sky and
the entire earth. It's like a web of magic, like a *māẏā mantra*. There's
no end to the numberless fragments of words that I conjoin to my
tunes—so many one-line songs accumulate and are then discarded
throughout the day. I don't feel like sitting down to systematically
turn them into complete songs. I sit on this chair drinking in the
golden sunlight from the sky while my eyes fall like an affectionate
touch upon the moist lichen's new softness, allowing my mind to
fill up easily and lazily with whatever comes spontaneously to it—I
cannot try any harder at the moment than this. I can remember
the two or three lines in the most simple of Bhairabī rāginīs that I
spent the entire morning continuously reciting, so I'm attaching
an extract as an example for you below —

    ogo tumi naba naba rupe eso prāṇe.
        (āmār nityanaba!)
      eso gandha barana gāne!
  āmi ye dike nirakhi tumi eso he
  *āmār mugdha mudita naẏāne!**

  (Oh, come to my heart in new and newer forms
      [My constant newness!]
    Come as a fragrant song of welcome!
  Whichever direction I look, you come to me
    To my entranced, shut eyes!)

* This is the way the words of the song are written down in the letter. The words
of the song as it appears in the *Gītabitān* have changed a little from this version.

153

On the way to Dighpatia
20 September 1894

The water on the other side of the Padma is receding, but it is time for the water to rise on this side. I can see this on every side. There's no end to the different kinds of waterways we're travelling through—marshes, canals, rivers. Large trees have submerged their entire base in the water and stand with all their branches bent over the water—there are boats tied within dark forests of mango and banyan trees, and the village people bathe there, hidden from sight. Occasionally, a village hut remains standing in the stream, the areas all around it completely immersed in water. There's no way one can see any sign of a field, only the tips of rice stalks raise their heads over the water slightly. The *boat* slides through the rice fields with a scraping sound and suddenly enters a pond—there's no grain there—white lotuses bloom in lotus groves and black kingfishers dive into the water to catch fish. Then again, as we go on, at one place we suddenly enter a small river—there's a rice field on one shore and, on the other, a village surrounded by dense vegetation—in the middle, the full stream of water goes on its winding way. The water enters wherever it can—I don't think you all have ever seen the land so defeated. The village people come and go from one place to another sitting on large, round clay tubs plying a plank of wood for an oar—there's no trace of any roads on the land. If the water increases even slightly, it will enter the houses—and then they'll have to use ladders and live on the upper floors, the cows standing day and night in knee-deep water will die, their edible grass become increasingly scarce, snakes will abandon their flooded holes and come and take shelter in the roofs of huts, and all the homeless insects and reptiles of the world will come to live by the side of men. As it is the villages are dark, enclosed on every side by forest cover—and then on top of that the water enters even there and all the leaves and creepers and shrubs begin to rot, with all the garbage from the cattle shed and people's homes floating around on every side, the water made blue with the stink of rotting jute, and naked children with swollen stomachs and sticklike hands and legs keep splashing around here and there in the water and the mud while clouds of whining mosquitoes hover above the still, putrid water like a layer of fog—the villages in this region assume such an unhealthy, comfortless aspect in the rainy season that one feels nauseated just travelling past them. When I see the housewives getting drenched in rainwater, wet saris wrapped around their bodies in the cold, wet wind, the material pulled up above their knees so they can do their everyday domestic work, patiently pushing aside the water, it is impossible to like what you see. I can't think how men put up with so much hardship and such lack of comfort—on top of this, in every house people suffer from arthritis, swollen feet, colds, fever, there's the continuous whining and crying of boys suffering from an enlargement of the spleen, and they are simply beyond saving—they die one by one. One cannot accept the existence of such neglect, ill health, ugliness, poverty and barbarism in man's places of habitation. We are defeated by every sort of power—we tolerate the depredations of nature, we tolerate the tyranny of kings, and against the intolerable oppressions of the śāstras through the ages we don't have the courage to say a word. Such a race of men should run away from the world and become absolute deserters—they bring the world no happiness, beauty or convenience.

154

On the way to Boyalia
Saturday, 22 September 1894

Today it's cleared up on every side and there's a wonderful sun up, Bob. A small river, a fierce current which, as we pull against it, creates a constant *kal-kal, chal-chal* sound that comes to the ear. After getting wet in the rain all these days, the trees and villages on both sides of the river express such a feeling of leisurely joy in the new sunlight of śaraṭ! Today the memories of bad days have all been completely wiped away from the sky and the earth. As if the world had never ceased to be joyful. This skyful of golden sunlight has spread itself completely over my mind as well—there the home of all my happiest memories has taken on an amazing and magical aspect in this śaraṭ light. When I think that only thirty-two seasons of śaraṭ have come and gone in my life, I find it very surprising—yet it seems as if my memory's path becomes increasingly obscure and misty as it travels towards the beginning of time, and when this cloudless, beautiful morning sun comes and falls upon that large world of my mind, then I seem to be sitting at the window of my magical palace, looking out unblinkingly towards a magical mirage kingdom spread out as far as can be seen, and the breeze that comes and touches my forehead all the time seems to bring with it the entire unclear, mixed, mild fragrance of the past to me. How I love the light and the air! Perhaps because of the appropriateness of my name. Goethe had said before he died: *More light!*—if I had to express a wish at a time like that I would say: *More light and more space!* I've said in one of my poems—

> *śūnya byom aparimāṇ,*
> *madyasama kariba pān*
> > *mukta kari ruddha prāṇ*
> > *ūrdhva nīlākāśe.*

> (The empty sky without measure
> I shall drink like wine
> > Freeing the imprisoned heart
> > Into the blue sky on high.)

I am not yet satiated with what I have drunk of this sky. Many people don't like the fact that Bengal is on level ground, but that's exactly why I like the vista of its fields, its riverbanks, so very much. When the evening light and the evening peace begin to descend from above, the entire unfettered sky fills up like a sapphire cup; when the motionless, tired, silent afternoon spreads out its cloth of gold, there are no obstructions anywhere—there's no other place like this to keep looking and looking, and to fill up one's heart by looking. That's why I love the seashore so much more than the mountains. The day I arrived at the seashore in Puri—with the white sands stretching desolately in one direction, and, on the other, the dark blue sea and the pale blue sky spread out till the limits of one's vision—one can't quite talk about how my entire inner soul had filled up on that day. That's why I had really wanted to build a small house by the sea in Puri and just be there. Even now, that unhomely roar of the waves comes to my ears like a distant dream. If I could travel as sannyāsīs do so easily from one place to another, then I would give myself up into the hands of this unbounded earth and travel once to many other countries. But the sky calls out with both its arms extended and the home too pulls you back by both your hands. A lot of trouble comes from being an amphibian creature. I'm an amphibian in all respects—the world of the mind and the material world both tie me down equally.

155

Boyalia
Monday, 24 September 1894

You've written that those who have a greater power to feel are those who suffer more in this world—there's no doubt about that at all—because the capacity to experience sorrow depends on the ability to feel. But I've frequently thought that whether I'm happy or unhappy is not the last word on the subject for me. Our innermost nature continues to feel and to grow through all our joys and sorrows. Our momentary life and our eternal life may be joined together, but they are not the same—this I can clearly comprehend at times. Our experiences of joy and sorrow in this transient life feed the sources of eternal life. You know perhaps that the green leaves of trees analyse the sun's rays and help in the collection of a substance called *carbon*, and it is that *carbon* which results in fire when we burn trees. The leaves of the trees spread themselves out in the sun and dry up and fall, and then new leaves grow—the transient life of the tree is experiencing the sun and then drying up and falling in the same heat—the eternal life of the tree is gathering an unburnable eternal fire within it. Our leaves of every day, every moment, too spread themselves on every side to experience the joys and sorrows of the world as they flow, and then, burnt by the heat of those joys and sorrows, fall one by one, but our eternal life cannot be touched by those momentary flames—it continuously keeps collecting that energy within itself in an unnoticed and unconscious way. The tree whose leaves are not green is not a tree of the highest class, and its store of *carbon* too is negligible. The man whose ability to experience the everyday joys and sorrows of each moment is poor also does not burn, and his reserves for eternal life too are extremely insignificant. His transient life stays protected from the heat of life's joys and sorrows and he lives for longer—that is, one often sees that the small social world of the day-to-day, the narrow limits of a narrow way of life are enough for him; this doesn't dry up or fall off. They keep the transient relatively stable by covering it in insensitivity; they keep a small number of days so fresh that you would think them eternal; they turn the insignificant business of life into something extraordinary. But life has a rule of checks and balances everywhere which is called '*the law of compensation*'. If you try to protect your everyday to keep it alive, you turn your eternity into a dead thing. Those who are completely satisfied with themselves within the narrow boundaries of the material world, those worldly, materialistic men are healthy and happy in the transient world, but the deep joy of eternity is beyond their imagination, outside their conception—they think of it as the rhetoric of poetry; they don't believe in it with all their hearts. That's why they think it is their life's mission to forsake the happiness that is not of this world and the unhappiness that is of it, and nobody can make them believe in a higher ideal than this, to make them understand that 'Even those who are suffering from the greatest of sorrows are no more an object of pity than you are.' I don't know if I've made myself clear to you, Bob. The real thoughts of our minds live so far inside that to articulate them properly, to make someone else see them in their true form is very difficult—that's why initially one hesitates to even try. That which is the deepest truth above all for me—that which lives in the innermost sanctum of our lives—that's something we express unconsciously and fragmentarily in many forms, many words and many deeds. But to make it discernible to someone else all at the same time, in fact even to one's self, is very difficult—one is afraid if perhaps the thing that is completely true for one's innermost being may take on an imaginary aspect once it tries to emerge from within.

156

Boyalia
24 September 1894

I'm ashamed to admit it and it makes me very unhappy to reflect on it, but human company usually makes me terribly uncomfortable, it keeps chafing away at me inside—I want to be like everyone else, to mix easily with everybody, to be happy with simple pastimes and amusements—I keep lecturing myself about this at great length every day, but there is such a barrier surrounding me on all sides that I am unable to cross it however much I try. I am a new creature among men, I never become completely familiar with them—I'm very distant from even those I have been friends with for a very long time! Since I'm a naturally distant person, I find the forced proximity of men for social reasons very tiring. Yet it's not as if it's natural for me to be completely removed from the company of men; I feel like dropping into the midst of gatherings from time to time—to see what sort of work goes on in which places, what revolutions are taking place—I too feel like participating and helping with those—the warmth of life that comes from human contact seems essential for the mind to stay alive. These two opposing impulses come together when you're in the company of those who are like your very close relations, who don't wear down your mind by rubbing it the wrong way; in fact, they give joy, and so help the mind to work enthusiastically and easily in all its natural activities.

157

Boyalia
25 September 1894

Think about it, when we undertake a very major kind of self-sacrifice, why do we do it? A noble passion then separates our insignificant transient life from ourselves, and its joys and sorrows cannot touch us any more. We suddenly see that we are greater than the sum of our joys and sorrows, that we are free from the insignificant bonds of our everyday lives. The principal rule of our everyday life is the effort we make to attain happiness and to avoid unhappiness; but, occasionally, a time comes when it's possible that we discover a place within us where those rules don't work—where sorrow is not sorrow and happiness is not even counted among the things we aspire towards—where we are beyond all the small rules, independent. Then we derive a certain pleasure from defeating our transient lives, we exult in making a garland of our sorrows to

wear—we think that it is the strength of our inner independent
manhood that allows us to attain, through the joy that resides within
all our joys and sorrows, the accomplishment of our character. But
then again society, the company of men and everyday conversations,
hunger and thirst, grow strong all around us and hide that innermost
independent field from our eyes—it becomes very difficult to release
ourselves completely and self-interest appears more forcefully again.
The principal difference between great men and lesser men is that
great men manage to live in that field of independence within
themselves, that inner sanctum of eternal life, for most of the time,
while for lesser men that place remains inaccessible and unknown
most of the time. Bob, when I stay alone in the mofussil, the inner
beauty and joy of nature opens the door to my self's concealed abode
of joy, and unites the outer and inner worlds, and then the figure
of the immediate world recedes into the far distance—just as the
melody of a song confers immortality upon its insignificant words,
so too the material manifestation of the everyday world attains an
eternal splendour through the inner eternal rāginī of joy present in
the world of my mind. All our relationships of love and affection
then glow with the essence of a humble, self-forgetful dharma of
meditation—it's not as if the sorrowfulness of sorrow goes away, but
it seems to cross the limits of my self-interest and spread out across
such a vast sky that a beauty seems to emanate from therein—just as
the light at sunset casts a melancholy shadow over the land, water and
sky, but there is yet a cool, soft joy of beauty mixed in it. This time
on the boat I wrote a poem called 'Antaryāmī' [The God Within]
in which I have tried to express these thoughts about my inner
life to some extent. I don't know if I've been successful, because
expression doesn't always depend only on the writer's abilities, but
also upon the reader's experiences. Sometime ago I received a letter
from you where you expressed this inner life of yours and it made
me very happy—I'm sure there are many occasions when you have
experienced the true manifestation of your inner self, but you don't
want to express it because you don't believe in yourself. You have

doubts about whether these occasional feelings are true or if it is the insignificant everyday which is true. Don't have such doubts, Bob. Because if you doubt the truth then often that is tantamount to destroying the truth. If we mark those auspicious moments of our lives when we feel ourselves to be much bigger than ourselves, then, with the help of our memory, they become resources for us, guiding us in the future in the right direction. It is because I have made my radiantly beautiful moments of joy figurative through language again and again that the path of my inner life is slowly becoming more accessible—if those moments had been spent in transient enjoyment then they would have always remained like obscure and distant mirages, they would not gradually have become clear as the expressions of a firm belief and definite feeling. For a long time now, consciously and unconsciously, the inner life of the world, the inner life within our lives, the celestial nature of love and affection have taken form for me by being marked in language—my own words have been of help to me—I would have never have got so much from the words of others.

158

Calcutta
29 September 1894

It's very surprising, but nowadays when I hear my poems being praised, I don't feel as happy as I should. Actually, that's because I don't entirely grasp that the person who is being praised by people is the same person who writes the poems. I know I haven't been able to write all the good poems I've written just because I wanted to—if a single line in them gets lost, I doubt I'd be able to reconstruct it, however hard I try. The moment I hear praise, I wonder if I'm equal to it—perhaps the best writing I've done will never be bettered. Because the power that makes me write is outside of my abilities. I'm sending you a review that appeared in one of the papers. This person has played quite an *original* hand. He's abused my poems, but praised my short stories to the sky. There's another group of people who travel along the exact opposite route. I'm left sitting in the middle, both puzzled and amused. As long as I'm a writer there's no end to the number of different opinions I will have to hear. And then again, there's another group of people who say that all the rest of my work will be short-lived, it's only the songs that will ensure my immortality among men. I think to myself, if fame is the ultimate aim of man's ambition, I don't need to worry—I've been sitting around throwing stones into the darkness of eternity; out of the whole lot, you never know, one might hit the mark. But it's one thing to hit the mark by fluke just once, and another thing to hit it for all time. No one can say what will endure eternally and what will not, and I too don't want to enter into any sort of argumentation about it—for a writer, true immortality is when you yourself experience a joyful feeling of success. Unfortunately, that joy is felt to a greater or lesser degree by almost all writers, from the very best to the very worst.

159

Calcutta
5 October 1894

All the rain and storm came to an end yesterday. A beautiful sun is out this morning. The morning breeze today has the slightest nip of winter in it, just enough to make you shiver. Tomorrow the Durga Puja starts, so this is a beautiful preamble to it. When ripples of joy flow through all the people of the country* and in

* Rabindranath uses the word *deś* throughout to mean Bengal.

every home, then even if you don't belong to the same society, that
joy touches your heart. Day before yesterday on the way to Suresh
Samajpati's house in the morning I saw images of Durga, ten hands
aloft, being built in the courtyard of almost every mansion—and
all the boys of the houses all around had become very restless.
Observing this, I thought how both the young and the old in the
country all become like children for a few days and together begin
to play with dolls on a very large scale. If you think hard about
it, all the higher pleasures are comparable to doll-playing, in the
sense that there is no ambition or profit in it—if you look at it
from the outside it seems like a sheer waste of time. But something
that brings a feeling of joy, a huge enthusiasm, to the people of the
entire country can never be wholly barren or insignificant. There
are so many people in society who are hard and dry and worldly,
for whom poetry and song are all completely meaningless, yet even
they are affected by the pervasive feeling of anticipation for the
festival and become one with everybody else. Surely this deluge of
feeling every year *humanize*s men to a large extent; for a few days it
engenders a feeling of such empathy and softness in the mind that
love, affection and pity can easily germinate there—*āgamanī*, the
songs of *bijaẏā*, the meeting of friends, the melody of the nahabat,
the śaraṭ sun and the transparent sky, all of it together composes
a joyful poem of beauty within the heart. In the article this time
on '*meẏeli chaṛa*' [womanly rhymes], I have said in part that the
joyfulness of boys is the ideal of pure joy. They are able to take an
insignificant pretext and imbue it with the fullness of their mind's
feelings—children make an ordinary, ugly, incomplete doll come
alive with their own life force and their own joys and sorrows. The
person who is able to preserve that power until he's older is the one
we call a thinker. To him, all the things around us are not merely
things that are visible or audible, but are full of an inner significance
as well—their narrowness and incompleteness made complete by a
song. You can't ever expect that sort of capacity for thought in all
the people in a country, but at a time of festivity such as this, most

people's minds are overflowing with a stream of feeling. Then, that which we see from afar hard-heartedly as a mere doll is dressed by the imagination and sheds its doll-like form; then such a vast feeling and life moves through it that every person in the country, whether appreciative or not, is anointed with that holy stream of bliss. Later, when the doll becomes a doll once again, they throw it into the water. All things in the world are like that doll. Those whom we love may only be a person of a particular look or form to others, but to me they may be lit from within by an amazing light; to me they may seem endless and eternal. Those who lack an ear may think of song as merely sound, but to me, that same sound is song. To those who cannot see the beauty of this earth, the earth is a lump of mud encircled by water. But that same lump of mud encircled by water for me is the world. So if you look at it one way, all things are dolls; but if you look at it from the heart, through your imagination, you recognize them as gods—there's no limit to them. And so, if I were to think of her, who has occasioned every person in Bengal to be moved by joy and devotion, as a mere clay doll, I'd only betray a want of feeling in myself.

160

Calcutta
7 October 1894

I too know, Bob, that the letters I've written to you express the many-hued feelings of my heart in a way that hasn't been possible in any of my other writings. Even if I wanted to I couldn't give these to the people to whom I give my published writings. I just don't have it in me. When I write to you it never crosses my mind that you might not understand something I may say, or may misunderstand it, or disbelieve it, or think of those things which are the deepest truths to me as merely well-composed poeticisms.

That's why I can say exactly what I'm thinking quite easily to you. When I know in my own mind that my readers don't know me very well, that they won't quite understand a lot of what I want to say, nor will they try to understand it empathetically, that they won't accept on trust all the things that don't match their own experiences, then the heart's emotions don't want to flow easily in language, and whatever little is expressed is often substantially disguised. Therefore I feel that our highest expressions cannot be given to anybody at will. That which is deepest, loftiest or innermost within us is beyond our reach; we don't have the power to gift it or sell it; if we weigh it up and try to sell it then all you get is the outer cover, while the real thing slips away from our grasp. How many people in the world have been able to leave behind that which is their very best? How many have even managed to grasp it? That's why I don't believe in autobiographies. We reveal ourselves by chance; we cannot divulge ourselves to others even if we want to or try to—it's beyond us to express ourselves even to those we spend every hour of the day with. It's not just because you've known me for a very long time that I'm able to express my feelings to you; you have such a genuine nature, such a simple love for the truth, that the truth expresses itself spontaneously to you. That's by your particular talent. If the best writings of any writer are to be found in his letters alone then we must surmise that the person to whom they are written also has a letter-writing ability. I have written letters to so many others, but nobody else has attracted my entire self to themselves in writing. One of the main reasons for that is that different people are of different sorts, with different ways, and one has to navigate through those differences when one communicates. One's words are quite easily broken and bent by the time they reach people set in their own ways—and they too see everything in their own way—so that people around them reveal themselves to them only in their own measure. Your genuineness has such a simple transparency in it that it reflects the truth quite unhindered. That German girl who was happy to tell

you all her innermost thoughts—that was because of your own
natural, calm clarity. You have the ability to easily attract the truth
to yourself. By truth I mean the genuine, innermost thought, the
thought that we don't even always know ourselves—not just chatter
and gossip and conversation and laughter and fun. The letters that
Byron wrote to Moore expressed not merely Byron's character,
but Moore's character as well—however well written those letters
might be, Byron's innermost nature is not completely revealed in
them; they've acquired a particular form by bouncing off Moore's
character! Both the person who listens and the person who speaks
are together responsible for the composition—

'*taṭer buke lāge jaler dheu,*
     tabe se kalatān uṭhe.
bātāse banasabhā śihari kaṅpe,
     tabe se marmar phuṭe.'

(The waves beat upon the shore's breast,
     Only then does its murmur rise.
The assembled woods tremble in the wind,
     Only then does that rustle materialize.)

161

Calcutta
9 October 1894

The śāstras say that we have been constructed in several layers. For
instance—there's the strata of food, of life, of the mind, of science
and of joy. When I am in Calcutta, it's the strata of food and of
life that take over the most forcefully, overwhelming all the other
finer instincts. Like the majority of Bengal's people, I too eat and
drink and sleep and roam around and chat, made completely inert
by being trapped in the material web of everyday routine—the

leisure or the inspiration required to think, feel, imagine or express my feelings slowly departs—all of it seems to get rice-smothered. Yet, within me, day and night, a constant niggling feeling of restlessness persists—the weight of inertia becomes unbearable with every passing moment. Plain living and high thinking is actually my ideal. Comfort, dressing up or small habitual practices seem to smother me like a heavy feather quilt on a hot night. When all around you it's quite simple and empty, one can give the mind some space, otherwise the more the furniture and the servants and the arrangements multiply, the more the mental vista's *perspective* is obstructed until comfort becomes more plentiful than joy. I like the thought of what one hears of Japanese home decor—a single spotlessly clean bamboo mat, a single-flower arrangement in a vase upon a wall—no other furniture crowding around. If you want to give your eyes some pleasure, then make your arrangements so that when you open the windows you have boundless sky and beautiful trees all around. It's very tiresome to surround yourself on all sides with meaningless furniture—because if things are going to become the master then that's unbearable for the mind. I'm beginning to think of escaping from here. I'm planning to go to Bolpur quite soon. I can quite see that when I go there and sit by myself in the large easy chair on the carriage veranda on a śaraṯ evening, smoothing out my creased inner self and spreading it upon Bolpur's horizon-extended green fields, my entire life will be anointed by the deepest peace.

162

Calcutta
Thursday, 11 October 1894

I've spent this beautiful śaraṯ morning lying quietly on a *couch*—the plants and shrubs in my flowerpots were trembling in the lovely breeze that came and touched my body. I really just wanted to lie there and have somebody in the next room play some pieces one after another on the piano as they pleased. And that Chopin of mine would be one of the pieces played. Even if a desire of this sort remains unfulfilled after you wish for it, there's a sort of happiness in the desire itself. The greatest suffering is when you don't even feel that desire—that's when the mind has becomes inert and heavy. There's a continuous music in nature which works within our minds in the form of an extraordinary anguished desire when we compose music—those desires have a beautiful rāginī of their own, like a very tender, melodious morning song—and that rāginī then makes even those unfulfilled desires peaceful and charming. It is when nature's music resounds desolately in the far-distant shadows of the mind and finds no returning echo that the mind really becomes joyless, inactive and inert. Then, even if there's no particular sorrow in your heart, its weight presses down on you like an immovable heavy stone. . . .

The bīṇā was played quite wonderfully. Somewhat as that Badri had done—the melody seemed to be wrung out of it heart-wrenchingly, and occasionally the *jhaṅkār* [resonance] of all the strings, from the minor to the major, being struck all at the same time created a fast-paced sequence of waves that played upon the mind from one side to the other and left, and then again after a while, a very slow, tender, faint rustle seemed to smooth out those waves with a pair of soft hands right up to the farthest horizon of the mind and leave. Who will comprehend all the various things the instrument was speaking of—it was as if it nestled up to your breast and unburdened itself of all it wanted to say—at times, when the generous pity of the deep manly tones of the bass strings broke upon you, one felt that the world was completely false and that it was so full of an eternal sorrow and limitless beauty exactly because it was false, and that was why it contained so many rāginīs, such modulations. . . .

After staying up last night, this morning I lay on the couch, tiredness in my limbs—that's why to my half-shut eyes, the sun and the trembling of the plants and the breeze upon my tired body felt so sweet. The śaraṯ morning today seemed to shimmer, full to the brim with memories of the idols' immersion and the festivities; as if all those melodies of the nahabat that had stopped playing had silently spread themselves across the clear sky, and the vacant, sighing tiredness and lassitude engendered by the ending of the festival has today therefore melted into the śaraṯ sun and spread itself out over the entirety of the land, water and sky, wrapping it in a silent melancholy.

163

Calcutta
17 October 1894

Yesterday I was talking with B—— about the 'meẏeli chaṟā' essay. He was saying he couldn't understand why I wanted to lecture ordinary folk on such an insignificant and pointless subject. I asked him, why did Kalidasa write *Śakuntalā* and why has that endured till today? There are so many ways of looking at all the big and small things that exist around us and that arrive at every moment, and one can discover so many kinds of joy in them, that they constitute the most important subjects for our analysis. The education that makes the human mind conscious and gives it the strength to experience the world in many ways is the most valuable education of all. Literature has no other palpable result except that it makes the character of man more sentient—that is, it makes man's nature larger, so that it extends its domain to regions that were outside its purview before. The ability to receive is a far greater strength than any immediate result—that's why in literature one doesn't pay as much attention to the subject as to the composition, the imagination, the expression. But I'm not very sure that B—— quite understood all these thoughts.

164

Bolpur
18 October 1894

We arrived in Bolpur yesterday in the evening. This morning, I
woke up at dawn, had a bath, and came and sat in the south room;
all the lassitude in my heart seems to have been dispelled. The
mornings are so deeply quiet and beautiful and bright that I feel as
if my mind has been completely immersed in a clear and cool light
and emerged clean and cured. A plate heaped with *śiuli* flowers
as new as childhood and as expressive as youth has been kept by
my side—the *śarat* sun falls upon the veranda, the bed sheet is a
glimmering white, everything is clean and empty, no crowds, no
everyday chores, bird call to be heard, and where the row of trees
up ahead ends, a great deal of green expanse can be seen. Sitting in
the south room over here it feels like it used to in the sun-warmed
veranda at Simla, where the deep blue, leaf-covered landscape
seemed to appear right in front of your eyes, your breast and your
body as you stood there. It's not exactly alike, but the same peace
and beauty descends slow upon the mind. It's as if all of you are
present in the next room as you were there, with your affection and
your care ready and waiting for me. For me, that affection of yours
has now melted into the landscape—this *śarat* morning's slow, cool
breeze contains your caring, affectionate touch. It's so completely
silent all around, Bob! It's as if this endless, clean, refreshing blue
sky silently embraces my inner soul alone. And the soft, plump
whiteness of the *śiuli* flowers seem to rain down tenderness upon
my eyes. If my god separates me from all the chains of my routine to
exile me here, I can calmly, quietly and completely immerse myself
in the sky outside and my own inner self and get on with my own
work. . . . I feel like throwing myself down upon the mattress in
——'s room with a pencil and an exercise book and begin some
piece of writing. The morning is quite calm and new, perhaps its

best to start now. . . . My mind is so replete that it seems I can almost touch her, hear her tone of voice very close by.

165

Bolpur
Friday, 19 October 1894

Yesterday all I did was lie down flat upon my stomach on the bed to write a small poem and to read a book about travels in Tibet. I really love to sit alone in secluded spots like this one and read travel books. I can't touch novels in places like these. Alone in this first-floor room with all the doors and windows open and a mattress laid out, amidst such empty fields and forests of śāl, the tender sound of birds filling the dreamlike śarat afternoon, an English novel is so completely out of place. The great convenience of travel books is that they have a continuous motion, yet no plot—the heart finds an unfettered freedom there. Here the desolate field has a red road running through it—when two or three people or a bullock cart or two move very slowly down that road, all of it has a great pull for me, perhaps because that little bit of motion seems to make the completely motionless desolation all around even more sharply evident—the fields seem to stretch away even more endlessly, and there seems to be no address towards which these people travel. Travel books too seem to similarly draw a faint line of flow and motion in my emptiness of mind—as a result I seem to be able to feel my mind's spread-out, silent, lonely sky even more keenly. The traveller is a Frenchman, that's why he knows both how to travel and how to write. In one place, the man comes from the mountains suddenly upon a desert, and this gives rise to a feeling he calls the 'sensation of the desert'—there he says he prefers this sort of vast desert to mountains and hills:

Solitude is a true balm, which heals up the many wounds that the chances of life have inflicted; its monotony has a calming effect upon nerves made over sensitive from having vibrated too much; its pure air acts as a douche which drives petty ideas out of the head. In the desert too the mind sees more clearly, and mental processes are carried on more easily.

In society or at work the mind disciplines its full strength to assume a much smaller form. But when it wants rest it becomes necessary to provide it with a huge bed extending up to the horizon for it to sleep on; it wants to occupy an entire country all on its own; then it does not find enough space for itself in the entire city, it cannot make do without a free sky and meadows and seas. I doubt that any English traveller would have found this 'sensation of the desert' exactly happiness-inducing. Almost all the English travel books I have read display their proud, brutish nature and their arrogance. They're unable to do justice to other races or love them. Yet god has given them the responsibility of looking after a greater variety of races than he has to almost any other.

166

Bolpur
Saturday, 20 October 1894

Clouds have gradually been accumulating since last night. But there's also some sun. Heaps of black clouds have gathered on the margins of the sky, and in the light of the sun their borders have turned a silvery white. All around the fields the new crop of *āman* rice has assumed a dark and luscious green colour, and the cool lustre of the clouds above it looks lovely. I remember when I first came to Bolpur with Bābāmaśāẏ I was about nine or ten years old—I had never seen rice fields before, and I was very curious to see them. We reached Bolpur at night; while travelling to the house in a palanquin I didn't look out properly on either side in case my curiosity was dispelled to some extent in that unclear evening light. The moment I woke up at dawn I came outside and looked—but there were only fields all around, no sign of any rice plants anywhere. In places, the ground had been dug up; I heard that was where crops had been grown. At that time, I had so much curiosity bottled within me like corked *champagne*—now I've seen more or less everything of the world, yet the joy has not lessened, rather its intensity has increased even more. That first sight of Bolpur—I remember so many things about it. I used to write poetry even then. I had an idea that if you wrote poetry under a tree with the open sky above you, you were accomplishing something truly poetic. That's why I woke up at dawn and with an old *Letts' Diary* and pencil in hand, sat under a small coconut tree in one corner of the garden and wrote a heroic poem called '*Pṛthvīrājer parājaẏ*' [The Defeat of Prithviraj]. It took me about seven days to write it. Where's that diary, and where's the poem now! I don't remember a single line of it. I only recall that Baṛ-dada had liked that poem. I was very particular in those days about exactly how a poet should be—in the afternoons I would sprawl in the shade of a cave in the khoẏāi region across the fields, a faint trickle of water flowing across the sand in front of me, and I would feel like a real poet. Small clusters of dates would be ripening on wild date trees—you couldn't possibly enjoy eating them, but still, to think that I was plucking wild dates from wild date trees by myself at the edge of the desert and eating them made me feel very proud. There was a small pond in the khoẏāi called Āmānidobā which had small fish in it—I'd take off my clothes and go and jump into it and believe that I was bathing in a waterfall. No people around anywhere, no regulations, no discipline; I would spend the entire day playing the poet by myself in those caves within the fields—some days I would feel scared of dacoits, but there was poetry even in that fear. It's true that I still write poetry, but I don't think of myself any more as a poet described in history or in novels—in fact, when I read my own poetry I don't feel as if I've written it; almost as though I write good poems by accident, not because I want to. Whatever else may happen, it's impossible for me sit under a tree and write poetry any more; I get distracted too easily.

Anyway, if I ever find that *Letts' Diary*, I'd like to sit once more at dawn under that coconut tree in the garden and reread 'Pṛthvīrājer parājaẏ'.

167

Santiniketan
Tuesday, 23 October 1894

It's become progressively cooler since day before yesterday, making everything all around even more pleasant. That tired air the breeze had seems to have gone. In the mornings when I come and sit here after a bath in clean clothes and this cool morning breeze touches my body, it is as if it collects a little more calm—the light that comes and falls upon the eyes seems anointed by refreshing dew and full of the cool smell of śiuli flowers. The skies are blue, the plants and trees shimmer, the green rice fields in between seem wrapped in the soft, pale light of the sun, there's no saying from how far away the wind comes unobstructed across the fields, kissing the dew-wet tips of grass—one cannot say where the desolate red road winding across the middle of the empty fields came from or where it is going—in the midst of all this, I'm sitting here overjoyed, submerged in a flood of ice-clean *hemanta* [autumn] light, greeted in body and mind by the dew-wet breeze, a plate piled high with śiuli flowers in front of me—there's no one to disturb me here, all three rooms on the first floor are entirely my own and all eight hours of daylight are for my independent use alone. The large, clean white bed with its pillows and bolsters in the bigger middle room seems to be waiting for my convenience—I feel like a proper *nabāb*. Remember Satya had said to me, 'There's an air of luxury about you, like the Muslim nabābs'?

That's not entirely true; in the sense that my nabābi is a mental nabābi—there, in my own kingdom, I don't want any restrictions on me, I want an unchecked right in my domain. But the sort of nabābi that the nabābs indulged in was something that obstructed mental nabābi; it required so many possessions and trappings and people and foot soldiers and equipage and outfits that that entire heap of material things simply smothered the mind and killed it. I try and escape the tyranny of things at every opportunity—if it's constantly excited and amused, my inner self becomes secretly rebellious; there seems to be somebody there within myself who becomes jealous the moment I'm seen in proximity with the outside.

168

Santiniketan
Wednesday, 24 October 1894

Truth be told, when you concentrate properly on managing an estate, its intoxication slowly takes over. One then gets completely absorbed in many different sorts of inquiries, instructions and planning for the future. I would perhaps have been ashamed to admit to such an unpoetic fact at the time when I used to sit in the coconut groves with my torn *Letts' Diary*, writing 'Pṛthvīrājer parājaẏ'. But the expression of emotion and the work of business have a certain unity, and that's where they give pleasure. There's a great happiness in turning the incipient into the realized, the incomplete into the complete, in creating order and design from *chaos*. If, despite all the obstacles, you can express your thoughts in a well-rounded way, you experience the pleasure of creation; and in a large jamidāri estate, if you can exercise certain rules and impose some sort of order, that too gives you a similar feeling of pleasure. There's a certain satisfaction, of course, in the increase in revenues, but the greater pleasure is in the fact that the job is being done well.

I firmly believe that if I had come back as a *barrister* or a *civilian*, I would have been immersed in my designated work, and wouldn't have felt it necessary to pay any attention to literary writing. My entire attention would have been constantly occupied with the nitty-gritty of the finer points of the law, with cutting through the arguments of the opposing side, with constructing an organized history and opinion from disorganized witness statements, and I would have derived a particular pleasure and self-forgetfulness from these things. Thank god I didn't come back as a *barrister*!

169

Bolpur
25 October 1894

There has been intense rain since last night. There was fierce wind and pounding rain all night—this morning the wind has abated, but the skies are clouded over and it's raining. As it is Bolpur is deserted, but on top of that a dark curtain of cloud has been drawn across the stage of the sky, making it seem even more deeply solitary. You can hear the running sound of rain upon the leaves of the trees. On such a day as this, does one feel like writing a *political* essay on the Hindu–Muslim riots! I've been sitting here since early morning with a restless, absent air, turning over the leaves of the *Padaratnābalī*, and in an imagined kingdom of separation and togetherness called Bṛndāban I can see—

> Daylight has been submerged in the sky
> One cannot tell if it is day or night
> The trees sway in the wind on every side
> Fine drops of rain fly clamouring through the air everywhere
> The fair maid walks on the city path
> In temple after temple, the doors close.

On a rainy day, every house has shut its doors as Gauri walks on an empty, cloud-covered road through Bṛndāban—the trees and plants sway in the restless breeze, and drops of rain scatter and fly in the air across the universe—there is no sign of where the sun has sunk to, and day and night are as one. I've been wanting to write an essay explaining exactly where the attraction of Vaishnava poetry lies, but let it be today—today I have to finish a half-completed *political* essay. . . . God alone knows of what use writing it will be. The Bhāgabat Gītā says that we have a right only to action, not to the fruits of action—that is, we must work without thinking about the results we may or may not obtain from it. In our country we must work knowing we'll never get any results.

The rain is pressing down harder with the passage of morning— in the darkness of the cloud and rain it's difficult to tell whether the morning is moving on or not, it's as if time has taken the entire day off today. In my childhood when I used to study at the Normal School the teacher would stop teaching on rainy days such as this when the room would become too dark—though we couldn't leave the classroom, still, we'd shut our books and joyfully take pleasure in the sound of the rain and the clouded darkness. Perhaps it's because of that old habit that even today on a rainy day such as this I feel like taking leave from the hard *schoolmaster* named duty and shutting all the manuscripts and books to be free to follow my own whims in my own way. But the publishing deadline for *Sādhanā* looms, and I simply must try and finish the *political essay* today as best I can.

170

Bolpur
Friday, 26 October 1894

You're completely wrong if you think from far away that nowadays by mingling freely with people, conversing and socializing, I've become quite the swaggering *public man*. Ducks and fish are two different species altogether, although the duck may occasionally dive into the water and the fish may leap up to gulp down a mouthful of air. From a distance I sometimes think that this time I'm going to really mix with people and go around participating in all their work and political agitation, but all of that stays only in the imagination. Just like imagining that one is cutting across a choppy sea with sails aloft and breeze behind—yet of course all one's nerves go for a toss in an instant when you are on choppy seas—similarly, my soul is afflicted the moment I spend time in the agitations of a sea of people, and then I have to return to my own solitary space with twice as much eagerness as before. . . . You've written that if I mix with people I could achieve some good by virtue of my *personal influence*. But *personal influence* is disseminated differently by different people—some may take people along the desired path by being present, by speaking to people and by dint of character, others may capture people's hearts by staying out of sight and by expressing the best part of their nature as beautifully as they can. Those minds that are sensitive to all sorts of impressions, those whose nerves vibrate and resound with every blow, big or small, are people who can never be influential by living in the midst of people—in fact they do more harm than good, and so destroy their power to influence—they need to run away from society and conceal their own joys and sorrows and pain within themselves completely so that they can spend their lives working safely in solitude and calm—only then will the glory of their work be safeguarded. Otherwise, why should anybody be bothered with trying to understand their real nature after dealing with all the hundreds of problems and obstacles in their lives! It is those who can be aloof and unresponsive to a great extent when in the midst of people who can be influential. That song from '*Māyār khelā*' [The Play of Maya] works in this context as well—

tāre kemane dharibe, sakhi, yadi dharā dile!

(How shall you catch him, friend, if you are caught yourself?)

171

Bolpur
Saturday, 27 October 1894

As it is we're Indian Hindus, and then on top of that if you become fat I suppose you've accomplished a corporeal nirvana! I've observed that one has to constantly try and snub thoughts of renunciation and indifference in one's mind. Quite often, a meditative state will come and ruin whatever enthusiasm for work one has. But again, the problem lies in the fact that renunciation is a very logical thing in this world. It is true that everything is transient, that death mocks every effort of life with a calm smile—it's doubtful whether a race, going against the tradition of its ancestors, can fight against nature and manage to make a success of a very large and ambitious enterprise. All this *philosophy* comes up in the mind on its own.

172

Bolpur
28 October 1894

It isn't eight o'clock yet, but it feels like midnight—everything is very silent and deep asleep—only the sound of the crickets can be heard. I don't know what all of you are doing now and I can't guess either. All those whom we know in the world we know like a dotted line; that is, there are gaps in the middle which we need to fill in as best we can. Even those we feel we know best have to be made complete by our own imaginative powers. There are so many breaks in between, the footsteps on the road are lost, things remain uncertain, unclear and obscure, but still the creative mind wants to put together all the broken pieces and make a whole of it so that it can be kept within one's possession. If even the most familiar people remain as fragmented pieces sown together by our imagination, then with whom or what may we say we are fully acquainted—and, on the other hand, who can say that they know me wholly? Every man is known completely only to his god and disconnected from everybody else. But perhaps because they're at a remove there is space to add our own imagination to them—and that's exactly why in some respects they are even closer to us, perhaps that is why we manage to come together with each other to a great extent. Otherwise, as impure individuals, we are perhaps impermeable to everybody except god. Our own selves too we know only partially, we merely turn ourselves into the heroes of a self-composed story in our imagination—god has kept these gaps so we can use these fragmented materials to construct ourselves by ourselves.

173

Bolpur
30 October 1894

The sort of deep peace and quiet I get at Bolpur would not have been possible anywhere else. Darjeeling's *sanatorium*s are paradoxically crowded, the districts too have work and people arriving all the time, while in Bolpur, there are no duties and there's no disturbance—no sound except the unceasing song of the birds and no visitors on my first floor except for the squirrels. In the afternoons I can hear a drone like the buzzing of bees, and it seems to me as if all the happiest memories of my life have travelled to me from a great distance, borne upon a curious, mixed rustle of sound. The afternoons are so deep and silent and secluded and full that they overwhelm all my heart in whatever I do—writing, reading, thinking—this extensive, vast and piteous afternoon encircles me silently and affectionately. Nowadays, with winter here, the moment my hands and legs feel a little cold I go and sit in the south veranda and nature embraces me like the warm touch of a mother's lap; the sun comes and falls near my feet, the green fields can be seen till the remote edge of the blue horizon, an unceasing humming sound keeps coming from the insects in the trees all around, and it seems as if everybody's affection and care surround me from every side to infuse life into my body.

174

Bolpur
Wednesday, 31 October 1894

The north wind that blows the whole day when winter first starts has begun this morning—the wind comes whistling and the yellow leaves on the rows of *āmlakī* trees fall trembling to the ground, completely covering the ground beneath its feet—the wind dries the skin of your face and the skin on the palm of my hands is peeling. It is as if the jamidār's bailiff is visiting the woods—everything trembles and falls and sighs anxiously. The afternoon sun feels good, it drowns one in a sort of restful melancholy, and the endless cooing of the pigeons from within the dense mango orchards turns the entire field and sky and wind and dreamlike long hours of the dappled afternoon into a song of separation's sorrow—even the sound of the clock on my table seems to have merged with the tender melancholy of the afternoon's rustle of sound. Inside my room, the squirrels run around all through the afternoon. It has become a part of my daily routine to sit lazily for a long time after lunch observing the various ways of these animals. Fluffy tails, a soft, furry body drawn with black and grey lines, two restless eyes like small little dots, and a completely harmless yet extremely busy air—one feels very affectionate towards them. There is a steel-meshed cupboard in the corner of this room in which dal and rice and bread and other eatables are hidden away from these sort of greedy, speedy creatures—they spend the entire day circling around it with their curious noses, searching for an opening. The few grains of dal and rice that remain scattered outside the cupboard are picked up and nibbled at with their small, sharp front teeth and eaten with the utmost satisfaction—sometimes they sit up straight on their haunches and, joining their two small hands together, arrange the tiny bits of grain tidily and conveniently in their mouths—if I move even the slightest bit they immediately raise their tails up on their backs and run off, quick as a flash—on the way out, they might suddenly stop halfway on the doormat and give their ear a quick scratch and then turn back again—in this way the entire afternoon passes with nibbling and racing and the clatter and tinkle of plates, forks and spoons. . . .

I don't feel like leaving this place—when I return to Calcutta, these pleasant mornings and lonely afternoons will constantly come to mind—the peace and beauty of this place will seem so attractive! But what to do! Let's go happily to the workplace, suppressing all selfish desires. The beauty of this place seems to grow even more appealing when it is time to leave; the day today has been flooded by just such a tender rāginī.

175

Calcutta
19 November 1894

I've observed from my childhood onward that those cries of the *pheri*-wallah [itinerant hawkers] have always affected me—the sharp call of the kite in the desolate, silent afternoons too had a great impact; I haven't heard that call for a long time now. I don't think that's because the kite doesn't call any more nowadays, but because I have a lot of work and a lot of thinking to do now—I don't have that same intimate connection with nature any more.

There was a time when I would spend entire afternoons alone on the second floor near the south entrance lying on a *couch*—I would drink in every sound, every shiver of the long afternoons and their inner tender essence to the dregs. Now it's impossible to waste that much time; I think, let me read something or write. Even if I don't feel like harnessing the mind to any particular work, still, one has to try and get some work done, so it becomes necessary then to at least try and read a book, however absent-mindedly. But this is in Calcutta. When you're in the mofussil, just sitting quietly and looking fills your heart with satisfaction, you're not a blind slave to work. There's one sort of work which is tied to one's duties, there's nothing to be said against that, but when there's no immediate work at hand or when for some reason one is unable to do one's work properly, and then if one tries to root around looking for some work merely to pass the time out of sheer habit—and if one cannot be at peace with just oneself, draw companionship from one's surroundings—then one must concede that the situation is quite bad. Work is merely a means to an end. Man is not just an instrument of work. The ability to be at rest in a fulfilled and satisfied way should not be lost—because there is much in it that belongs to a higher humanity. No doubt work is a very good thing, but work has a narrowness about it which conceals man. Day and night are the correct metaphors for work and leisure. During the day, there is nothing for us but the world; it is at night that we establish a connection with the endless universe through the planets and constellations of stars. When we work, we belong to this world, when we are at rest, we are of this universe. When we work we need to see the world clearly in the light of logic, argumentation and science; when we rest, the world's grip must be loosened—then we must see the everlasting connection that we have with eternity as the most important one. Then we should keep all our effort at work at a great distance and feel the intimations of eternity in the ever-present beauty of all the smells, colours and sensations of the world with our bodies and minds.

One shouldn't leave out either of these two modes of being. In the morning when we wake up we should know that we are a person of the world, and when the day comes to a close, we must feel that we inhabit the universe. The vast universe remains forever hidden to those who are too busy with work.

176

Calcutta
Tuesday, 20 November 1894

To continue with the thought I had brought up in yesterday's letter to you, it seems to me that just as day and night have divided work and rest between themselves, so too have people divided prose and poetry in literature into two sections. Prose clearly belongs to work and poetry to an immense leisure. That's why you do not need to say anything necessary in poetry. Our everyday relationships seem to have almost disappeared in the world that is created for us in poetry. If that wasn't so then the ever-present beauty of the world, the world of feelings, would not have been visible to us. When both these things are true in man's life, and both truths, like day and night, cannot be seen together, then there's a necessity for both prose and poetry. That is why poetry, with its metre, scansion and language, has pushed all connection with the everyday world to a distance; in place of necessity, it has introduced beauty—it has tried to convey to us in many ways and through many gestures the news that completely outside of our field of necessity there is an endless ocean of joy extending boundlessly. I was discussing this division between prose and poetry and the need for that distinction with Thakurdas Mukherjee not so long ago. He thinks that in the future prose will become beautiful to the extent that the particular requirement for poetry will be gone. If what was being said had been pure argumentation, it would have been much easier, but because there was a great deal of feeling involved, it became very difficult to explain in conversation. I only said briefly that while it's true that level ground is extremely useful for all our work—nobody can deny that—but when you want to act, you need a separate *stage*; if you come down amidst the audience to perform then the illusion is not created in that way in their minds. The subject of performance must be separated from its surroundings and elevated a little and lit up with lights, scenery and music and held up for display, only then will it succeed in imprinting itself upon the mind in a complete and independent way. The language and metre of poetry is like that *stage* and that music—it is because the subject is separated by being encircled by all that beauty that it's able to have such a powerful and complete impact upon our minds, that's why it can take us out of the surrounding poverty to a land of beauty, and we realize we are no longer in our field of work at first glance itself—we make ourselves ready in an instant. But it's very difficult to explain all this properly. Thakurdas-babu did not seem too convinced with what I said. He seemed to think that it is my prose rather than my poetry that's a great deal more poetic in expression, and in his opinion that's what is more natural. He's asked for some of my most recent books of poetry—perhaps he'll write an essay proving that my poetry is my prose and my prose, poetry.

177

Calcutta
21 November 1894

Aban is sitting in the ground-floor room in that house playing an ālāp on the *esrāj* in Bhairabī which I can clearly hear sitting in the corner room on the second floor of this house.* You too have written in your letter about Matang's Bhairabī ālāp. Nowadays, before you know it, it's ten or eleven in the morning and then noon—as the day grows warmer, the heart too grows equally detached and melancholy; over and above that, when your ear repeatedly picks up the extremely tender, plaintive tug of the Bhairabī, a tremendous feeling of renunciation spreads across the sky and the sunlight. The melting notes of the Bhairabī rāginī extract the eternal, deep sorrow of this work-laden, suspicion-prone world, made sorrowful by separation, and bring it to you. The raga Bhairabī unlocks from within our hearts the tearfulness of the daily grief, fear and supplication that is a part of man's relation with man; it establishes a connection between our pain and the pain spread across the universe. It is completely true after all that nothing we have is permanent; but nature, by some strange magical power, makes us forget that fact all the time, which is why we are able to do the world's work enthusiastically. That eternal truth, that pain of death, finds expression in the Bhairabī; what it tells us is that nothing will remain of what we know, and that we know nothing of what will remain eternally.

178

Shilaidaha
Sunday, 25 November 1894

Go—— has survived this time. I didn't sleep almost the entire night the day before yesterday. His boat was right behind mine—I could

---

* Aban: Abanindranath Tagore, famous artist and nephew of Rabindranath, who lived in the neighbouring Tagore household at No. 5 Jorasanko. His grandfather, Girindranath, was Debendranath Tagore's brother; when Debendranath opted for the Brahmo Samaj, his family resided at No. 6 Jorasanko, while the other branch chose to remain with the household Hindu deity at Dwarakanath Tagore's house at No. 5. Relations between the two houses always remained cordial.

hear his groans from time to time and was distressed thinking that he might die. It was a silent night, and my room was completely dark. Lying there on my bed I kept thinking how the life and death of man was shrouded in a terrible mystery—at times the still, silent, everlasting time surrounding me on all sides seemed very cruel. In relation to it, our lives, our greatest joys and sorrows, our noblest hopes and desires are so insignificant—it matters little to it whether I die today or tomorrow. Whether I die alone or whether a million people die swept away in the floods is also of no consequence. The sun will die out completely one day with its entire solar world and everything will freeze up, but even that is nothing to it—so many such extinguished, dead worlds, concealing their millions of years of life and play, wander around the skies today. Every layer of the earth contains the fossils of so many lost life forms, not a single descendant of theirs is extant today. So I was lying on my bed and thinking to myself, to whom should I say, on behalf of this dying man, in this endless darkness, 'Oh, this poor man is suffering so much'? Who shall understand the value of his life if not helpless people like us? For whom is his pain true? If death is an unavoidable, inevitable occurrence for every living thing, why should one suffer such terrible agony? Unless we think of our most personal and heartfelt joys and sorrows and desires as having an eternal recourse somewhere, a dwelling of eternal empathy, everything seems like the cruellest farce! A son's death takes the form of an absolutely unbearable pain for a mother, but if that has no meaning at all to the eternal, then why this māyā? My love may mean so much to me, but if it has no place at all in eternity, then it is merely a dream. We are doing our utmost for our country, giving our lives for human progress. But our country is a country only for us, that is, greater than the entire world—man is man only for us, that is, greater than all other living things in the world—if you look at it from the outside then these thoughts and, along with them, all our lifelong efforts are totally farcical. Go—'s impending death seemed terribly grave, terribly important to me; but that was only because

I am a man, because I am acquainted with him and near him—was there any real depth or significance in it? Ants die, mosquitoes die all the time, why do we think those deaths to be so insignificant? When a leaf dries and falls, when a lamp is extinguished by the breeze, why aren't those reasons for grief too? They are no less of a change. To eternity, a solar world dying out, a leaf falling, a man dying, are all the same—so all our grief and our joys and sorrows are only our own. I sometimes think that this world is a battlefield of two opposing forces—one of these is within us and trying to live all the time, and the other is attempting perpetually to kill it—if that were not so then death would have seemed entirely natural to us, it wouldn't have seemed in the slightest bit terrible—we were one way at one time, and at another time we have become something else—there would be no sorrow or grief or wonder entangled there. But our nature says from within, 'I want to live', it says 'Death is my opponent—I must conquer it'—yet nobody has ever been able to conquer it. But we go on trying. That's why we feel the pain of death, the grief of death—when the eternal desire of staying alive is repeatedly defeated by death.

179

Shilaidaha
Wednesday, 28 November 1894

This year, the sandbanks are exactly as they were the first year I came to Shilaidaha by boat, when the limits of the sandbanks could not be seen from this shore. The white sands stretch desolately for miles right up to the farthest limit of the horizon; there is no grass, nor are there any trees, houses or anything at all—that time there were a few wild jhāu clumps, this time even those aren't there. You'll never be able to imagine such vast emptiness unless you see it with your own eyes. We are used to the emptiness of the skies and the seas, and don't expect anything else there; but the emptiness of land seems the emptiest of all—no movement anywhere, no life, no variety of colour, not a hint of softness anywhere—not a blade of grass in a place that could have been full of the fluidity of grain and grass and birds and animals—just an indifferent, hard, endless bondage of widowhood—the Padma River flows by on one side, on the other side the ghat, tied boats, people bathing, coconut and mango groves—in the evenings the murmur from the bazaar next to the river can be heard and the rows of trees on the Pabna side appear like a dark blue line—deep blue in some places, pale blue in some, green in some, and in between is this bloodless, deathlike pale white—silent, inert, desolate. In the evenings, at sunset, when I walk upon this sandbank I feel a deep expansiveness and boundless freedom in my heart. Nothing anywhere, nobody around, just me, alone. Everything that I have to say, I can spread out upon this land without a mark or a boundary; I am my own companion, my own happiness, I can make everything on my own. Yesterday I was thinking that when our senses cannot feel anything then our minds feel everything for us, the senses are merely the gateway to the mind, so why should we not think that whatever presents itself to our minds even without the help of our senses is true as well? Or why should we not find an equal amount of happiness from it as from truth? I think that's merely because of habit. From the beginning, we are used to experiencing everything through our senses. Now, even if our minds can independently construct many things with the help of the imagination, unless we feel all our joys and sorrows through our senses we aren't able to enjoy them completely. For instance, it is the mind that writes, not the pen, yet for those who are used to writing with a pen, it isn't possible to organize their thoughts orally in the same way as they can when they sit down with a pen in hand. I definitely think that if we can just concentrate a little and prepare and practise, the materials of the imagination can be used in lieu of the materials of the senses to experience things in the closest, most intimately attainable way. Unfortunately, the powers of the imagination are not always as clear, as detailed or as definite as that all the time. In the mofussil, these powers of mine blossom fully, and I can fill the distance of time and place with my imagination; but in the filth of Calcutta god knows where these magical powers disappear, and my only recourse then is to beg and cry at the door of the senses.

180

Shilaidaha
Thursday, 6 December 1894

Normally on other days it gets quite warm by this time, and one has to take off one's jobbā—today it's exactly the opposite. The wind outside has begun whistling sharply, the river's waters have become restless and make a splashing sound, yet there's no sign of any clouds, the sun is shining brightly, the birds that root around in the mud are jumping around, their tails dancing, upon the muddy banks by the river, and the porpoises are turning a somersault in the water from time to time. If the wind remains like this in the evening too, I won't be able to go for a walk today. I've recently changed my position a little. I've brought the boat to the middle of the river where a sandbank raises its head above the water and have tied it there. Remember that rhyme?—

epār gaṅgā, opār gaṅgā, madhyikhāne car
tāri madhye base āche śib-sadāgar.

(This side Ganga, that side Ganga, sandbank in between
In the centre of it all sits the merchant-man Shiva.)

I'm sitting here exactly like that śib-sadāgar. In the evenings when I go for a walk on the shore I have to take the *jolly boat* and row a short distance; as a result, I get to both row a bit as well as walk. It is the Śuklapakṣa nowadays—as soon as I have walked for a little while, the moonlight blossoms, and the limitless white sands of the sandbank assume such a shadowy, imaginary form that it seems to not be the real world at all—as if it's an amazing manifestation of my own mind. God knows when in my childhood I had once heard a description in a fairy tale told by Tinkari-*dāsī* one night while lying under the mosquito net, '*tepāntar māṭh—jocchonāẏ phul phuṭe roẏeche*'★ [A desolate expanse of field—flowers blooming in the moonlight]—whenever I go walking on the sandbanks in the moonlight I remember those words of Tinkari-dāsī. That night in my childhood I had become very restless hearing this one description of Tinkari's—a vast field stretching desolately with sparkling-white moonlight upon it, and a prince on his horse, riding on for some unknown reason—how thrilled I was to hear this! Besides, the prince would inevitably find an incredibly beautiful princess, you see, which made me even more agitated. I had a hope against hope ingrained in my mind that I too, when I was older, might pull off some improbable feat of this sort, and that after facing many trials and tribulations, a certain breathtakingly beautiful being might not be absolutely impossible to attain in some such place. As I walk on the sandbank in the moonlit night, that childhood feeling of the pull of a joyful heart under the mosquito net rises up again in me; wherever I look, everything seems so unreal that all that is impossible attains form, and I walk around enchanted amidst the mirages of my own imagination—it has no limits anywhere, or obstacles.

★ The word *jocchonāẏ* is rendered here as pronounced by the illiterate maidservant.

181

Shilaidaha
7 December 1894

Nowadays the evenings upon the sandbanks are so wonderful
that it's beyond my powers of description. When I walk alone,
often after a while Shai—— comes to keep me company and
discusses work-related issues. He came yesterday as well. After
discussing the arrangements for the transfer of property to another
name on the rent roll, etc., for a while, the moment he stopped
speaking—I suddenly saw the eternal universe standing silently
in front of me that evening. And I was surprised that one man's
inconsequential voice near your ear could drown out the silence
that fills this infinite sky—in that bare, silent universe what were
the rent rolls and the Birahimpur estate records! I didn't reply to
what Shai—— was saying, so he thought I hadn't heard him. He
asked me again, and I again did not reply, avoiding the matter. He
was very surprised and became quiet. The moment that happened,
immediately, as I stood watching, a peace descended from that
entire silent constellation of stars and filled my heart. I too found
a seat in one corner of the meeting at which uncountable millions
of stars had soundlessly gathered. Just as they are one each in
that endless space, so too was I one, standing beside the Padma
upon the desolate sands stretching to the horizon; both they and
I had found a place in this astonishing thing called existence.
After walking on the moonlit sands till very late at night, I finally
returned to the boat, lit the lamp, closed the door, stretched out
on the long easy chair and once again began a discussion on the
Birahimpur rent rolls. Four pieces of luci with the help of *natun
khejur gur* and a glass of milk were consumed. Then, after a little
literary discussion, it was time to sleep.

182

Shilaidaha
11 December 1894

Nowadays I go out for my walk very early in order to avoid ——;
after a long time of walking alone, Shai—— arrives. By that time
I've made my mind calm and cool and swept away all the worries
of the day and the scattered refuse of work to a far distance.

For a very little while it seems as if all the profit and loss and
joy and sorrow of this world are as nothing. Then suddenly when
Shai—— asks, 'You haven't been feeling ill after drinking the milk
today, have you?' or 'Did the nāyeb maśāi present all the accounts
to you today?'—how strangely disconnected it sounds! We live in
the exact centre of two perpetual opposites called the everyday and
the eternal! Although they are eternally joined together and have
always been neighbours, still, each finds the other so laughable!
When you're thinking of the spiritual it seems very incongruous
to speak of clothes to wear and food for the stomach, yet the soul
and the stomach have been living together forever. My estates exist
exactly at the spot where the moonlight falls; yet the moonlight says,
'Your estates are a fiction,' and the estates say that the moonlight is
all a sham! I, as an individual, am right in the middle.

183

Shilaidaha
Wednesday, 12 December 1894

You've written, Bob, asking, 'When will world and idea unite?'—
they never will completely. Because the more the world tries to
catch up with the idea, the idea will proceed further on its path.

Exactly as though the idea is the older brother of the world, and there's no chance of one catching up with the other in age. So, as of now, if we can somehow make the best of what we have—in whichever way possible—we think of our lives as having been successful. Especially when we can't even always decipher which the *highest ideal* is—perhaps that which is the *nighest* is the *highest*, perhaps the *sacrifice* of your own personal *ideal* is the *higher ideal* sometimes, perhaps if I keep my life well preserved, high up somewhere my life will be fruitless, perhaps I need to descend a little in order to find some success in this world in accordance with my abilities. The solutions to all these problems are with each of us individually, Bob. The world is so tremendously complicated altogether that one doesn't have the courage to show someone else the way, because differences in personalities make each person's way of walking so different from another's! Perhaps it's best not to think too much and take the path that is nearest and then face the problems that arise on the way with as much sincerity as possible— that might be the easiest option. He who has turned our lives into such an intractable problem may eventually in the end provide a very simple solution, and then perhaps we will feel like laughing at the thought that we had been so perplexed about it in the past.

184

Shilaidaha
14 December 1894

Today I'd wanted to walk for a while on the sandbank in the morning, but seeing there was fog, I retreated. The sky had a few fragments of clouds floating in it as well, like yesterday and the day before. But yesterday at sunset the evening light upon these fragments of clouds looked so wonderful that I can't tell you. Small bits of pleated, curled-up clouds had turned golden at one place in the west and assumed a new sort of beauty. So many colours had blossomed all around that for a well-known colour-blind person like me to try and describe them would be sheer impertinence. The magic of colour had suddenly affected not only the sky, but the waters of the Padma and the sandbanks as well. And then again the blue waters of the Padma were shivering and trembling a little from top to bottom in the north wind—as a result all the colours and shades of the sun's rays upon the river were set into such astonishing motion that I was simply awestruck. On the other hand, the water was calm in those places in the middle of the Padma where there were sandbanks under the water; there, in those still waters, the clear golden light fell in a completely smooth, fluid, bright, soft, luminous way—in the midst of all the variety of colour and dance everywhere, that still, sad, unmoving glow of the sunset had turned extraordinarily beautiful. And then the brush of sunset had fallen upon the banks of sand as well. These sandbanks had been under the water at some point, you see, so in places the sand bore the imprint of the waves of water up to quite a distance—in many other places, however, they were quite level and stretched for miles—the myriad shiny colours of light as they fell upon the wavy sand arranged in pleated layers made it look like the multicoloured skin of an enormous snake. I thought to myself—it is true after all that the Padma is a huge she-snake that used to live at one time upon these vast sandbanks, and now only an enormous empty skin lies glinting upon the sand—I was reminded also of the way in which she had raised her thousand hoods during the rains and struck repeatedly at the shore with a roar, thumping her large curved tail furiously again and again, swelling up as she moved—now, like a snake in the winter, she grows leaner by the day, half-entering her hole to hibernate through the long sleep of winter. As I walked, gradually these various colours began to slowly fade away, and the sky, water and land were bathed in the monotone of white moonlight—and no sign remained anywhere in the world that the day had dawned in the east once.

185

Calcutta
14 January 1895

Spring is slowly preparing to arrive. Yesterday it was quite hot the entire day—I couldn't concentrate, and I spent the entire day wandering around quite mindlessly. A—— came yesterday, and making polite conversation with him was also becoming quite impossible for me. All these days it was winter and there was an enthusiasm for work—I thought I could spend my entire life editing *Sādhanā*. Now, the moment a warm wind has begun to blow, it seems to me that I would much rather be the poet that I was than an editor. I feel like lying next to an open window with a slate in hand, humming to myself as I scan the metre, and continuously write poetry—in front of me green leaves and branches can be seen on the body of the bright sky and the breeze comes and touches my whole body. Even if I don't write poetry, there's always song composition; I really like doing that too in this sort of mood. The music of song can change the appearance of the entire world completely and a wonderful intoxication buzzes in the mind. But it's also better for me to remain serious and calm and careful as the editor of *Sādhanā* rather than be restless with joy, heedless and thirsty like an inebriated, plaintive and self-forgetful madman. There's an eternal youthfulness in the world of poetry and song that is not always compatible with real life. On some days, when the morning grows warmer, then suddenly, catching a glimpse of the sunlight outside, I feel instantly happy, yet worried—then I feel afraid and discouraged as I realize that this poetry resides within the marrow of my bones—it is my constant companion; at least once every year it will break out into leaf and flower from within my bones—and it will make me forget that there is no empathy at all between my inner life and outer world.

186

Shilaidaha
4 February 1895

It's very cold here now, Bob—I wish this fierce winter weather would end and a spring breeze blow just once to its heart's content; I would undo the buttons on this ākcān and make my bed on the roof of the open *jolly boat* with my feet stretched out and leave this path of duty to concentrate solely for a few days on the completely unnecessary. If I could be editor of *Sādhanā* for six months and somebody else for the other six then that would be the most convenient arrangement—because while a man may not be able to behave madly for an entire calendar year, it's equally difficult for someone like me to maintain my *sanity* for a whole year. This enormous earth changes its seasons every couple of months—then how do small men like us keep up an equitable display of politeness all twelve? The huge problem for man is that he goes against nature when he has to function according to the laws of society in exactly the same way all three hundred and sixty-five days of the year—actually, he has to shyly and fearfully hide the eternally new, eternally mysterious core that is within him and make himself appear absolutely like a mechanical device driven by the daily operations of routine. That's why men go wrong from time to time; become rebellious; that's why men want to take shelter in literature in order to truly understand themselves; that's why the workplace is a prison and the imagination a place of freedom. That's why literature narrows down its enormous potential if it becomes *conventional*; that's why thoughts that cannot be raised in polite *drawing room* conversations gain depth and generosity in literature and freely and beautifully express themselves. In fact, to imprison literature in the civilized environs of tea-drinking and *drawing room* meetings would be a bit like dressing the generous universe in a chintz *gown*.

187

Shilaidaha
12 February 1895

I've found a walking companion for the evenings on this bank. The man's name is Tha———; he's quite intelligent and literary, middle-aged, the thinking type, plainspoken, and experienced in handling jamidāri work. . . . Every day during my walks I discuss a variety of ideas with him. I was explaining to him the particular way in which I look at the world, that I have a very intense, intimate, real and living relationship with all of nature, and that it is that love and that relationship which I feel is my truest and highest dharma, and that unless you understand this inner character of mine you will not be able to enjoy, in fact, even understand most of my poetry. I saw that he understood it very well—not only understood it, but was quite absorbed by it. He correctly intuited the exact source of my intoxication with this world. This dharma of mine is an everyday dharma; I meditate upon it all the time. Yesterday there was a mother goat sitting on the grass by the road, serious, relaxed and calm, with her infant snuggled up against her in a completely dependent and totally relaxed way—the deep sensuous experience of love and wonder with which my heart filled up on seeing that is what I call my religious discourse. The moment I see a scene like this I feel the entire world's inner joy and love in a very real and substantive way in my inner heart. If there are any *dogmas* that I don't know or understand, and see no possibility of understanding, I'm not in the least bit anxious about it. What little I *positively* know is enough for me, and gives me complete happiness. If you attempt to turn that into a *system* by adding false analyses and evaluations

to it, then its inner felt reality too is threatened. I know just this
much, that there's a certain joy and love in this world—there's no
need to know any more than that.

188

Shilaidaha
16 February 1895

Temperatures seem to be dropping suddenly all over the world.
We hear from the newspapers that Europe has been wrapped in
ice from head to toe, that England is experiencing a desert-like
winter—perhaps the impact of that has partially reached the shores
of the Bay of Bengal as well. I can't remember such out-of-the-way
cold weather in the month of Phālgun in Bengal ever. I remember
experiencing this sort of winter weather in the months of Phālgun
and Caitra when I had gone with Bābāmaśāẏ to Amritsar as a child,
where bathing-time every day would be a time of great regret.
This cold has brought those memories from long ago to mind,
also reminding me of sitting alone there in the long afternoons,
listening to the creak and whine of the mechanism by which the
cows drew water from the large well nearby, the farmers singing a
monotonous modulation at a very high pitch; there was a mulberry
tree leaning over the well from which I picked ripe mulberries
and ate them, and I kept feeling homesick all the time. That leads
to the memory of my first sight of the Himalayas when we were
climbing up towards Dalhousie. My heart was smaller then, you
see, so it was as if it just couldn't contain that quantity of wonder. I
still remember a very large wood of pine trees there—dark, lonely,
deep, cool, and shadowy. I feel like visiting Dalhousie once again; I
want to see whether I feel anything like the first feeling of wonder
I felt in my childhood. One huge convenience of that time was that
one never needed to think about one's own needs in those days.

189

Shilaidaha
17 February 1895

Although it's pretty cold this morning, there's no strong north
wind blowing as on other days—the river water is quite still
and calm, like a mirror. There, on the other side, a boat moves
slowly; three men, like three black lines drawn upon the pale
background of the sandbank, tow the boat along—that's it—
there's no restless current of work anywhere, no sound, no
movement—the morning sun falls stilly upon the water and the
sand, the morning doesn't seem to move, but rests silently in a
tired, calm sort of way. I should have completed a lot of work by
now, but I too was enjoying the lazy beauty of this morning in
a lazy way—while wondering from time to time why those two
or three men towing the boat slowly upon the desolate sands on
the other shore should appear so especially exquisite to my eyes.
Those who pull it are driven by hunger and are actually working
very hard; the particular picture of peace and pleasure that they
compose in my eyes is certainly not reflected in any feeling of
peace or contentment or beauty in their minds. Whatever it is,
I was not particularly worked up about finding a solution to all
these thoughts—just as that slow movement of the towing of the
boat was a small interlude in one corner of the all-encompassing
silence of this morning, so too this little, gentle, lazy thought
was a small intermission in the far corner of my mind's peaceful
enjoyment: it merely added some variety to the calm. Nowadays,
with the everyday compulsion of writing for *Sādhanā*, I don't find
the time any more to come effortlessly and wholly face-to-face
with this enormous expanse of nature—there's always something
or the other working within me, making me forgetful of the
fact that there is anything outside. Beauty too is a thing that is
a little *jealous*, it doesn't allow itself to be caught unless it can

claim the entire mind. That's the reason why I always say that you need a sufficient amount of solitude and peace in order to really understand and enjoy poetry or literature—it's not something you can do in a hurry, there's no way you can take in a little flavour of it in a short interval between two tasks. That's why the number of people who really like poetry is so limited. They don't have any unoccupied space or time in their minds, which are like small, overcrowded spaces. I'm afraid to open a book of poetry in Calcutta—I wait to come to the mofussil. Otherwise, maybe the thing will be spoiled for me, so that I may not like it even when the time is right. A thing like poetry is terribly cowed down in Calcutta—there it seems terribly small. Here, in this solitude, I can experience its fathomless depth and truth in the right frame of mind. Then I understand how essential it is for our character that we do so, and how starved our minds were in the city.

190

Shilaidaha
18 February 1895

It's such a silent and lovely day today that I yearn to immerse myself in the complete rasa of idleness. But I still have to finish the 'Brief Reviews' for *Sādhanā*. I'll have to read two unreadable books and write an unfavourable review. An absolutely worthless task—it's wrong to have to do such work on a day such as this. But this is the irony of fate—in the lonely leisure of this tranquil Phālgun afternoon, sitting on this private boat upon the still waters of the Padma, with the golden sunlight, blue skies and ashen sandbanks before me, I'm having to embark upon a review of *Dewan gobindarām* published by Sri Yogendranath Sadhu. Nobody will ever read the book, nor will anybody read the review, but this precious day today will be wasted as a result. Just think about it, how many days like this does one get in one's life! Most days, after all, are broken and fragmented and joined together—but the day today has blossomed completely and fully like a full-blown lotus upon this silent river, drawing my mind into its secret inner chamber of meaning. And then what's happened is, a big, glossy, blue-coloured bee in a yellow cummerbund is flying around my boat with a buzzing sound in a restless way. I've always laughed at the saying that the humming of bees in springtime increases the pain of separation in a beloved's heart. But I first discovered the real sweetness and meaning of the bee's hum one afternoon in Bolpur. That day I was wandering wildly about on the south veranda like a vagrant—the afternoon had stretched itself out to lie upon the field and a peaceful, silent shadow had spread its reign across the dense, secret masses of the trees' leaves—there was an ache in my heart—and just then, from a neem tree adjacent to the veranda, the lazy hum of a bee tied the entire melancholy of the vast afternoon into a melody. That was the day that I first properly realized that the fundamental tune of an aimless and tired afternoon is the hum of a bee. I quite understood then that it's not at all impossible that the pain in a lover's heart might increase even more on hearing it. Actually, the thing is—if a bee enters a room and instantly begins to buzz in your ear then that certainly will not increase anybody's happiness or unhappiness, but the tune it composes among the trees and beneath the open sky hits exactly the right note. This golden *mekhalā*-wearing bee of mine today too is hitting the right notes—it's certainly not reviewing a book, but why it keeps circling unceasingly round my boat on every side is beyond my grasp. There'd be some meaning to it if I were Sakuntala, perhaps, but even the most unbiased person will concede that I am not Sakuntala. Just this moment another boat passed by mine. One of its Muslim oarsmen was lying flat on his back with a book on his chest and loudly reciting from a poem. That man too has an appreciation for life—I'm sure you wouldn't be able to sit him down to review *Dewan gobindarām* even if you beat him up.

191

Shilaidaha
22 February 1895

As a result, the day has passed today in some business-related work, some letter-writing, some newspaper-reading, and some editing of essays. It's now past four, and I will go out for my walk as soon as the sun recedes. Days that you cannot devote entirely to either work or leisure are wasted days. Our Multān rāginī is for this time of the day—around four or five o'clock—and it expresses just that feeling—'I have not done anything at all today'. Some ustad must have woken up after his afternoon nap and composed this rāginī. Today, in this shining afternoon light—on the water, the land, space, everywhere—I can see that Multān rāginī with its tender high notes of the *antarā* [second movement] visibly—it evokes neither happiness nor unhappiness, only the melancholy of inertia and its inner secret sorrow. Unhappiness has a particular sort of ache, but there is a certain rasa within even that. And there is another sort of ache that is beyond sorrow or feeling, inert and hidden—that's very dry, without generosity or the beauty of imagination. There's another big problem—lots of mosquitoes—which is really irritating. It's impossible to preserve the sweetness of a feeling or the depth of a thought if you're constantly slapping your hands and legs and body; the mind becomes prone to aggression and frustrated with failure. These sorts of small irritations—the mosquito's bite, the helpful literary review, sand in the *mohanbhog*—do not teach men to be brave in any way, I can say that much. I can say it especially because there was sand in my mohanbhog today—and I can clearly recall how I felt then—such feelings were unworthy of a Christian or a Brahmo . . . or of a good Muslim too.*

---

* A sweet preparation made with semolina, sugar and raisins cooked in ghī.

192

Now spring [*basanta*] has arrived. It would have been great if I hadn't had any trying tasks on my shoulders at this time. I could have loosened the reins of my imagination and let it run free through the fullness of my leisure. I could have gone and relaxed by the window and given myself up completely to writing, reading and thinking. Nowadays, I get easily distracted while writing for *Sādhanā*, and my mind travels instantly towards anything happening outside—a boat passes by and I raise my head to watch it—the ferry crosses from this side to that and quite some time is spent looking at that too—on the shore, very near my boat, the slow-moving buffaloes fill their big mouths with grass and move about with much heavy breathing and sound of chewing, swishing flies from their backs with their tails as they walk—then a very small, thin, weak, almost naked boy comes along and prods this gentle giant of a beast on its back with a short staff, making a *hut-hut* sound—the animal glances at this tiny child of man once from the corner of its large eye, tears up a few more blades of grass and leaves, and calmly and slowly moves away a little—and the boy thinks he has done his shepherd's duty. I'm yet to penetrate the mysterious *psychology* of these shepherd boys—exactly what they accomplish by shooing away a cow or a buffalo from a place where it's contentedly eating food of its own volition to another spot a little distance away is quite beyond me. Perhaps it's to establish their lordship over the animals. Perhaps it's a habit with men to unnecessarily torture tame animals in order to feel powerful. But I get very angry with these shepherd boys. I like watching cows or buffaloes feed on dense, moist clumps of grass. It's quite worthwhile to watch those who have no higher nature go about their business of eating, sleeping, sitting. It's like the happiness you feel watching very poor people squat before their ordinary dal and rice and eat. But the lengthy thirty-six-course affairs that the rich and mighty organize are extremely annoying. Look what I started to say and what I've ended up talking to you about. What I was going to say was that just when I'm engaged in gathering all sorts of elevated resources for the readers of *Sādhanā*, my entire attention is attracted towards the ordinary sight of cows and buffaloes grazing on the grass and shrubbery by the river. I think I told you in a previous letter about a couple of bees that frequent my boat and how they've been flying restlessly around or inside my boat with a futile humming in an unsuccessful investigation. They appear every day at around nine or ten in the morning—quickly darting around my table, under my desk, on the coloured sash, by the side of my head, and then exit with a whoosh. I could quite easily think that this was the manifestation of some unfulfilled ghostly spirit in the form of a bee visiting everyday from the beyond to see me, circling around me once and then leaving. But I don't think so. It is my firm belief that these are real bees, the black bee, which is sometimes in Sanskrit called the *dvireph*.

193

Shilaidaha
Thursday, 28 February 1895

I'm somewhat relaxed today after having completed a story for *Sādhanā* last evening. The afternoon too is very quiet and warm and peaceful and still—the feeling in my mind today is like the sort of melancholic yearning I felt as a very small child when school got over at one, and I sat in my empty classroom by the window looking out at the vacant, silent ranks of the terraces in Calcutta, listening to the sharp cry of the kite in the distant sky. I'm reminded of those deep, dreamlike, wild childhood imaginings of mine—it doesn't seem like too long ago. Yet half of my mortal life is already gone. We manage to come to the end of our lives treading across every moment and every day, but taken all together, it's very brief. One could encompass it all within the space of two hours of solitary thought. Shelley spent thirty years of his life occupied with a thousand daily tasks and a thousand endeavours for his life's story to be told in only two *volumes*, and that too with a lot of unnecessary talk and commentary from Dowden saheb interspersed in its pages—both may easily be read in the space of a week. Our thirty years would perhaps not even fill up two whole *volumes*. That's all it comes to—such a brief affair, but such a lot of planning—so many arguments, so many battles and so much herculean effort! So many businesses, estates, and people just to provide it with supplies! I sit quietly on this one-and-a half-cubit-long chair—but I occupy so much space in this world in so many ways! If you edit out all of that, all you're left with is just two hours of thought—and that too not for long. Today I was remembering that storehouse that in my childhood used to stand by the edge of the pond on the south side. Iru was very small then, but she too was part of our group. Think of how far Iru has travelled from that small centre-point of the storehouse, and of how far I too have come along another track.* And then if you keep drawing these lines straight outward from that south-facing Jorasanko storehouse, there's no saying what sort of mysterious darkness you will have to enter. This feeling in me today on this afternoon alone on the boat, these thoughts, the languid fantasies of this one day—who knows where it falls upon that long track and where it disappears? Will this lonely, full afternoon upon the silent sands by the still Padma's shore leave even a very tiny golden mark upon my eternal past and eternal future? There's such a particular feeling of renunciation in the Indian sunlight that nobody has the power to evade it.

* Iru: Irabati Debi, daughter of Baṛ-didi.

194

Shilaidaha
Thursday, 28 February 1895

I've received an anonymous letter today. It starts—

To give up one's life at another's feet
Is the utmost one can give!

Then there's an excess of admiration expressed. They've never seen me, but nowadays they can see me in *Sādhanā*. So they write— 'The sun's rays [*rabikar*] have fallen upon your efforts [*sādhanā*], so however small or far away the seekers of the sun [*rabi-upāsak*] may be, the sun's rays emanate for them too. You are a poet of the world, yet we think that today you are our poet too', etc., etc. Man is so eager to love that in the end he begins to love his own *idea*. To think of the *idea* as any less true than *reality* is merely one of our illusions. What we get through our senses is something that philosophy and science tell us has been created by our senses, but nobody really knows what it is—and what we get through our *idea*s is constructed by our minds, and nobody can say what that really is either. Still, people believe in their senses' creation more than they do in their mind's creations. Yet those who know me through their senses by spending time in my company may still be very far from my real self—and this anonymous devotee of mine who knows me only through *ideas* may perhaps know me relatively more truly. Every person has an *ideal* person inside themselves; one can reach a little of that self only through love and devotion and affection; the endless *ideal* that resides within every boy can only be felt by his mother with her entire heart and soul—she cannot see that *ideal* self and that ineffable truth within other boys. *Reality* often hides that *ideal* self from view. Our imagination may enable us to feel affectionate towards children, but when we see a real boy's shabbiness, ugliness and whining, we just cannot imagine what it is in him that could make his mother want to sacrifice her life for him—what makes her think of him as the most precious and most beautiful thing in the world! The thing which makes the mother think of her son in such a way that she can give up her life for him—is it false? And what I think about her son that makes me incapable of sacrificing my life for his—is that the greater truth? I say that there is something in every boy and every old man for which one can lay down one's life. It is because we don't have enough love in our nature that we cannot discover that *ideal*. Christ's sacrifice of his life for mankind and for every man has just such a truth hidden within it. Every living thing is a treasure for eternal time and eternal care, and has a limitless appeal. Look how one thing has led to another. The fundamental thing is—in some respects I'm unworthy of receiving the gift of love my devotee gives me; perhaps if they had known me intimately in my everyday life, they would have been unable to offer me this sort of love; but in another reckoning I do have the right to receive this sort of love; in fact, maybe even much more than this. This is what is at the heart of the Christian and Vaishnava religions. This afternoon I sat and wrote a letter to you which had a lot of talk about renunciation, and now in the evening I'm writing another letter in which the talk is all about love!

195

Shilaidaha
1 March 1895

When you don't receive a letter one day, and get one the next, you feel a very distinct new pleasure—the mind and its daily machinery of routine, which was temporarily out of order, suddenly begins to work enthusiastically again, creating a feeling of joy. When the world is not exactly as you desire it to be, you often feel despondent, but certain days arrive when you feel the world is just as it was before, and that makes the blood flow more rapidly through your heart. I liked the Christina Rossetti poem you sent me. But it's only the first four lines that are good, and what it has to say is said in those four lines itself. After that, the rest of the poem is an add-on which doesn't drive the feeling onward but, rather, weakens it. There are some songs, for instance, in which the *āsthāyī* [first movement] is quite good, but the antarā is fake—the entire expression of the melody has been accomplished in the first part itself, but a second unnecessary antarā has been added only because the rules require it. Like my song '*bājila kāhār bīṇā madhur svare*' [Whose bīṇā is played so sweetly]—in which the tune accomplishes its work right at the start, yet, because the poet still has something to say, the song is not allowed to stop where it wants to but is dragged on. Poems too have a melody, and in this poem of Christina Rossetti's, the real melody is finished in its first four lines. You've written, 'I don't know to this day if I like a poem because it expresses a feeling well, or because of its "style", the manner in which it turns pithily around, for its cleverness of language.' Actually, the thing is that for us the majority of feelings are old; and the dharma of our minds is such that we are unable to appreciate the complete flavour and beauty of old and habitual things—that's why when a poet attracts our attention by using language, metre and a new form of expression for an old feeling, we are able to taste the essential flavour of that thing again—then that eternal old thought resounds in our minds and in our ears in the form of a new song. One of the chief tasks of a poet is to always keep the world fresh for us—the green of the trees, the blue of the skies, the golden of the evenings, all of it would have become blanched and dull and wrapped in dust for us by now unless poets had used their imagination upon them. The mind of man becomes easily ripe with the heat of thought, so the poet's task is to dampen it with a sprinkling of imagination's nectar so it can stay alive and full of flavour for all time. He doesn't give you anything new; he just tries to keep your thoughts new.

196

Shilaidaha
6 March 1895

There's an argument in your letter today about whether to give the practice of beauty or the practice of convenience greater importance, Bob. That depends largely on the situation and the amount of inconvenience faced. *For instance*, the example you gave of riding a horse with an umbrella over your head doesn't really address the issue of beauty in any way. Because while it might not be unbeautiful to ride a horse while holding an umbrella, it might actually be inconvenient. But to my mind, it's unnatural. There's an *association* between horse riding and manliness; that's why people might automatically think, if you are riding a horse, why use an umbrella? Inconvenience, ugliness and unnaturalness—it's necessary to avoid all three, but perhaps the last most of all. Even if a man looks nice wearing a sari, and doesn't find it inconvenient, still, it's better not to embark upon so strange an endeavour. The shyness one has with regard to that is a natural one. Actually, one naturally feels timid about attracting too much attention to one's self—the sort of behaviour that in English is called '*loud*' is reprehensible for exactly these reasons, and true politeness is habitually reticent. The sort of unnatural or strange behaviour that attracts excessive attention to itself should make people feel ashamed—just as it's not too much to ask that one should be very self-aware, so too, one should be disinclined to hurl one's self violently upon someone else's consciousness. If I go out to meet some gentlemen in my night clothes it might not create an upheaval of mythic proportions, and it might even look good, but it's not exactly good manners to suddenly assault people with such unnatural behaviour. This sort of thing has a limit, but that limit is very distant. If I think of some prevalent custom—some countrywide practice—as wrong and harmful to most people or if I think that some new practice is good for us, then I mustn't feel hesitant to assault the public forcefully on that issue; then the argument about what is natural or unnatural is a very minor one. But I must have a steady aim and high ideals. In our country, women do not carry umbrellas over their heads or wear shoes, so the woman who is the first to do so will have to face the disapproval of others—in that case it won't do for her to bow down before general opinion. But, ordinarily, the convenience of behaving as most people do is that other people are not disturbed, and you yourself find it easier to go on your way—else, other people are inconvenienced and you too face unnecessary obstacles. If one has to fight with general opinion and habit even for the little conveniences of life, then it's exactly like setting up a canon to fire at a mosquito—an unnatural and strange affair. One cannot then find an appropriate higher purpose that might mitigate the irritation or oddity of that unnatural act. In that case you might just venture out in civilized clothes in civil society and the moment you feel hot, take off your cāpkān and kāmij and sit there happily barebodied—if one must *philosophize*: where's the harm in that? Why should I bother about what people might say when the heat is making me feel ill? I might be lecturing, but I myself have indulged quite often in behaviour that goes against socially acceptable norms. But I don't want to defend that—I know that that's my whimsicality, my madness. I don't think anybody could say that Baṛ-da's wrong-side-up jobbā and tricycle-riding costume was very acceptable to received opinion, but since we're arguing about *principle*, one shouldn't bring up individual instances. The basic thing is—when it is a question of only one's self, one needs to try and practise both convenience and beauty, but when one is talking about society, one needs to synchronize convenience, beauty and naturalness, all three things. The argument has almost filled up the letter—the good thing about small-size letter paper is that one has to restrict one's argument as well, or this would have turned into a long essay.

197

Shilaidaha
7 March 1895

I was thinking after reading your letter yesterday that it's true that women are far more vigilant than men about keeping their surroundings beautiful, but does that really mean that they are somehow more appreciative of beauty than men? One generally cannot come to any conclusion on these sorts of issues; because individual men and women have different talents according to who they are—when we speak on issues like these we usually think of ourselves as representative of our genders. I might want to keep everything around me beautiful, but I'm frequently unmindful about it for a variety of reasons—often everything becomes quite untidy and it's not as if I always keep myself very neat either. But I have no doubt at all about the fact that beauty makes me crazy— nothing else can make me feel its endless depth with all my heart as beauty and love can, and when one is really immersed in such a feeling then one's own personal appearance and neatness don't matter so much—when the mind is filled with the rasa of beauty, then just that is sufficient. I remember Biharilal; the man might have been unadorned and loose and untidy—but if you read his writing, you would have had no doubt about the fact that he was drunk on beauty. There's also no doubt about the fact that at one time Bar-dada, like a true poet, used to enjoy every aspect of beauty, but there's also no doubt that he never ever kept his surroundings or himself beautiful. It's natural for women to want an *association* between their own things and beauty. Whenever you recall her,

her fragrance, her appearance, her neatness must be evoked—it's very necessary to notice the golden lotus alongside the goddess Lakshmi. If you have to make yourself the ideal of beauty, your surroundings too must be beautiful. Women have a tender affection for all sorts of lovely things such as flowers—it's as if all of those things were their own, special things, to which they are tied in a relationship. But men feel differently about beauty—for us the attraction of beauty is much stronger, and the meaning of beauty much deeper. I might not be able to express myself properly, and if I do, it might sound like unworldly poetry—beauty for me is a felt divinity—when my mind is not troubled and I look properly, a *plate* full of roses are to me a particle of that most abundant delight about which the Upanishads have said: *etasyaibānandasyānyāni bhūtāni mātrāmupajībanti* [on a particle of this very bliss other creatures live].* The endless deep spirituality within beauty is something only men have experienced. That's why for men there is a universality about women's beauty. The other day I was reading a book of poetry called Śankarācharya's *Ānandalaharī* in which he was looking at the entire universe in the form of a woman—the sun, moon, sky, earth—all of it was encompassed by the beauty of woman—until he transformed all the description and all the poetry into a single line expressing a single exalted thought. Biharilal's book of songs, the *Sāradāmaṅgal*, too is of that class. Shelley's *Epipsychidion* too has the same implication. Most of Keats's poetry brings a similar feeling to mind. One realizes the true meaning of beauty when it actually touches, not only the eye or the imagination, but one's soul, like a felt experience. When I'm alone I feel its evident touch every day, and I quite understand what a living truth it constitutes in the eternity of space and time—and even a quarter of what I have understood I cannot make others understand.

* 'Thus did Yājñavalkya instruct [Janaka]: "This is his [the seer's] highest goal; this is his highest treasure; this is his highest world; this is his greatest bliss. On a particle of this very bliss other creatures live."' From the *Brihadāranyaka Upanishad*, IV.3.32.

198

Shilaidaha
8 March 1895

When I reach Shahjadpur, I'll find a heap of letters accumulated
there. There are lots of valuable gifts in this world, but the
insignificant letter is not a small thing. The invention of the *post
office* is a new addition to men's happiness. This is a new type of
happiness. I'm not talking about convenience here, that's there
of course. But letters have created a new joy in the world. They
connect men to one another in a novel bond. We gain something
by seeing people, and we gain by speaking to them, but now when
we receive letters we gain another sort of insight into them. It's
not just that we compensate for face-to-face conversation through
letters, by talking to each other even in our absence—there's an
additional flavour in them that is not exactly there in everyday
conversation and meetings. We express ourselves in conversation
in a manner that we don't in our writing, but again, the opposite
is also true. Both situations have an element of incompleteness
in them that can become complete only when the two come
together. That's why, in men's relations with men, letters convey
a new pleasure and communication that was not there before. It
is as if a new sense has been added to enable us to see men, to
find them. When ordinary conversation and discussion are caught
within the frame of a letter, they assume a new aspect—the thing
which evades us in conversation and which becomes artificial
in essays is easily captured in letters. I think that those who are
always in each other's company twenty-four hours, who haven't
had the opportunity to write letters to each other, know each
other incompletely—they don't have any way of knowing many
delicate, many true and deep things about each other's characters.
Just as the cow's udders fill with milk as soon as the calf comes

near, so the mind fills up with particular flavours only at the instance of a particular excitement and not any other—the exact spot in your heart that this four-page letter is able to touch cannot be reached through conversation or essays. I think the envelope has a particular attraction—the envelope is an important part of the letter—it's a major discovery. Perhaps we need to thank the French for that.

199

Shilaidaha
10 March 1895

This time I've decided that when I go to Calcutta I won't enter into any arguments—I'll read and write quietly with a calm and peaceful heart. There's no greater happiness than that. It is perhaps the thirteenth day of the lunar fortnight today—there will be a lot of moonlight—in these three or four days I will have to take my moonlit sandbank by the Padma and load as much of it as I can into my heart to take back with me. Quite possibly, when I return again the next time this spread-out, white sandbank will no longer be there. In its place will be either the waters of the Padma or ploughed land. Nowadays I don't manage to walk alone any more. I'm often accompanied by Shai—— and Tha—— babu. In the middle of their conversation suddenly sometimes the entire moonlit peaceful scene and the endless silence filling up the sky come and stand in front of me for a little while—they pull that old, familiar curtain of mine to one side and reveal themselves to me from time to time. Then my whole heart fills with an amazing fulfilment—as if a very big, soft, deep embrace has wrapped around my whole body, and a soundless, still, intense love comes from the stars and envelops me. To suddenly experience such a serious and momentous arrival in the middle of all that dry, work-related talk astonishes even me, and my two companions on either side appear completely out of place. The three of us are walking together, but for a while I am not in their presence as they walk. My serious, silent, moonlight-drowned world suddenly lets me know in the momentary break of conversation, 'Don't think you have only two companions, we too are by your side today as we have always been before—'

> I sit here day and night,
>> Come when you remember me.

I've written about the comic [*kautukhāsya*] in *Sādhanā*. On these moonlit, desolate sandbanks by the Padma, as I keep listening to the seresta's reports from Tha——— babu, and in the gaps between those reports when the star-filled sky keeps playing hide and seek, sometimes I feel it's joking with me—somebody's sweet smile of mischief is within it somewhere.

200

Shilaidaha
11 March 1895

There are a number of things that never grow old for me—perhaps when I'm far away their brightness may dim under the pressure of other material things, but then, as soon as I come face-to-face with them again, immediately all the old feelings are refreshed in my mind. There are times when my exile in the mofussil becomes a faded memory in Calcutta, and then I may think that my Padma's shores have perhaps grown old—but the surprising thing is that the moment I come here I see that everything is still bright and full of wonder, like that first glance at each other on your wedding day [*śubhadṛṣṭi*]. Every day in the evening as I walk on the sand I think of this—that which I found novel the other day still feels new to me today—exactly the same feeling fills my heart in exactly the same way, as if I had come here for the first time today. This is a thing of great joy and wonder for me. I think that perhaps all the letters I have written you from all these places for such a long time have the same feeling in them. Again and again I've said the same thing, expressed the same enthusiasm in the same language. I can't help it—it's because I experience the same feeling in a new way every time. I often wish I could take all the letters I've written you and, reading them, travel again through the narrow path of my letters' old familiar landscapes gathered over the mornings, afternoons and evenings of so many days. I have tried to hold on to so many days and so many moments—these must be captive in your box of letters—the moment I set my eyes on them, those old days will surround me on every side. The stuff in them that's to do with my personal life is not that valuable—but the things that I have gathered from outside, which are each an item of rare beauty or invaluable enjoyment, are the incomparable earnings of my life—those are things which perhaps nobody else but I have seen, and which are kept only within the pages of those letters, and nowhere else in the world—nobody will perhaps appreciate their value more than me. Give me your letters once, Bob, and I'll copy out just the experiences of beauty from them into an exercise book. Because if I live for a long time then I'm sure to grow old; then all these days will become things of remembrance and consolation. At that time I will want to walk slowly in the evening light within the accumulated beauty of the days of my past life. Then this Padma's sandbank of today and the soft, peaceful, spring moonlight will return to me afresh in exactly the same way. My days and nights of joy and sorrow are not woven together like this anywhere else in my poetry or prose.

201

Calcutta
15 March 1895

I'm not exactly sure what I've been doing this morning. I haven't done any work at all, perhaps I haven't thought very much either. There was a bit of breeze from the south, and every joint of the body had loosened with the warmth; I was lying quietly by myself, rolling around, turning the pages of the newspaper, knowing all the while that there were letters to be written, *proof-sheets* to be corrected, writing to be done for *Sādhanā*, kāchāri work to be completed, accounts to be presented to Bābāmaśāẏ, and yet I felt no regret at all for this laziness—perhaps the body and mind lacked the energy for regret. But this basanta morning breeze really wastes me. Just letting this generous warm wind caress the whole body seems like a duty worth doing—it seems as though the flow of this sweet breeze is a conversation that nature holds with me. That I was born in this world, that the spring breeze came and touched me, that the smell of the *kanakcāṅpā* flower filled my head, that occasionally a morning such as this came to me in obeisance like a message from the gods—in the brief life of a man how can this be insignificant! Not just the writing of poetry or the editing of *Sādhanā*—all these forgotten, unconscious moments too are an important part of a successful life. That's why sometimes this sort of overflowing laziness doesn't give rise to any regret. If this time had been spent listening to a good song one would not have regretted that either. On some days, for me, nature functions exactly as a song does. This breeze, this light, all these small sounds, make me completely inert. Then I can quite comprehend that there is a pleasure in merely 'being'—that 'I am' is in itself a tremendous affair—in all of nature this is the most ancient and all-encompassing joy of all. It is when your mind is completely relaxed in this way that your relation with the outside is the most intimate.

202

Calcutta
16 March 1895

The argument about good and bad is an endless one, Bob. Based on what must we judge the good or bad in men: the contour of their mind or the results of their work? If we were to judge only from the results, then someone who has hurt a man accidentally and someone who has done so intentionally will both be found equally guilty—we would give the same punishment to the man who has done the deed in a fit of anger and one who has calmly planned it. Of course, whether an act is good or bad is one thing, and whether a certain man is good or bad is quite another. We aren't all-knowing; it's true that we sometimes judge a man by his work. And that's exactly why we don't always judge correctly. But the example you give from Shelley's life is entirely different—it proves that even if a man may be good at many things, in some contexts he may be morally unresponsive; that he may, in a particular scenario, be blind to the hurt he causes others because he is so immersed in his own pleasure—that's not a quality that deserves praise. There's no legitimate reason to sit down and try to turn Shelley's faults into good qualities. But just because he had a fault doesn't mean he did not have any talents. Many much less talented people might not have hurt other people like he did. Shelley's life does not prove in any way that depending on the person a bad deed may become a good one. But it does prove that no man is completely good. The good and the bad in every man are weighed and he's labelled good or bad according to the weight of the good in relation to the bad. Depending on their own character, some people praise Shelley highly and some people criticize him—but only god knows the real Shelley. Since man's relation with man is temporary, it is natural that men should judge each other on the basis of their impermanent lives alone—he with whom man is tied in an eternal relationship has a completely different method of judgement. Quite possibly, many reprobates will find a higher seat in heaven than many saints. St Paul, St Augustine—if they had died young, who would have known of their real greatness? But that doesn't mean one should deceive one's self by saying these things. A wrongdoing is a wrongdoing—since we have come to this world for a short time it is better if we can leave it after trying our best to make each other happy and by creating a permanent source of happiness. We have all gathered together in this guest house for just one evening—if I spend that little bit of time making others happy by helping them, comforting them, and so on, only then will I be a good man. If, in pursuit of my own pleasure, I torture somebody else needlessly, that person will call me a bad man, and I don't think it's reasonable to sit and disprove that by any sort of sophistry.

203

Calcutta
Monday, 18 March 1895

A majority of readers generally really liked that story published in *Sādhanā* in Māgh—that's why a lot of people are very annoyed with the review in *Sāhitya*. It's impossible to gauge why people like or dislike something—and even if you do, you cannot shape your talent in response. That's why I think that the assessment of those on the outside is completely useless and often harmful for me. A man's polestar and refuge is the ideal that he has within him. It's necessary to elevate that ideal as far as one can by reading, listening, thinking and practising literature. The manner in which literary analysis is engaged with in our country is completely uneducated. There's no point in hearing: 'I liked it' or 'I didn't like it'. That only gives you a particular person's opinion; it doesn't give you the truth of that opinion. If that opinion comes from somebody who is sufficiently capable of appreciation or experienced in literary affairs then even that might make you think a little. But just any person's opinion has no value at all. Our country lacks good reviewing skills—and the primary reason is that the people of our country do not have an intimate acquaintance with literature. They don't exist in the midst of literary creativity. They don't have any real experience of what's easy, what's hard, which is genuine and which made-up, what is impermanent and what is permanent, which is *sentiment* and which *sentimentalism*. Until a great variety and quantity of good literature is published in our country, the time for literary analysis will not arrive. First we must create an ideal, then analysts can begin their education from that ideal. Just as you cannot swim if there is no water, so too you cannot have good criticism without good literature. I've noticed that the older I get, the less dependent I become on the opinions of others—praise or criticism doesn't create as much of an impact—perhaps one has gotten used to both to a great extent. Trust in my own judgement too is perhaps gradually becoming firmer and more deep-rooted.

204

Calcutta
20 March 1895

Do you know why one particularly likes Shelley more than many other important people? His personality was not prone to doubt; he never analysed himself or others—his character was, in a way, whole. That's why one has a special affection for children or, in many instances, women—they're easy, natural; they haven't deconstructed and then constructed themselves around their own debates or *theories*. The beauty of Shelley's character is that there's no trace of any arguments, disputes or discussions in it. He has become what he has through his own inexorable creative strength. He's not responsible for himself at all—he's not even aware of when he has hurt someone or when he's made someone happy—and others too cannot be sure that they know him with any certainty. Just this much is clear—he is what he is—there was no way he could have been anything else. He's characteristically generous and beautiful, like outdoor nature, and his personality too is naturally without doubt or hesitation with regard to himself as well as others. There's an immense attractiveness about people with this completeness of character. Such people are always forgiven and indulged—no fault seems to stick to them with any degree of permanence. Their nature seems naked, like Adam and Eve were at the dawn of time, and, for that very reason, by another reckoning they seem eternally mysterious. They have not yet tasted the fruit of knowledge from the tree and so they live in a constant age of truth. It is very difficult to easily fall in love with those who think, who discuss, who exercise their judgement before they act, who know what good and bad are. Such people may be respected, looked up to, and trusted, but they are not readily loved. They may be able to sacrifice themselves, but others don't sacrifice their lives for them. I have written this in many of my essays, that man's mind is worthy of respect, but it is not an object of love—the real, genuinely important people are unthinking and spontaneous: they attract people towards themselves without effort, without logic, simply because they're irresistible.

205

Calcutta
2 April 1895

I was stuck with that lecture the whole day today as well. It's so difficult to express one's self in Bengali exactly as you want that writing becomes a form of wrestling. It's difficult not only because the language is inadequate—those who're going to hear it are the sort who have generally never thought about anything in depth, that's why it becomes necessary to unpack all the layers and explain everything at length. As a result, something that would have shown its *originality* and its brightness had it been written with more economy and brevity is diluted and over-worked, and this makes it completely worthless—making me feel terribly dissatisfied. I have repeatedly seen that Bengalis cannot easily follow a thread of argumentation, they just want to revel in the excitement of *feeling*—there's no account of the hundreds of things that are lost in transition between an essay and a lecture.

206

Calcutta
4 April 1895

Nowadays, impelled by work, I've descended to the first floor. The wooden nest bounded by a balcony that I had constructed for myself in one corner of the south veranda has now become my *āddā* [rendezvous]. There's no furniture in the room, only that Chinese desk you people had given me at the centre of it, and just one chair. You might say that this is a new discovery for me—I've never been able to put my mind to writing in my second-floor room, and I've always thought it was Calcutta's fault, but now, ever since I've moved to this room, I see that there's no problem with writing and that I can concentrate quite well. . . . Also, not having any furniture in the room is a great help. I see that there's a great necessity for *plain living, high thinking*—one must tear up one's ties with material objects as far as possible. Material objects do not establish any cerebral relation with the mind, they don't bring any news to it that's new—the furniture remains in the same shape and form forever, only becoming shabbier with time, functioning unnoticed as weighty obstructions to the mind. If one collects as much of the sky and light as one can and lets them occupy as much space as possible around the furniture, then the mind completes its work freely and enthusiastically. Gagan's garden being located right in front is also a great help. If I could have a garden next to the Ganga, and in a corner right next to the river, a neat and tidy room of paved stone, clear and calm, with a *couch* to sit and lean back upon and a *desk* to write on, and all the rest only garden and sky and water—the fragrance of blossoming flowers and the call of birds—then I could quietly keep doing my duty as a poet. One can make do with far less than this in the world, and far more than this often brings not an iota of happiness to many.

207

Calcutta
6 April 1895

You know how I cite the breezes of India as an excuse for rebellion against undertaking my duties? There's a deeper significance to that, Bob. There is a type of work which is composed in part of leisure, which sucks out the juice of leisure in vast quantities, or it cannot grow. My entire education and personality make me feel that I was born for that kind of work—if I labour on and on at work every moment, then the natural and proper duty of my life may suffer. One shouldn't judge work or duties with a measuring tape—if that were the only criterion of evaluation then the job of ploughing the land would have received the *first class prize* above all others. While working for *Sādhanā*, for my family, for the welfare of society, my innate character sometimes presents its own demand; it says, 'Let your work be done later; for the time being, extract as much flavour as you can from the sky and the light and the earth in a most leisurely way.' That might seem like laziness and neglect of duty to the outsider, but he whose mind it is knows that this enjoyment of leisure is the food required by his nature—without this little bit, all his leaves, flowers and fruits will not be able to flourish. Trees are of use for lighting ovens even when they become dry wood, but their most important work is to stay alive and bear flowers and fruits, and if they have to do that work they need a lot of leisure, sky and light. Now the question is just this: if I may accomplish something greater than just earning my wage, then is it not my duty to do so? Great work, by its very nature, demands, like a great tree, a lot of time and space—that is exactly what I call leisure, renunciation, meditation.

208

Calcutta
9 April 1895

The clock strikes ten with a clanging sound. Ten o'clock on a Caitra morning is quite late—the sun is blazing away; I don't know why the crows are making such a din; the *locket*-orange and sweet-and-sour mango-wallah is passing by our main gate, calling out loudly in a sing-song voice as he goes; my mouth is a bit dry—I feel like drinking a glass of cold curd *sarbat* with some ice. . . . I feel like going to some foreign country or the other. A country that's quite like a picture—with mountains, waterfalls, dense green moss on rocks, with cows grazing on the undulating hillside far away, the blue of the sky very calm and deep, the slow and rich sounds of birds, insects and leaves all mixed up rising in a languid, wavelike motion to the head. Oh, to hell with it—I don't think I'll put my hand to any more work today—I'll take myself off to Dwipu's room on the south side and sit there all alone stretched out with a travel book, a travel book with lots of pictures and new, uncut pages. There's a travel book on China at hand, but I've read about China in lots of books. There's a Persian travel book written by a woman, but women are not good travellers, and it doesn't have a sufficient number of pictures. I've finished reading Tibet, and I'm done with Africa. If I had a good book on South America with lots of pictures, then I'd read that. But I couldn't find anything I really liked in Thacker's. There are thousands of books in the world that are good for a discussion, for moral upliftment or for imparting an education. But books to be lazy with are very few in number. You need a special talent to write that sort of book, and that's a very rare talent. It's quite difficult to achieve both sides—to write so that you don't destroy the leisureliness of leisure—instead make it a little more colourful, a little more flavoursome—and at the same time to stoke the fire of reading. It shouldn't cut your mind with a steel nib, but fly over it with a feather quill—that creates a spread-out country, time, colour and flavour all around your mind. A good travelogue is the most weightless thing and the best thing to read in your free time. But one doesn't feel like picking up such books in Calcutta—because one never has that sort of wonderful uninterrupted leisure in Calcutta. I keep such books in store to take with me to the mofussil. It's very relaxing to sit down with that kind of thick book in hand on a completely secluded afternoon or evening—such princeliness [nabābiānā] is very rare in this world. Satya used to say that there's something of the nabāb in my character—that there is.

209

Calcutta
14 April 1895

Yesterday I had to travel around a lot the entire day. . . . If it had been any other day I would have been half-dead, but yesterday it was very cool—the sky was overcast, with the occasional drizzle—I was enjoying it. Although there's nothing in the least bit poetic about honouring invitations and going about presiding over meetings, still, yesterday in the time between travelling from one place to another a keen poetic ache filled my heart—exactly as if I were listening to a song—and I couldn't quite gauge the meaning of the indescribable feeling that rose up within me. The essential flavour of all the poetry I have read over the years, all the songs I've heard, and everything I've imagined is stored away somewhere in some corner of my mind. Why its alluring, intoxicating fragrance escapes on certain days or occasions I really don't know, nor do I know what to do with it, how to use it and where—I don't comprehend what its spiritual meaning or spiritual fulfilment may be. But its limitlessness, its depth and its mysterious plaintive note fills the mind with unrest, and it's impossible to think that this is in any way untrue or impermanent—even its impatient restlessness seems to be good. The material comfort and satisfaction of life in Calcutta seems very lowly in comparison with it. Last night at Jyo——'s place, A—— sat down with an esrāj—outside it was raining, and the breeze was full of the sound of the leaves on the trees. First I sang '*Bharā bādar*' [Rain clouds]. After that I sang '*Āmāẏ bāṅśite dekeche ke*' [Who calls me with a flute]—my voice was in good form, my heart too was full and the new year sympathetic, everything seemed to fall into place—and I wondered—this amazing realm of melody and feeling—is this only in my mind? Is there nothing like it anywhere else? Is it just a mirage?

210

Calcutta
24 April 1895

Today I've been afflicted with the deepest inertia since morning . . . I've just been wandering around in circles through the empty first-floor rooms of our Jorasanko house like a vagrant. All the joints of my body seemed to have been loosened, and I didn't have the strength to put my mind to any writing or reading. And then in no time at all the entire sky was suddenly overcast with clouds, thunder began to rumble, and a strong wind made all the large and small trees in the south garden sigh and moan. The afternoon became calm and shadowy and very intimate. An inexplicable restlessness made me inwardly agitated—whatever work my mind was given was rapidly flung out. . . . The mind's ways are like the sky's—unpredictable. For twenty-nine days in the month it works perfectly well with all the minor everyday work it has to do—no fuss—but suddenly, on the thirtieth day, it wants to kick that work away. It says, 'Give me something that's very large—in which all my days and nights, all that is big and small, the past and the present, can be swallowed up in a single gulp.' At that moment, what can one give it from what's near at hand—one can only keep wandering around the rooms and verandas at will. We say the mind is healthy when it is made to jump around among the scattered fragments of social duties, and when it wants to impatiently engage in a larger enterprise with the utmost fervour so that it may achieve a self-forgetful singleness of purpose, we consider it sick! But I think that man's true and natural state is attained when he wants to give up his entire life to be tied in chords of unity with that one strong passion—not everybody can achieve that unity, and for them, the scattered mechanical jobs of society are appropriate—but the deepest aspirations of the mind are towards that larger unity. That's the reason why, while living every day in this society, on certain days one thinks—

Āmāy bāṅśite dekeche ke!
[Who calls me with a flute!]

211

Calcutta
2 May 1895

Today the sound of the nahabat playing somewhere can be heard. The morning nahabat makes the mind terribly pensive. To this day I've been unable to determine what the significance is of the indescribable feeling created in the mind when you hear music. Yet, the mind tries to analyse and understand this feeling every single time. I've seen that as soon as the melody of a song unfolds fully, as soon as the wine hits the palate, this social world of life and death, this country of coming and going, this workaday world of light and shade, all move very far away—as if to stand on the other shore of some immense Padma River—from where everything appears like a picture. To us, our everyday life is not exactly proportionate— some insignificant part may seem immoderately large, and every present moment may be made thorny with the smallest of things, minor details, petty squabbles, hunger and thirst, work and rest; but music, through some irresistible attraction it exerts because of its own inner beauty and proportion, seems in a moment to give such a particular *perspective* to this life that those small, impermanent irritations become invisible to the eye—the world seems whole and vast and harmonious like a picture, and man's life and death, tears and laughter, past and future, all seem to sound upon the ear like the tender rhythm of a poem. At the same time, our own individual forcefulness or sharpness relaxes, and we loosen up, so that we can drown ourselves easily in a music-filled expanse. The inconsequential and artificial ties of society are particularly useful for society, yet music, or any of the higher *Arts*, reminds us of their insignificance in a moment—that is why *Art* by its very nature has a certain amount of social destructiveness within it—that's why our hearts become restless when we hear a good song or poem, the social fabric of our ties in this world is pierced, and our mind makes futile war for the freedom to enjoy the beauty of the everyday—the experience of beauty results in an inner war within us between the daily and the eternal, creating a sorrow beyond reason.

212

On the way to Patishar
1 June 1895

Returning again to my secluded *boat* after a long time, I'm feeling very much at ease. It feels as if I've returned home from abroad and someone is saying to me from time to time, 'You've come, I'm very happy to see you.' Solitude seems to stroke my head, my face, my body. It wasn't too hot today during the day—the sun was up, but the cool breeze felt very sweet. The river is small—the fields on either side are green as they roll towards the shore, there are cows grazing, women drawing water or bathing, and naked boys calling loudly to their distant companions upon catching sight of the *boat*. Small and big villages of all types, all with different sorts of names—as I watch them go past, I think, these villages are merely a momentary image for me, but for so many people they are their entire world. The people who descend to the water to bathe or sit on the shore scraping wood, will, at the right time, go to their homes hidden somewhere behind those dense trees. That is the stage upon which they will enact their everyday lives and work. The unknown and unremarkable people of that place are their most familiar and influential neighbours. I can't say that these thoughts are terribly wonderful or unique, but still, if you think along these lines, you see things in a new way—all of us are so big to ourselves, yet so small to most other people—that's what primarily comes to mind. It's evening now—those in the villages on both sides have lit their lamps in their homes and are sitting down by themselves without any work to be done, conversing, smoking, sleeping—only this solitary *boat* of mine goes on its way through the middle, the sound of its oars making a *jhup-jhup* splashing sound; I have no relation at all with the people on either side.

213

Patishar
3 June 1895

All of a sudden, '*gahana ghana chāilo gagana ghanāiȳā*' [densely, intensely, darkness covers the sky]—as much storm as rain. The wind is blowing sometimes from the east and sometimes from the west—the rain strikes hard against the sides of the boat with a *chaṭ-chaṭ* slapping sound . . . the wind rages across the sky moaning like an enraged beast. . . . There's no let-up in the thunder and lightning as well. All the sashes of my windows are closed—I've opened just one shutter on the side where there is no wind and am writing by the dim, cloudy light. The rain has intensified to the extent that I feel like writing the letter not in prose but in verse—but if I do that then perhaps the storm will come to an end before my poem does. After all, the storm doesn't have to rhyme its syllables as it goes. At this time it would have been good to sit and plot a story as well. That's what I might have done, but Shai——— is sitting here next to me—you can't write with someone sitting near you. But there's a great sense of joy within—the storm's blows, the cloud's shadows, the incessant *jhar-jhar* sound of rain, the roar of thunder—it seems to raise a storm in my heart—I want to do something, at least think of happy things, dream impossible dreams—if I could sing a song in the Kānāṛā or Malhār raga at the top of my voice that too would pass the time quite well—so many cloudy days, so many skies above the second-floor terrace, so many memories fly across my mind like scattered clouds!

214

Patishar
6 June 1895

And then, after having sent everyone off, I sat down to write a
story for *Sādhanā*—the month is almost over after all. So with firm
resolve, great intensity and a lot of concentration I've just finished
writing it. It's now past seven. But the summer evenings are long,
so it's still quite bright. As long as one is writing something, the
mind is at peace—the moment it finishes, one has to wander
around everywhere like a lost soul, a vagabond, in search of a new
subject. . . . A person writes something with so much thought,
effort and hard work, but the reader reads it with such indifference
and idiocy, and most of the time doesn't read it at all. To bemoan
the fact is cowardly, and I don't usually do that. But when you're
tired after an entire day's work and sitting alone in the evening, it's
impossible to avoid a temporary pensiveness. Then one feels like
departing the battlefield and hiding one's self away completely to
live one's life as one pleases, doing what one wants and relaxing as
one wants in a solitary and unknown space of one's own. Nothing
is more tiring for man than the public. His only place of rest is
in the generosity of nature and in the depths of love—everything
else brings only tiredness.

215

Calcutta
Monday, 24 June 1895

After quite a few days of out-and-out rain and storm, the sun has
appeared today from behind the clouds. I remember there was
a time when days like these would quite overpower me. Such a

trembling feeling of joy would rise within me that it is impossible to express it properly. I was reminded of that today. I had gone to Park Street this morning to meet Bābāmaśāẏ. On the way to see him, I was reading the *Amrita Bazaar Patrika* as I went, but on the way back, I happened to suddenly look out on to the meadows of the *gaṛer māṭh**—the world is much the same as it used to be, but I don't have the time any more—the youthful, graceful morning sunlight fell upon the field, covering its green beauty—so unruffled and succulent and clear and new—with a pensive peace, making it calm and beautiful. For a brief while, my heart resounded as it used to with the quiver of an unspeakably tender and beautiful rāginī's notes. These days there are so many things that tie me down, encircling me on all sides, that I no longer come face-to-face with the world—the intimate relation and everyday connection between my conscious self and the character of the world is slowly slipping away—the musician who plays upon the bīṇā of the world and wakes the waves in the rivers, who makes the flowers of spring bloom in a moment, who enlivens the land, water and air with the murmur and chatter and hum of birdsong—that musician's live, self-aware trembling fingers do not touch the strings of my heart any more. I'm afraid if too many days pass in this way then those heartstrings that used to resonate all the time may gather dust and become rusted, and the mind may become increasingly old and inert. Men who work without rest become hard and old. I realize that that hardness is necessary—that to be worthy of society it's absolutely necessary to be of a certain age too—but still, I really dislike it a great deal. But you must keep ślokas such as '*sukhaṃ bā yadi bā dukhaṃ priẏaṃ yadi bā priẏaṃ*' [happiness or unhappiness, dear or not dear], etc., in mind and give up such futile regrets in the face of what will certainly be, and prepare yourself for all the work that is at hand and every situation that

---

* *Gaṛer māṭh*: literally, the fields of the fort; refers to the fields of the well-manicured grassland around Fort William in Calcutta, also referred to as the Maidan.

confronts you. Nowadays, that has been accomplished to some extent—one has managed to bind one's mind quite firmly to the tree of circumscribed duties—and the blinkers are firmly in place over one's eyes too, so that one can keep going round and round in the circles of everyday routine in order to manufacture the maximum oil and become an indispensable animal for this world. Oil is much more useful than music—one needs it for cooking as well as for lighting the lamps at dusk. So I'd better stop now, Bob, and resume my circumambulation around the oil press—the kāchāri letters have been delivered, and the *proofs* of *Sādhanā* lie in a heap.

216

Shahjadpur
28 June 1895

I've been sitting and writing a story for *Sādhanā*; it's a bit far-fetched [āshāḍhe]. I was feeling really irritated and reluctant when I began, but that's not the case any longer. Now I've jumped midstream into the imagining of it—as I write a little at a time, the entire light and shade and colour of the scenery outside filters into my writing. This stream of rain and sun, the forests of reeds on the riverbank, this monsoon sky, the shady village, the fields of grain made happy with flowing water, all of it surrounds from every side the scenes and people and events that I imagine and make them come alive in truth and beauty—my own imaginings have become quite delightful for me. But readers will not get even the half of it. They get only the cut grain, but the sky and the breeze on the fields of grain, the dew and the cloud-like darkness, the green and gold and blue are all left out. Along with my story, if I could give them this small river and its riverbank bathed in sunlight from this cloud-free rainy-season sky, the shade of this tree and the peace of this village, all complete and whole, then how sweet and alive my story would appear! How easily everyone would comprehend its inner truth! Then no one would have the courage to criticize it. A lot of the flavour stays within the heart, it's impossible to give it all to the reader. God has not even given us the ability to wholly give what we have to another.

217

Shahjadpur
2 July 1895

I've left the boat and come up to the Shahjadpur bungalow since yesterday. It's exactly as I thought. I'm really liking it. The ceiling is quite a bit above my head and because there are two open verandas on either side, immense quantities of light from the sky keep raining down upon my head—and it's a very sweet feeling to write and read and sit and think in that light. Another good thing is, while I work, every time I turn my face in any direction a section of blue sky mixed with green earth is present right outside my room. As if nature, like a curious village girl, was peeping in through my doors and windows all the time. Every part of my room and my mind—of my work and my leisure—is happy and satisfied, full of flavour and life, new and beautiful. The light of this sky free of rain, this village and the lines of water, this shore and that, the open field and the broken road are all a heavenly poem, enrapt in the notes of Apollo's golden lyre. How I love the sky and the light with all my heart! The sky is my *sāqi* [wine bearer] holding an upturned clear-blue glass cup; the golden light enters my bloodstream like wine and makes me coeval with the gods. At the place where my sāqi's face is happy and free, at the place where this golden wine of mine is the most golden and clear, that is where I am a poet, that is where I am a king, that is where I have my thirty-two thrones [*batriś siṃhāsan*].* I feel the deep, silent, heartfelt love and endless peaceful consolation of this sky in every part of my body and mind. This storehouse of the sky, this light, this peace will never be depleted—if I can maintain this same uninterrupted felt connection with this calm, blue, light-filled limitlessness forever, my life will never be completely dry.

218

Shahjadpur
5 July 1895

Yesterday they were playing tunes from devotionals [kīrtan] at the nahabat long into the night—it felt quite wonderful, and very appropriate in this rural atmosphere—as simple as it was tender. There was a soft breeze and sparkling moonlight last night, and the nahabat was being played in lingering detail. I kept the windows open and went to sleep listening to that music. This morning I woke up to the same music. In the olden days, kings had court musicians who sang at specific hours by which you could tell the time; that aristocratic habit seems very desirable to me. In my childhood when we lived in the garden house at Peneti, the nahabat would play three or four times a day from the Dakshineshwar Shiva temple next door—I used to think then that the moment I grew up and became independent, I would employ a nahabat like it. The stone god who is deaf to the unbearable din of the brass bells does not need to hear the opening notes of the ragas of the nahabat four times a day. Far better if some pious soul made an arrangement for such a nahabat to play for gods [ṭhākur] like us, then the music would not be played in

* *Batriś siṃhāsan*: refers to the legend of the thirty-two thrones of King Vikramaditya.

vain.* Then this daily inconsequential life would become so much more pleasurable, and the day's work and duties would not induce such feelings of unbearable weariness and renunciation. The moment I hear music or song I realize how thirsty I had been feeling all the while for music—that's why I really wish sometimes that someone close to me would learn how to play a musical instrument really well.

219

Shahjadpur
6 July 1895

Yesterday our annual ceremonial rituals here came to an end. A huge number of our tenants [prajā] had come. I was sitting and writing when suddenly they began to arrive in streams for an audience with their king [rājdarśan]—the room and the veranda filled up completely. I have an old devotee; his name is Rupchand Mredha—a real dacoit-like specimen—tall, muscular, truthful, tyrannical, and a devoted subject. He loves me like a very close relative—he touched my feet in greeting, stood up straight, and said, 'I've come to see your beautiful moon-face [chāṅdmukh].' On hearing this, 'beautiful moon-face' perhaps began to blush a little. Rupchand said, 'I'm seeing you after so long—it must be a year since I last saw you!' Women's love, of course, may feel very sweet, but this sort of simple, forceful man's genuine and unswerving devotion too has a wonderful charm—an absolutely pure and ancient empathy of man for man finds expression in it—the particular strength and hardness that accompanies it, and the sincerity and *directness* it conveys, perhaps make this full, beautiful love seem so much more

---

* *Thākur*, meaning the gods, is being punned on here, as it is also, of course, Rabindranath's family's surname in Bengali.

valuable. Bearded men, as simple as children and unable to express their inner feelings, came one by one to kiss my feet and take its dust—occasionally, some of them would literally kiss the feet. One day I was sitting on a chair in a field in Kaligram when a woman suddenly came up to me and put her head upon my feet and kissed them—I should of course mention that she wasn't a young woman. Many male subjects too kiss the feet. If I was the only jamidār these people had, I would have kept them very happy—and their love would have made me very happy too.

220

On the way to Pabna
9 July 1895

We're travelling through the winding Ichamoti River now. I've written so many letters to you while journeying through it, coming and going. This small whimsical river, with its green sloping banks on either side, deep and dense kās forests, fields of jute and sugar cane, and rows and rows of villages—they are like the lines of a poem that I recite every time, and which feels new each time. Rivers like the Padma are so large that they cannot be learnt by heart. And this small, winding river of the rainy season seems to become especially my own—there are no steamers on this river, no crowd of boats, only my *boat* seems to lord it over this rural river as it passes. The sky has been overcast since yesterday. Everything is calm and green, both shores peaceful. Human settlements are insignificant to the Padma, but the Ichamoti is a river close to men—her peaceful stream of water merges beautifully with the flow of man's everyday work routines. She is a river for boys to fish in and women to bathe in—all the gossip that the women bring to it when they bathe mingles harmoniously with its laughter-filled babble. In the month of Āśvin, Menaka's daughter Parvati leaves her mountain home at Kailash once to come and visit her parents and see if they are well; so too is the Ichamoti invisible throughout the year, but filled with joyful laughter in the rainy season when she comes to find out about her friends and relations in these settlements—then, after listening to the village news brought by the women to every ghat with the intimacy of a friend, she leaves again.

221

Shilaidaha
10 July 1895

It's almost evening—the sky is dark with clouds. Thunder rumbles and the jhāu trees on the shore sway in the stormy wind. Jackals call from the forests, there are no boats on the river—the women have abandoned the ghat and the riverbank is completely deserted—two or three cows walk homeward through the bāblā forests. There is a darkness as black as ink in the bamboo forests on the shore, and the pale grey light of twilight falling upon the water appears like an unnatural excitement. In this weak light, I'm bent over a sheet, writing—all the papers on the table scatter in the wild wind and are ready to fly away. Then again the restless river is making the boat rock a little, which makes it difficult to maintain a straight line while I write. But I really love the splendid arrangement of the heavy rains upon this small river—I feel like sitting and writing a letter at this time. A letter that is like continuous low conversation in a small, secluded room in the cloudy, twilit darkness. But that is only a wish—I'm not sure how exactly to turn it into reality. That is, I don't have the ability to turn the letter into the stories told in that secluded room. Our simplest wishes are the ones that are really the most impossible to fulfil. Either they are fulfilled on their own or they are never fulfilled. It's sometimes easier to make war than to make stories work.

222

There's a new idea in my '*pañcabhautik*' this time that is at least worth thinking about, but I see that none of my readers have quite understood it.* I've said that if there was no death, our imaginations would have been confined to the material world, and the world would not have had any *suggestion* of the eternal in it. The material world is an unshakeable *reality*—but our imagination and our spiritual sense are not satisfied by it. If we want to satisfy them, we need to create an *ideal* world, and where should we establish that *ideal* world? Where death has created a gap in this material world. It is in the space beyond death that we have our heaven, our gathering of gods, our completeness, our eternal existence. If the world kept us fenced in with an immovable, hard wall, and if death had not opened up windows in it from time to time, we would have been completely limited to only what is there. We would never even have imagined that something else could exist. Death has opened a doorway to endless possibilities. There is no end to what we may be after death, and it is because death removes the old that the limitless futurity of the new can nourish our *ideal* hope. The most important poetic quality in a good poem is *suggestiveness*. The way this world is made means that in it, *suggestiveness* is to be found in death—that's where we get to feel that there is much more, and that much more can happen. Just as we can see an indication of the immensity of the universe in the dark night sky alone—for in daylight it is only this world which is illuminated—so too do we

---

* A section of *Sādhanā* was devoted to the discussion of something called the *pañcabhautik sabhā*, which roughly translates as 'gathering of the five elements', where personifications representing the five elements debated particular issues. The topics of discussion could vary from 'The Significance of Poetry' [*Kābyer tātparya*] to 'The Satisfaction of Beauty' [*Saundarya sammandhe śantosh*].

experience intimations of our relation with the eternal in death; if there were no death, we would have been strictly imprisoned within our meagre, poor existence; we would never have received even a hint or an indication of that space that contains the human soul's most noble poetry, the next world and the world of the gods, where our spiritual sense and appreciation of beauty are satisfied. Besides which, if our existence had not on occasion found a gap, it would have become dangerously ugly. True beauty is constructed at the confluence of clear *definiteness* on one side and endless *suggestiveness* on the other—just as the same death puts a limit to our lives on one side and also frees us from those limits on another. Looked at personally, death is terrible, and we gain no reassurance from it. But looked at from the point of view of the whole universe, death is very beautiful and the actual place of comfort for man's soul.

But I've seen again and again that the kernel of the questions I raise in my *pañcabhautik* is usually not understood by anyone. Actually, perhaps that's because I cannot explain it very well—it is also very difficult to explain.

223

Calcutta
3 August 1895

One has to admit that there's a great intoxication in fame, but, like other intoxicants, fame too can be very wearying and tiring. After the first surge of excitement, everything seems empty and false—one feels like taking the utmost care to keep one's distance from this drug that's so insulting and degrading for the soul, so that it doesn't turn into an addiction. Firstly, people's praise immediately makes you feel doubtful about your own abilities, and then one feels terribly uncomfortable thinking that you've obtained all this false praise by deception—yet it's not as if I really think I'm unworthy of the affection of the ordinary Bengali reader—that's the strange thing. Yet day by day the more famous I become, on the one hand I'm happy, but on the other I feel an increasingly strong desire to leave it all behind, and, pushing aside the crowds, take refuge in a secluded corner of my own *private* residence. To see my name in the public eye as it appears repeatedly in *Sādhanā* every month is really irritating. I can quite see that this fame thing is not good—it doesn't quench the thirst of one's soul, only increases it.

224

Shilaidaha
14 August 1895

The more I put my hand to many different sorts of work, the more I respect this thing called work. Of course I already had a general idea that work was an excellent as well as a very superior thing. But all of that was textbook stuff. Now I see quite clearly that man's ultimate worth lies in his work. Work engages quite a few of man's faculties—you have to evaluate the worth of goods and of people, and maintain a relationship with the business field. A new kingdom has opened up for me now. I have plunged into the vast arena of commerce in which millions of people from many different countries are already striving to their limits—I have experienced for the first time the chains that tie man to man and the generosity of his work as it spreads across far distances. One feels quite a sense of pride in labouring and thinking as one learns and knows all this. One of the great things about the work men do is that when they work, they have to ignore and curtail their personal joys and sorrows and keep going. I remember, one morning in Shahjadpur when the khansama there turned up late for work I got very angry; he came and did his everyday habitual salaam and said, in a slightly constricted voice, 'Last night my eight-year-old daughter died.' Saying this, he put the duster on his shoulder and went off to dust my bedroom furniture. I felt horrible—there's no time to stop for the most heartfelt grief in the hard workplace. But what's the point of taking that time either? If work can free a man from the ties of futile regret and propel him forward, then what better education than that! What is not to be is beyond our reach, while what can be is quite enough and available ready at hand. I can do nothing but grieve for the daughter who has died, but for the son who is still alive I must work really hard. I look at this worldwide workplace of man through my mind's eye—everybody is working hard on either side of the royal road of life—some are employed in offices, some do business, some are farmers, some labourers—yet, beneath this workplace, at every moment, secretly and hidden from view, there flows so much death, so much grief, sorrow and hopelessness—if these win the day, in a moment the wheel of work would stop spinning. Personal joys and sorrows flow on underneath us and above it all is constructed a bridge made of hard stone upon which the train of work chuffs on upon its steel tracks with a whistling sound with its millions of people—except for its designated stops, it doesn't stop for anyone. There is a hard comfort in this cruelty of work.

225

Shilaidaha
18 August 1895

There's one aspect of living in a hut that I don't mind—though one can't exactly call living with *tables*, *chairs* and *camp*-beds proper living in a hut. Still, to get up on to land and see the green world of the rains felt good. A lot of time was spent sitting for a long time watching the cows and goats grazing on the abundant wet grass, and in observing the accompanying shepherd girls. It feels very sweet to observe, from up close, those human situations in which men live right next to trees and crops and cows and calves and single-storeyed mud huts—absorbed in cropping grain, sailing boats, drawing water, washing clothes. Some say that the happiness we imagine them experiencing is not founded in fact. But that's not true. They are a bit like children, that's why they can experience happiness and satisfaction with their entire hearts. Our joys are terribly complicated and difficult to attain and in most instances have become quite artificial. Our minds are not easily charmed, we can't easily forget ourselves completely, we can't embellish the little we have with our simple imaginations— instead, our critical analysis reduces what we had in plenty. That doesn't mean I want to become a farmer—I just want their satisfaction and their simplicity without letting go of my own reserves of intelligence or erudition.

226

Shilaidaha
20 August 1895

The cloud and the rain have given way since yesterday to the clear, bright, beautiful feeling of the śarat season. In the last few days the river water has decreased and the river has suddenly acquired a very calm, unruffled air—the fishermen near the sandbank on the other shore have got down into the waist-deep water to catch fish, and there are cows grazing by the riverbank on this shore—a very vast, beautiful, bright peace sits with its generous maternal lap extended over the land and water and air; it comes very close to me and kisses my head. On mornings such as this, all the sweet days of the past mingle with the present and appear as a complete whole. I've said to you once before, Bob, if I could stitch together all my letters, leaving out all the insignificant personal detail and selecting only my opinions, descriptions and enjoyment of beauty, I could then have access to a concentration of all the sweetness of a greater part of my lived life—that would be like a large, spread-out grove for me to wander in—if at any time the delicate ability for enjoyment ebbs away, if the new world begins to close its doors on me one by one, then that invaluable old world of mine would stay with me as my ultimate shelter. My thoughts on my most intimate relationship with the universe are truthfully there in these letters in a way that they are not to be found anywhere else—if I could access that part, my life would become that much larger.

227

Shilaidaha
23 August 1895

I was wondering why the monsoon river's enormous torrent and unceasing murmur keep me so satisfied in their company. I can quite see why, but it's difficult to express the thought. The river is like a huge living thing—a powerful stream of energy comes pouring proudly and carelessly down from a great distance. When we see this, our hearts respond with a tremor of intimacy. If one sees an unconquerable wild horse running with the powerful joy of freedom upon a field, our hearts are rocked with a feeling of power. I've thought about it many a time—the deep and secret joy we get from nature is only because we feel a great sense of relationship and familiarity with it—these ever-fresh, green and simple creepers, grasses, trees and bushes, this flowing water, moving air, the revolving, ceaseless shadow-world, this cycle of seasons, the stream of stars and constellations moving across the limitless sky, the numberless living things of this world—we have a connection of flowing blood and beating pulse with all of it—

we are set to the same rhythm as the rest of the universe—when there is a caesura or a reverberation in this rhythm, our hearts respond in agreement from within—if we were not of the same family as every atom and molecule that the world is made up of, if eternity had not pulsed with life, beauty and a concealed joy, we would never have been able to feel this genuine pleasure when in proximity to the real world. We have a secret path that connects us to that which we unfairly term insensate; otherwise, there could never be such an irresistible tie of love between life and inert things, between the mind and material objects, between inside and outside. It is because there really is no caste division between me and the tiniest particle of this universe that we have all found a place in this world together—else, two different worlds would have been created for both of us. When I become earth of this earth, even then my tie with this eternal, living world will not be severed—I feel this with my own simple inner joy. I have no logical reason for it.

228

Shilaidaha
24 August 1895

The fact that we have a certain concealed, delightful relationship with this autochthonous, limitless, skyful of habitually pulsating and whirling atoms and molecules is a truth that sometimes fades from our minds and becomes near invisible—perhaps it stays written somewhere in my memory as a result of a very old habit, but I cannot feel it any more in my inner heart like a real and illuminating thing. Then one makes the mistake of considering it a poetic fancy. What better proof do we have of it than that we feel it within our own hearts? But the mind is often led astray by all sorts of work and all sorts of thoughts, so that the delicate ability of the imagination to feel dries up for the lack of nourishment, and consequently that calm, deep and fulfilled expansiveness of the inner self vanishes, in whose deep silence one could hear the distant footsteps of truth resonate clearly, just like one's inner thoughts. Then it all gets mixed up and muddy, and one thinks of the outer confusion alone as the truth and keeps mistaking the heart's eternal thoughts as dreamlike imaginings. If that were not so, if the living attraction of this endless universe could be exprienced absolutely clearly and truly at all times, then what else would've given me comparable peace and comfort? Then I could have embraced the earth of this world, so full of life, and held it close, extending my heart into its all-encompassing beauty. The sad thing is that unless you have a little peace, this unbroken peace outside cannot be reflected in you; unless you have some joy, you cannot connect with this whole and entire joy. That's why occasionally when I come here to the mofussil this truth manifests itself before me suddenly in a single moment. But if with the passing of time this vitality of my imagination fades, if the material world appears inert due to my own mental inertia, then what I feel today as the most intimate truth will be thought of as the fancy of a certain time of my youth—as if it were quite a beautiful *theory*—perhaps it will evoke a dry smile when I am older. But this felt experience of intense joy is contained in so many of the letters I have written you—that perhaps when I see them my dry heart will gather sap from them—and I will regain that *religion* which is peculiar to my character.

229

Shilaidaha
20 September 1895

Today the storm has abated, and the sun has been trying to rise little by little this morning, although it hasn't been completely successful yet. The clouds are scattered across the sky, the wind blows fiercely from the east. The blooming forests of kāś on the other shore tremble like flames in the wind. You can hear the distant Padma's roar from here. Yesterday and the day before the scene was exactly as in that new song of mine—*jharajhara barashe bāridhārā*—

> Drops of water rain down—
> The wind moans
> In the deserted endless fields—
> The restless Padma's waves cry out—
> Dense clouds fill the sky—

And then, this wretched, homeless person got completely soaked from head to toe on the roof of the steamer and turned into mud. I was wearing that enormous silk *ālkhāllā* [long coat], and it began to fly about in every direction in a most laughable way—the spectacles in front of my eyes became blurred with water—the cover of the book in my hand began to shed continuous coloured tears. In the last couple of days I'd been singing that song quite frequently. As a result, the flow of the rain, the moan of the wind, and the sound of the Gorai River's waves all assumed a new life of their own—their speech began to become clear on every side, and I too took up my stance as one of the main actors in this vast dance drama of storm and rain. There's no greater magic than music in this world—it is a new lord of creation. I can't decide whether music creates a new world of māyā or if it unveils the wondrous, innermost, everyday kingdom of the old world. There are some things like songs that say to men, 'However hard you try to explain everything in this world clearly and logically, its real essence is indescribable,' and it is with that that the meaning of our existence has the most heartfelt connection—it is the cause of all this sorrow, this happiness, this yearning.

230

Shilaidaha
21 September 1895

I certainly know that if I can once force my head down and engage myself in composing something, the writing flows on speedily, and the more I immerse myself in it, the more I'm filled with pure joy. But the surprising thing is, just before I begin to actually start writing I don't seem to be able to take my mind in hand. My mind says, 'All my writing is done; and I don't have anything to write about either; my ability to write too is almost spent—when I'm in this state don't prod me to write and embarrass myself in front of the public.' I say to it, 'That's what you keep saying, but you keep writing nevertheless.' My mind is like a particular class of horse that begins to shy and kick and move backward the moment the reins are pulled, but once you manage to whip it and coax it and make it take a couple of steps forward it runs ahead on all four legs the rest of the way. Now it is bending towards its stables in Calcutta—but the moment it regains complete authority over its own ability to compose or imagine, the moment it goes forward a bit, it will think that the material world actually really exists in this imaginary world. As I write, I enter my own secret life of the mind more and more deeply, and once there, I see that the honey I collected from my life's flowers of desire has mostly remained stored there. One doesn't always manage to find the entrance to that everyday kingdom of the mind.

The clouds have cleared since yesterday and the new śarat season has flooded my surroundings, that's why I drown in my dew-wet memories this way.

231

Shilaidaha
25 September 1895

Men have, by their own hand, made this social world of theirs
so complicated and entangled that it's become a huge problem
simply being happy or making others happy. But sorrow is perhaps
a very necessary thing for man, perhaps more essential than war or
striving or tolerance or sacrifice or being happy. Unhappiness turns
a man into a man, and that humanity has some value somewhere
or other. Those who peddle religion say that god makes those he
loves suffer. That might often sound like devious 'cant', but that
doesn't mean it's completely without foundation. Suffering is
the one and only value of our souls, our loves, our most precious
treasures. . . . The unfortunate thing is that we don't have the
wherewithal to alleviate another's sorrow. That's why making
money doesn't seem a small thing. If I can make some money
through this business of ours then I'll be able to quell many of my
heart's sorrows—one cannot deal with someone's unhappiness in
this *material* world by wishes alone.

232

Shilaidaha
26 September 1895

I see no signs of a storm coming, though—there are very few
clouds in the sky, the river is very calm, the daylight is clear
and bright—the *boat* races ahead in the current with a whistling
sound and the breeze blows softly—a certain happy languor fills
my heart. Today is the last day of my solitary existence; besides

all my other work, from tomorrow I'll have to concentrate on hospitality. . . . I still haven't started writing for *Sādhanā*. I've kept up only a partial relationship with Saraswati through some discussion of music. Nature is so close to you here, her pulse and heaving breath can be felt from up close to such an extent that one doesn't feel like expressing one's self in anything that needs more effort than music. Nothing is closer to nature than song—I know for certain that right now if I look outside my window and begin to intone the Rāmkeli raga, this endless sun-coloured, greenish-blue scenery shall come into my inner essence like a mesmerized doe and begin to caress me. Every time it rains on the Padma, each time I think, let me compose a song for the rains in Meghamallār, but where's the strength? And after all, the audiences don't have this daily attraction of the rains in front of them; they'll find it monotonous. Because the words are the same—it rains, it's cloudy, lightning flashes. But its inner ever-new passion, its autochthonous, never-ending sorrow of separation [*birahabedanā*] can only be expressed partially in the melody of a song.

233

Shilaidaha
30 September 1895

I see you're really annoyed with the writer of 'Us and Them' ['*Āmrā o tomrā*']. But the man is sitting there thinking, 'What fun'. The problem is, you cannot explain rasa to a man who doesn't understand it because the appreciation of rasa is sensory and has to be experienced. So much so, that even persons who have a sense of rasa may have differences of opinion when they evaluate good or bad. That's why the task of reviewing seems like such a chore and the same goes for the work of writing. Still, the work of judging good or bad continues in the world, and not too badly either—although differences of opinion are not scarce, with the passing of time a certain unanimity is arrived at in public opinion. Somewhat like *natural selection—variation* manifests itself in many forms every day, but that which does not endure falls by the wayside for different reasons, and that which does attains a certain unity. If the seeds that we writers sow have a truly lasting worth in the minds of people, then however critical a reviewer may be, that seed will not go in vain. Actually, man's mind is not something one can know well—I can say with some certainty what I will like or dislike for now, and can even speculate on what others will like or dislike, but the moment it becomes a little fine or complex, it's only the most skilled or knowledgeable critic who can account for it. And even the most skilled critic can sometimes make mistakes. The mark of a good critic is that his understanding is as nuanced as his empathy is all-encompassing and his literary experience vast. He should be able to transcend his own likes and dislikes, and with the help of his powers of empathy access different tastes and different situations. That sort of person is very rare. Rather, one may find many good writers, but a real critic is very rare. But the surprising thing is—even then, it is only good writing that goes on to establish itself in the affections of the ordinary reader. So, whether there is anything like an ideal taste isn't something one can conclude through nuanced argument; yet, ordinarily, a certain ideal of taste is constructed in human society through use and nothing that's totally ugly ever survives as beauty—mistakes are made, and those are then corrected as well. If that were not so, the talented would not have been trying so hard through all time to achieve completeness in the creation of beauty—they cannot prove that there is an imperative ideal of taste, yet they devote their staunchest efforts to that truth.

234

Shilaidaha
4 October 1895

With the rain and the clouds gone, it's turned out to be a very
beautiful day. Today the śarat season has been properly established.
The word 'beautiful' is used often for many different purposes—
that's why the word has become almost unusable; yet there aren't
that many words that one can use instead of it. Whatever it is,
today is a precious and rare day—my heart is completely full with
this light, this silence, this clear, white, transparent sky. Some
unknown magician has stroked a nectar-filled intoxicant upon my
eyes with tender hands, so that this still river in mid-afternoon
and the sandbank on the other shore embroidered with glad kāś
flower forests seem to me as pleasurable as a distant memory. I'm
filled with a very selfish regret when I think that I will not be
able to access these deep śarat days as completely as this when
other people arrive on the *boat*. Perhaps it's in anticipation of
that impending interruption that today's enjoyment of silence
and solitude is all the more intense. It's as if the hurt and proud
companion of my exile, with her tender, steadfast gaze, has come
to bid me farewell. It's as if she says to me, 'What's the point of
this domesticity and these ties with your relatives—I am what
you have been meditating upon for all time, I am the beloved of
all your past lives, your only familiar acquaintance among all the
numberless fragments of your eternal lives—do not, for any reason,
neglect my precious company, for your inner soul does not receive
the ultimate fruits of beauty, happiness or sorrow from any other
hand than mine.' But all these words will sound unreal and baseless
before the present workplace and the real world—although if you
look at it from a distance and review the matter a little deeply,
you will see that it's not such an invalid thought after all. It is no

small thing for me to keep the layers of my soul watered in the abundant peace of this śaraṯ. If I go and stay at some inaccessible place in the interests of the jute business, people will praise me, and my sense of duty too will be at peace, but if I disappear for a few days without any work, then it's difficult not to make either myself or others anxious. All that gives me the deepest satisfaction and pleasure in this life is stored in this sort of moment of solitude and beauty alone—it's become impossible for me to gather that in a fragmentary or diluted way from the social world. A new truth is rising gradually from the depths of my heart—I get only its merest hint. For me, it is a permanent everyday resource, the pure liquid gold extracted from the mines of my entire life experience—the crop of nectar within all my sorrow, grief and pain—if I can obtain it in a clear, expressive and dependable form, it is more to me than all my money, status, fame, happiness—even if I don't obtain it completely, just orienting the natural and necessary flow of my heart in that direction is something of a major accomplishment. If I were always happy, if I had attained all that I wished for after having completed all the work of my days to spend my days in ease, how little would I have got out of this human birth—what would I have known!

235

Shilaidaha
4 October 1895

Nowadays the days have turned extremely sweet—the breeze is cool, the sky is bright, the shoreline is green, the river is calm, the heart is a refuge for dreams, there's little work, all my writing has ceased, the holidays are all around, and beauty flows both within and without. The gurgle of the water seems to have somebody's very tender tones of love mixed in it; the clear blue sky too is bent with the weight of affection, and the calm waters are full of queries of love; all these colours—this deep brownish-orange [*geruā*] of the water, the white of this shore, the green of the other shore, the blue of the sky, the gold of the sun—all this shines in the rays of śaraṯ in so many outfits and with such smiling glances! The entire sky, like an infinite heart, seems to hold me in its embrace. The astonishing thing is that day after tomorrow when there will be a crowd of people over here, all this will seem to not be here at all—when men arrive, nature seems not to find a place in nature any more. Man takes up so much space, wastes so much!

236

Kushtia
5 October 1895

Who is it who tells me to look at everything with depth and seriousness, who inclines me towards listening to the ancient music of this world with so much attention and absorption, who recites a mantra of melancholy over me so that all my restlessness fades away day by day, allowing me to experience all my finest and most forceful connections with the outside in this secluded, silent, alive and self-conscious way! I have starved often and for long periods in this life to keep penance—it's a result of this *tapasyā* [meditation] that the world's limitless and mysterious depth is almost always spread like an ocean before me. No good is done to man if his heart is gratified at every moment—that only produces a limited amount of happiness and wastes an unnecessary number of ingredients, and more time is spent on the preparation rather than the enjoyment. But if you live your life by practising austerity, you will see that even a little bit of happiness is a lot, and that happiness is not the only pleasurable thing on earth. If you want to keep the heart's faculties of sight, sound, touch and thought vigilant, if you want the ability to receive all that you can receive to remain sharp, you must keep the heart always hungry—you have to deprive yourself of abundance. I have kept something Goethe said always in mind—it sounds simple, but to me it seems very deep—

> *Entbehren sollst du, sollst entbehren.*
> *Thou must do without, must do without.*

Not only food for the heart, outer pleasures and comforts and things too make us inert—it is only when everything outside is scant that you can find yourself. That's why the relative comfort of Calcutta begins to prick me after a short while, as if its small pleasures and enjoyments were making it difficult for me to breathe.

Yet tapasyā is not something I have wanted of my own will, happiness is very dear to me, but since god has forcibly created in me an inclination towards tapasyā, maybe he wants some special results from me; at the end of it all—dried, ground-to-dust, burnt, scattered—perhaps something hard will remain from this life that will endure. Sometimes I can feel a shadowy premonition of this. The dharma we get from the śāstras never becomes my dharma; it is only a sort of habitual bond with it that develops over time—for me it's only the dharma that is *crystallised* in the unbearable heat within my life that is the real thing. I can't explain this to anybody else, and there's no need to either—they will not be able to understand the inner meaning of it, and even if they do they'll distort it—but to take that and allow it to grow within one's self is man's best evidence of his humanity. You give birth to it in the greatest pain, give your own blood to make it live—and then, even without having been completely happy in this life, it might be possible to die contented:

Entbehren sollst du, sollst entbehren.

237

Kushtia
6 October 1895

I'm letting my days float away one by one in a stream of laziness like Rathi's paper boats. Only occasionally do I compose a song or half a song, and then I sit on the chair in an idle way, humming the tune; I keep forgetting the tune and I make it again, and then I remain lying there, curled up in this sweet-memory-filled, melancholy-soft śarat season. I don't quite know when I'll be able to tighten my belt and get down to some serious work. A breath rises from this vast water and riverbank and falls upon my body—a very intimate and live presence full of life and love and feeling has attached itself to me, both within and without, and I just cannot tell it to go. This unbounded, light-filled blue sky seems to be bent over my heart, the light has entered my blood, the all-enveloping silence has embraced my breast with both hands, a tender, tear-wet calm kisses my eyes, my forehead—I'm encircled by an all-encompassing yet secluded beauty. Everybody has left their work and come home for the Puja holidays, and this is my home too—my home-body snatches away my exercise books and says, 'You've worked a great deal, now stop for a while.' I too comply and stop without protest; after this, work will get a hold of me at some time and grab me by the throat—then this home-body of mine, this mistress of my holidays, will have disappeared and it will be impossible to find any trace of her. Nowadays, I frequently think to myself that I shall sink the *Sādhanā*, monthly and quarterly, in the waters of the Padma and leave. But I know that even if I sink it, it shall drag me along in its wake.

238

Shilaidaha
10 October 1895

I cannot say that I have attained what is ordinarily called religion
in a very clear or firm way within me, but, increasingly, there
are times when I can feel the living thing that has gradually been
created in the interiors of my mind. This is not a specific belief
of any kind but a secret awareness, a new inner sense. I can quite
see that gradually I will be able to establish a certain proportionate
balance of my own within myself; I will be able to give my life—
my joys and sorrows, outside and inside, beliefs and behaviour—a
certain totality. I can't say whether what they write in the śāstras is
true or false, but those truths are often completely inapplicable to
me—really, it's fair to say they have no relevance for me whatsoever.
My ultimate truth is that which I will be able to construct with
my entire life in a complete form. When we experience all of life's
joys and sorrows in a scattered and evanescent way, we don't quite
understand this limitless mystery of creation within us—just as one
cannot understand the unity of feeling and meaning in a verse if you
begin to spell each word aloud separately. But once you experience
the unbroken source of unity of this creative power within yourself,
you can feel your connection with this eternal, created universe;
then I comprehend that just as the planets and stars and moon and
sun have been created as they whirl around through time, there is
a certain creation going on within me as well from the beginning
of time—my joys and sorrows, desires and pain have taken their
own place within it—I don't know what will come of it, because
we don't know even a single particle of dust, but when I connect
my own flowing life with the eternal life that is outside of me,
I can see that all of life's sorrow too may be collected within a
larger source of joy—I am present, I am functioning, I am going
on—these are the things I then understand as a large, vast affair. I

am and, along with me, everything else is; without me not even an atom or molecule could exist in this limitless world; the connection I have with this calm, beautiful śarat morning is no less than the intimate connection I have with my relatives; that's why this light-filled space soaks up my inner soul in this way—otherwise, would it have been able to touch my heart even fractionally? Would I have been able to feel its beauty? Would I have been able to see all my dreams and desires reflected so completely within it? The everlasting secret connection between me and this life of the world is evidenced in the diverse language of colour, smell and song—all around us, the never-ending manifestation of this language rocks our hearts in seen and unseen ways—the conversation continues day and night.

239

Shilaidaha
15 October 1895

The sun is blazing down, the water shimmers, there's a slight winter breeze blowing, the river water is as still as a mirror, occasionally one or two boats pass by with a splashing sound. If I were alone I would be lying, engrossed, on a long armchair near the window—I would daydream, I would be able to hear the deep notes of the Bilāwalī rāginī that is within this sky so bright with sunlight, and I would feel my own existence dissolved, spread across, rocked in the waves of this sunlight, water and breeze—I would experience myself lying down on a bed of unfragmented, endless time—I would feel myself flow in the chatter and gurgle of the ever-rippling waterfall of life that wells up in the form of grass and shrubs, leaves and creepers, birds and animals throughout this world—my own personal envelope of personhood would dissolve in this śarat sunshine and become a part of this clear sky, and I would be beyond time and place. But, right now, in this situation, it is difficult to quite immerse myself in such a self-forgetful feeling. That I am who I am, that is, someone's father, someone's husband, someone's friend, Mr so-and-so—all sorts of evidence to that effect is present everywhere.

240

Shilaidaha
16 October 1895

Last night, I couldn't sleep till very late, and lay on the *jolly boat* for a long time—after that I came to the *boat* and sat on a bench at the bedroom window and spent a night all alone after a long time. The river water was as still as a mirror—the light from the stars had made the night's darkness transparent; it was as if the entire universe could be seen through a dark glass. Although it was very late, the night was not completely silent because the two women who were in my neighbouring boat were talking and laughing as they lay on the bed, and a couple of boats had arrived and were creating a commotion—the other shore looked peaceful under the cover of the calm darkness—the tall coconut trees in the garden of our wooden bungalow were standing still like sentries, and you could hear the sound of a kīrtan being sung far away. There was no breeze at all. The clusters of the white flowers of kāś on our deserted sandbank seemed to softly nod off to sleep—eventually, after sitting there for a long time, when my head too seemed to bend down with the weight of sleep, I went to bed. This morning, after having had my bath, I feel as if I haven't slept enough. The ennui my body feels is pleasant—I can quite see that right now if I could stretch myself out on the bed and pick up a travel book and feel this slow winter breeze on my body, I should find it very relaxing. That's why I really like this feeling of slight tiredness in the morning—one can abandon all one's work without regret and take a holiday for half a day. Nowadays my holidays are rationed—but I don't like this state of uselessness. When the body is fully fit, it searches out work on its own, making men restless. But today it's quite calm, feeling its own spinal cord to be a bit of a weight, and will be relieved if it can be spread out upon the bed.

241

On the way to Patishar
22 November 1895

My *boat* makes its way through this small river—I've been alone the whole day, not having had to say a single word to anybody. The river here has almost no current, and the floating moss emits a new sort of fragrance. The sails fill with a gently pleasant breeze—the *boat* is moving very slowly, a particular soft light upon the water, and on the near shore, a succession of many different vivacious green colours and scenes of secluded villages all ranked together gradually draw me out of my own ego, untying life's complicated knots one by one and calming the sharp edges of my self-absorbed heart. The reverberation of all the rough handshakes of Calcutta still courses jarringly through my nerves—but I can feel that gradually all of it will come to a stop, and I will know the world as eternal and vast, and all my connections with the world will become simple and easy. When you first jump into this calm, deep solitude, you feel the pull of your many ties to the world and, for a while, it hurts—but then, when I feel the embrace of a limitless affection within this deep comfort, when I feel myself intimately bound in this extremely intense, private, heartfelt relationship, the accumulated warmth in my innermost self breathes a deep sigh and attains freedom; then I understand that 'happiness is very simple and easy', that true fulfilment resides in the depth of one's own heart, and that no unkind fate can deprive me of it. The moment you step out of your ego you can see the vast, joy-filled world spread out before you, full of life, youth, beauty—then I feel I am blessed to have been born in this world, I am blessed that I shall be in this world for eternity—all that I know, all that I have got, all that I have felt, is such an astonishing amount for this one heart!

242

Patishar
25 November 1895

We're such domesticated animals that the moment we take a couple of steps outside of Calcutta and arrive at Kaligram, we think we've accomplished something really great. Our feet are tied to the peg of our homes on such a short leash that the slightest movement pulls you back—what's the point of all this writing of letters and waiting for letters! No doubt my family hasn't fallen into a bottomless ocean the moment I've come away. God has not given the sons of Bengalis the right to wander about freely and joyfully across the vast universe, we are all cows in cowsheds—at the most, the village field is the outer limit of our wanderings—and even then the cowherd is always behind you, stick in hand. Last evening I was reading an essay on Goethe by Dowden—there I saw that Goethe had left everything behind to go and spend two years in Italy in order to immerse himself in art analysis and the appreciation of beauty and had gained something of a new life and new riches in the process, and how this experience had instantly produced amazing results, transforming his talent and endowing his entire temperament with immense peace and a great sense of worth. Reading this agitates the hearts of prisoners like ourselves—then one thinks one has not managed to be even the half of what one could have been, that there is a lot to learn and prepare for yet. I think—if I had the good fortune of Goethe, if I hadn't been born in Bengal, if there were appropriate food for the soul to be found here, then I would have attained immortality in the entire world—at present I am largely an object of pity, and poor. If I can, I too shall set out into this world at some point—that's what I really desire.

243

Patishar
28 November 1895

I've been wanting to put my hand to some writing, but I still can't get my mind to concentrate on work—I don't know how long it's going to take to dispel this deep apathy, perhaps by then it will be time to return to Calcutta. It seems like a long time since I've come to the mofussil and that I've spent all these days being continuously useless—if I'd been obsessed with composing songs the days would have been filled with an incessant humming and passed intoxicated and the hours would have been spent unconsciously addicted to music. Of late I've been looking after jamidāri work, reading newspapers, reading books and eating my meals. If I could only force myself somehow to throw myself midstream into the flow of writing, I wouldn't *care* for this world one bit any longer—my world would then be my own world, there I alone would be king, there I would be the god of all happiness, unhappiness and beauty. How many days am I made up of, after all, and how long will my joys and sorrows exist—but the stream of *ideas* that wells up from a source at the beginning of time and flows through a thousand minds towards eternity—that is the connection between me and all of the past and the future—in that kingdom of thought I am a complete man, not a particular individual named Rabi—there my joy and my pain permeate the universe. The unfortunate thing is that the established goddess of that kingdom of thought is far more restless than the restive goddess Lakshmi—when I want her, she doesn't always appear, but when she wants me, then I cannot delay for a moment. I have to set aside the most urgent of tasks in the world and report my presence at her feet. In Calcutta, when I become frantic and fatigued with all the confrontations and the battles, I imagine my muse sitting, bowl of nectar in hand, in some distant secluded corner—but when I finally arrive there I see that stony Calcutta has followed me and my muse has hidden herself again in the most distant seclusion. Perhaps one day in the evening she will come silently and stand behind me in the starlight upon the roof of the *boat* and slowly rest her soft hand upon my shoulder, and I, gradually lifting my face, will see her mute face in the endless, mute sky—and there will be no more incompleteness.

244

Patishar
29 November 1895

There's no doubt any more about the fact that I have written to you many times about Kaligram, but still, unless you repeat yourself you cannot maintain a correspondence, and perhaps it might not exactly even be repetition—because old things too strike us in new ways; every time I renew my acquaintance with my ever-familiar favourite things, it is always partly a fresh acquaintance; a new sense of wonder appears from somewhere each time. Kaligram is not a place that is among my favourite things, but once I arrive here, its old familiar features acquire a new attraction for me. I'm really enjoying this very small river and completely domestic sort of landscape. The river bends right ahead, just where there's a small village and a few trees, ripening fields of grain on one side, and on the high bank of the river five or six cows shooing away flies with their tails, munching on grass with a chewing sound, while on the other side the empty fields stretch on and on—there's moss floating on the river water, the occasional bamboo pole planted by fishermen in the water; a kingfisher sits upon a bamboo pole still as a picture; a flock of kites fly in the sky's bright sunlight. It is afternoon, and in front me blossoming mustard flowers on a parcel of a mustard field near the milkman's house blaze like fire—the women of the house draw water and feed the cows; in the mopped courtyard, the tethered cows bury their heads in tubs and eat their fodder; straw has been kept in heaps; a pond is being dug near the milkman's house for our kāchāri, and Hindustani women in colourful clothes take the soil in baskets on their heads and dump it in a nearby pit of water. Here everything is close at hand. On both sides of the river, this side and that, there is a not-very-large lake that disappears within the bend of the river—on either side of this lake are the only two villages. Sitting in the middle of this lake, I'm surrounded on all sides by all the everyday work and business of these two villages. This is my whole world. These people sit in front of their houses and smoke, bathe and wash clothes; they cross the small river on small canoes, paddling the water with their hands; in the afternoon one or two idle women sit unmoving for a long time on the side of the house that is shady, watching the world go by as the day passes; the village schoolboys return home carrying their shabby books in a bundle—in the evening, lights are lit in the rooms, the cowsheds are wafted with smoke, the two villages fall silent like two nests—I've lifted up the spine of the shutters on my window and absorbed myself in studying the accomplishments of Goethe in the royal court at Weimar. Where am I, in a boat in Patishar by the banks of the river Nagor, and where the court poet Goethe of the work-abundant royal court of Weimar.

245

Shahjadpur
4 December 1895

A very old thought has been constantly coming up in my mind
since morning—that the world is transient. Yet grief, sorrow and
death affect us in such a way as though the world were permanent.
Even if it's all a mirage, māyā, or whatever, still the widowed wife
has to rear her infant children on her own—the philosophy of the
Vedanta will not make the affection in a mother's heart disappear!
However irrevocable and powerful death may be, the bonds of
love are not any less strong. Even after repeated defeats since the
beginning of time, why does this endless conflict between given
certainty and futile desire continue unabated? I was sitting and
extending my imagination into the future a hundred years from
now. I was thinking of what it was like a hundred years ago, that
on an Agrahāyan morning in 1795 there would have been just
this sort of winter, this sort of sunlight, this sort of commotion
of people—but there's not a trace of that morning in this one. In
those days too, so many festivals, so much grief, so many births
and deaths, tears and laughter must have appeared like burning
truths. And then again, the morning of the 19th of Agrahāyan
will appear at the appointed time over the world in the year 1995
too. This same sort of dew-wet grass, this winter breeze, the mild
sun—but not the slightest shadow, not a trace of the memory
of Jna———'s death or his bereft widow and orphaned children's
severest grief and sorrow will be cast upon that day—and I too,
who, on a morning a hundred years before was thinking of myself
as an aspect of the complete and living truth as I felt myself firmly
established among my friends, relations, and near and dear ones,
adjacent to the limitless world and the beginning of time—not a
trace shall remain anywhere of me in the entire memory of the
awakened human heart on that morning! On that day I will be

without sorrow, without desire, without regret—yet this earth and
this sky will be here.

246

Kaligram
6 December 1895

I had written to you saying that everything in Kaligram is small-
scale and near at hand. But that's only when I'm staying in the *boat*
upon the river. The river is a small one, both its banks are high,
and the boat too is narrow, so you can't see very far all around—
only a limited rural scene can be seen. Yesterday after a long time
I climbed up on the riverbank on the opposite shore after sunset
to walk there—as soon as I went up there I suddenly saw that the
sky had no beginning or end, that the deserted field stretched
wide open till the horizon—how far those tiny little villages of
mine were! How narrow the little line of water at one end! On the
fields at Shilaidaha, one can see trees and villages and woods—here
there is nothing all around, only blue sky and white earth, and in
the middle, a lonely, homeless, endless dusk—it seems as if a bride
veiled in gold walks alone through the limitless field with the veil
barely pulled across her face. Slowly, slowly, she travels this entire
circular earth, across so many thousands of villages, rivers, fields,
mountains, seas, cities and forests, throughout the ages, alone,
with her astonished, tearful, wan gaze, silently, with tired steps—if
she has no husband then who has dressed her up in this golden
wedding attire! On which eternal western shore is her husband's
house? Yesterday, upon ascending that field, a certain rhythm and
music and poetry seemed to well up suddenly in my head. But I
couldn't give it form, and perhaps it was impossible to do so. As
impossible as attempting to collect all the glitter of dusk to melt into
a single golden image. That inner fervour I felt has been dispersed

into that soundless, silent dusk above the field at Patishar, and has
set with it. If my mind has drawn a golden line or two of its own
upon the limitless canvas of that evening sky—will that be visible
any more? When that dusk comes again to that field today, it will
bring no sign of yesterday with it.

247

On the river
Saturday, 7 December 1895

The *boat* set off again today at dawn—we left the narrow river
behind and emerged into an expansive marsh. The bright sun and
the keen winter breeze are enjoyable. The dew-bright world looks
like a morning flower newly blossomed in the sky. Having emerged
from the small cave-like river at Patishar after a long time, my mind
today has spread its wings across the sky, my *boat* floats along, I
seem to be flying through this calm, clear sunlight. This place too
is quite wonderful. The land and water are like conjoined twins,
brother and sister—there's no great difference between the two;
water and land are on the same level; one part shines like steel in
the sun, while another part is green with layers of herbivorous soil
and mossy grass. Many varieties of herons and kites fly around, from
white to brick-red, cormorants with long, shiny, black necks take a
dive into the water and swim playfully around, chests puffed up; the
fishermen have hung out their nets on bamboo poles—that's where
the long-beaked kingfishers have their āddā. Before we know it, the
banks on either side grow higher at a certain place, and land and
water divide—river in the middle, banks on either side, Agrahāyan's
yellow fields of grain on the banks; their heads bent, cows graze
absorbedly upon the high banks, and near their mouthfuls of grass
the *śālik* birds dance around, hunting for worms—on occasional
islands of high ground are two or three straw huts surrounded by

a few banana and kul trees and pumpkin vines, on whose porches stand naked children and curious housewives, staring amazed at my *boat*—black and white ducks huddle in groups by the waterside, busily cleaning the feathers on their backs with their beaks—far away, bamboo groves and dense rows of trees stand blocking the horizon—a little further away empty fields on either side—then again suddenly at one place the shouts of boys, the laughter and chatter of bathing women, the wail of a grieving older woman, the slapping sound of clothes being washed—I lift up my head at the sound of splashing bathing-water and see that we have arrived at the ghat of a densely shaded village; there are a couple of boats tied here and a reluctant bawling boy is being forcibly held down by the arm and bathed by his mother.

248

On the river to Shilaidaha
Sunday, 8 December 1895

I've been on the river since yesterday. We'd hoped to make it to Shilaidaha by today, but I don't see any sign of that happening now. I'm not unhappy about that—the few days I get en route are days of unadulterated holiday for me—no work to be done apart from what I want to think or do of my own volition. I'm looking out of both windows, reading and writing—on every side there's white sand and pale blue water, in the distance green fields and blue sky above. Occasionally in one or two places there was a touch of danger—the Padma's waters are receding now in the winter, you see, which is why the narrow flow of water becomes tremendously forceful at certain spots. The water seems to cut the bottom of the boat with the scraping sound of a steel knife as it flows. Your eyes begin to hurt if you look at that fast-flowing water. I've been sitting the entire day with my rough book for poetry open, pencil in hand, writing a few lines now and then, and lazily gazing in this or that direction. I woke up at four in the morning today—got up and swathed myself in some warm clothes, lit the lamp, and finished a poem called '*Urbaśī*', then I went to have my bath at seven-thirty—in this way I've completed two quite long poems in these last couple of days. If you can get this sort of free time, uninterrupted and whole, over entire days of open sky and unlimited light, you can then nurture a poem in all its colours and flavours just as nature causes her flowers to bloom and fruits to ripen. Or else there's always a sense of hurry within—willingly or unwillingly, the mind is chased and harried down so many paths and wrong turns where the imagination receives no help at all. That's why sometimes I think that if I can travel by *boat* for a month or a month and a half and keep going west—separating myself from all news of home and all discussion of work—to completely disappear from sight into forgetfulness and cessation like that distant bird rising in the sky—then I could complete so many pieces of writing in that abundance of leisure. I have no greater duty than that of writing. I have accepted this injunction within my heart and come to the world—when I obey it, my joys and sorrows are all lighter, when I don't, then a horde of joys and sorrows are at my throat like a pack of greyhounds—what sort of terrible torture is this for a man!

249

On the way to Shahjadpur
11 December 1895

Ore bās re! What a terrible affair! We've just gone past the kāñcikāṭhā—an enormous hurdle has been crossed. This place is like a narrow, winding canal—an enormous amount of water rushes through this small space falling like a foaming, puffed-up waterfall—the angry water grabs, tears and pulls the entire *boat* along by the tuft of its hair—it runs along like lightning, so that there's no time to even think of what has happened or what is happening—the oarsmen and boatmen begin to shout and cry out loudly—the water gurgles and splashes, the stunned heart stops breathing, astonished, and then in ten minutes you cross over the danger spot and absolutely leap into the lap of safety. We've left behind the marshes of Kaligram and reached the river now. Now, with the help of a supportive current, we'll fly along with a whistling sound through high and winding banks of ripe grain and blossoming mustard fields on both sides. The smell of these mustard fields entrances me, bringing I don't know what picture and atmosphere of beauty to mind—something like a field full of sunlight seen many years ago, a cool, calm breeze, a winding village road by a pond, a veiled bride with a pitcher at her waist, and, along with all that, I'm reminded of a generous, clear sky permeated with the mild fragrance of a mustard field—as if the smell of those mustard flowers were somehow entangled with the deep, happy memory of a time of satiated love and fulfilling peace.

250

Shilaidaha
12 December 1895

The other day I was suddenly quite surprised by a very small and minor incident. I've written to you before that nowadays in the evenings I light a lamp on the *boat* and sit and read until I feel sleepy, because one's own solitary company is not always desirable, especially in the evenings. There's a proverb that says that people who have no work indulge their aunts by accompanying them on a pilgrimage to the Ganga—a conveniently gratuitous aunt is rarely to be found close at hand when you need one, so then you have only your own mind to occupy yourself—rather than that, I think it's better to keep yourself occupied with a book. The other evening, I was sitting and reading an English critical work on poetry and beauty and art and other such gobbledegook—while reading the dire argumentation around all this significant stuff there are times when I feel, tiredly, that everything is an empty mirage—that all twelve annas of it are made up, just words on top of words. That day too, as I read, I was filled with a dry, jaded feeling, and a mocking monster of doubt appeared in my mind. As it was getting quite late at night, I slammed the book shut with a bang, flung it on the table with a thud, and blew out the lamp with the intention of going to sleep. The moment the light was extinguished, moonlight flooded into the *boat* from the open windows on all sides and scattered all around. How astonished and taken aback I was! My tiny little ray of lamplight had been smiling the dry smile of a villain, yet that completely insignificant smile of contempt had entirely obscured the limitlessly deep smile of this universe's love! What had I been searching for in the heaps of sentences of this dry book—the one I had been looking for had been standing outside all this time, silently filling the entire sky. If by chance I had not seen her, and gone to bed in the dark, then too she would have had no objection to that small wick of my lamp, but would have set silently. If I hadn't caught a glimpse of her even for a moment in this life and had gone to bed for the last time in the darkness of the last day of my life, then too that lighted lamp would have won, for she would still have spread across the entire world in the same sort of silence and with the same sweet smile—she would not have hidden herself, nor would she have shown herself.

Since then, nowadays in the evenings I've begun to put out the lighted lamp.

251

Shilaidaha
14 December 1895

Nowadays, between my writing and my leisure, I've begun to read a slim biography of the poet Keats little by little. Just in case it finishes in one go, I read it slowly, savouring it and saving it—I've been enjoying reading it. Of all the English poets I know, I feel the most intimate connection with Keats. There may be many more important poets than him, but none so much after my own heart. Unfortunately he died young, and was given little time to write. . . . Keats's language is full of the sincerity of a very real experience of joy. His *art* and his heart have come together in the same melodic pattern—whatever he has created has always had a pulsating connection with his heart. The poems of a majority of the modern poets such as Tennyson or Swinburne have the air of having been carved in stone—they write poetically, and there is a great beauty in what they write, but the inner heart of the poet is not a witness to the truth of that writing. Tennyson's poem 'Maud' has a wellspring of *lyricism* that is both multi-hued and intensely heartfelt, it's true, but still, Mrs Browning's sonnets are far more intimately true. The unconscious poet in Tennyson writes lines that are then coloured over by the brushstrokes of the self-conscious artist Tennyson and increasingly obscured from view. In Keats's writing, the natural and deep joy of the poet's heart radiates outward, full of life and brightness, through the skilful craft of his compositions. That's what attracts me to it so much. Keats's writing is not holistic and almost no poem of his achieves perfection from the first line through to the last, but by the strength of their particular genuinely beautiful living quality, they are able to give intimate company to our living hearts. When I get back to Calcutta I'll give you this biography of Keats to read. His incomplete short life is so tender and sad.

252

Shilaidaha
15 December 1895

The days pass in this way. And then, in the evenings, by the time
I row to the sandbank on the other shore, walk and return, it is
already night. I've tried to describe the incredible beauty of the
evening upon the still, silent river and the trees on the other shore,
but it's beyond description—you can't imagine that beauty and
that peace if you are far from it. When I return to Calcutta even
I may not be able to recall it exactly. Last evening, after having
immersed my entire heart, mind and will in this evening scene,
when I was slowly returning in my *jolly boat* through the golden
dark, suddenly, from an unseen boat far away came the sound of a
violin playing at first the Pūrbī and then the Imankalyāṇ ālāp—and
the entire still river and silent sky filled up completely with the
human heart. Before that I had been thinking that there is perhaps
no equivalence to this evening scene in the world of man—but the
moment the melody of Pūrbī began to play I felt that it too was
an amazingly deep and limitlessly beautiful affair, that it too was a
crucial creation—how easily the rāginī blended with all the magic
of the evening, without a break anywhere—my entire heart filled
up. After returning to the *boat* I sat down with the harmonium
again after a long time. One by one I sang a number of newly
composed songs slowly in a low tone—I felt like composing a few
songs again—but I haven't managed to do so yet.

Notes

Introduction

1. Buddhadeva Bose, *Āmār chelebelā*, cited in Samir Sengupta (ed.), *Buddhadeb basur jīban* (Calcutta: Bikalpa, 1998), p.14.
2. Rabindranath Tagore, *Chinnapatrābalī*, edited by Kanai Samanta, first published October 1960 (Kolkata:Visva-Bharati Press, 2004).
3. Rabindranath Tagore, *Chinnapatra* (Calcutta, 1912).
4. Rabindranath Tagore, *Glimpses of Bengal: Selected from the Letters of Sir Rabindranath Tagore 1885–1895* (London: Macmillan, 1921).
5. Tagore, *Chinnapatrābalī*, p. 355.
6. Introduction to Tagore, *Glimpses of Bengal*, p. v.
7. Prasantakumar Pal, *Rabijībanī* (Rabi's Life) (Calcutta: Ananda Publishers, 1984),Vol. 3, pp. 39–40.
8. Gautam Chakrabarty, *Ananda Bazaar Patrika*, 5 December 2010.
9. Subhash Chaudhuri (ed.), *Indira debi pramatha chaudhuri patrābalī* (Letters of Indira Debi and Pramatha Chaudhuri) (Calcutta: Ananda Publishers, 1987), pp. 28 and 7.
10. Chitra Deb, *Thākurbāṛir andarmahal* (The Inner Quarters of the Tagore Household) (Kolkata: Ananda Publishers, 2010), p. 81.
11. '*Nāsik haite khuṛār patra*' (An Uncle's Letter from Nasik), *Bhāratī*, Bhādra-Āśvin 1293 BE (Bengali Era).

12. Giribala is to be found in the story 'Megh o roudra' (Cloud and Sunlight), first published in *Sādhanā*.

13. For a discussion of this essay, see Amit Chaudhuri, Introduction to *Clearing a Space: Reflections on India, Literature and Culture* (Delhi: Penguin, 2013).

14. Roland Barthes, 'The Rustle of Language' in *The Rustle of Language* (Berkeley: University of California Press, 1989), p. 76. For a detailed discussion, see Rosinka Chaudhuri, Chapter Seven, *The Literary Thing: History, Poetry and the Making of a Modern Cultural Sphere* (New Delhi: Oxford University Press, 2013).

15. Biswajit Roy, *Ananda Bazaar Patrika*, 8 May 2011.

16. Nirad C. Chaudhuri, *Bāṅgālī jībane ramaṇī* (A Social History: Women in Bengali Society) (Calcutta: Mitra and Ghosh, 1967), p. 78.

17. My translation. Ranajit Guha, *Chaẏ rtur gān* (Song of Six Seasons) (Calcutta: Charchapad, 2009), p. 80.

Letter 44 (page 114)

1. This paragraph (beginning 'When Khoka sits there') is from the manuscript of *Jibansmṛti* in the Rabindra–Bhavana: No. 146, pp. 7–8, Santiniketan. Inserted by the editor of *Chinnapatrābalī* in 1960.

ALSO BY RABINDRANATH TAGORE

Gitanjali

Translated by William Radice

**A critically acclaimed translation that renders
with beauty and precision the poetic rhythm
and intensity of the Bengali originals**

Described by Rabindranath Tagore as 'revelations of my true
self', the poems and songs of *Gitanjali* established the writer's
literary talent worldwide. They include eloquent sonnets such as
the famous 'Where the mind is without fear', and poems that are
intense explorations of love, faith and nature, and tender evocations
of childhood.

In his arrangement of Tagore's original sequence of poems
alongside his translations, William Radice restores to *Gitanjali* the
structure, style and conception that were hidden by W.B. Yeats's
edition of 1912, making this book a magnificent addition to the
Tagore library.

Poetry
Rs 350

Gora

Translated by Radha Chakravarty

The Nobel Prize–winning author's most ambitious work

Gora unfolds against the vast, dynamic backdrop of Bengal under British rule, a divided society struggling to envisage an emerging nation. It is an epic saga of India's nationalist awakening, viewed through the eyes of one young man, an orthodox Hindu who defines himself against the British colonialist culture and finds himself approaching his nationalist identity through the prism of organized religion. First published in 1907, *Gora* questions the dogmas and presuppositions inherent in nationalist thought like few books have dared to do. This new, lucid and vibrant translation brings the complete and unabridged text of the classic to a new generation of readers, underlining its contemporary relevance.

Fiction
Rs 399

Home and the World

Translated by Sreejata Guha

'There is nothing static, earthbound or lifeless about it . . . It has the complexity and tragic dimensions of Tagore's own time, and ours'—Anita Desai

Set against the backdrop of the partition of Bengal by the British in 1905, *Home and the World* (*Ghare Baire*) is the story of a young, liberal-minded zamindar Nikhilesh, his educated and sensitive wife, Bimala, and Nikhilesh's friend Sandip, a charismatic nationalist leader whom Bimala finds herself attracted to. A perceptive exposition of the difficulties surrounding women's emancipation in pre-modern India, and a telling portrayal of the chasms inherent in the nationalist movement, *Home and the World* has generated endless debate and discussion. This classic novel was first published in Bengali in 1916, is now available in a lucid new translation.

Fiction
Rs 299